Critical Pedagogy and Predatory Culture

This book is a major contribution to the radical literature on culture, identity, and the politics of schooling, especially as it addresses the challenge and the promise of school and social reform through what the author calls a "critical multiculturalism." Peter McLaren's approach to "predatory culture" and his exploration of recent debates over the role of public institutions, the state, and social agents offers the discerning reader a unique combination of neo-Marxist and post-structuralist theory – referred to as "resistance postmodernist critique." Readers are invited to construct a politics of resistance at the level of everyday institutional life and within other public spheres. Such a politics of resistance is discussed in detail as a form of critical pedagogy which the author develops from the work of the Brazilian educator, Paulo Freire, and from a range of theorists and practitioners on the educational left including Deleuze, Guattari, Derrida, Foucault, and Lyotard. Critical pedagogy is seen as a means of investing desire in a project of the possible.

Written by one of the pioneers of critical pedagogy in North America, this book presents a unique and far-reaching challenge for educators, cultural workers, researchers and social theorists.

Peter McLaren is Associate Professor in the Graduate School of Education and Information Studies at the University of California, Los Angeles.

"Sous ce masque un autre masque.
Je n'en finirai pas de soulever tous ces visages."

Claude Cahun (Lucy Schwob), 1930

Critical Pedagogy and Predatory Culture

Oppositional politics in a postmodern era

Peter McLaren

London and New York

First published 1995
by Routledge
11 New Fetter Lane, London EC4P 4EE

Simultaneously published in the USA and Canada
by Routledge
29 West 35th Street, New York NY 10001

Phototypeset in Times by Intype, London
Printed and bound in Great Britain by
Biddles Ltd, Guildford and King's Lynn

British Library Cataloguing in Publication Data
A catalogue record for this book is available from the British Library

Library of Congress Cataloging in Publication Data
A catalogue record for this book has been requested

ISBN 0–415–06424–4 (hbk)
ISBN 0–415–11756–9 (pbk)

For Jenny McLaren, the love of my life

Contents

Preface

Paulo Freire

For quite some time, on account of my own personal experiences, I have convinced myself of the existence of what I have become accustomed to calling "intellectual kinship" among people who otherwise would be strangers in that they have no blood relationship. "Intellectual kinship" – involving similarity in the manner in which facts are assessed, comprehended and valued – is also comprised of dissimilarities and incongruencies.

I am referring to this mysterious sensation which begins to "reside" within us, when, immediately upon meeting someone, it seems as though we have somehow always been tied to them by an enduring friendship. It is as though the very concrete fact of having met him or her is felt by both parties as a sort of déjà-vu. It is as if encountering this person for the first time were in reality a long awaited re-encounter. Sometimes this "kinship" is of little importance, even less significant than it appeared in the beginning; sometimes, however, an even stronger similarity may fan the spark to a flame.

The state of "intellectual kinship" provokes in its subjects the feeling of finding oneself immersed in a pleasant ambiance in which intercommunication takes place easily, with a minimum of disturbances; an ambiance in which the themes discussed have been learned by both individuals through similar experiences of epistemological approximation to them. It is one in which a mutual affection, "softening" the "rough edges" of the subjects involved, helps them in building their relationship as opposed to hindering them.

It is interesting to observe how at times this same phenomenon occurs between us and different parts of the world that we visit. When for the first time I set foot on African land, the sensation that overtook me was one of returning and not one of having just arrived. Perhaps it can be said that the Africanism which I as a Brazilian of the Northeast carry within me makes it natural that arriving in Africa I would feel as though I was returning to her. But on the other hand, something very similar occurred within me at Cambridge, particularly in Harvard Square: that is, the sensation of an old, very old camaraderie. The same can be said for San Francisco, Buenos Aires, Amsterdam, Lisbon . . .

Along the journey of my long life I have had, on different occasions, the enjoyable experience of "intellectual kinship." I once met a woman in Greece, for example, with whom I lived out this experience. After a long conversation, in which I almost always knew what she was going to say next, I visited her library and found in it old and new companions of reading and study. It is of no importance whether the subjects who live out this experience belong to the same generation or even the same culture.

Sometimes we may suspect that this kinship exists merely through the reading of an individual's work, but it is in the personal encounter that such discourse finds its completion and that the 'intellectual kinship" is confirmed. And it is at this moment that great friendships take root and prosper across the years, almost always resisting the inevitable changes in the particular way subjects comprehend the world at the time that they initially recognized themselves as "intellectual relatives."

If someone should ask if intellectual kinship is a sine qua non to our ability to influence or to be influenced, to work together, to exchange points of view, build each other's knowledge, I say no. When such a kinship develops we need to cultivate within ourselves the virtue of tolerance, which "teaches" us to live with that which is different; it is imperative that we learn from and that we teach our "intellectual relative," so that in the end we can unite in our fight against antagonistic forces. Unfortunately, as a group, we academics and politicians alike expend much of our energy on unjustifiable "fights" among ourselves, provoked by adjectival or, even worse, by purely adverbial differences. While we wear ourselves thin in petty "harangues," in which personal vanities are displayed and egos are scratched and bruised, we weaken ourselves for the real battle: the struggle against our antagonists.

Peter McLaren is one among the many outstanding "intellectual relatives" I "discovered" and by whom I in turn was "discovered." In reality, such an "intellectual kinship" is mutually discovered and, moreover, reaches its fulfillment or its consummation through the mutual effort of its subjects. No one can become a relative of the other if the other does not also recognize that they belong to the same "intellectual family." Based on certain similarities and affinities, the kinship is "invented" and reinvented and is never considered completed.

I read McLaren long before I ever came to know him personally. In both encounters (of coming to know his work and meeting him in person) our "intellectual kinship" occurred because another very close and dear "relative" of ours, Henry Giroux, mediated the mutual discovery.

Once I finished reading the first texts by McLaren that were made available to me, I was almost certain that we belonged to an identical "intellectual family." It is of no importance that we may have assumed, then or now, different positions when faced with the same problem. To belong to the same "intellectual family" does not signify the reduction of one into the other, for it is the very autonomy of each which constitutes the stone upon which an authentic kinship is founded.

A love for autonomy, the struggle to sustain it, the search for creativity, the defense of the idea that friendship is to be cherished; the maintenance of intellectual responsibility and rigorousness in discussing any subject; the search for clarity; the courage to expose oneself; the relishing of risk-taking; a kind of purity without puritanism; a humility without servitude: these are all aspirations in pursuit of concretization, and that, through the life and work of McLaren, challenge me and make me his "cousin" to the extent that I am constantly seeking to allow myself to be touched by these qualities.

Paulo Freire
São Paulo, February 1994

(Translated by Maria del Pilar O'Cadiz, Marcia Moraes and Cesar Rossatto)

Acknowledgements

I wish to thank the following publishers for permission to reprint materials previously published (sometimes in different form).

In the Introduction, from "Education as a Political Issue: What's Missing in the Public Conversation about Education?' by Peter L. McLaren, in *Thirteen Questions: Reframing Education's Conversation* edited by Joe L. Kincheloe and Shirley R. Steinberg (249–62). Copyright 1992 by Peter Lang. Also from "Critical Pedagogy and the Postmodern Challenge: Toward a Critical Postmodernist Pedagogy of Liberation" by Peter McLaren and Rhonda Hammer 1989, in *Educational Foundations*, vol. 3, no. 3 (29–62).

In Chapter 1, from "Radical pedagogy as cultural politics" by Henry A. Giroux and Peter L. McLaren, 1991, in *Theory/Pedagogy/Politics* edited by Donald Morton and Mas'ud Zavarzadeh (153–86). Copyright 1991 by the University of Illinois Press.

In Chapter 2, from "Schooling the postmodern body" by Peter L. McLaren, 1991, in *Postmodernism, Feminism, and Cultural Politics* edited by Henry A. Giroux (144–73). By permission of State University of New York Press, copyright 1991.

In Chapter 3, from "Border disputes: multicultural narrative, identity formation, and critical pedagogy in postmodern America" by Peter L. McLaren, 1993, in *Naming Silenced Lives* edited by Daniel McLaughlin and William Tierney (201–35). Copyright 1993 by Routledge.

In Chapter 4, from "White terror and oppositional agency: towards a critical multiculturalism" by Peter L. McLaren, in *Strategies*, no. 7 (98–131).

"In Chapter 5, from "Pedagogies of Dissent and Transformation (a dialogue with Kris Gutierrez)," 1994, in *Critical Multiculturalism* edited by Barry Kanpol and Peter L. McLaren. In press, Bergin & Garvey.

In Chapter 6, from "Postmodernism, post-colonialism and pedagogy" by Peter L. McLaren, 1991, in *Education and Society*, vol. 9, no. 1 (3–22).

In Chapter 7, from "Multiculturalism and the postmodern critique: toward a pedagogy of resistance and transformation" by Peter L.

McLaren, 1994, in *Between Borders* edited by Henry A. Giroux and Peter L. McLaren (192–222). Copyright 1994 by Routledge.

In Chapter 8, from "Critical pedagogy, political agency, and the pragmatics of justice: the case of Lyotard" by Peter L. McLaren, forthcoming, in *Educational Theory*.

I want to thank Chris Rojek and Ann Gee for their advice and support throughout the writing of this volume. I also want to thank Dan MacCannell and Marc Pruyn for their editorial assistance. The support of Diane Stafford was also invaluable. I would like to acknowledge the many conversations with friends, colleagues and reviewers who have directly and indirectly contributed to this volume: Joe Kincheloe, Henry Giroux, Colin Lankshear, Donaldo Macedo, Shirley Steinberg, Kris Gutierrez, Joanne Larson, Lisa Chin, Nick Burbules, Mike Apple, Carlos Alberto Torres, Carl Weinberg, Marcia Moraes, Dennis Carlson, Christine Sleeter, Richard Quantz, Cameron McCarthy, Stephen Haymes, Antonia Darder, Jo Anne Pagano, Bill Pinar, David Purpel, Jim Giarelli, Larry Grossberg, Bernado Gallegos, Richard Lichtman, Gustavo Fishman, bell hooks, Bradley J. Macdonald, Michele Wallace, Jeannie Oakes, Justine Zhixin Su, Dean MacCannell, Paulo Freire, Barry Kanpol, Stanley Aronowitz, Doug Kellner, Rhonda Hammer, Michael Pavel, Bill Tierney, Tom Oldenski, James T. Sears, Adriana Puiggrós, Michael Peters, Harold Levine, Tom Popkewitz, Svi Shapiro, Nize Pellanda, Alicia de Alba, Edgar Gonzalez, Bel Schaeffer, David Llewellyn, Bertha Ovozco Fuentes, Lourdes Chehaibar, María Teresa Bravo, Tomaz Tadeu da Silva, Khaula Murtadah, Tomasz Szkudbarek, Jeannie Brady, Sol Cohen, Maria del Pinar O'Cadiz, Concepcion Valadez, Alfredo Artiles, Cesar Rossatto, Richard Smith, Amy Wells, Michael Pavel, Annette Street, Heinz Sünker, Lech Witkowski, Valerie Scatamburlo, Darlene Emily Hicks, Donald Morton, Donaldo Macedo, Michael Peters, Mas'ud Zavarzadeh, Teresa Ebert, Donaldo Dippo, Jim Cummins, Barbara Flores, Antonia Darder, Lois Weis, Michele Fine, Michele Wallace, David Theo Goldberg, Glen Hudak, Jim Bruno, Diane Brunner, Bill Tierney, Lauren Langman, Lilia Bartholme, Bebel O. Schaefer, and members of Movimento Boneco. I would also like to express my appreciation to the Communication Processing Center at U.C.L.A.

Finally, I would like to pay tribute to my friends and companions at Cafe La Sopa, and La Universidad Veracruzana, Xalapa City, Veracruz, Mexico, for providing inspiration for the final revisions.

Introduction
Education as a political issue

Hypocrite lecteur, – mon semblable, – mon frère!

(Baudelaire)

I will not mince my words. We live at a precarious moment in history. Relations of subjection, suffering dispossession and contempt for human dignity and the sanctity of life are at the center of social existence. Emotional dislocation, moral sickness and individual helplessness remain ubiquitous features of our time. Our much heralded form of democracy has become, unbeknownst to many Americans, subverted by its contradictory relationship to the very object of its address: human freedom, social justice, and a tolerance and respect for difference. In the current historical juncture, discourses of democracy continue to masquerade as disinterested solicitations, and to reveal themselves as incommensurable with the struggle for social equality. The reality and promise of democracy in the United States has been invalidated by the ascendancy of new postmodern institutionalizations of brutality and the proliferation of new and sinister structures of domination. This has been followed by an ever fainter chorus of discontent as the voices of the powerless and the marginalized grow increasingly despondent or else are clubbed into oblivion by the crackling swiftness of police batons.

Although pain and suffering continue to pollute the atmosphere of social justice in the West, the dream of democracy and the struggle to bring it about has taken on a new intensity, as recent events in Eastern Europe attest. In its unannounced retreat in the United States over the past decade, democracy has managed to recreate power through the spectacularization of its after-image, that is, through image management and the creation of new national myths of identity primarily through the techniques of the mass media.

The prevailing referents around which the notion of public citizenry is currently constructed have been steered in the ominous direction of the social logic of production and consumption. Buyers are beginning culturally to merge with their commodities while human agency is becoming absorbed into the social ethics of the marketplace. Social impulses for equality, liberty, and social justice have been flattened out by the mass media until they have become cataleptically rigid while postmodern images threaten to steal what was once known as the "soul."

ARE WE HAVING FUN YET?

We now inhabit predatory culture.[1] Predatory culture is a field of invisibility – of stalkers and victims – precisely because it is so obvious. Its obviousness immunizes its victims against a full disclosure of its menacing capabilities.

In predatory culture identity is fashioned mainly and often violently around the excesses of marketing and consumption and the natural social relations of post-industrial capitalism. Life is lived in a "fun" way through speed technology in anticipation of recurring accidents of identity and endless discursive collisions with otherness because in predatory culture it is virtually impossible to be cotemporal with what one both observes and desires. Predatory culture is the left-over detritus of bourgeois culture stripped of its arrogant pretense to civility and cultural lyricism and replaced by a stark obsession with power fed by the voraciousness of capitalism's global voyage.

It is a culture of universalism compressed into local time. The predatory culture naturalized by and entrenched in primitive accumulation has exceeded even its own wildest fantasies of acquisition and has dropped its facade of civility and its window-dressing compassion. It can stand naked in its unholy splendor; it can make no claims to be just and fair; it can now survive thrillingly without artiface or camouflage.

Abandoning the historical criteria for making ethical judgments, predatory culture – as you will see in the chapters that follow – refuses to wager on the side of radical hope; instead, it cleaves false hope out of the excrement of image-value. It collapses all distinctions between the real and the imaginary, and seeks to conceal under its cloven hoof its own simulating activity. Predatory culture is the great deceiver. It marks the ascendancy of the dehydrated imagination that has lost its capacity to dream otherwise. It is the culture of eroticized victims and decaffeinated revolutionaries. We are all its sons and daughters. The capitalist fear that fuels predatory culture is made to function at the world level through the installation of necessary crises, both monetary and social. Computers have become the new entrepreneurs of history while their users have been reduced to scraps of figurative machinery, partial subjects in the rag-and-bone shop of predatory culture, manichean allegories of "us" against "them," of "self" against "other." The social, the cultural and the human has been subsumed within capital. This is predatory culture. Have fun.

Given the current condition of end-of-the-century ennui and paranoia, we have arrived at a zero-degree reality of the kind that once graced only the pages of surrealist manifestos or punk fanzines. André Breton's "simplest Surrealist act" – firing a pistol into a crowd of strangers – is no longer just a symbolic disruption of the grudgingly mundane aspects of everyday life or a symbolic dislocation circulating in avant garde broadsheets. It is precisely in the current North American historical conjuncture that people are really shooting blindly into crowds: at children in hamburger establishments, at employees and employers in factories, at teachers and classmates in schools, at civil servants in employment offices and at female engineering students in university seminar rooms. In Montreal, at Ecole Polytechnique, Marc Lepine massacres fourteen women. He is at war with females. And in the U.S., thrill-seeking arsonists destroy thousands of homes in L.A. and the Southern California coastline. In some urban settings, children are murdering other children for their status-line foot gear – not to mention the lurid reality of L.A. "drive-bys." In Ohio, a 5-year-old boy sets a fire that kills his baby sister, apparently through the influence of *Beavis and Butthead.* A new secret weapon is unveiled by the F.B.I.: the music of Mitch Miller. The old-time friendly sounds that Americans used to "sing along with" while following the bouncing dots that kept them in time with the music are blasted at David Koresh and his Branch Davidians along with sounds of rabbits being slaughtered, chants of Tibetan monks, and Nancy Sinatra's "These Boots Were Made For Walking" (apparently, to no avail) as a form of psychological torture. Similar psychological tactics are used against Noriega in Panama. In this case groups include AC/DC, Twisted Sister and David Bowie. Songs include "Crying In The Chapel," "Eat My Shorts," "Give It Up," "I Fought The Law," "Never Gonna Give You Up," "Paranoid," "One Way Ticket," "Waiting For You," and "Wanted Dead Or Alive." Lorena Bobbitt becomes enshrined as an emblem of radical feminist resistance; Mr. Bobbitt's penis surgery does more damage to Freud's castration complex than the controversial theories of Jeffrey Masson.

In Los Angeles, Aurelia Macias, a Mexican immigrant and battered wife, snipped off her husband's testicles with a pair of scissors as, she claimed, he was about to rape her. According to newspaper reports, the male prosecuting attorney told her she could have easily escaped her abusive husband by leaving him and "working as a cleaning lady." It was the same attorney who reportedly snapped at a female psychologist serving as a witness: "You're a woman. You know about jealousy." Ms. Macias was acquitted of the most serious charges. Hollywood might work this into an episode of "L.A. Law."

An eighth-grader at Mary McLeod Bethune Middle School, Astrianna Johnson, is reportedly suing the Los Angeles Unified School District for preventing her from wearing packaged condoms on her clothes and shoes to promote safe sex and AIDS awareness among her fellow students.

L.A. can be a cruel place for those who want to make awareness legal. Chart-topping pop songs replace somber hymns at British funerals: a recent survey by the Cremation Society reveals that songs by Whitney Houston, Kylie Minogue and Phil Collins are among the most frequently requested songs at funerals, prompting crematorium managers to invest considerable sums of money in high-tech C.D. players.

Esteemed scientists are helping to propel genetics into the age of the body-as-theme-park. Stargene Company, co-founded by a U.S. Nobel Prize-winning scientist, reportedly makes plans to market celebrity D.N.A. strands as fetish objects for the star-struck. D.N.A. will be magnified until it is visible to the eye, then laminated alongside a photo and a short biography of the star and mass produced for public consumption. In New York City, manufacturers of bullet-proof vests are starting special fashion lines for toddlers and elementary school children who might absorb stray bullets from homeboy dealers in pumps and gold ten-dollar tooth caps and who carry customized A.K. 47 assault rifles. The guns are not fashion accessories – yet. But gas masks are. After the war in Iraq, New York celebrity fashion designer Andre Van Pier announced a new spring fashion line based on the theme "Desert Storm." Its stated intent was to capture the "Gulf War look." Fashion accessories included neon-colored camouflage patterns, canteen purses, and gas masks slung renegade-chic over the shoulder. About the same time, a major New York manufacturer of baseball cards revealed a new line of Gulf War cards that are supposed to be "educational." Included were photos of the major American military hardware and portraits of the generals but the only item represented from Iraq in the collection was a "Scud" missile. These cards compete with serial killer cards. In the winter of 1993, just as Attorney General Dan Lungren is to arrive at a Long Beach California high school to speak about the dangers of guns, a teenager is shot in front of a Long Beach high school while trying to register.

Today's social ugliness that makes the bizarre appear normal is no longer just a (white, male) surrealist fantasy or proto-surrealist spin-off, or a Baudrillardean rehearsal for a futureless future. This scenario is the present historical moment, one that has arrived in a body bag – unraveled and stomped on by the logic of a steel-toed boot. Serial killer Ted Bundy has donated his multiple texts of identity to our structural unconscious and we are living them. We are now in the age of recombinant subjectivity. There is no escape. A funky nihilism has set in; an aroma of cultural disquiet. Marc Lepine and the Russian cannibal mass murderer, Andre Chikatilo, live comfortably in the interstices of our manufactured desires, waiting to audition for the role of central protagonist in the agitated dramas of our daily existence and the next television movie. Recently the Galerie at Tatou in Beverly Hills, hang out for movie stars, venture capitalists, and other "fun" people, was selling the paintings of serial killer John Wayne Gacy. Gacy was recently executed by lethal injection for the sex-torture slayings of thirty-three boys and young men in the Chicago area. For as little as $10,000 per painting, it is possible to purchase Gacy's illustrations of Christ, Elvis, a skull with teeth dripping blood ("Jeffrey Dahmer Skull"), Adolf Hitler, and the smiling Seven Dwarfs rendered in bright colors. A special item in the collection – and a consistent best seller – is Gacy's painting of Pogo the Clown (Gacy enticed many of his victims to his home using Pogo the Clown routines). Gacy can be considered a "star" of promotional, predatory culture for the considerable success he enjoyed in strangling all but one of his victims by wrapping a rope around their necks and twisting it with a stick prior, during, or shortly after having sex with them. There is a yearning today for a daily apocalypse where salvation is unnecessary because chaos is always sublime, morality is frictionless and heaven can always be had, M.T.V.-style, between a pair of bubble-shaped buttocks. If you're in doubt, just witness music video's reverential display of holy buns, the hard, glistening, ghetto onions on rap videos that make grown men groan for babes who got "back." Buttocks have become the new icons of social resurrection, the cultural promise that will selflessly defy gravity for us – just to keep us feeling young and satisfied.

Hair stylists are also giving the social order new hope for redemption. José Eber, famous for his teal-colored eyes and beauty salon in Beverly Hills, and who specializes in trichology (the study of hair and scalp), facials using aromatherapy, Balayage hair painting, and manicure and pedicure, has found a solution to the violence in Los Angeles: he gives "empowering makeovers" to battered women who live in inner-city shelters (Garneski 1993). Just prior to Gacy's execution, almost any predator could be empowered by phoning 1–900–622-GACY, to listen to a recording of Gacy's voice. They could let their fantasies of having sex with a serial killer fly loose and easy in the privacy of their bedrooms. It cost a mere $1.99 per minute and was more fun than being pampered by a hair stylist – even a famous one.

The unsettling contradictions of our age are reflected in the transnational assault on "difference" – that form of difference that eludes the profit motive or refuses commodification or revision in the interests of the logic of capital. Feelings of despair about the global condition have gone high-tech: we can now eroticize our depression and rearrange and reterritorialize our feelings by entraining our central nervous system with the electromagnetic spectrum via T.V. waves and fend off depression with designer M.T.V. moods.

We now live in an age where we can make our own dreams come true. In Inglewood, California, a woman recently turned 40 and because she had not yet found a man to marry, she married herself. She had a three-tiered wedding cake at the ceremony, and was probably unaware of the implications her actions had for Lacanian feminists. Also in California, the Supreme Court upheld the right of a dead man to leave his sperm to whomever he desires. Beware of strange packages in the mail. The ghost of Charles Bukowski drools bourbon-flavored ectoplasm and delights in a hot wet shit as he watches everyday life in the United States conform to the dark vision of his fiction.

The erosion of the American dream has forced today's youth to occupy, if not a dystopian parody of *The Cosby Show*, then paracriminal subcultures of sardonic nihilism focusing on drugs and violence, apotheosized in movies like *A Clockwork Orange* and *Colors*. Corporate rock's celebration of the subversion of adult authority gives its youthful listeners the illusion of resistance but not a language of critique or hope. It works to produce a politics of pleasure but simultaneously functions as a form of repression and forgetting – a motivated social amnesia and forced disavowal of the nation's complicity in racial demonization and colonialism. Narcissistic entrepreneurs of hype and ideology, Camille Paglia, Howard Stern, and Rush Limbaugh, are all on the nation's bestseller lists. Children are collecting trading cards of serial killers. University students read Mexican deformity comics during lunch breaks along with *American Psycho* and *Zen Gives You the Competitive Edge*. Afraid of falling prey to the Wimp Factor, fraternity students plan date rapes after spending a few inspirational hours with *Physical Interrogation Techniques*, a C.I.A.-authored torture manual. Charles Manson smiles from his prison cell and his face appears on Axl Rose's T-shirt while a nation mourns for Polly Klaas, a young girl stolen from her bedroom during a slumber party by a stranger, then murdered.

DO YOU SECRETLY DESIRE TO HAVE SEX WITH A CANNIBAL KILLER?

The current culture of the United States makes it fun to be an abomination, to be a simple, run-of-the-mill predatory killer and even more fun if you happen to co-construct your subjectivity along with the state as an over-achiever murderer. It's the most fun thing of all, of course, to be a serial killer. You might even inspire a movie starring a famous Hollywood actress about a housewife serial killer, and perhaps even pave the way for making serial killers more acceptable as parents. In fact, you don't have to be very successful in normative terms to be a celebrity murderer. You don't have to be much more than just a plain human butcher who likes to attend church bingo games, watch television game shows and comfortably gnaw human gristle. You don't even have to cook the limbs or flayed tissue at all, let alone prepare them from a Hollywood celebrity chef recipe.

Jeffrey Dahmer T-shirts are big sellers at heavy metal concerts but it's safe to conclude he must have some admirers who listen to classical music. But classical music lovers who are secret fans of cannibal killers would *never* be seen in a Dahmer T-shirt (they might wear them privately, of course). You don't have to attend a musical concert of any kind to thrill at Dahmer's exploits of dismembering seventeen delicious young men. There is a comic book available that you can enjoy privately although you will probably want to let your friends know you have one. Adoring fans have showered Dahmer with over US$12,000. Dahmer's father wrote a book about what it was like to raise a cannibal murderer, proving that even guilt-ridden fathers of cannibals can become bestselling celebrities.

Predatory culture makes it possible to be a Henry Lee Lucas or a Richard Ramirez and be adored. Ramirez, better known as California's "night stalker" who killed thirteen people, has a devoted following of women who write to him regularly. But Dahmer is probably more popular because, after all, he's a cannibal. Seventy-five of the approximately 160 worldwide serial killers over the last twenty years were found in the United States (Toufexis 1994). Baudrillard is right on at least one count: America is the "*only remaining primitive society*" (1988:7). And that's a blessing for "fun guy" churchgoing handyman, John Famalaro, who kept the slain body of Denise Huber in a freezer on a rented storage unit so he could visit her frequently.

In predatory culture we need not worry too much. Our politicians can console and reassure our fears about enjoying violence and feeling pleasure while witnessing human suffering – especially the suffering of darker-skinned peoples – by plugging us into the myth machine: television. The New Right has used the media effectively (and affectively) not simply to transform gangsters or actors into politicians through the services of high-tech image consultants, but even more impressively, to seduce U.S. citizens into cultural nostalgia and social amnesia as a way out of the postmodern ambience of retreat and despondency. Now that the Cold War is over, many students feel a hunger for a new and culturally different enemy. In the wake of burying alive tens of thousands of what some U.S. patriots referred to as "sand niggers" in the trenches of Iraq, there exists in the U.S. a nostalgia for the Persian Gulf War as it was ideologically produced through C.N.N.

The drama surrounding O.J. Simpson's arraignment on charges of murdering his ex-wife and her friend has given him another starring role in predatory culture, this time an even more thrilling role in the public imagination's gleeful obsession with the glamor of a celebrity hero gone bad. Everybody loves a handsome and middle-aged football hero turned rent-a-car spokesperson who charges through airports like his old running-back self and helps Americans find the car that they need in a hurry. O.J. helped us dream that maybe we could marry a beauty contestant one day. And haven't we all wished at one time that we could exchange our rent-a-car for the junker that's parked in our oil-stained garage? It's hard not to remain a fan, even if you believe it was his powerful hand that was responsible for the multiple stab wounds that ripped apart the flesh of his victims, including the gash in his ex-wife's neck that was so deep it exposed her spinal column.

The Menendez brothers are not football stars but they can be stars of predatory culture because they're cute murderers in crew neck sweaters. Young women have even forgiven one of them for wearing a toupe because Eric and Lyle know how to display anguish for the camera and you can feel sorry for them. In predatory culture you can empty dozens of shotgun shells into the bodies of your twitching and bleeding parents and then use your dead parents' money to buy yourself a Rolex watch and hire a personal tennis coach. You can even buy yourself a restaurant. In order to get a hung jury (at least the first time around) all that you have to do is convince at least half of the jury that you were savagely butt-jacked by your father. That shouldn't be too difficult because in predatory culture such horrors are commonplace. In predatory culture there are endless possibilities for clean-cut "preppy" murderers.

Capitalism can be fun for students, especially if you happen to live in Memphis, Tennessee. Memphis City School District now has Weapon Watch in its 104,000-pupil district and already more than seventy students have been arrested. Students are given rewards of $50 if they turn in fellow classmates who bring guns to school. What's fun about it is that a Weapon Watch representative arranges to meet secretly with and pay off the informants. Anonymous tipsters are given code numbers to protect their identities. Already an 11-year-old has been caught with a sawn-off rifle and dozens of guns have been confiscated including a 9mm pistol, a 380mm automatic and a .38-caliber revolver (Natali 1994). Guns can be fun but it's more fun to turn in those who bring them to school. At least that's what predatory culture teaches. And in the end the school doesn't have to invest in expensive metal detectors like so many other schools.

It's less fun to be in Wedowee, Alabama for high school students. That's because high school principal, Holond Humphries, threatened to cancel the school prom rather than allow "mixed" couples to attend. This didn't jive well with ReVonda Bowen, a student who has a white father and black mother. Humphries reportedly said that his edict was designed to prevent more "mistakes" like her from happening. Predictably, the Ku Klux Klan supported Humphries on the grounds that he was supporting Biblical edicts (Harrison 1994).

Ironically, today's increasingly "disorganized" capitalism has produced a gaudy sideshow that has managed to promote a counterfeit democracy of flags and emblems – one that has managed to harness the affective currency of popular culture such that the average American's investment in being "American" has reached an unparalleled high the likes of which has not been seen since the years of the McCarthy hearings. The question that needs to be asked is: How are the subjectivities (experiences) and identities of individuals and the production of media knowledges within popular culture mutually articulated?

What isn't being talked about in today's educational debate is the desperate need within our schools for creating a media-literate citizenry that can disrupt, contest, and transform media apparatuses so that they no longer have the power to infantilize the population and continue to create passive, fearful, paranoid, and apolitical social subjects.

George Gerbner (1989/90) and others have pointed out that American television viewers are accepting a distorted picture of the real world "more readily than reality itself." Television reality is one in which men outnumber women three to one, where women are usually mothers or lovers, rarely work outside the home, and are natural victims of violence. It is a reality where less than 10 per cent of the population hold blue-collar jobs, where few elderly people exist, where young Blacks learn to accept their minority status as inevitable and are trained to anticipate their own victimization (they are usually portrayed as the white hero's comic sidekick or else drug addicts, gang members, and killers). It is a world in which eighteen acts of violence an hour occur in children's prime time programs. Violence in television demonstrates the social power of adult white males who are most likely to get involved with violence but also most likely to get away with it. It also serves as a mass spectacle reflecting the allocative power of the state. And this is occurring in a country that in 1990 reported the largest number of rapes against women in its history and a prison incarceration rate of Blacks that exceeds that of South Africa. A country where there are more gun stores than gas stations; where rich Angelenos are hiring private police; where the wealthy neighborhoods display signs warning Armed Response! and where security systems and the militarization of urban life are refiguring social space along the line of the postmodern film *Bladerunner*. The veins of Latin America opened by C.I.A. mobsters and generations of foreign policy bureaucrats in starched shirts are bleeding northwards, pumping the Third World into the heart of Los Angeles. We are facing a crisis of predatory culture forged through the unholy symbiosis of capitalism and technology (technocapitalism), a crisis that has profound global implications. Our eyes and ears no longer belong to us. They've been replaced by John Wayne Bobbitt's penis and Tonya Harding's beefy thighs.

What educators need to realize is that a New World Order cannot be realistically achieved without creating a new moral order at home first (and that means in the classrooms and the living rooms of the nation) – one that refuses to challenge the received truths or accepted conventions that have provoked the current crisis of history and identity. So far Bush and Clinton have been successful in reproducing a moral order in which young people are able to resist being motivated to enter into any logic of opposition through counterpublic spheres of cultural resistance, despite the understated extravaganzas of Clinton's electronic "town hall" meetings.

It is sad that the supposed "education president", George Bush, invested more in the intelligence quotients of his weapons of war than in those who grow despondent inside of the walls of the nation's schools. While politicians self-righteously decry the retrenchment of the conservative "hard-liners" in Russia, they fail to see the ideological affinities with their own political positions; incredibly, they see *their* conservative position as somehow more enlightened and the politics they support immune to the ideological terrorism of a Vladimir Zhirinovskii. This has blinded them to the ways in which dominant social order continues to shut the colonized out of history – even in this so-called era of interculturalism and growth of poly-ethnic and poly-lingual communities.

Missing from the debate over public education is a serious examination of the way in which contemporary forms of schooling reproduce national images of citizenship modeled on the Ramboizing of America and captured in Rocky Balboa's "Go for it!" and Clint Eastwood's "Go ahead. Make my day!", cliches which adorn the discursive fountainhead of United States bravado culture. These intoxicating slogans, like Walter Cronkite's "And that's the way it is," have become cultural aphorisms that reveal a great deal about the structural unconscious of the United States – phrases that constitute a combination of insurance company rationality, the politics of Sunday School charity drives, and the patriarchal, zenophobic and militaristic logic of terror. Both Ronald Reagan and George Bush used "Go ahead, make my day!" during their time in office. When Clint Eastwood delivers the line in the movie *Sudden Impact*, he is daring a black man to murder a woman so that he (as Dirty Harry) can kill him. As Michael Rogin (1990) has pointed out, Eastwood/Harry is willing to sacrifice women and people of color in the name of his own courage. Reagan had made women and Blacks his targets by destroying their welfare-state tax benefits – an act he was defending when he dared his detractors to "Make my day!" George Bush adapted the film's messages to his own purposes in the creation of "Willy" Horton, as he attempted to reorganize American politics around the ominous image of interracial rape (Rogin 1990). Rogin brilliantly articulates the use of movies such as *Rambo* and *Sudden Impact* as political spectacle which operates as a form of social amnesia (1990: 107).

The kind of curriculum focus needed in today's schools is one that actively contests the historical amnesia created by contemporary cultural forms found in the mass media. Students should be invited to explore why they identify with Dirty Harry and Rambo, and begin to historicize such an identification in the context of the larger political and social issues facing the country.

It should come as little surprise that public opinion among those groups most advantaged by wealth and power is more supportive of the public school system and current reform efforts than those disempowered on the basis of race, socioeconomic status or gender. For those very populations that will be increasing in numbers in the coming decades – particularly African–American and Latino youth – conditions in this country's school systems have worsened appreciably. Groups actively lobbying for minority positions on issues dealing with race, social and welfare concerns, are now being labeled within the conservative agenda by spokespersons such as Diane Ravitch, Roger Kimball, William Bennett, Lynne V. B. Cheney and others as "ethnocentric" or "separatist." Within such an agenda, which arrogates to itself the task of preserving the unconditional principles of civilized society, the call for diversity is sanctioned only when the converging of diverse voices collapses into a depoliticized coexistence based on capitulation to the hidden imperatives of Eurocentrism, logocentrism and patriarchy. Those educators and students who refuse to genuflect before the Western cultural tradition and regard it thrillingly and glowingly as the apogee of cultural and political achievement are branded as perverse, ignorant and malicious sophists who have "defiled reason" (Kimball 1991; see also Ravitch 1990). What this ideological position effectively does is sound an alarm for the impeding demise of white culture: "If white people have any pride in their heritage, now is the time to act because your history is under assault!" This clarion call for white authenticity embalms the past for people of color and shrouds their histories in the thinning strands of the moral and social consciousness of a nation plagued by social amnesia. It also wraps domination in a white sheet of race, class, and gender purity by exiling questions of racism, sexism, homophobia, and class oppression.

What Anglocentric educators who teach under the sign of "First World" fail to understand is that our schools are failing large numbers of minority students precisely because too much emphasis is already being placed on trading in on the status of one's cultural capital. Ironically, those students who populate urban settings in places such as New York's Howard Beach, Ozone Park, El Barrio, etc., are likely to learn more about Eastern Europe in contexts designed by *soi disant* metropolitan intellectuals than they are about the Harlem Renaissance, Mexico, Africa, the Caribbean, or Aztec or Zulu culture. The sad irony is that test scores based on information filtered from the Western canon and bourgeois cultural capital and developed in the bourgeois salons of the Prozac generation are used to justify school district and state funding initiatives. The reality of schooling is that U.S. society is composed of differentially empowered publics, and mainstream schooling ensures that those publics which already enjoy most of the power and privilege in society will transmit their advantage for succeeding generations. In this way, intergenerational continuity is ensured: working-class students get working-class jobs; affluent students get the kind of employment that will advantage their life chances and those of their children.

WHAT YOU BE ABOUT?

Gangs in predatory culture are situated in what Dwight Conquergood (in press) calls a "media demonology" that foments "moral panics" about gangbangers who are categorized as social defectives, who occupy a subterranean rogues' gallery of the half human *untermensch*, who have been socially identified as the expendable human excrement *par excellence* of predatory culture. As Conquergood notes, public opinion of gangs, largely motivated by the media, deflects attention away from the "political and economic macropatterns of exclusion and displacement which shape the microtexture of everyday struggle for poor and socially marginalized people" (p. 54). Shunted aside is the necessary realization that the criminalization of gangs is directly linked to deindustrialization, disinvestment, economic polarization, residential segregation, real estate speculation, gentrification, and the abandonment, neglect and collapse of civic institutions such as schools in the name of retrograde fiscal responsibility (p. 54). We demonize those who, like gang members, are physically threatening predators, lavishly decorated with the tattoos and piercings of the hostile subordinate classes and also the less dangerous, eyesore predators such as the homeless whose disturbingly neglected physiognomies are left to decay in doorsteps and over sewer grates, and who serve predatory culture as little more than an affront to bourgeois sensibility and decorum.

According to Conquergood,

> Before they tattoo their bodies with gang insignia, urban youth are always already inscribed and branded by stigmatizing images of poverty, prejudice, and pathology, which are produced by the official discourse of the media, legal system, and public policy institutions – those authorities and experts who have the power to know, name, and label. Gangs are constructed in public discourse as the cause, effect, and aberrant response to social disorder and urban decay. The demonized figure of the violent gangbanger is the sensational centerpiece in a self-righteous morality play called "the urban underclass" playing currently in mainstream media and social-policy institutions.
>
> (in press, pp. 53–54)

Schools in predatory culture keep youth stupid. Here, literacy becomes a thesaurus to be memorized by students aspiring to become active, engaged citizens. Yet when culture is despairingly viewed as a storehouse of dead facts, a time capsule of frozen memories detached from historical context, then the concept of difference, when applied to issues of race, class, gender, age, sexual preference, or disability, can be absorbed into what I call "dead pluralism." Dead pluralism is what keeps at bay the need to historicize difference, to recognize the hierarchical production of systems of difference and whose interests such hierarchies serve, and to acknowledge difference as a social construction forged within asymmetrical relations of power, conflicting interests, and a climate of dissent and opposition. The "pluralism" that supposedly already undergirds our so-called multicultural society in the vision of Diane Ravitch and Roger Kimball is one that is based on uncoerced consensus, interracial and intergenerational harmony and zero-degree public unity – a perspective shrouded in the lie of democratic ubiquity. When Ravitch and Kimball call for pluralism over separatism they are really buttressing the status quo against disempowered minorities seeking social justice.

The real danger facing education is not simply the refusal of the general public to recognize its embeddedness in relations of power and privilege at the level of everyday life, but rather the fact that the public prefers to act as if there exist few – or no – such political linkages. The danger is not an apathetic nation, nor a cynical one, but rather the ability of the public sphere to exist relatively uncontested. Why? I believe that it has to do with the ability to the larger public sphere to mobilize desire, and secure the passion of the public, and the relative inability of progressive educators to analyze the social, cultural, moral and political implications of such an ability.

Work within the field of critical pedagogy is currently being undertaken in the United States and Canada during what I consider a precipitous and precarious time. We live in a moment of particular urgency and importance for the future of democracy as we bear witness to two conflicting potentialities which manifest themselves in the struggle on an increasingly worldwide basis between democratic forms of social life and those which can be labeled totalitarian and autocratic. A significant dimension of this crisis involves the politics of meaning and representation. Attention must be paid to the cultural logic or sensibility currently organizing aspects of everyday life, a logic which has been variously theorized under the term "postmodern." Recognizing that there exists a lack of shared understanding of what constitutes a "real" postmodern political or cultural agenda, I use the term here only in its most general sense to refer to, among other things, the rupturing of the unitary fixity and homogenizing logic of the grand narratives of Western European thought – what Lyotard refers to as the *grands recits* of modernity (the dialectic of Spirit, the emancipation of the workers, the accumulation of wealth, the steady march of progress leading to the classless society, the mastery of nature, etc.). The term also covers the cultural reproduction of subjects produced from the consumer myths and images fed by the global dispersion of capital, the social construction of unfixed identities, and the leveling of the opposition between high art and popular art. In a very broad sense, it also suggests the rejection of truth claims that have a grounding in a transcendent reality independent of collective human existence, an abandonment of the teleology of science, the construction of lifestyles out of consumer products and cultural bricolage, and cultural forms of communication and social relations that have evolved from the disorganization of capitalism.

The debate surrounding postmodernity is not gathering momentum solely in literature, but also in social theory, cultural studies, education, and legal studies. A central thesis of postmodernism is that meaning is increasingly becoming severed from representation. Peter Burger puts it thus: "[I]n our society the sign no longer refers to a signified but always only to other signs, so that we no longer encounter anything like meaning without speech, but only move in an endless chain of signifiers" (1989: 124). In other words, the unity of the sign and its ability to anchor meaning has been significantly weakened. The average individual lacks a language for making sense of everyday life. Burger writes:

> The modern culture industry robs individuals of "languages" for interpreting self and world by denying them the media for organizing their own experiences. The consciousness industry does represent a public sphere of production, but one that takes consciousness as "raw material" or that constantly tries to sever the connection between concrete experiences and consciousness.
>
> (1984: xxviii–xxvix)

Lawrence Grossberg echoes this theme when he writes that

> Contemporary ideological structures seem incapable of making sense of certain affective experiences. . . . But this does not mean that we do not continue to live within and experience ourselves in terms of particular ideological meanings and values; simply that these are increasingly unrelated to our affective moods, that they cannot speak to them.
>
> (1988c: 180)

As a result of the postmodern condition, the alienation of the subject associated with modernism has been replaced by the fragmentation of the subject, what Madan Sarup (1989), citing literary critic Fredric Jameson and economist Ernest Mandel, refers to as a

> refusal to engage with the present or to think historically . . . a random cannibalization of all the styles of the past . . . [an increasing incapacity] of fashioning representations of our current experiences . . . [and] the

> penetration and colonization of Nature and the Unconscious [by contemporary forms of multinational capitalism].
>
> (1989: 145–6)

I should add here that it is not necessary like Sarup to hold that poststructualist and postmodernist theories which have emerged in recent years to engage and explore our location within the postmodern condition are necessarily antagonistic to the project of emancipation.

Postmodernity positions us within the tension produced by modernist and postmodernist attempts to resolve the contradiction of being both the subject and and object of meaning. We refer here to two distinct ways of ordering reality discussed by David Holt (1989: 174). Holt describes these orderings as being reflected in the following questions: Does meaning generate life or does life generate meaning? The first question is posed within the discourse of modernity in which it is assumed that our lives should be lived out as an explanation of a meaning prior to life, a transcendental meaning that is codified in a conception of metaphysical truth. The second reflects the advent of postmodernity and the shattering of the notion of "truth" based on metaphysical assumptions. To live life as if it generated meaning is to live within the contingency and uncertainty of the present, a present in which ethics, tradition, and agency are revealed to be social constructions or cultural fictions. Living within the tension created by these two questions generates further questions: Do we act in order to represent meanings or do we act for the sake of the possible effects of our actions? Does action create identity or does action follow from identity? While these questions have always occupied the projects engaged in over the centuries by philosophers of various stripes, the postmodern condition has turned our attention boldly to the interface between such questions (Holt 1989).

Throughout this book I have tried to emphasize that it is the educator's task to help students critically engage the politics and ideologies which inform these questions, as they begin to understand themselves as both a product and producer of meaning. It is precisely by critically engaging the dialectical tension between these two questions that we must assume our role as active social agents. Living as a critical social agent means knowing how to live contingently and provisionally without the certainty of knowing the truth, yet at the same time with the courage to take a stand on issues of human suffering, domination, and oppression. This is the "postmodern" task of the critical educator – to live with courage and conviction with the understanding that knowledge is always partial and incomplete – a task to which this book is directed.

Bauman lists as characteristics of postmodernity "the widespread aversion to grand social designs, the loss of interest in absolute truths, the privatization of redemptive urges [e.g., self as opposed to social transformation], the reconciliation with the relative – merely heuristic – value of all life techniques, the acceptance of the irredeemable plurality of the world" (1988/89: 39). He notes that these characteristics are a consequence of the fact that the abolition of strangeness has been raised to the level of a universal human condition.

Ineradicable plurality is now a constitutive quality of existence and represents a refusal to overcome differences for the sake of sameness. Values so central to modernity – uniformity and universalism – have become ruptured, and replaced by coexistence and tolerance. Bauman writes that "in the plural and pluralistic world of postmodernity, every form of life is *permitted on principle*; or, rather, no agreed principles are evident which may render any form of life impermissible" (p. 40). Bauman distinguishes between the modernist (cognitive) and postmodernist (post-cognitive) questions. Modernist questions "How can I interpret this world of which I am a part? And what am I in it?' have been replaced by postmodernist ones: "Which world is it? What is to be done in it? Which of my selves is to do it?" (p. 40).

The so-called cognitive questions, upon closer inspection, turn out not to be cognitive at all, but questions that "reach beyond the boundaries of epistemology" (p. 42); they are fundamentally pre-epistemological. Modernist questions such as "What is there to be known? Who knows it? How do they know it and with what degree of certainty?" are replaced by questions which do not locate the task for the knower but attempt to locate the knower: "What is a world? What kinds of worlds are there, how are they constituted, and how do they differ?" (p. 42). Questions demanding certainty, such as "How is knowledge transmitted from one knower to another, and with what degree of reliability?" are positioned against "What happens when different worlds are placed in confrontation, or when boundaries between worlds are violated?" (p. 42).

Bauman's insights into the shift from a modernist quest for certainty to a postmodernist attempt to understand shifting contexts are extremely important, for they speak to a growing tension between these two positions which possess both empowering and constraining potential for the struggle against oppression and the quest for human freedom. While we should welcome the breaking down of grand theories informed by Eurocentric and patriarchal assumptions and epistemological certainties, we are aware that questions related to oppression and liberation have a greater propensity to become lost in a new postmodernist relativism, where the question of "How can we eliminate suffering?" collapses into the question, "What is suffering?". Bauman captures this tension when he writes: "It seems in the world of universal strangeness the stranger is no longer obsessed with the absoluteness of what ought to be; nor is he disturbed by the relativity of what is" (p. 42).

I do not wish to enter into an extended discussion of postmodernity here, except to note that there are both utopian and dystopian currents to the postmodern condition and post-structuralist theorizing. But what is important to recognize in this ongoing debate is that postmodernity has brought with it not only new forms of collective self-reflexivity but also new forms of ideological colonization. Critics as diverse as Andreas Huyssen, Todd Gitlin, and Fredric Jameson have pointed out that postmodernism has a specifically, though not exclusively, American strain. Cornel West (Stephanson 1988b: 276) refers to this as "a form of Americanization of the globe." The rise of postmodernism has been materially tied to the rise of American capital on a global scale, dated to the late 1950s and early 1960s, an era of interimperialist rivalry and multinationalization. Jameson has argued that the persistence of the ancien regime in Europe precluded the same kind of development there, but in the United States a whole new system of cultural production emerged and a new, specifically American cultural apparatus or "cultural dominant" began to serve as a form of ideological hegemony, forcing Third World countries into the untenable positions of playing "catch up" (Stephanson 1988a: 8).

Postmodernity has also been described as the era of the death of the Cartesian subject and a retreat from history. Dean MacCannell (1989: xiii) goes so far as to say, following Lévi-Strauss, that after Hiroshima and Nagasaki and the stockpiling of nuclear weapons by strategic nuclear planners, American society has deemed it too risky to have history and therefore has effectively abandoned it as its motive power of development, entering instead the "reversible time" of so-called primitive societies which, though they are immersed in history, nevertheless try to remain impervious to it.

One strand of contemporary postmodernism has grown out of juxtaposing currents in American culture: emancipation and the rise of immigration in the late nineteenth century and assimilation into the American myth of the melting pot. Here difference becomes flattened out, accommodated to the values of white patriarchal capitalism. This is reflective of MacCannell's notion that a mere celebration of difference can become an insidious higher form of "sucking difference out of difference, a movement to the still higher ground of the old arrogant Western Ego that wants to see it all, know it all, and take it all in, an Ego that is isolated by its belief in its own superiority" (1989: xiv–xv).

A critical understanding of the relationship between the self and other is one of the crucial challenges of current pedagogical practices in the age of postmodernism. This is especially true in light of MacCannell's observation that two dominant activities shaping world culture are the movement of institutional capital and tourists to remote regions and "the preparation of the Third World into the First" by which he means the movement of refugees and displaced peoples "from the periphery to the centers of power and affluence." For instance, in the case of the

United States, MacCannell notes the profound implications which follow from cultural implosions such as the following:

> Entire villages of Hmong peasants and hunters, recently from the highlands of Laos, have been relocated and now live in apartment complexes in Madison, Wisconsin. Refugees from El Salvador work in Manhattan, repackaging cosmetics, removing perfume from Christmas gift boxes, rewrapping them in Valentine boxes. Legal and illegal "aliens" work the agricultural fields of California.
>
> (1989: xvi)

The implication here for educators is to construct a pedagogy of "difference" which neither exoticizes nor demonizes the "Other" but rather seeks to locate difference in both its specificity and ability to provide positions for critically engaging social relations and cultural practices.

Like Grossberg (1988c), I do not conceive of postmodernity as a "total historical rupture" that constitutes the ideological representation of late capitalism, the commodification of our decentered subjectivities, the implosion of the difference between the image and the real, or the collapse of all metanarratives, but rather as a sensibility or logic by which we appropriate in the contemporary context, cultural practices into our own lives. That is, I wish to call attention to postmodernity as a process significantly less totalizing, as "determining moments in culture and everyday life" (Grossberg 1988c: 39). Postmodernity in this view refers to a "growing distance, an expanding series of ruptures or gaps, between . . . various aspects of everyday life, between the available meanings, values and objects of desire which socially organize our existence and identity, and the possibilities for investing in or caring about them which are enabled by our moods and emotions" (p. 39). Grossberg is referring here to a feeling or sensibility that life no longer has any fundamental purpose to which we can passionately commit. He remarks that our " 'mattering maps' no longer correspond to any available maps of meaning" (p. 40). Postmodernity is, in short, a crisis of meaning and feeling: "a dissolution of what we might call the 'anchoring affect' that articulates meaning and affect" (p. 40). One of the dangers of postmodern culture is the establishment of what Grossberg calls a "disciplined mobilization" by which he means "the construction of a frontier as an unbridgeable gap between the livable and the unlivable, the possible and the impossible, the real and the unreal" (p. 37). A disciplined mobilization refers to the temporal and spatial articulation of texts through social practices which give us both stability and mobility within everyday life. It "defines the very possibilities of where and how we move and stop, of where and how we place and displace ourselves, or where and how we are installed into cultural texts and extended beyond them" (pp. 36–7). Such a "typography of cultural practices" defines the sites within culture we can occupy, the investments we can make in them, and the places along which we can connect and transform them. Grossberg is especially concerned here with the increasing ability of the New Right to develop ideological and affective alliances among social groups. That is, looking at the postmodern frontier as a site of struggle among discourse, material practices, and representation, it can be argued that the New Right has been able to rearticulate, reconstruct, and reterritorialize the "national popular" (the family, nationalism, consumerism, youth, pleasure, heroes, etc.) against itself as affectively charged but ideologically empty. One example of this is the ability of New Class neo-conservatives to manipulate traditional populism (Piccone 1987/88: 21).

PREDATORY CULTURE: "HOPELESS BUT NOT SERIOUS"

In this postmodern era, ideological hegemony in the United States, while irredeemably condemnable and undeniably powerful, is more like a buffer than a monolith. Students often see the critical educator's concern for community and social justice as a threat to their general ideological commitments. Critical pedagogy becomes, for many students, an uncomfortable and self-contesting exercise. They are reluctant or refuse to question meanings, preferring instead to live them.

It is not the purpose of this book to absorb student apathy about politics and social change into traditional political categories and end up by offering yet another "blaming the victim" analysis of the ideological formation of today's youth. Rather, I want to acknowledge that there are historical conditions which account for youth resistance and apathy. For instance, Grossberg notes that "youth inserts cultural texts into its public and private lives in complex ways" and we need to be aware of the complexity and contradictory nature of youth's social and political positions (1988b: 139). Grossberg rightly recognizes that in our postmodern era, young people exist within the space between subjectification (boredom) and commodification (terror). Our media culture has become a "buffer zone," a "paradoxical site" in which the youth of today lives out a difficult if not impossible relation to the future. In fact, Grossberg argues that American youth have largely been formed out of the media strategies of the "autonomous affect" in which politics, values, and meaning have been reduced to individualized images of morality, self-sacrifice, and community. Young people are living the surface identities of media images in which the politics of interpretative insight is replaced by the politics of "feeling good."

Grossberg points to one cultural struggle in which the New Right has taken the lead: the attack on the counterculture of the 1960s and 1970s, in part through its ability to reconstruct the history of the war in Vietnam. A brief treatment of such a reconstruction will help to illustrate his point.

Vietnam was a war fought by youth and became "the symbol of the moment when the identification of the postwar youth generations with America fell apart and consequently, the moment when America lost, not only its center but its faith in a center" (Grossberg 1988c: 56). Yet popular narratives in the media now attempt "to place the war back into the familiar frameworks of traditional war narratives or personal drama" (p. 57). The existence of the counterculture at that time is generally ignored in popular representations of the war. Rather, the war is interpreted as an attack on America and its sacred values – "the moment when the postwar youth generations lost their faith, not only in America, but in the possibility of ever finding a center, an identity, in which it could invest" (p. 58). The effect of ignoring the counterculture is to displace "any ideological content from youth culture and [transform] it into purely affective relations" (p. 59) – or to create "affective nostalgia." That there exist few grounds presently available to students upon which to imagine constructing an oppositional or counter-hegemonic pedagogical stance in a cultural center with no real ideological content – only feelings – makes the challenge of critical pedagogy all the more acute and all the more pressing.

Aside from youth's subjective formation through the "affective alliances" of mass media, part of the problem with the refusal of youth to engage in issues of class oppression and social injustice both inside and outside the classroom has to do with the fact that in the United States, domination and oppression are not as overt as in many Third World countries. North American civil society is less obviously structured by divisions based on the conflict of labor and capital. Consequently, class relations do not appear to cause social inequality and there is a greater focus on oppressive instances of gender divisions, age differences, and ethnic conflict. In other words, we do not live within structures of terror such as those found, for instance, in El Salvador or Guatemala, where workers are frequently dispatched by a coup de grâce through the forehead. Furthermore, collective action does not seem as necessary within a climate of political and cultural pluralism, although the presences of the black underclass and the homeless are somewhat changing this spectatorial detachment from human oppression. The point is that class, gender, and racial oppression do exist, regardless of the perception by the public at large (Baum 1987).

Grossberg admits that given the New Right's incursion into the frontier between affect and ideology, where only or mainly emotional responses are possible without the benefit of ideological understanding or commitment, there is little room for Gramsci's "optimism of the will" so necessary for political struggle, for understanding and confronting affective commitment outside of the system of cultural power within which such an investment is constructed, and for assuming a necessary relationship between affective investment and external systems of meaning. For instance, the desire among conservatives and die-hard "patriots" to make flag burning a crime (whether by constitutional amendment or civil blasphemy statute) as a reaction against the recent United States Supreme Court ruling, is an excellent example of affective commitment in which patriotism is construed, in Grossberg's terms, as an "empty center" devoid of the kind of ideological engagement that makes it impossible to undermine any definition of what American means other than absolute commitment to America itself.

This book takes the position that in relation to what is happening on the popular front, critical pedagogy must become a strategic and empowering response to those historical conditions which have produced us as subjects, and to the ways we are inserted on a daily basis into the frontier of popular culture and existing structures of power. I will argue that a clarification of some of the practices of critical pedagogy can, as a form of intellectual labor, have transformative effects, enabling us to deconstruct and move beyond affective investments "to a higher level of abstraction in order to transform the empirically taken-for-granted into the concretely determined" (Grossberg 1988c: 68).

Dare we conspire to create a critical pedagogy that is able to provide conditions for students to reject what they experience as a given; a pedagogy that includes a sharpened focus on the relationship among economies of capital investment, political economies, moral economies, economies of "free" expression, sexual economies, economies of belief and identity formation and the construction of desire and formation of human will; a pedagogy of discontent and of outrage that is able to contest the hegemony of prevailing definitions of the everyday as the "way things are;" a pedagogy that refuses the hidebound distinction between lofty expression and popular culture, between art and experience, between reason and the imagination? We need a critical pedagogy in our colleges of education that can problematize schooling as a site for the construction of moral, cultural, and national identity, and emphasize the creation of the schooled citizen as a form of emplacement, as a geopolitical construction, as a process in the formation of the geography of cultural desire. Dare we transform teaching practices in our schools into acts of dissonance and interventions into the ritual inscription of our students into the codes of the dominant culture; into structured refusals to naturalize existing relations of power; into the creation of subaltern counterpublics?

It only makes sense that a curriculum should have as its focus of investigation the study of everyday, informal, and popular culture and how the historical patterns of power that inform such cultures are imbricated in the formation of individual subjectivity and identity. Pedagogy occurs not only in schools but in all cultural sites. The electronic media is perhaps the greatest site of pedagogical production that exists – you could say it is a form of perpetual pedagogy. In addition to understanding literacies applicable to print culture, students need to recognize how their identities are formed and their "mattering maps" produced through an engagement with electronic and other types of media so that they will be able to engage in alternative ways of symbolizing the self and gain a significant purchase on the construction of their own identities and the direction of their desiring. It is in such an investigation that teachers and students become transformed into cultural workers for self and social emancipation. I am calling for a pedagogy of critical media literacy that is linked to what Paul Willis (1990) has referred to as a "grounded aesthetics" designed to provide students with the symbolic resources for creative self- and social formation in order that they can more critically re-enter the vast, uncharted spaces of common culture.

I am further suggesting that students need to make critical judgments about what society might mean, and what is possible or desirable outside existing configurations of power and privilege. Students need to be able to cross over into different zones of cultural diversity and form what Trinh T. Minh-ha (1988) calls hybrid and hyphenated identities in order to rethink the relationship of self to society, of self to other, and to deepen the moral vision of the social order. This raises an important question: How are the categories of race, class, gender, and sexual preference shaped within the margins and centers of society, and how can students engage history as a way of reclaiming power and identity? The critical media literacy of which I speak is structured around the notion of a politics of location and identity as border-crossing. It is grounded in the ethical imperative of examining the contradictions in U.S. society among the meaning of freedom, the demands of social justice, and the obligations of citizenship on the one hand, and the structured silence that permeates incidents of suffering in everyday life on the other.

It is important that critical educators do not choose the chronic dream of totality and completeness in their theoretical formulations. Rather than undertaking the task of charting out a grand theory, critical educators should begin to connect the cause of social transformation to a more inclusive view of the project of critical pedagogy unburdened by the narrowness of vision that has characterized so many radical educational projects of the past which have allowed themselves to work simply within the context of ideology critique, class analysis, or gender analysis. By recasting the task of critical pedagogy in a language of possibility, they can connect it more persuasively and passionately to a view of what it means to be truly empowered. In doing so, critical educators must seek to create social spaces which break down the tightening grasp of social division and hierarchy and build upon what Roberto Unger calls "the ennoblement of human solidarity" (Unger 1987: 212), a task that makes it "possible to achieve a wholehearted engagement in our societies that does not rest on illusion and bad faith" (p. 212). That is, it remains the task of critical pedagogy to construct a praxis for teachers that urges an active solicitude for the marginalized and dispossessed, both male and female, those who have been vanquished by the incursion of the logic of capital into both the rural and urban landscapes of North America.

The praxis to which I refer throughout this book is one which is lived in solidarity with all victims struggling to overcome their suffering and alienation. The irruption of the poor in our towns and cities over the last decade demands a relocation of schooling in a praxis of solidarity where the individual and personal is always situated in relation to the collective and communal (without the simple-minded cohesiveness that these terms usually imply). It is a praxis that seeks to engage history with the intent of helping the powerless locate themselves in it. This means calling teachers to a cosuffering with the oppressed as they struggle both to transcend and transform the circumstances of their disempowerment (Chopp 1985). In other words, we need to resituate the challenge of teaching as a task of empowering the powerless from states of dependency and passivity as both an informed movement for revolutionary social and economic transformation and as means of achieving what Brian Fay calls a "state of reflective clarity" (1987). This is a state of liberation "in which people know which of their wants are genuine because they know finally who they really are, and a state of collective autonomy in which they have the power to determine rationally and freely the nature and direction of their collective existence" (p. 205).

In searching for the nonidentity constitutive of a genuine experience of liberation, I seek to avoid becoming trapped within a totalizing negativity – what I refer to as an incipient anti-utopianism, Left malaise, or an entrenchment in despair characteristic of those who have abandoned a language of hope and possibility. In addition, my theoretical approach is deliberately cast to avoid following a pre-established scheme, formula, or script, and it is self-consciously multidisciplinary as I have chosen to enter into collaboration with many different types of contemporary scholarship: semiotics, hermeneutics, critical theory, liberation theology, and post-structuralism. But in doing so, I maintain I am not moving away from the concrete but rather towards the complexity of the concrete. In the words of Matthew Lamb:

> Theory is not an impoverished abstraction away from . . . reality. Instead theory as critical is a profound effort to understand processive reality ever more adequately. Theory, then, does not move away from the concrete, only to be returned to it in the form of some sort of practical application. Instead, theory is continually moving toward the complexity of the concrete and, in the measure that it is correct in

> indicating the underlying concrete and contradictory tensions in reality, it is capable of guiding the transformation of reality.
>
> (1982: 49–50)

The pedagogy of the concrete which this book addresses is grounded in a politics of ethics, difference, and democracy. It is unashamedly utopian in substance and scope, and articulates a vision of and for the future, maintaining that if we have no idea of what we are working towards, we will never know if, in our struggle for human freedom, those conditions have been met. Our thoughts and actions are thus deliberately designed to rupture the unitary fixity and cohesiveness of social life and resist attempts at asserting the homogeneity of the social and public sphere. I am referring here to a pedagogy that is grounded in the importance of the "other" and the necessity of developing a common ground for linking the notion of difference to a publicly shared language of struggle and social justice (Giroux 1988b). Like MacCannell, I believe the positive potential within postmodernity "depends on its capacity to recognize and accept otherness as radically other ... the possibility of recognizing and attempting to enter into a dialogue, on an equal footing with forms of intelligence absolutely different from [our] own" (MacCannell 1989: xv). However, Rosaldo makes the point that radical otherness may not be as radical today as it once was, since:

> Rapidly increasing global interdependence has made it more and more clear that neither "we" nor "they" are as neatly bounded and homogeneous as once seemed to be the case. . . . All of us inhabit an interdependent late-twentieth-century world marked by borrowing and lending across porous national and cultural boundaries that are saturated with inequality, power, and domination.
>
> (1989: 217)

The politics of difference that undergirds the critical pedagogy discussed in this book is one in which differences rearticulate and shape identity such that students can actively refuse the role of cultural servant and sentinel for the status quo in order to reclaim, reshape, and transform their own historical destiny. The pedagogy I am calling forth, incanting, and incarnating throughout the pages that follow is not premised upon a common culture, or a transcendence of local knowledges or particularisms. It is not, in other words, committed to Enlightenment epistemology nor economic liberalism but rather a new socialist imaginary grounded not in specific forms of rationality but in forms of detotalized agency and the expansion of the sphere of radical democracy to new forms of social life. It is a move away from what Arnold Krupat calls "unself-critical humanistic universalism" and toward a "critical cosmopolitanism" (1991: 243) which does not ask people to discard their ethnic and local attachments for more global commitments but rather interrogates *the universal already contained in the local* and examines how the ethnic and the regional *is already populated by other perspectives and meanings.* We make our homes, we come "homeys" in this zone of contest between local and global, dominant and subordinal meanings and social practices, seeking to rearticulate them in the interests of greater social justice and freedom. Our pedagogical homes, our "hoods" need to become cultural spaces where students are able to form interlaced networks of intracommunal negotiation, spaces that work toward the construction of intimacies and coarticulated communal patterns in classrooms and the surrounding communities and that take the project of human liberation and social justice seriously.

The challenge of critical pedagogy is a daunting one at this time of historical amnesia, when our public mentors have been replaced by cultural snipers and urban poachers, when counter-hegemonic identities are exchanged for more domesticated aesthetic productions, when the vision of what education should be looks like a mixture of the "rah rah" spirit of an Anglican boys' school outdoor excursion, the learning opportunities of a boot camp for young criminals, and all the intellectual fodder that can be sifted from a jar full of fossilized brain matter. The global curriculum for late-capitalism's civics instruction is being written by Abfab's Edina and Patsy, as education is being transformed into just another commodity theater for lifestyle aficionados, a subsector of the economy designed to serve the entrepreneurial interests of promotional, accelerated culture. The future looks empty and intense. Oliver Stone's film, *Natural Born Killers,* gives us a glimpse of the "fun" Citizen Golem that capitalist culture is producing, and the fab time that awaits us in predatory culture. Prepare yourselves, teachers, for curriculum *agitado.* It's going to be real.

Part I

Pedagogy, culture, and the body

Chapter I

Radical pedagogy as cultural politics

Beyond the discourse of critique and anti-utopianism

With Henry A. Giroux

Within the last fifteen years a radical theory of education has emerged in the United States. Broadly defined as "the new sociology of education" or "a critical theory of education," a critical pedagogy developed within this discourse attempts to examine schools both in their historical context and as part of the social and political relations that characterize the dominant society. While hardly constituting a unified discourse, critical pedagogy nevertheless has managed to pose an important counterlogic to the positivistic, ahistorical, de-politicized discourse that often informs modes of analysis employed by liberal and conservative critics of schooling, modes all too readily visible in most colleges of education. Taking as one of its fundamental concerns the need to re-emphasize the centrality of politics and power in understanding how schools function within the larger society, critical pedagogy has catalyzed a great deal of work on the political economy of schooling, the state and education, the politics of representation, discourse analysis, and the construction of student subjectivity.

The expurgatorious writings of critical pedagogy have provided a radical theory and analysis of schooling, annexing new discourses from various strands of critical social theory and developing at the same time new categories of inquiry and new methodologies. Critical pedagogy is not physically housed in any one school or university department, nor does it constitute a homogeneous set of ideas. Critical educational theorists are, however, united in their attempts to empower the powerless and to transform social inequalities and injustices. Constituting a small minority of the academic profession and of public schoolteachers, the movement nevertheless is substantial enough to present a challenging presence within the teaching profession.[1]

One major task of critical pedagogy has been to disclose and challenge the ideological privilege accorded the school in our political and cultural life. Especially within the last decade, educational theorists have come increasingly to view schooling as a resolutely political and cultural enterprise. Recent advances in the sociology of knowledge, the history of consciousness, the critical study of colonial discourse, cultural Marxism, continental social theory, and feminist theory have provoked a conceptual recasting of schools as more than simply instructional sites. They may instead be considered as cultural arenas where heterogeneous ideological, discursive, and social forms collide in an unremitting struggle for dominance. Within this context, schools have generally been analyzed as sorting mechanisms for human capital, in which groups of students are privileged on the basis of race, class and gender; and less frequently as agencies for self- and social empowerment.

This new perspective has ushered in a view of the school as a terrain of contestation. Groups from dominant and subordinate cultures negotiate on symbolic terms; students and teachers engage, accept, and sometimes resist the ways school experiences and practices are named and legitimated. The traditional view of classroom instruction – of learning as a neutral or transparent process antiseptically removed from the concepts of power, politics, history, and context – can no longer be credibly endorsed. In fact, researchers within the critical tradition have given primacy to the categories of the social, cultural, political, and economic, in order to better understand the workings of contemporary schooling.

Theorists within the critical tradition examine schooling as a form of cultural politics. From this perspective, schooling always represents forms of social life and is always implicated in relations of power, social practices, and the privileging of forms of knowledge that support a specific vision of past, present, and future. In general, critical educational theorists maintain that the cultural politics of the schools historically and currently inculcate a meritocratic, professional ideology, rationalizing the knowledge industry into class-divided tiers; reproduce inequality, racism, and sexism; and fragment democratic social relations through an emphasis on competitiveness, androcentrism, logocentrism, and cultural ethnocentrism.

While remaining indebted to specialized frameworks appropriated from European intellectual traditions, critical pedagogy also draws upon a uniquely American tradition. That tradition extends from the mainstream progressive movement of John Dewey, William H. Kilpatrick, and others, to the more radical efforts of the social reconstructionists of the 1920s, such as George Counts and John Childs, to the work of Theodore Brameld, and finally to the more current theoretical contributions of revisionist educators.[2]

Fundamental to the principles that inform critical pedagogy is the conviction that schooling for self- and social empowerment is ethically prior to questions of epistemology or to a mastery of technical or social skills that are primarily tied to the logic of the marketplace. Concern over education's atrophied ethical dimension has provoked leftist scholars to undertake a socially critical reconstruction of what it means to "be schooled." Their efforts stress that any genuine pedagogical practice demands a commitment to social transformation in solidarity with subordinated and marginalized groups. In its broadest possible sense, this entails a preferential option for the poor and the elimination of conditions which promote human suffering. Such theorists are critical of liberal democracy's emphasis on individualism and autonomy, questioning the assumption that individuals are ontologically independent or that they are the autonomous, rational, and self-motivating social agents that liberal humanism has constructed. The theoretically and historically unsituated analyses of schooling promulgated by liberal and conservative critics alike represent different ideological aspects of the dominant society; each perspective privileges the interests of the dominant culture with equal facility. The liberal perspective especially has been shown to be reappropriated by the very logic it purports to criticize. By contrast, the radical perspective involves a critical reinscription of liberalism in a concerted attempt to displace its Eurocentric, patriarchal, and logocentric assumptions. Employing theoretical strategies that allow the unstated and submerged grammar of schooling to be more insistently critiqued and transformed, radical educators work to reveal the social and material conditions of schooling's production and reception.

Challenging the dominant assumption that schools currently function as a major mechanism for the development of the democratic and egalitarian social order, radical educational theorists have argued that schools do not provide opportunities for self- and social empowerment. They have also challenged the dominant assumption that schools currently constitute major sites of social and economic mobility, arguing instead that American schooling has defaulted on its promise of egalitarian reform. In this view, the economic, social, and political returns from schooling are far greater for the economically affluent than for the disadvantaged. Curriculum becomes both a "selective tradition" and a duplicitous practice that provides students with particular forms of knowledge, ideologically coded in ways similar to the goods and services that have been subjected to the logic of commodification.[3]

In their efforts to explode the popular belief that schools are fundamentally democratic institutions, radical critics have attempted to demonstrate how curricula, knowledge, and policy depend on the corporate marketplace and the fortunes of the economy. They warn against being deluded into thinking that either conservatives or liberals occupy a truly progressive platform from which educational decisions can be made on the basis of transparent and disinterested standards. Furthermore, their critique has revealed that the application of rigorous standards is never innocent of social, economic, and institutional contexts. In this view, schooling must always be analyzed as a cultural and historical process in which select groups are positioned within asymmetrical relations of power. Radical scholars refuse to accept the task capitalism assigns them as intellectuals, teachers, and social theorists: to service the existing ideological and institutional arrangements of the public schools, while simultaneously discounting the values and abilities of minority groups. In short, educators within the critical tradition regard mainstream schooling as supporting the transmission and reproduction of what Paulo Freire terms "the culture of silence."

Central in their attempt to reform public education has been a critical rejection of the worst aspects of the modern Enlightenment project, defined in terms of a debilitating positivism, instrumental reason, and bureaucratic control, which have been tacitly lodged in models of curriculum planning and dominant approaches to educational theory and practice. Bolstered by certain strands of feminist theory and postmodernist social theory, critical pedagogy continues to challenge the often uncontested relationship between school and society, effectively unmasking mainstream pedagogy's development as a purveyor of equal opportunity and its claim to access such virtues as egalitarian democracy and critical inquiry. Rejecting the conservative claim that schooling is a politically opaque and value-neutral process, critical pedagogy has attempted to empower teachers and researchers with more critical means of understanding the school's role within a race-, class-, and gender-divided society. Radical pedagogy has generated categories crucial for interrogating the production of student experiences, texts, teacher ideologies, and aspects of school policy that conservative and liberal analyses too often leave untouched. In effect, critical pedagogy has sharply etched the political dimensions of schooling, arguing that schools operate mainly to reproduce the discourses, values, and privileges of existing elites.

Critical pedagogy commits itself to forms of learning and action that are undertaken in solidarity with subordinated and marginalized groups. In addition to interrogating what is taken for granted or seemingly self-evident or inevitable regarding the relationship between schools and the social order, critical pedagogy is dedicated to self-empowerment and social transformation.

At the same time, many current trends in critical pedagogy are embedded in the endemic weaknesses of a theoretical project overly concerned with developing a language of critique. Critical pedagogy is steeped in a posture of moral indignation toward the injustices reproduced in American public schools. Unfortunately, this one-sided emphasis on critique is matched by the lack of ethical and pragmatic discourse upon which to ground its own vision of society and schooling and to shape the direction of a critical praxis.

How does one redefine the purpose of public schooling and rethink the role of teaching and learning in emancipatory terms? More orthodox radical educational theorists have been unable to move from a posture of criticism to one of substantive vision, from a language of critique to a language of possibility. Drawing inspiration from the traditional perspectives of Marxism and socialism, of liberalism and democratic theory, critical educators have constructed a powerful critique of the culture and knowledge industries; yet they have been unable to conceive of pedagogical and curricular reform outside of the most debilitating metaphysical assumptions of the Enlightenment. At the same time they have failed to achieve the most ennobling goals of modernity, which are to link reason to values and ethical reflection to the project of individual emancipation and social justice. These critics have been unable either to adequately mobilize key public constituencies or to challenge the current conservative attack on the schools (Giroux and McLaren 1994a) and the philistinism of the federal bureaucrats at the U.S. Department of Education. This theoretical and political impasse appears to mark a fin-de-siècle frustration with political economy models of educational reform and a failure of liberal progressivism. To a great extent their work remains fettered by a mode of analysis that hovers over, rather than directly engages, the contradictions of the social order that their efforts seek to transform.

Generally speaking, critical educators have been unable to develop a critical discourse that provides the theoretical basis for alternative approaches to school organization, curricula, classroom pedagogy, and social relations (Giroux and McLaren 1987). Nor have attempts been made to redefine the individual social actor – whether teacher or student – as constituting multiply organized subjectivities that are both gendered and discursively embedded in complex and contradictory ways. The programmatic impetus of much radical educational reform remains fettered by the limited emancipatory goal of making the everyday problematic. But while calling into question the ideological dimensions of classroom transactions – i.e., the structural positioning of thought in relation to the larger social totality – is certainly commendable as a starting point, it cannot further the project of democratizing our classrooms unless united with the larger goal of reconstituting schools as counterpublic spheres (Giroux and McLaren 1986a). The language of critique that informs much radical theorizing is overly individualistic, Eurocentric, androcentric, and reproductive; radical educators fail to acknowledge that the struggle for democracy, in the larger sense of transforming schools into democratic public spheres, takes political and ethical precedence over making teachers more adept at deconstructive "double readings." That is, this language's programmatic suggestions are locked into the limited posture of reproduction and resistance theories (Giroux and McLaren 1986b). In general, critical pedagogy can be accused of purveying either a mechanical and deterministic view of the social order or a liberal, humanist, and Cartesian view of human agency. Its emphasis on individual student subjectivity constructed within particular discursive alignments and power/knowledge configurations has deflected attention from the concept of collective struggle. While we recognize, along with feminist theorists and others, that we must challenge the claims of a unitary female experience and universal experiences based on race or class, we remain optimistic that critical pedagogy will be able to address these issues while at the same time discovering new ways of establishing itself as a collective countervailing force with the power to inscribe a condition of radical possibility, what Laclau and Mouffe refer to as the construction of a "radical imaginary" (1985: 190).

CRITICAL PEDAGOGY AS A FORM OF CULTURAL POLITICS

Despite the advances of critical pedagogy over the last decade, there remains the problem of how cultural politics is to be defined and developed. The problem results from the one-sidedness of the critical tradition's analysis. Critical pedagogy has failed to articulate a vision for self-empowerment and social transformation; consequently, the term "critical pedagogy" needs to have its meaning specified in more precise terms.

"Pedagogy" refers to the process by which teachers and students negotiate and produce meaning. This, in turn, takes into consideration how teachers and students are positioned within discursive practices and power/knowledge relations. "Pedagogy" also refers to how we represent ourselves, others, and the communities in which we choose to live. The term "critical pedagogy," by distinction, underscores the partisan nature of learning and struggle; it provides a starting point for linking knowledge to power and a commitment to developing forms of community life that take seriously the struggle for democracy and social justice. Critical pedagogy always presupposes a particular vision of society. As Roger Simon reminds us, a critical pedagogy is based on a project of empowerment. Without a vision of the future – without asking, "Empowerment for what?" – critical pedagogy becomes reduced to a method for participation that takes democracy as an end, not a means. In Simon's terms, critical pedagogy must be distinguished from teaching:

> To me "pedagogy" is a more complex and extensive term than "teaching," referring to the integration in practice of particular curriculum content and design, classroom strategies and techniques, and evaluation, purpose, and methods. All of these aspects of educational practice come together in the realities of what happens in classrooms. Together they organize a view of how a teacher's work within an institutional context specifies a particular version of what knowledge is of most worth, what it means to know something, and how we might construct representations of ourselves, others, and our physical and social environment. In other words, talk about pedagogy is

> simultaneously talk about the details of what students and others might do together and the cultural politics such practices support. In this perspective, we cannot talk about teaching practice without talking about politics.
>
> (Simon 1987: 30)

Unfortunately, the New Right has naturalized the term "critical" by repeated and imprecise usage, removing its political and cultural dimensions and its analytic potency, leaving only the sense of "thinking skills." Teaching is thus reduced to "transmitting" basic skills and information and sanctifying the canons of the dominant cultural tradition. The moral vision that grounds such a view encourages students to succeed in the world of existing social forms. Critical pedagogy, as we are using the term, refers to a form of cultural politics aimed at enhancing and transforming the social imagination. Our task here is to outline what such a conceptualization might mean for education.

Critical pedagogy as a form of cultural politics attempts to redress the ideological shortcomings of current analyses of schooling and mainstream discussions of pedagogy, particularly as found in teacher education programs. For instance, student teachers are often introduced to a one-dimensional conception of schooling. Student teachers often encounter schooling as a set of rules and regulative practices that have been laundered of ambiguity, contradiction, paradox, and resistance. Schools are presented as free of all ideological contestation and struggle. Educators usually think of struggle in schools as "behavioral struggle" – attempts to delegitimate certain forms of unruly behavior – a perception enforced by myths of the "culture of poverty" or the naturalness of cultural or racial "deficiencies," which we read as a perception of students' "lack of whiteness" on the part of many teachers from the dominant white culture. Classroom reality is rarely presented as socially constructed, historically determined, and mediated through institutionalized relationships of class, gender, race, and power. This dominant conception of schooling vastly contradicts the economies of power, privilege, and subject-formation in which student teachers are actually located during the practicum, especially in a working-class school. Student teachers are often taught to view their own cultural capital and lived experiences as constituting a meaningless subjective referent; what counts most, in the dominant view, is not the fragility or importance of one's own voice and beliefs, but the "force" and imperatives of a technocratic logic that unifies subjectivity in a masculinist regime of power and authority. In mainstream schools of education, teaching practices and methods are often linked to a menu of learning models employed in stipulated conditions – conditions where questions of culture and power are completely annulled or else shunted to the margins, in favor of questions having to do with procedural proprieties, learning strategies, developmental theories, and behavioral outcomes.[4]

In effect, critical pedagogy as a form of cultural politics speaks to a form of curriculum theory and application that stresses the historical, cultural, and discursive in relation to classroom materials and teaching practices. As such, it speaks to a fundamental intersection between social and curriculum theorizing. It also seeks to render problematic the experiences and needs of students as the basis for exploring the interface between their immediate lives and the constraints and possibilities of the wider society. Critical pedagogy as a form of cultural politics attempts to provide educators with an opportunity to examine, dismantle, analyze, bracket, de- and reconstruct pedagogical practices. How is meaning produced? How is power constructed and reinforced in classroom and school life? Deconstructive strategies from postmodern social theory are instrumental tools for answering such questions through radical critique. Central to such a perspective is not simply the critical appropriation of semiotic, hermeneutic, or Marxian strategies, but also a commitment to hope and emancipation and a desire to link educational practice to the public good. Underscoring this commitment is an understanding of curriculum as an expression of struggle and an acknowledgment that curriculum constitutes a primary agent for introducing, preparing, and legitimizing forms of social life.

Critical pedagogy as a form of cultural politics is also concerned with constructing a language that empowers teachers to take seriously the role of schooling in joining knowledge and power. Teachers need critical categories that probe the factual status of white, Western, androcentric epistemologies that will enable schools to be interrogated as sites engaged in producing and transmitting social practices that reproduce the linear, profit-motivated imperatives of the dominant culture, with its attendant institutional dehumanization. By conceptualizing radical pedagogy as a form of cultural politics, we are underscoring the idea that school culture is not neutral, but ideological. It consists of stipulated social practices and diffuse configurations of power, as well as historically mediated ideas and world-views that often work to sustain the interests of dominant groups. In this view, schooling does not reflect the dominant ideology but constitutes it. That is, schooling is an integral (though mediated) aspect of the dominant ideology and provides the social practices and material constraints necessary for ideology to do its work. Part of this work consists of a disciplining of consciousness by selective languages of analysis and the reproduction of specific social and cultural forms in which pedagogy occurs; it also consists of constructing relations of race, class, and gender dependency and generating feelings of self-negation and defeat, all of which are underwritten by a victim-blaming psychologization of school failure that rests on a conception of the masculinized and privatized

Cartesian ego. This position highlights the need for educators to explore how the experiences of students are produced, contested, and legitimated at school; in addition, it points to the need for educators to remake schools into sites for greater social probity and equity and deeper challenges to dominant definitions of truth and structures of power.

CURRICULUM AS A FORM OF CULTURAL POLITICS[5]

To conceive of critical pedagogy as a form of cultural politics is to underscore the importance of understanding schooling and pedagogy as an expression of radical social theory. In recent years, leftist educational theorists have employed critical social theory to increase our understanding of schooling as an essentially political enterprise, a way of reproducing or privileging particular discourses, along with the knowledge and power they carry. As a result, many educators have come to recognize schooling as both determinate and determining, constraining and enabling. The conceptual core of radical scholarship over the last decade has been strongly influenced by the rediscovery of Marx and has involved unpacking the submerged connections between schooling and the economic sphere of capitalist production. We are certainly sympathetic with this position, especially with Ernest Mandel's argument that we are now entering a form of corporate capitalism in which capital has expanded into areas previously unsullied by the language and logic of commodity exchange (Mandel 1975). We also agree that forms of power and control have become more difficult to uncover because they are now disguised within circuits of electronically produced signs and meanings that saturate almost every aspect of public and private life (Brenkman 1979; Aronowitz 1981). But this position has failed to escape the economic reductionism that it attempts to press beyond. Such reductionism, in its more sophisticated forms, is evident in the continuing work of radical educational theorists who overemphasize the relationship between schools and the economic sphere, even as they neglect to interrogate the role of signs, symbols, rituals, narratives, and cultural formations in naming and constructing student subjectivities and voices.[6]

State capitalism is much more than a series of economic determinations, and the economic process is not always causally related to the appearance of new symbolic and cultural discourses that sustain as well as disrupt and decenter important dimensions of modern social life. While economic forces and the intervention of the state are important determinants of school policy, they require re-examination in light of theoretical considerations that stress the mutually constitutive roles played by language, culture, and power in affecting how teachers and students impose, resist, and negotiate meaning in the classroom. Questions about how students make meanings and create their cultural histories cannot be answered with sole recourse to discussions of social class and economic determinism; rather, we must analyze how the discursive mediations of culture and experience intersect to constitute powerfully determining aspects of human agency and struggle. Capitalism, however, is far from being ignored.

A curriculum as a form of cultural politics stresses the importance of making social, cultural, political, and economic issues the primary categories for understanding contemporary schooling (Giroux and Simon 1984). Within this context, school life is to be conceptualized not as a monolithic and iron-clad system of rules and relations, but from the perspective of a theory of culture that insinuates elements of discontinuity and indeterminacy into what is usually perceived by educational researchers as uniform and determinate. School life can best be seen as a turbulent arena of conflicting discourses and struggles, a terrain where classroom and streetcorner cultures collide.

To conceptualize curriculum as a form of cultural politics is to acknowledge the overriding goal of education as the creation of conditions for social transformation through the constitution of students as political subjects who recognize their historical, racial, class, and gender situatedness and the forces that shape their lives and are politically and ethically motivated to struggle in the interest of greater human freedom and emancipation.

The project of "doing" a curriculum of cultural politics consists of linking radical social theory to a language of critique and possibility through which teachers can dismantle and interrogate preferred and officially sanctioned educational discourses. Our concern here is not just with developing a language of critique and demystification; we are more concerned with developing a language of possibility that can create alternative teaching practices capable of shattering the syntax of dominant systems of intelligibility and representation, both within and outside schools. We are committed to articulating a language that can examine public schooling as a new public sphere, one that seeks to recapture the idea of critical democracy and build alliances with progressive social movements.

Schools are historical and structural embodiments of ideological forms reproduced through uneven discursive alignments that privilege certain groups, and asymmetrical relations of power that sustain such privilege. They signify reality in unitary ways that fail to acknowledge the heterogeneous, multilayered, and often contradictory process of subject formation. Schools in this sense are ideological and political terrains out of which the dominant culture, in part, produces its hegemonic "certainties" and popular assurances of received orthodoxies; they are also places where dominant and subordinate groups define and constrain each other in ongoing battles over discursive positions and material conditions.

Schools are not ideologically innocent, nor do they simply reproduce dominant social relations and interests. At the same time, schools do produce forms of political and moral regulation intimately connected with technologies of power, which in turn "produce asymmetries in the abilities of individuals and groups to define and realize their needs" (Johnson 1983). More specifically, schools establish the conditions under which some individuals and groups define the terms by which others live, resist, affirm, and participate in the construction of their own identities and subjectivities. Roger Simon illuminates some of the important theoretical considerations that must be addressed within a radical pedagogy:

> Our concern as educators is to develop a way of thinking about the construction and definition of subjectivity within the concrete social forms of our everyday existence in a way that grasps schooling as a cultural and political site that embodies a project of regulation and transformation. As educators we are required to take a position on the acceptability of such forms. We also recognize that while schooling is productive it is not so in isolation, but in complex relations with other forms organized in other sites. . . . [Moreover,] in working to reconstruct aspects of schooling [educators should attempt] to understand how it becomes implicated in the production of subjectivities . . . [and] recognize that existing social forms legitimate and produce real inequities which serve the interest of some over others and that a transformative pedagogy is oppositional in intent and is threatening to some in its practice.
>
> (Simon 1986: 176–7)

Simon rightly argues that schools are sites of contestation and struggle; as sites of cultural production, they embody representations and practices that construct as well as constrain the possibilities for social agency among students. Developing a radical pedagogy consistent with a focus on cultural politics involves rethinking the very nature of curriculum discourse. At the outset, this demands understanding curriculum as representing a set of underlying interests that structure how a particular "story" is presented, represented, and legitimated. In this respect, curriculum itself represents a narrative or voice, one that is multilayered and often contradictory but also situated within forms of representation and relations of power that in the majority of traditional institutions favor white, male, middle-class, English-speaking students. We can discuss the classroom as a site of discursive production and reception, and we can learn from the deconstructive and textual strategies now finding their way into the critical educational tradition. Curriculum discourse and pedagogic practice are now viewed as orderings and transformations of time, text, and space that position both teachers and students within particular renderings of authority and experience but do not automatically reproduce the messages they carry and legitimate. Curriculum and pedagogical practice are thus considered as offering the possibility of contestation and resistance. Without overlooking the degree of struggle and resistance possible among both teachers and students, it is important to extend the practice of post-structuralist critique to the development of narratives and reconstituted histories, values, and representations that also point to new visions of social life.

To speak of curriculum as a form of cultural politics is to assert that curriculum cannot be understood outside a theory of interest. Such a conceptualization of curriculum is only possible if it can justify both its particular assumptions and the presuppositions that constitute its analytic framework. First, since all knowledge and social practice become intelligible only within the ideologies and systems of representation they produce and legitimate, it is essential to analyze curricula in relation to the interests that structure the questions they raise, the version of the past and present they legitimate, and the social relations they either affirm or marginalize. Second, since curriculum implies a picture of how to live, it cannot be understood outside a theory of experience. Curriculum is deeply implicated in the production and organization of student experiences within historically produced social forms such as language usage, the organization of knowledge into high- and low-status categories, and the affirmation of particular teaching strategies and tactics. Third, as a form of cultural politics, curriculum not only represents a configuration of particular interests and experiences; it also represents a site of struggle over whose versions of authority, history, the present, and the future will prevail in schools. Finally, critical curriculum theorists want to restore to educational theorizing a public language that interrogates the ways in which the voices of teachers and subordinate groups are produced and legitimated.

Curriculum must attend to the contradictory nature of student experience and voice and therefore must establish the grounds whereby such experiences can be interrogated and analyzed. This often means refusing the very frames of reference that split off the marginalized from the dominators, and creating new vocabularies of resistance that do not separate curriculum from gender politics, values from aesthetics, pedagogy from power. The concept of "voice" in this case not only provides a theoretical framework for recognizing the cultural logic that produces, contains, and enables learning; it also provides a referent for criticizing the kind of romantic celebration of student experience that characterized much of the radical pedagogy of the 1960s and the culturalism of the 1970s.

At issue here is linking the pedagogy of student voice to a project of possibility: students affirming and celebrating the interplay of different voices and experiences, while at the same time recognizing that such voices must always be interrogated for their metaphysical, espistemological, ethical, and political interests. Voice becomes a pedagogical site for asserting and interrogating spoken/unspoken interests. As a form of historical, textual, political, and gender production, student voice must be rooted in a pedagogy that allows students to speak, to appreciate, and to practice the emancipatory politics of difference. Such difference is more than a function of democratic tolerance; it is also a fundamental condition for critical dialogue and the development of forms of solidarity rooted in the principles of trust, sharing, and a commitment to improving the quality of human freedom. While we recognize that a pedagogy of voice is in itself fraught with difficulties, we believe such a pedagogy allows students to believe that to be critical is to be present in history, to make a difference with respect to the future. This type of curriculum must be developed around a politics of difference and community that is not rooted simply in a celebration of liberal pluralism. Rather, such a pedagogy must be grounded in a particular form and vision of human community in which a politics of difference becomes dignified (Young 1986). Such a vision means acknowledging the different ways in which the generative themes that suture and codify the materiality of our experiences are produced, affirmed, and disconfirmed according to ruling discourses. This is not to suggest that community must be constructed mainly out of supportive discourses or actions at the expense of oppositional ones. Rather, a language of possibility must provide a version of community that offers serious consideration of political and pedagogical alternatives under nonrevolutionary as well as revolutionary circumstances.

CRITICAL PEDAGOGY AND THE POLITICS OF EXPERIENCE

Critical pedagogy as a form of cultural politics takes as one of its most fundamental aims an understanding of how the socially constructed and often contradictory experiences and needs of students might be made problematic. Such experiences can then provide the basis for exploring the interface between their own lives and the constraints and possibilities within the wider social order. Traditionally, radical educators have emphasized the ideological nature of knowledge (either as a form of ideology critique, or as ideologically correct content to convey to students) as the primary focus for critical educational works. Central to this perspective is a view of knowledge suggesting that it is produced in the head of the educator or teacher/theorist and not in interaction. In short, knowledge is theoretically abstracted from its own production as part of a pedagogical encounter. The notion that knowledge cannot be constructed outside a pedagogical encounter is lost in the misconception that the propositional logic or "truth content" of knowledge is the most essential issue to be addressed in one's teaching. In this way, the relevance of the notion of pedagogy as part of a critical theory of education is either under-theorized or merely "forgotten." This view has often brought about the following division of labor: theorists who produce knowledge are limited to the university, those who merely reproduce it are seen as public schoolteachers, and those who passively receive it at all levels are students.

We propose a critical pedagogy as a form of cultural politics that is fundamentally concerned with student experience in a threefold sense. First, a post-structualist concept of student experience allows subjectivity to be analyzed outside the exigencies of humanist psychology. In this perspective, experience and subjectivity do not collapse into the humanist notion of the integrated ego as the source of all actions and behavior. If student experience is viewed as constituted out of and by difference and rooted in contradictory discursive and nondiscursive practices, then the experience that students bring to schools, as well as the cultural forms out of which those experiences are produced, operate within tensions that are never closed or unassailable. The concept of the nomadic and postcolonial subject that emerges from our view of student experience as a terrain of struggle is articulated by Larry Grossberg: This "post-humanistic" subject does not exist with a unified identity (even understood as an articulated hierarchical structure of its various subject-positionings) that somehow manifests itself in every practice. Rather, it is a subject that is constantly remade, reshaped as a mobilely situated set of relations in a fluid context. The nomadic subject is amoeba-like, struggling to win some space for itself in its local situation. The subject itself has become a site of struggle, an ongoing site of articulation with its own history, determinations and effects (Grossberg 1986a).

We are suggesting that one way of opposing and transforming the unified, singular, monolithic subject of patriarchy is to formulate a concept of subject formation that stresses negotiation among discourses and subject positions as social practices that are both determined and determining. Second, a pedagogy of student experience encourages a critique of dominant forms of knowledge and cultural mediation that collectively shape student experiences. Such a pedagogy emphasizes the link between experience and the issues of language and representation. Third, it attempts to provide students with the critical means to examine their own lived experiences, deep memories, and subordinate knowledge forms. This means helping students analyze their own experiences outside of frames of reference produced in the "master's house" so as to illuminate the processes by which they are produced, legitimated, or disconfirmed. Student experience, as the fundamental medium of culture, agency, and identity formation, must be given pre-eminence in an emancipatory curriculum; therefore, critical educators must learn how to understand, affirm, and analyze such experience. This means not only understanding the cultural and social forms through which students as embattled subjects learn to define themselves, but also learning how to engage student experience within a pedagogy that is both affirmative and critical.

Knowledge must be made meaningful to students before it can be made critical. School knowledge never speaks for itself; rather, it is constantly filtered through the experiences, critical vernacular, and mutual knowledge that students bring to the classroom. Unfortunately, most approaches to teaching and learning fail to consider the critical justification for local knowledges and belief-claims that students use to give relevance and meaning to their experiences. Nor do teachers often invite students to consider the ideological ramifications of their commonly held beliefs and routine social practices. David Lusted is worth quoting on this issue:

> Knowledge is not produced in the intentions of those who believe they hold it, whether in the pen or in the voice. It is produced in the process of interaction, between writer and reader at the moment of reading, and between teacher and learner at the moment of classroom engagement. Knowledge is not the matter that is offered so much as the matter that is understood. To think of fields or bodies of knowledge as if they are the property of academics and teachers is wrong. It denies an equality in the relations at moments of interaction and falsely privileges one side of the exchange, and what that side "knows," over the other.
>
> (Lusted 1986: 4–5)

Moreover, for critical cultural producers to hold this view of knowledge carries its own pedagogy, an autocratic and elite pedagogy. It is not just that it denies the value of what learners know, which it does, but that it misrecognizes the conditions necessary for the kind of learning – critical, engaged, personal, social – called for by the knowledge itself.

This position is exemplified by teachers who define the success of their teaching exclusively through the ideological correctness of the subject matter they teach. Sharon Welch speaks directly to this issue by arguing against using theory as a form of social control. She points out that the most important concern in teaching is to support the process of theorizing and not the mere exposure to correct ideas. Welch is all too aware of the trap that theory-building often creates, the use of theory to silence the voices of others:

> I find it difficult, yet essential, to avoid the trap of more traditional educational methods, the use of theory as a form of social control. This takes several forms, all ways of containing and eventually destroying the boldness of students. One obvious strategy is the smug reminder that a student's ideas – whether critical or constructive – are not new, and giving the long list of all those who have already formulated a similar notion with, of course, greater sophistication and rhetorical

power. Another way of preventing boldness is encapsulated in the aversion to "reinventing the wheel." Theories are taught in their final form, and the complex process of engendering them, moving through the requisite understanding of particular forms of oppression, particular visions of liberation, is ignored. I think we would do well to take as a model for our work one that is used in some elementary education.

(Welch 1990)

Students are actively encouraged to reinvent the wheel – they are given the problems that led to creating a formula for finding the area of a rectangle, the volume of a box. By creating the formulae themselves they understand the mathematical theory more thoroughly, and as a not so incidental side-effect, gain confidence, boldness if you will, as thinkers. The fact that the formulae they derive are not new, the fact that others have reached the same conclusions, can be presented after the fact as confirmation of the students' work, as an affirmation that they are not alone or crazy, outside the bounds of communal discourse.

Teachers are often apprehensive and defensive about letting students tell their own stories. Teachers must be careful not to silence students unwittingly through the unacknowledged play of discourses in their own pedagogical practices.

To have a voice means knowing when to express and assert it. In this respect, students should be encouraged to listen as well as to speak, especially if their voices tend to dominate and control others. But teachers should never tell students that their stories don't count. Michelle Fine provides an excellent example of one teacher who unwittingly silences a student during an attempt to establish a lively debate on an issue relevant to the lives of her students.

In early Spring, a social studies teacher structured an in-class debate on Bernard Goetz, New York City's "subway vigilante." She invited "those students who agree with Goetz to sit on one side of the room, and those who think he was wrong to sit on the other side." To the large residual group who remained mid-room the teacher remarked, "Don't be lazy. You have to make a decision. Like at work, you can't be passive." A few wandered over to the "pro-Goetz" side. About six remained in the center. Somewhat angrily, the teacher continued: "OK, first we'll hear the pro-Goetz side and then the anti-Goetz side. Those of you who have no opinions, who haven't thought about the issue, you won't get to talk unless we have time."

Deidre, a black senior, bright and always quick to raise contradictions otherwise obscured, advocated the legitimacy of the middle group. "It's not that I have no opinions. I don't like Goetz shootin' up people who look like my brother, but I don't like feeling unsafe in the projects or in my neighborhood either. I got lots of opinions. I ain't bein' quiet 'cause

I can't decide if he's right or wrong. I'm talking." Deidre's comment legitimized for herself and others the right to hold complex, perhaps even contradictory positions on a complex situation. Such legitimacy was rarely granted by faculty – with clear and important exceptions including activist faculty and paraprofessionals who lived in central Harlem with the kids, and understood and respected much about their lives (Fine 1989).

The social studies teacher in Fine's anecdote had unreflectively privileged her own ideological position; consequently, she had undermined and delegitimized Deidre's refusal to oversimplify what she considers a complex issue. Student experience frequently becomes unintentionally devalued despite the best political and ethical intentions; as a consequence, any sense of equality in the exchange between teacher and students is lost. A teacher's own pedagogy can thus become unknowingly elitist and automatic.

CRITICAL PEDAGOGY AND THE POLITICS OF THE BODY[7]

Any critical pedagogy as a form of cultural politics must take seriously the premise that learning occurs relationally. Knowledge as a form of ideology cannot be reduced to social practices that simply mirror, follow from, or obey cognitive operations. As important as it is to link learning to the production and legitimation of particular discursive positions, it is equally important to understand learning as taking place within historically situated practices involving political regimes of the body. Ideology needs to be understood as lived experience constructed as common sense, and hegemony as the process whereby students not only unwittingly consent to domination but sometimes find pleasurable the form and content through which such domination is manifested. Knowledge cannot be theorized in terms of rationality, nor can ignorance be relegated to the status of inadequate or inappropriate information or to distorted communication. Such a view denies that ideology is fundamentally related to the politics of pleasure, the typography of the body, and the production of desire.

To say that ideology is related to the domain of the affective is to assert that ideology must be understood as operating within a politics of feeling – structures of desire that both enable and constrain emancipatory struggle. As Larry Grossberg writes,

> Affective struggles cannot be conceptualized within the terms of theories of resistance, for their oppositional quality is constituted, not in a negative dialectics, but by a project of or struggle over empowerment, an empowerment which energizes and connects specific social moments, practices and subject positions. Thus, if we want to understand particular cultural practices, we need to ask how they empower

their audiences and how the audiences empower the practices; that is, how the very materiality (including ideological) of cultural practices functions within an affective economy of everyday life.

(Grossberg 1986a: 73–4)

For instance, *Schooling as a Ritual Performance*, my ethnographic study of Portuguese Catholic students in Toronto, attempted to draw attention to the importance of the body as an organ of mediation in the construction of student resistance to the authoritative pedagogy of the school.[8] While engaging in the life and language of the streets, students acquire and react to information viscerally; that is, students make affective investments in certain kinds of knowledge.[9] Knowledge, in this instance, is not something to be "understood;" it is always, understood or not, felt and responded to somatically, that is, in its corporeal materiality.

Streetcorner knowledge is epistemologically different from traditional conceptions of school knowledge. It is a type of mimesis or visceral/erotic identification. For the Italian and Portuguese students in the study, knowledge acquired in the streets was "lived" and mediated through discursive alignments and affective ideological investments not found in school. In the streets, what mattered was always somehow "felt," whereas classroom knowledge was often sullied by an inflated rationalism and logocentrism. In the streets, students made use of more affective engagement with symbols marked by the emotive rather than the rational, and the inchoate rather than the homogeneous. Classroom knowledge was more formally differentiated, but because such knowledge was not a lived engagement it remained distant, isolated, abstract. Students chose not to invest affectively in this kind of knowledge. It was knowledge that had become safely insulated from the "tainted" production of desire, a knowledge that had been congruent with the discourse of the Other, one whose elaborated code speaks for the students but one to which they have little access without relinquishing the ritual codes that affirm their dignity and streetcorner status. Students whose subjectivities were "decentered" or displaced in school – in the sense of having their voices disconfirmed and delegitimized – could reclaim their sense of subjective continuity and social and cultural agency through affective investment in the popular realism of street life.

Students battled daily to reconcile the disjunction between the lived meaning of the streets and the ideological boundaries and fixed lines of desire produced through the pedagogical and social practices of classroom life. In school, inordinate emphasis was placed on knowledge *about*, on the digital dimension of learning (univocality, precision, logic) as opposed to knowledge *of*, or the analogic dimension (equivocation, ambiguity, description) experienced by students outside. Classroom instruction constituted what Robert Everhart calls "reified knowledge" – knowledge that is given, linear, relatively unproblematic, and that places the student in the role of passive recipient (Everhart 1983). Resistance to this type of knowledge in the classroom mirrored student behavior at home, and constituted a ritualized attempt to bring the hybridized and transgressive discourses of the street into the school. In Everhart's terminology, the knowledge gathered through such resistance becomes a form of "regenerative knowledge" that attempts to assert creative control over the knowledge-production process. This type of knowledge, "ritual knowledge," is essentially interpretive and provisional and does not draw upon assumed categories. Furthermore, it is established to resist the role that students occupy in the labor process of the school.

We are suggesting that classroom instruction must be understood within a reformulated theory of ideology that problematizes the classroom as a gathering point for the construction of Otherness in which racial, class, and gender determinations are tightly woven.

Power mediates and structures the pedagogical relation between teachers and students, the politics of knowledge production, the availability of critical discourses, and the social and cultural forms in which student subject positions are made available. Furthermore, power must be seen in relation to the production of affective investment – i.e., to the production of knowledge as the object of desire. This demands a critical attentiveness to the sentience of human subject formation and the process by which meaning is transcoded through the body – a process we refer to as "enfleshment."

Enfleshment refers to the mutually constitutive (enfolding) of social structure and desire; that is, the dialectical relationship between the material organization of interiority and the cultural forms and modes of materiality we inhabit subjectively. This is similar to the process that De Certeau refers to as "intextuation" in *The Practice of Everyday Life* (1984) or the transformation of bodies into signifiers of state power and law. We are suggesting, however, that power is not simply oppressive but works relationally and that schooling promotes and provokes relations of power that are both normalizing and resistant.

Schools serve as sites for locating students in subject positions that do not contest the discursive assumptions, dispositions, and dimensions of the dominant culture. Yet the classroom can also become a site of resistance, where students combine the countervailing and transgressive possibilities found in streetcorner culture; that is, where discourses laden with concreteness exist as possibilities, where self-negation, despair, and denial do not become the primary referents for the construction of racial, gender, and class identities.

Rather, the sensuous body becomes the primary referent for the politics of knowledge construction. The students of *Schooling as a Ritual Performance* reacted against the eros-denying quality of school life, where they became fetishized objects of surveillance and control. Intellectual labor had little affective currency for the students because it served to displace the sensuous body as a prime signifier for the organization and investment of meaning. This brings us to the important idea that ideological hegemony is not inscribed solely in the sphere of rationality, but through the fusion of politics and ethics at the level of the body.

Throughout classroom life, student gestures become reified into corporeal manifestations of hegemony. The cramped, defensive posturing of students and the brusque, authoritative gestures of teachers reveal the relations of power that have been grafted on to the medium of living flesh. Student bodies became tablets upon which teachers encoded a belief in their own class and cultural superiority.

Every body carries its own history of oppression, residues of domination preserved in breathing tissue. The bodies of the students in the study were ideologically swollen with surplus, polyvalent meaning. Accordingly, their bodies became sites of struggle. Resistance became a way of gaining power, celebrating pleasure through the shattering of sanctified codes, and fighting oppression in the lived moment and in the concrete and social materiality of the classroom. To resist meant to fight the monitoring of passion and desire and the capitalist symbolization of the flesh. Student resistance constituted a rejection of the historical subject reformulated as a docile object compliant with the grammar of capitalist domination. It was a reaction against the purging of the body's opportunity to invest in the pleasure of transgression and illicit knowledge in favor of a disembodied ideal of what constitutes "proper" modes of desire and patterns of conduct demanded by civil society. Resistance constituted a willingness of students to struggle against the prospect that their indigenous constructions of gender, sexuality, and identity would become rewritten and demonized by the subjectively defined tropes of Anglo male authorities and through narratives defined by the division between the high-status knowledge and culture of the middle class and the degraded knowledge and cultural Otherness of the subaltern.

We must pay more attention to the affective power invested in particular ideologies, cultural formations, and social practices and the body's sensuous relationship to the popular and everyday. Grossberg recognizes that fields of discourse are organized both ideologically and affectively:

> In order to understand the relation of this totalized subject to reality it is necessary to recognize that the world is affectively as well as semantically structured. I am using the term *affect* to refer to the intensity or desire with which we invest the world and our relations to it . . . this process of affective investment (through which the body is inserted into its physical and social environment) results in the very possibility of a totalized sense of reality.
>
> (Grossberg 1986b: 185)

A reformulation of ideology that accommodates a political economy of affective investment is in order if educators are to better understand knowledge as more than a semantic construct. Ideology is fundamentally related both to the production of discourse and to the domain of bodily investment – that is, to the politics of pleasure.

Students' inability to be "literate" may constitute less an act of "ignorance" than an act of resistance. That is, members of the working class and other oppressed groups may consciously or unconsciously refuse to learn the cultural codes and competencies legitimated by the dominant culture. In this respect, it is important to view student behavior not as a measure of learned helplessness but as a form of moral and political indignation. Students resist what the school has to offer, including subtextual contours of instruction – what is now commonly referred to as "the hidden curriculum" – in order to survive with a modicum of dignity the vagaries of class and cultural servitude. Such resistance should be seen less as an unqualified act of conscious political refusal than as an opportunity to investigate the political and cultural conditions that warrant such resistance. The interests that inform such acts never speak for themselves; they must be analyzed within a framework that links the wider context of schooling with the interpretation students bring to the act of refusal. The "refusal" to learn may provide the pedagogical basis for engaging in a critical dialogue with those whose traditions and cultures are often the object of a massive assault by the dominant culture.

To help create and guide a liberating praxis, critical pedagogy must seize a concept of resistance that will allow teachers to construct pedagogical practices that resonate with their students' experiences without romanticizing them or affirming what might constitute racist, sexist, or otherwise oppressive ideologies and practices. Teachers would do well to tap the hidden utopian desire in those resistances. Within the current dominant forms of pedagogy, teacher and student produce oppositional discourses within unequal power relations. In a critical pedagogy, as we envision it, teacher–student dialogue cannot be framed within such stark binary oppositional discourses. On the contrary, as the work of Paulo Freire and others has made dramatically clear, a critical pedagogical encounter will represent the interplay, modification, and mutual exchange of teacher–student discourses set against structuring principles that promote human capacities which acknowledge a multiplicity of positionalities along the axes of gender, race, class, and sexual orientation and social forms compatible with a reconstituted democratic imaginary and public life.

BEYOND THE DISCOURSE OF ANTI-UTOPIANISM

While leftist educators and social theorists have constructed detailed and sophisticated forms and methods of ideological critique, they have, for the most part, failed to develop a radical notion of hope and possibility. Some radical educators have, in fact, argued that the notion of hope as the basis of a language of possibility is really nothing more than a "trick of counterhegemony," and that hope is employed for ideological effect rather than for sound theoretical reasons. In other words, hope as a vision of possibility contains no immanent political project and as such has to be sacrificed on the altar of empirical reality. Ironically, this position makes the very notion of counterhegemony untenable, since all struggle implicitly signifies an element of utopian possibility.[10] In this case, the concept of hope is actually used to discourage political action. Such a theoretical and political dead end is the antithesis of what it means to speak the language of possibility while engaging in radical practice. It runs counter to the idea of challenging oppression while simultaneously struggling for a new kind of subjectivity and alternative forms of community.[11] These new kinds of subjectivities and alternative forms of community must recognize the multiplicity, contradictoriness, mutually informing and historically discontinuous character of discourses and social practices. This suggests, for us, the self-conscious production of post-colonial modes of subjectivity and multiple communities of solidarity and resistance which actively contest oppression both as a conscious subjective act and as forms of collective political praxis as part of an ongoing effort to rethink the social world from the perspective of the omnipresence of oppression. There is always the danger that critical modes of subjectivity may become reterritorialized by Eurocentric discourse, and that social practices may become recolonized by phallic desire, technocratic rationality, bourgeois instrumentalism, and the logic of fascism. There is also the danger of considering race, class, and gender relations independently or assuming that they produce effects equal in their oppressiveness, rather than examining such relations in their interlocking relatedness, contextual specificity, and within particular historical circumstances. Critics of schooling must examine how race, class, and gender intersect in specific contexts and in complex ways to create – such as in the case of working-class black females – forms of triple oppression.

The exercise of hope and possibility that we are advocating as part of a critical pedagogical praxis bears a significant comparison with, and indebtedness to, new developments in liberation theology, political theology, and feminist theology. Arguing that both Protestant and Roman Catholic theologies have too often overlooked the biblical theme of oppression/liberation and the politically empowering message of the messianic mission of the Gospel, liberation theologians claim that such an oversight has functioned as an "unconscious hermeneutical option which served the political and material interests of the institutions both of established Christendom and of the rising middle class, and which today serves the interests of the American capitalist empire."[12]

Protestants such as Miguez Bonino, Roman Catholics such as Juan Luis Segundo, and other "theologians of the periphery" including Sharon Welch, Rebecca Chopp, Mary Daly, Cornel West, Elisabeth Schusser Fiorenza, Jurgen Moltmann, Rubem A. Alves, Leonardo Boff, Clodovis Boff, Gustavo Gutierrez, Enrique D. Dussel, Hugo Assmann, Severino Croatto, and Luis Metz (many of whom are Third World Roman Catholic pastoral theologians) articulate their theological positions not from the ahistorical, decontextualized, and putatively value-free commitment of the Gospel – that is, from the sovereign or authoritative Enlightenment perspective of a fixed reading of scriptural truth – but from a post-Enlightenment understanding of history, class struggle, and patriarchy, and from the point of view of the oppressed and the struggle for liberation. This position is a "hermeneutical wager" affirming "God's bias" in favor of the poor, the disenfranchised, the marginalized, and the oppressed. From the perspective of critical pedagogy, liberation theology is more than an ecclesiastic addendum; it is fundamentally a contestatory ethical stance, in its fundamental challenge, for example, to repossess the symbols of the Gospel "that have been employed by successive rulers in southern Africa to divert the unquestionable right of the oppressed to be free" (Villa-Vincencio 1989: 463).

Liberation theology has much to offer critical educational theory. It confronts those forces that hold history captive and challenges the reactionary and patriarchal image of a God often championed by the forces of the New Right, a God "whose providence justifies passivity and resignation . . . a God enshrined in devotions and sacraments that lead to semi-fatalism" (Segundo 1980: 18). It is, in effect, an attempt to "break with anything and everything that hinders real and effective solidarity with those who are suffering from a situation of injustice and spoliation" (Gutierrez 1983: 9).

Liberation theology offers critical educational theory a way of reconceiving hope without falling prey to either cheery optimism or righteous certainty. Invoking a "theology of hope," Alves (following Moltmann) argues that history must not be understood as "immanent process" but rather "as the creation of the word" (Alves 1975: 57). Hope, in this critical sense, is not created simply out of an act of negation or the language of critique, but out of a utopian conception of the future. This utopian form of hope can be conceived metaphysically as well as historically.

Richard Bernstein decries the "abstract scepticism" of much postmodernist social criticism, which takes aim at metaphysics in its attack on certainty, totality, the reconciliation of differences, and unquestioned ethical-ontological distinctions; Bernstein claims such attacks are based on a caricature of the metaphysical tradition, ignoring its spirit of critique, and especially its "commitment to critical encounter and dialogue, and its openness to what is different and other, a willingness to risk one's prejudgments seeking for common ground without any guarantees that it will be found."[13] Bernstein posits the important notion of "engaged pluralism" against other kinds of pluralism often (rightly) attacked by post-structuralist critics. What he calls "flabby pluralism" involves a simple acceptance of the existence of a variety of perspectives and paradigms, all regarded as virtually incommensurable, and a "decentered anarchistic pluralism" that can "take a despairing or celebratory form" – propelled in both cases by the recognition that we "live in a decentered, polycentric world in which there is no possibility of a unifying interpretation" (Bernstein 1988: 270). An engaged pluralism, on the other hand, accepts a lack of convergence of metaphysical speculation, even as it rejects the quest for certainty and absolutes; it does so while embracing a "critical encounter with what is different and other" (p. 272). Such an engaged pluralism recognizes that metaphysical assumptions are always contextually and historically situated and informed by modes of theorizing and interpretation that are themselves structured social and historical practices.

The spirit of such a perspective highlights the major thrust of Ernst Bloch's writings on the theme of utopianism. Writing in the 1930s, Bloch attempted to counter the nineteenth-century perspective that dismissed the concept of utopia because it could not be legitimated through reason or grounded in empirical reality. He argued that utopia was a form of "cultural surplus" in the world, but not of it: "it contains the spark that reaches out beyond the surrounding emptiness."[14] Bloch struggled to keep alive a redemptive and radically utopian spirit at a time of grave cynicism, when the Enlightenment tradition was being absorbed by the logic of fascism.

Bloch, of course, denied the ontological, regional, and psychological claims of the standard critique of utopia and argued that utopian thinking is fundamental to understanding both our humanity and the humanization of the world.[15] As Bloch himself writes, "Utopia extends so far and imparts itself so powerfully to all human activities that every account of man and the world must essentially contain it. There is no realism, worthy of the name, which abstracts from this strongest element in reality as something which is unfinished."[16]

Bloch's position has profound implications for radical educators: it represents the conviction that a Left unable to assert a utopian project consigns itself to political impotence, historical amnesia, and moral inertia. Such has been the case with many of the anti-foundationalist critiques of contemporary cultural and social formations, critiques that are marked by an apolitical aestheticism, polemics of skepticism, fetishism of the sign, and retreat into the Imaginary and into a negative metaphysics, all of which ignore the agony and smother the screams of the oppressed. Bloch reminds us that a utopian project not only uncovers the submerged longings inherent in all ideological distortions, but also attempts to reclaim those longings in ways based on both alternative and oppositional visions. Bloch's utopian project, as we have appropriated it for the construction of a pedagogy of postcolonial cultural politics, speaks to the elimination of forms of oppression and injustice. It demands educators' and students' recognition of the discursive and ideological underpinnings of the hidden curriculum and the manufacture of dreams and the mobilization of desire through the state's bureaucratic formations, institutional practices, and attendant culture industries, and through modes of subjectivity informed by the discourses and social practices of everyday life.

Bloch's work provides a basis for radical educators to consider how social institutions may be understood and developed as part of a wider political and educational struggle. Moreover, his work is instructive for those who perceive the benefit of combining a language of critique with a language of possibility, in an effort to broaden the social and political contexts in which pedagogical activity can function as part of a counter-hegemonic strategy.

Whereas Bloch links power to the collective struggle for unrealized emancipatory potential, Michel Foucault links truth with the most fundamental workings of power and knowledge. In doing so, he provides an important conceptualization of the role of the intellectual and of intellectual practice.

In Foucault's terms, truth cannot be viewed as existing outside power. Nor is it product and reward of those intellectuals who have freed themselves from ignorance. On the contrary, truth is part of a political economy of power. Foucault's oft-quoted passage bears repeating:

> Truth is a thing of this world: it is produced only by virtue of multiple forms of constraint. And it induces regular effects of power. Each society has its regime of truth, its "general politics" of truth: that is, the types of discourse which it accepts and makes function as true; the mechanisms and instances which enable one to distinguish true and false statements, the means by which each one is sanctioned; the techniques and procedures accorded value in the acquisition of truth; the status of those who are charged with saying what counts as true. . . . It seems to me that what must now be taken into account in the intellectual is not the "bearer of universal values." Rather, it's the person occupying a specific position, but whose specificity is linked, in a society like ours, to the general functioning of an apparatus of truth.
>
> (Foucault 1980: 132)

Foucault's analysis of the political economy of truth and his study of how "regimes of truth" are organized and legitimated provides us with a theoretical basis, consonant with Bloch's, from which to develop the concept of pedagogical practice as a form of cultural politics. Teachers as intellectuals must be seen in terms of their social and political function within particular "regimes of truth." That is, they can no longer deceive themselves into believing they are intellectuals serving truth, when in fact they are deeply involved in battles "about the status of truth and the economic and political role it plays" (Foucault 1980: 132).

If intellectual practice is to be tied to creating an alternative and emancipatory politics of truth, it must be grounded in forms of moral and ethical discourse and action that address the suffering and struggles of the oppressed. Such a practice must be attentive to the role of power in generating forms of knowledge that structure and legitimate particular forms of social and cultural life, that resonate with popular desires and everyday needs, and that construct particular ways of naming and understanding experience. Following Foucault's important insight, the knowledge/power relation produces dangerous "positive" effects as it creates particular needs, desires, and truths. Here Foucault's analysis can provide educators with the basis for reconstructing a radical social theory that links pedagogy to forms of critique and possibility. By illuminating the productive effects of power, it becomes possible for teachers as intellectuals to develop practices that take seriously how subjectivities are constructed within particular "regimes of truth"; it also highlights the importance of developing a theory of experience as a central aspect of radical pedagogy. This also points to the role that educators can play as bearers of dangerous memory.[17] Educators can serve as transformative intellectuals engaged in the task of excavating historical consciousness and "repressed" knowledge that points to experiences of suffering, conflict, and collective struggle. In this sense, teachers as intellectuals can begin to link the notion of historical understanding to strategies of social critique and transformation.

Finally, the construction of a radical pedagogy as a form of cultural politics means that radical educators need to engage in counterhegemonic struggles, transforming their classrooms into social laboratories where new cultural spaces open up. Such zones of possibility not only destabilize alliances among passivity, helplessness, dependency, and despair, but also invite teachers and students to form partnerships dedicated to reconstructing subjectivity and redirecting the paths of human desire.[18] They must think not in terms of civility, professionalism, and tenure promotions, but must redefine their role within political, economic, and cultural sites where "regimes of truth" are produced, legitimated, and distributed. Within such contexts intellectuals can confront the microphysics of power and work, building oppositional public spheres connected to the production of everyday life and to wider institutional spheres of power.

The utopian project we envision is not an a priori universal scheme for schools and society in general, masterminded by an elite cadre of radical intellectuals. Nor do we suppose that an idealized radical ethics can simply be mapped onto the social order and magically transform it. Rather, such a vision of hope involves constructing a radical public philosophy that rank-and-file teachers and popular alliances can engage critically, appropriate dialectically, and mediate concretely in communities and classrooms. This construction of a provisional morality necessary for emancipatory social change can be accomplished only by understanding both the productive and the debilitating roles that power plays in producing school subject areas and student subjectivities.

The language of possibility constitutes a powerful countervailing discourse set within a praxis-grounded politics of culture, one that eschews the formulation of a grandiose blueprint for change. Such a language of hope mitigates the relativistic implications of a universal curriculum by conceiving critical pedagogy so that fundamental principles and foundational referents of a socialist democracy can ultimately emerge within a praxis of the particular and the specific. Educational theory and historical struggle may be woven together so that just as theory is served and dialectically informed by practice, theory can also place itself at the service of pressing political goals within the public sphere of everyday human struggle. In this way the language of hope and possibility may avoid excessive indebtedness to pre-established standards and self-generating theoretical formulations that exist outside the crucible of concrete human struggle and historical inquiry. Such a language must acknowledge its role in the construction of subjectivity. In so doing, the language of hope must de-authorize and challenge the master narratives of liberal, postindustrial democracy and the humanist, individual, and patriarchal discourses that underwrite it, while at the same time undermining and reconstructing the idealized and romantic conception of the subject, a conception shaped by Eurocentric and androcentric discursive practices. Such language of hope refuses the class subjugation of the proletarian body through its sterile aestheticization by bourgeois categories of the flesh. It also refuses the inscription of patriarchy upon the female body and the enfleshment of masculinist ideologies.

Students must be provided with a language of critique and possibility that sets out to challenge and transform the violent repressiveness of modern bureaucracy, the barbarisms spawned by the technologies of androcracy, the systematic consolidation of class hierarchy by ruling elites, the logic of colonialism, and the demonization of racial minorities and the poor.

Finally, we emphasize that critical educators must function as more than mere agents of social critique. They must attempt to fashion a language of hope that points to new forms of social and material relations. Critical discourse then becomes more than a form of cultural dissonance, of deconstructive "double readings," more than a siphoning away of the potency of dominant meanings and social relations; it becomes, rather, part of an ongoing struggle for counterpublic spheres where the language of public association and a commitment to social transformation emerge as concrete social movements for change.

Within this perspective, and rooted in a dialectical logic that makes critique and transformation central, creative and critical teaching takes on an anticipatory character of possibility and hope. We support pedagogy whose standards of achievement are determined in relation to the goals of critique and the enhancement of social imagination, pedagogy that links teaching and learning to the goal of educating students to take risks within ongoing relations of power, and to envision a world that does not yet exist in order to alter the race-, class-, and gender-constituted grounds upon which life is lived.

Radical hope is always particular and specific. Without it, it becomes difficult to produce the conditions for human struggle and social transformation. Devoid of hope, we wither as social actors and merely echo the faint rustling of histories of resistance. Each act of hope is simultaneously an act of doubt; yet, in the case of radical hope, doubt refuses the totalizing logic that leads to a paralyzing despair. Radical hope – hope forged on the anvil of the particular and the specific – even when woven into the postmodern tapestry of pastiche, irony, and decentered and multiply organized subjectivities, deprivileges the will to cynical power in favor of a will to dream and to act upon such dreams. As postmodern dreamers, it has become our burden as well as our responsibility to transform our despair into compassion and commitment, to challenge our feelings of disorientation and hopelessness with an ethics of risk and refusal. A refusal of the totalizing logic of master narratives and a focus on specificity and particularity that a radical hope offers is not the same thing as rejecting the discourse of totality outright. While there may be a number of public and private spheres from which to wage an oppositional politics, and while a critical post-structuralism offers us the possibility of constructing new articulations of a deeper and more radical and indeterminate democracy (Laclau 1988), the educational left still needs to profit from a collective vision of the social totality to which education reform aspires. What needs to be abandoned are reductive uses of totality, and not the concept of totality itself. Otherwise we risk undermining the very concept of the democratic public sphere. I will return to this in later chapters.

To reject the language of possibility as an idealistic, abstract, impractical longing is to fail to comprehend it as expressing those elements of a critical praxis that have not yet been realized but that must be dialectically appropriated and grounded in a critical theory of culture and a politics of representation. In this context, schooling as a form of cultural politics is not an absolute category, but one that is critically provisional, concretely utopian, and culturally specific. A pedagogy of liberation is one that is necessarily partial and incomplete, one that has no final answers. It is always in the making, part of an ongoing struggle for critical understanding, emancipatory forms of solidarity, and the reconstitution of democratic public life.

Chapter 2

Schooling the postmodern body

Critical pedagogy and the politics of enfleshment

CRACKS IN THE HISTORICAL MOMENT

While educators in the United States are witnessing a reactionary and ultimately fatuous rearguard defense of the alleged transcendent virtues of Western civilization, a neo-corporatist assault on the New Deal welfare state, and what Jim Merod calls the "guiltless counterrevolutionary violence of state power" (1987: 191), they are also experiencing a new vitality in the realm of educational theory. The cultural/moral hegemony of mainstream approaches to curriculum, pedagogy, and epistemology are being fissured – and in some cases torn asunder – by new deconstructive postmodern strategies developed by and alongside predatory culture.

Largely imported from literary theory and influenced by continental post-structuralism, postmodern strategies (for example, Derridean grammatology and Foucaultian discourse analysis) have systematically problematized, if not dismantled, the epistemological certainty and transcendent claims to truth that characterize dominant strands of modernist discourse.[1] Suffice it to say that there exists a "crisis of representation" and a steady and sometimes vehement erosion of confidence in prevailing conceptualizations of what constitutes knowledge and truth and their pedagogical means of attainment.

Keeping in mind the conceptual inflation of the term "postmodernity" and its unwieldly semantic overload – which has come to designate a vast array of artistic, architectural, and theoretical practices – I want to make clear that I am using it in a severely delimited sense. While postmodernism crisscrosses numerous regions of inquiry, I am using it to refer to the material and semiotic organization of society, primarily with respect to what Stanley Aronowitz (1983) calls visual culture and the homogenization of culture (1981). That is, I am referring to the current tendency toward desubstantialized meaning or "literalness of the visual" in which students seem unable to penetrate beyond the media-bloated surface of things, and dismiss concepts such as "society," "capitalism," and "history," which are not immediately present to the senses (Aronowitz 1983).

According to Aronowitz, "In the last half of the twentieth century, the degree to which mass audience culture has colonized the social space available to the ordinary person for reading, discussion, and critical thought must be counted as the major event of social history in our time" (p. 468).

Our media culture has become a predatory "buffer zone," a "paradoxical site" in which youth lives out a difficult if not impossible relation to the future (Grossberg 1988b: 148). The former structuring principles of identity – family, peers, institutional life – have now taken on a vertiginous flux.[2] Situated as we are in the twilight of modernity, it is becoming more obvious that old forms of production and consumption have given way to a new universe of communication which celebrates the look, the surfaces, the textures, and the uniformization and commodification of the self. Cornel West notes that "the commodification process has penetrated cultural practices which were previously relatively autonomous" (Stephanson 1988b: 274).

Postmodernism has now been absorbed into advertising; the image – which no longer points to some extramundane transcendence or physical outsideness but simply refers back to itself – has now superseded reality with the latter dissolving into the artificial reality of the image. It is a world – a "teledemocracy" – "symptomatic of Reagan's America in its unquestioning materialism" (Kaplan 1987: 30), a terrain which Ihab Hassan describes as populated by "simulations rather than representations, intolerable to both Rightists and Leftists because it renounces the fiction of concealed truth, because it undermines the exercise of power – how does one punish or reward simulations of crime or virtue?" (1987: 228). Dick Hebdige offers a similar description of postmodern culture as "a parodic inversion of historical materialism [in which] the model precedes and generates the real-seeming" (1986: 84).

History is only glancingly recognized, and then only as the immutable truth of the past, as the temporal narratives which structure our political unconscious are replaced by the tyranny of the sign (Lash and Urry 1987: 292). The seductive symbolic power of goods has caused signs rather than products to become the primary foci of late capitalist consumption (p. 288).

Postmodern representation in the mass media has the effect of transporting meaning through the circulation of signs, the churning out of an apocalyptic hemorrhage of signifiers, thick with borrowed or rented meanings, all interchangeable, all bleeding into one another so profusely that any distinction between them is all but cancelled out. It is this fragmented and hazardous aspect of postmodern culture which provokes Hassan to proclaim, "The message no longer exists; only media impose themselves as pure circulation" (1987: 221).[3] The postmodern subject is reduced in this process to a semiotic orphan, clinging to the underbelly of consumer society. This is not far removed from Fredric Jameson's pronouncement of postmodernism as "an alarming and pathological symptom of a society that has become incapable of dealing with time and history" (1982: 117). Time has become so discontinuous and unfixed that present and future merge together as images on a screen. The pulsating beams from the T.V. screen become the shifting and perilous ground on which we form the judgments and decisions which forge our communal vision; a ground in which desire is infantilized, kept separate from meaning, and maintained in a state of narcissistic equilibrium.

By locating the subject within the surface meaning of the image and by making our subjectivities so malleable, postmodern culture contributes unwittingly to the demise and depoliticization of the historical subject – literally suctioning out its capacity for critical agency, then filling the battered husk with consumer desire.[4] Within the petrified thrall of predatory culture, the subject is unable to look to the past or the future to secure itself within a unified identity, but itself becomes a site of struggle in the arena of the present. As Lawrence Grossberg explains, "this 'post-humanistic' subject . . . is constantly remade, reshaped as a mobilely situated set of relations in a fluid context . . . struggling to win some space for itself in its local situation" (1986a: 72).

The current postmodern condition has not only witnessed the fracturing of the sovereign subject – which is, after all, a mythical product of Enlightenment rationality – but also its reconstruction as a decentered text. Francis Barker explains that the modern body, having been separated from its previous unmediated carnality through textual representation, has become supplementary to written communication. In effect, desire and meaning are becoming detached as the modern body becomes more "de-realized . . . confined, ignored, exscribed from discourse" (1984: 63). Within these recent developments, existence is reduced more and more to a form of "eventfulness" which, to borrow a phrase from Klaus R. Scherpe, reflects "the subject's becoming unable to feel pain, a state characterized by the absence of pain, in which the individual's capacity to resist gives up its last line of defense" (1986/7: 124). Even the body, in the torment of its death throes, is remorselessly aestheticized in various forms of discursive representation (witness the growing number of documentaries about people dying of various illnesses such as cancer and AIDS and the images of dying children produced in ads for relief organizations).

The real danger facing the politics of signification in the present historical conjuncture is a shrinkage of the body's powers "as signs come to surpass the body . . . [escaping] . . . its sensual control, dissevering themselves from the material world and dominating that which they are meant to serve" (Eagleton 1986: 97–8). In the regulated ignorance of today's commodity logic, which is inexorably tied to the profit motive, the codes of both signification and commodity partake of a general equivalence; that is, as Baudrillard has show us, an abstract equation has now been set up in which all meanings are made equal. While all meanings are not created equal, or are certainly not equal in their effects, they are now consumed as if they are. The free circulation of the commodity system anchors the postmodern world's new regime of terror. Our bodies are now regulated by a fascist economy of signs, precisely because they are now so fully detached from the body's service. The body in this process has become reduced to a sign of itself – abandoned for a better version of itself. The body is now just another idea for commodity logic to terrorize. In the postmodern world of easy reproductability and limitless circulation of signs, we are served up life as a continuous series of jump cuts to different representations with the same meaning.

THE POLITICS OF POSTMODERNISM

The ethical dilemma that has occurred as a result of this crisis has created an ideological vacuum ripe for the ascendency of a neo-conservative regime of truth. It is a regime which evinces a persistent tendency to instrumentalize knowledge, strip it of any serious socially emancipatory claims, and evaluate it in terms of its immediate payoff in the capitalist marketplace and its efficacy in transmitting a privileged "white man's" reading of Western culture (McLaren and Dantley 1990). The set of problems which postmodernity has brought to the fore is aptly summarized in a question put forward by Andrew Ross: "*In whose interests is it, exactly, to declare the abandonment of universals?*" (1988: xiv, italics in original).[5]

Social theorists on the Left cannot disclaim responsibility for the rise of the new cultural, political, and moral closure that is currently plaguing the United States. They have unwittingly helped this process along, not by advancing a crypto-positivism, but by turning postmodern social theory into a totalizing language of its own. On this point, Lawrence Grossberg is worth quoting:

> The descriptions offered by the postmodernists must be located within the broader social and cultural fields of everyday life and the struggles of power, domination, subordination, and resistance that take place within them. Moreover, postmodernism's tendency to totalize its own descriptions, to slide from a description of *a* determining structure to the identification of that level with the totality of our lived and historical realities, must be resisted.
>
> (1988b: 147)

Social theorists writing about postmodernity have often elided the contradictions which occur in the lived experiences of people who inhabit different class fractions and who are positioned asymmetrically in society in terms of race, class, and gender. In fact, the hegemonizing potential of forms of postmodern theorizing has prompted Hassan to remark that "the terms of our social discourse, its silent, constitutive metaphors, may now require reinvention" (1987: 227). It is a sentiment that is also shared by Barbara Christian, who decries the new critical literary discourse for being "as hegemonic as the world which it attacks" (1987: 55). The totalizing discourse that prevails in late capitalism often becomes a precondition for an alienated subjectivity since such language devalues individual experience and difference as a means of constructing resistant modes of subjectivity (Schulte-Sasse 1986/87).[6]

Except for a few dialectical gestures to the contrary, educational theorists of the Left for the most part have displaced politics from the struggle of dispossessed groups and their "walking nihilism" to a narrow radical engagement with the text. This engagement is too easily detached from what West calls the "reality *that one cannot not know*" (Stephanson 1988b: 277, emphasis in original), what he describes as the "ragged edges of the Real, of *Necessity*, not being able to eat, not having shelter, not having health care, all this is something that one cannot not know" (p. 287).

Left social theorists have not been able to effectively chart out points of resistance, counter-discourses, counter-identifications, and counter-practices in existing lines of forces, what Teresa De Lauretis calls "the blind spots, or the space-off of . . . representations . . . spaces in the margins of hegemonic discourses, social spaces carved in the interstices of institutions and in the chinks and cracks of the power–knowledge apparati" (1987: 24). Nor have they been able effectively to challenge the idea of the disintegrating subject which haunts the theories of Jean Baudrillard (1983) and his disciples and hagiographers[7] and which also terrorizes some versions of post-structuralist and anti-essentialist feminist theories.[8] We are faced on the Left with theories of bodies without organs, shadow bodies which are merely discursive fictions, or fractured bodies composed of solitary links along a signifying chain. Rarely do we discover body/subjects who bleed, who suffer, who feel pain, who possess the critical capacity to make political choices, and who have the moral courage to carry these choices out.

Under these conditions, the New Right has encountered little opposition in its flooding of the public arena with a host of seemingly unstoppable authoritarian discourses which have had little trouble colonizing the moral void left by the deconstructive dismantling of the Enlightenment project.[9]

THE POSTMODERN BODY: THE ENFLESHMENT OF SUBJECTIVITY

> There is a certain primordial *stupidity* of the body, a weird inertness and passivity, something that freely offers itself to all the categories of

> thought and representation, allows them to invest it and pass through it, yet somehow always effortlessly evades them.
>
> (Steven Shaviro, p. 207)

As sites of enunciation and cultural inscription, bodies are never "free spaces". They cannot be reduced to biological processes or medical explanations; neither can they be adequately conceptualized as discursive productions, such as those that have come to be fashionably articulated in recent years by bourgeois postmodern theorists for whom theory itself has become something of a *sanbenito*.

Bodies are not placeless, monadic, isolated sites but are the result of intellectual traditions and the way such traditions have disciplined us into understanding them; yet they are also compellingly complicitous in the constitution of the metaphors through which such traditions are constructed. Hence, there is no way of avoiding bodies. As evident as this might be, the educational establishment has been exceedingly successful in ignoring the body both in the theorizing of educational practice and in the practice of educational theorizing. The body can be overcoded as a virtual symbol in the hieroglyphics of hope (i.e. the sacrificial body of Christ) or constituted within the refracted signs of physical exchange, as when the tensile force of a police baton acts juristically to split the human skull in one swift disciplinary arc. The body is the central relay point – the *point d'appui* – in the dialectical reinitiation of meaning and desire. As body/subjects, we do not simply consume cultural knowledge, we are consumed by it. I have described this process in Chapter 1 as enfleshment. The description bears further elaboration.

> By enfleshment I mean the mutually constitutive enfolding of social structure and desire; that is, the dialectical relationship between the material organization of interiority and the cultural modes of materiality we inhabit subjectively. The idea here is that dreams are not only about flesh, as Freud would lead us to believe, but the flesh also *dreams*.... [Enfleshment] involves the entextuation of desire and the embodiment of textual forms.
>
> (McLaren 1994: 273–4)

Schools, prisons and other workplaces in advanced capitalist nations function (for the most part tacitly) as major sites of enfleshment through regulatory regimes of signification, majoritarian semiurgical grammars, and social and cultural practices – sites that are able to produce the fully assimilated "Western" body/subject, a developmentalist and orientalist identity cluster that conspires to contain socialist impulses in its construction of a protofascist subjectivity, an irrepressible authorial presence that can accommodate a post-utopian global society in ruins.

I want to make a case against some aspects of the Baudrillardian mode of postmodern theorizing and a case *for* the body as a site of resistance to the prevailing cultural and moral hegemony, and to tease out some implications this might have for a critical pedagogy.

"Body" is a promiscuous term that ranges wildly from being understood as a warehouse of archaic instinctual drives, to a cauldron of seething libidinal impulses, to a phallocentric economy waging war on women, to a lump of perishable matter, to a fiction of discourse. In this essay I will refer to the body as a "body/subject," that is, as a terrain of the flesh in which meaning is inscribed, constructed, and reconstituted. In this view the body is conceived as the interface of the individual and society, as a site of embodied or "enfleshed" subjectivity which also reflects the ideological sedimentations of the social structure inscribed into it. Furthermore, the body, as a form of socially inscribed intentionality, does not so much constitute a text as it does various modes of intertextuality – what I will refer to later as "modes of subjectivity."

THE DEMONIZATION OF THE EMPIRICAL REFERENT

Here I must sound my further hesitation with respect to the Baudrillardian tendency to dissolve the subject almost entirely into media text and the tendency of other critics of modernity to render the empirical world into complex strands of discourse. Both these positions are complicitous in the devitalization and derealization of the body, and its reductive cancellation; furthermore, they solemnly strip bodies of intentionality and volition and their capacity to resist the image systems which help shape their subjective awareness. It is a position which maligns the lived body as a material referent for the construction of oppositional subjective forms, material practices, and cultural formations – what I call "zones of emancipation." In effect, postmodern culture has taken the body into custody where it has become liquidated to the currency of signs. It is as if the flesh has been numbed in order to avoid the unspeakable terror of its own existence. As Alan Megill warns:

> All too easy is the neglect or even the dismissal of a natural and historical reality that ought not to be neglected or dismissed. . . . For if one adopts, in a cavalier and single-minded fashion, the view that everything is discourse or text or fiction, the *realia* are trivialized. Real people who really died in the gas chambers at Auschwitz or Treblinka become so much discourse.
>
> (1985: 345)

Here, too, we are faced with the postmodern "loss of affect" which occurs when language attempts to "capture the ineffable" experience of the Other (Yudice 1988: 225). There is also a danger of textualizing gender, denying sexual specificity, or treating difference as merely a formal category rather than having an empirical and historical existence: problems which Teresa De Lauretis (1987: 25) has discovered in the work of Deleuze, Foucault, Lyotard, and Derrida.

The warnings sounded by Megill and De Lauretis bring into important relief the fact that we cannot – and should not – escape the empirical referent. As Charles Levin points out, the body is inescapable and cannot be deferred or lost in a chain of reference or split into signifier and signified; we cannot adequately capture the reality of the body in terms of difference, indeterminacy, or the ideological constitution of the subject (Levin 1987: 108). Levin writes that "the body *is* the symbol; and while the relationship between what constitutes meaning and the functioning of the body can be separated out and arranged in the discrete markers of temporal sequence, its actuality is never exhausted by this or any other variation of linguistic meaning" (p. 108).

Terry Eagleton makes a similar point that while discourse functions to broaden and intensify the body, the body can never be fully present in discourse. Eagleton adds: "It is part of the very nature of a sign to 'absent' its referent. The symbol, as Jacques Lacan once remarked, is the death of the thing. In language we deal with the world at the level of signification, not with material objects themselves" (1986: 97).

It is important to acknowledge further the relation between linguistic meaning and "real" bodies, a relationship explicated by Silverman:

> [N]ot only is the subject's relation to his or her body lived out through the mediation of discourse, but that body is itself coerced and molded by both representation and signification. Discursive bodies lean upon and mold real bodies in complex and manifold ways, of which gender is only one consequence. Even if we could manage to strip away the discursive veil that separates the subject from his or her "actual" body, that body would itself bear the unmistakable stamp of culture. There is consequently no possibility of ever recovering an "authentic" female body, either inside or outside language.
>
> (Silverman 1988: 146)

Silverman recognizes that the body is "zoned and inscribed" in ways which have important implications for subjectivity. The issue here, of course, is to recognize and redress the discursive conditions under which women, minorities, and other groups are demonized by patriarchy and the social relations of capital so that their presence as racial, cultural, and gendered subjects are effectively struck out of the archives and current narratives of history.

Yet bodies are always cultural artifacts even before they are molded discursively. Since we cannot put on new bodies before we desocialize our old ones, the task at hand requires us to provide the mediative ground for a refleshed corporeality. This means the creation of embodied knowledges that can help us refigure the lineaments of our desires and chart the path towards the realization of our collective needs outside and beyond the suffocating constraints of capital and patriarchy. This knowledge cannot be objectively known in advance but rather only from a subject position or perspective which is always partial (Haraway 1988: 585). This means that we cannot act in and on the world *as* others if we want to see from these positions critically (Haraway 1988; Giroux 1988a). But we can articulate a vision and a praxis in order to liberate the contexts for a relocation of meanings inscribed in the body/subject.

Haraway is arguing for a politics and epistemology of location, positioning, and situation where rational knowledge claims are based on partiality and not universality, what Haraway (p. 589) refers to as "the view from a body, always a complex, contradictory, structuring, and structured body, versus the views from above, from nowhere, from simplicity." It is important to recognize that she is referring here to doing critical work in "unhomogeneous gendered social space" (what better description of the classroom can we get?) and in order to decode the conflicting discourses operative in such a space – or to liberate such a space – we must follow Haraway (p. 589) in seeking an approach that "is always interpretive, critical, and partial . . . a ground for conversation, rationality, and objectivity – which is power-sensitive, not pluralist 'conversation.' " This is what she refers to as "the joining of partial views and halting voices into a collective subject position." What this implies for critical educators is a sensitivity to the agency of the subjects' (students') generative bodies. Students as body/subjects are not passive biological resources to be mapped and manipulated by the latest advance in behavioral technology or from a subject position of moral certainty that exercises an authoritive closure on the meaning-generating abilities of the students in the name of a transcendent patriarch or imperial discourse.

THE POLITICS OF ENFLESHMENT

Either as a focus of theorizing or as part of a pedagogical strategy, the body carries little epistemological weight. Psychologist Howard Gardner conceptualizes bodily knowledge "as a realm discrete from linguistic, logical, and other so-called higher forms of intellect" (1985: 13). Largely as a legacy of Western Cartesian thought, such bodily-kinesthetic intelligence has been perceived as "less privileged, less special, than those problem-solving routines carried out chiefly through the use of language, logic, or some other relatively abstract symbolic system" (p. 208). Other cultures do not draw such a sharp distinction between the active and the reflective. In fact, J. L. Hanna writes that "of all possible media of communication the body is the least removed from our associations of personal experience" (1983: 7).

Brian Fay argues that learning is not simply a cognitive process but also a somatic one in which "oppression leaves its traces not just in people's minds, but in their muscles and skeletons as well" (1987: 146). That is, ideology is not realized solely through the discursive mediations of the sociocultural order but through the enfleshment of unequal relationships of power; it is manifested intercorporeally through the actualization of the flesh and embedded in incarnate experience. Fay describes it as "transmitting elements of a culture to its newest members by penetrating their bodies directly, without, as it were, passing through the medium of their minds" (p. 148). This is similar to Jacques Attali's concept of "autosurveillance" which, in Fredric Jameson's terms, "marks the penetration of information technology within the body and the psyche" (1987: xiii).

Taking seriously Fay's insight, it is important to recognize the essentially non-discursive penetration of flesh through the physical positioning, enforced postures and cultural tatooing of the body, the panoptic space of the school and its dress codes. Culture in this sense is inscribed both on and in the body by the sartorial extension of the flesh according to the market-enforced logic of the fashion industry (which is no small matter in a youth culture in which stressed leather bomber jackets become couture style, conjuring a "sons of Yale" era of patriotic reverie: "flyboys" in sheepskin and silk scarves and bush pilot adventurers emancipating us from the pressurized yoke of 1980s yuppiedom) and by the inscription into the musculature and skeletal system of certain postures, gaits, or "styles of flesh." This is our bodily knowledge, the memory our body has about how our muscles should move, our arms should swing, and our legs should stride. It is a way of being in our bodies.

Material production we inhabit subjectively occurs not just at the level of the materiality of the flesh, but through both the corporeal embodiment of symbols and metaphors into the flesh and the "fleshing out" of ideas at the level of cultural forms and social structures. That is, the body both incorporates ideas and generates them. This process is, of course, a dialectical one. It is important here to recognize that words and symbols are physiognomic and just as much a part of our bodies as our flesh. What this means is that language is not a disembodied mode of communication but rather constitutes what Denys Turner calls "an intensification of the bodily powers" (1983: 17) as well as an extension of these powers. By being inserted into the abstractive power of language, our bodies become intensified and extended. Ideas, therefore, have a "social materiality" (p. 182); they are enfleshed in ideologies and historical and cultural forms of subjectivity. Enfleshment can be conceived here as the mutually constitutive aspect (enfolding) of social structure and desire. Discourses neither sit on the surface of the flesh nor float about in the formless ether of the mind but are enfolded into the very structures of our desire inasmuch as desire itself is formed by the anonymous historical rules of discourse. It is in this sense, then, that the body/subject becomes *both the medium and the outcome of subjective formation.* Enfleshment, as I have been articulating it, refers not only to the insertion of the subject into a pre-existent or preconstituted symbolic order (what Silverman calls "discursive interiority" 1988: 149), but also an investment on the part of the subject of what Grossberg (1986b) calls "affect." Affective investment transpires during the subject's insertion into or engagement with various fields of discourse. To be enfleshed is not only to appropriate symbols but it is to be identified with the symbol that one is appropriating; that is, it is to identify oneself with that selfsame symbol and also to arrive at a correspondence between the subject position provided by discourse and the subject. It is, in other words, to mistake authorship of such a position for the anonymous historical rules which have constituted it. Furthermore, it is to repress or to forget the contradictions between the body/subject and the discursive position or multiple positions it has assumed. To identify unproblematically with the symbol which one has appropriated or the subject positions made available within any discursive field, is to be in a condition of enfleshment. Resistance as a form of enfleshment can still be accounted for, in this case, not by the randomness of the signifier or the surplus of meaning (polysemy) attached to any symbol but rather because of what Colin McCabe (1986: 214) refers to as "the body and the impossibility of its exhaustion in its representations . . . the specific positioning of the body in the economic, political and ideological practices."

What I have been describing as enfleshment is similar to the process which De Certeau (1984) refers to as "intextuation" or the transformation of bodies into signifiers of state power and law. Schools become sites of enfleshment in the sense that they serve as discursive arenas in which the norms of class- and gender-based social power are intextuated into the student body, reflecting the wider body politic of the society at large (cf. Fiske 1989).

It should be remembered that power is not simply oppressive but works relationally; schooling promotes a combination of relations of power – a certain "promotion of practices and techniques" which Michel Feher terms "a political regime of the body" (1987: 160). The body then becomes both the object of power – "the actualizer of power relations" – and resistance to power. The exertion of and resistance to power does not happen outside the body but operates as à tension within the body (p. 161). The question of disciplining the body becomes an ethical one: "What do we take our bodies for?" "What are our bodies capable of perceiving and doing?" "In the name of what are bodily activities disciplined or styled?" "What are the assigned goals of these ethical practices of the self-styling of the body?" In Feher's four questions (pp. 162–3) we see the importance of conceptualizing the body, not as a site for the reconciliation of conscious and unconscious struggles, but rather as a series of historically specific assemblages and techniques. Ian Hunter notes, after Marcell Mauss, that the body is, "the instrument and object of its own making . . . its own manufactory" (1993: 177).

The problem with schools is not that they ignore bodies, their pleasures, and the suffering of the flesh (although admittedly this is part of the problem) but that they undervalue language and representation as constitutive factors in the shaping of the body/subject as the bearer of meaning, history, race, and gender. We do not simply exist as bodies; we *have* bodies – not just because we are born into them, but because we *learn* our bodies, that is, we are taught how to think about and experience them. And in a similar fashion our bodies invent us through the discourses they embody (Turner 1984). We are not just male bodies or female bodies, but African–American bodies, White bodies, Chicano bodies, Jewish bodies, Italian bodies, Mexican bodies, and so on.

Many of us who write within the critical tradition and under the sign of liberation have attempted to address the importance of radically reproblematizing the subject from its sovereign monocentrism to a subject that is historical, raced, classed, and gendered (Giroux 1988). It bears repeating here that the consequences of excluding the voices of women, of minorities, of gays and lesbians, and "othering" or "occulting" them both in the discursive field of our pedagogies or in the specificity of our pedagogical practices carry serious political and moral effects. As Giroux (1988) has made clear in his discussion of voice, not all discourses carry equal weight and legitimacy in the classroom and critical pedagogy is only liberating to the extent that it palpably takes into account the patriarchal, class- and race-based interests which inform all forms of pedagogy, including those which claim to be critical. I would add here that we must be careful not to textualize marginalized voices by placing a fixed limit on the scope or means of their representation; nor must we posit a false equation among the various expressions of pain or modes of resistance that speak to the specificity of the oppression of African–Americans, Latinos, White women, African–American women, etc. We need to construct in our classrooms those cultural spaces for the constitution of difference that test the limits of existing regimes of discourse, including our own. As Carolyn Porter (1988: 78) writes: "What we do not need is a criticism which re-others those voices which were and are marginalized and disempowered by these dominant discourses." Rather, we need to find ways in which we can intervene in dominant cultural and political formations so that we can be attentive to difference, while sharing a "common ethos" of solidarity, struggle, and liberation. In this way, different manifestations of critical pedagogy can speak to the specificity of race, class, and gender oppression and to the *differentia specifica* of various group projects while at the same time to the construction of new spaces of possibility, cultural justice, and human freedom. The challenge is understanding how, in the virtual reality of enfleshed subjectivity in this age of predatory culture, our flesh remembers, how it creates history and historicizes the act of creation, how the flesh becomes phobic, how the memory abscesses, and how agency implodes into fear.

MODES OF DESIRE, MODES OF PRODUCTION, AND MODES OF SUBJECTIVITY

I want to argue that the constitution of the body/subject must be viewed as a complex process involving the production of subjectivity within various social and material practices. More specifically, it is a relationship which obtains among modes of desire, modes of production, and modes of subjectivity (Turner 1984). The term "modes of desire" refers to the different ways in which desire is socially constructed. It registers most acutely the fact that we cannot peel away the flesh to yield an unfettered access to some irreducible instinctual desire: the goals of desire are always kept in perpetual flight.[10] Unlike the Platonic conception, this notion of desire is never wholly free-floating but is lived out in historically and culturally specific forms and is mediated by desires for and of the other. As John Brenkman notes,

> The actual forms in which the dialectics of desire is played and lived are historical. These forms will open or close the play of satisfactions and recognitions in specific ways which must, in turn, be related to the institutional framework of society as it organizes the satisfaction of human desire and through the desire of others.
>
> (1985: 189)

For Jacques Lacan, needs are biological, and desire is the active principle of the physical processes which lies both *beyond* and *before* demand (Sarup 1989: 153). Desire may therefore be said to transcend demand because in essence it masquerades or conceals an absolute lack or unconscious desire for recognition by the Other. Madan Sarup (1989: 154) expresses Lacan's conception of desire as "the desire for desire." A desire is what cannot be specified by demand, since "the meaning of the demand is not intrinsic but is partly determined by the response by the other to the demand" (p. 24). According to Lacan, demands cancel need but need then re-emerges on the other side of desire. As Sarup (p. 25), summarizing Lacan, states: "Desire arises out of the lack of satisfaction and it pushes you to another demand."

Deleuze and Guattari support the idea that "lack" should not be seen as the universal pre-requisite of desire but as a social construction within a particular historical configuration (1983: 25).[11] Objects of desire are shaped not in a value-free laboratory or homogenizing sphere but by the often conflictual social and cultural forms in which desiring takes place. Desire does not, as Deleuze and Guattari claim, directly invest the social field in a manner which makes it immune to mediation. We must avoid seeing desire as a form of vitalism that is produced by the will in combination with testosterone or the yearning for pre-Oedipal bliss, for this is the surest way to lapse into a naive essentialism, biological reductionism or some form of naturalism (Holland 1988: 405–16).[12]

Ernst Bloch (1986) understood desire to be a form of dreaming, of searching for something beyond ourselves; he rejected Freudian explanations of motivation and drives which he rightly pointed out were saturated with bourgeois assumptions. According to Bloch, Freud's understanding of desire tended to disembody human impulses and ignored their socioeconomic aspects and historical mutability (Geoghegan 1987: 87–97). Capitalism engenders a socially constructed dialectics of desire – a libidinal economy of sorts – in which fantasy is mobilized in order to search for a substitute for a "lack," that is, to discover a material object to substitute for a mythical object we lack "in reality" and which we feel we *need* to complete our subjectivity (a notion which has its antecedents in the world of Jean-François Lyotard). It is important to recognize that forms of desire are linked historically and discursively to specific "modes of production" and "modes of subjectivity." Desire cannot be understood as a pre-social or biological force. Desire and its social determinations, its cultural objects of desire, cannot be seen separately but must be understood as mutually constitutive. Similarly, desires which students express in schools cannot be understood outside the manner in which they have become institutionalized and socially legitimated, or without taking into consideration the ends and purposes – both immediate and long range – for which they have been manufactured both in relation to established educational discourses and economies of power and privilege at work in the larger society. Bryan Turner notes that every mode of production has a mode of desire and that the social relations of material production structure particular relations – or modes – of desire (1984: 13). This amounts to saying that desire is always mobilized by the contingency of the social and its particular circuits of power which are often tied to the economic requirements of dominant modes of material and cultural production. Within capitalism, for instance, modes of desire are linked to the production of surplus labor and the process of consumption. In this context, consumer needs within predatory culture are often superimposed on the desires of the body so that "the subject's intention to satisfy the body must make a detour through exchange value; the response to the demands of the body is deferred, for the visible aim of laboring is the wage" (Brenkman 1985: 182).

MODES OF SUBJECTIVITY

I am using the term "modes of subjectivity" to refer to the way in which postmodern culture has penetrated the constitutive nature of our subjectivities. Jochen Schulte-Sasse (1987/88) calls this a logical organization of sentiments that is beyond the control of knowing subjects. It is a form of "psychological rearmament" that is semiotically arranged and based on the "postindustrial colonization of the id" and "ideological organization of super-egos" which have developed largely on the basis of new postmodern nonlinear narrative modes (1987/88: 127). By modes of subjectivity I am also referring to the fact that modern capitalism tends to foster modes of desire which contribute to what David Michael Levin refers to as "a reduction of human beings to the dual states of subjectified privatized egos and subjugated, engineerable objects" (1987: 486). Within postmodern culture, we have witnessed an erosion of symbolic processes that cathect body and communal vision. This erosion of communal modes of subjectivity has created pathologies conditioned by the duplicitous deterritorialization of the body under capitalist modes of production – what Levin has called "historically conditioned pathologies of the will." He writes that "the pathologies we are seeing today – the narcissistic character disorders, the schizophrenias, and the depressions – are pathologies distinctive of a society and culture in which the fate of the Self has been hitched to the ego's increasingly nihilistic will to power" (1987: 486). Grossberg echoes a similar theme when he maintains that "Postmodernity demands that one live schizophrenically, trying, on the one hand, to live . . . inherited meaning and, on the other hand, recognizing the inability of such meanings to respond to one's own affective experiences" (1988b: 148).

I am not simply equating modes of subjectivity with pathologies of the will produced by particular modes of consumer desire. I also wish to draw attention to the *moral technologies* which help structure these modes of production and desire. For instance, the moral technologies of technocapitalism have reduced the revolutionary body/subject, the suffering servant, to a dead corpse, placed in an easy-credit, no frills casket. Literary critic Terry Eagleton describes moral technologies as "particular set(s) of techniques and practices for the instilling of specific kinds of value, discipline, behaviour and response in human subjects" (1985/86: 96–7). Eagleton reveals how one such moral technology – that of English literature – serves to create a bourgeois body/subject which values subjectivity *in itself*. What Eagleton argues, convincingly in my view, is that within liberal capitalist society the lived experience of "grasping literature" occurs within a particular form of subjectivity which values freedom and creativity as an end in itself, whereas the more important issue should be: freedom and creativity *for what?* What the bourgeois body/subject does not recognize in this process is *the enfleshment of indifference to oppression*. Eagleton makes the important observation that "the shackling of the subject is from within – and that this shackling is itself nothing less than our very forms of subjectivity themselves" (1985/86: 100–1).

Eagleton stresses the point that liberal capitalism produces forms of subjectivity "free of any particular rigorous ends" whose moral formalism, for example, creativity, sensitivity, and interiority for its own sake, draws attention away from the fact that these very forms of subjectivity are colonized by specific capitalist interests and modes of domination. I have described this process as enfleshment.

THE RESISTING BODY: CRITICAL PEDAGOGY AND THE POLITICS OF EMPOWERMENT

Without denying my own ambivalence towards postmodernity, I shall attempt in this section to establish some pedagogical directions based on some of the insights provided to us by postmodernism with respect to the constitution of meaning and subjectivity. I have been arguing that the modes of subjectivity being formed within the postmodern scene are precisely those which give individuals the illusion of free choice while masking the means by which the parameters that define such choices have been constituted by the social and material practices of consumer capitalist culture. If it is true that there is a connection between postmodern pathologies of the will and the constitution of the body/subject, then it is important to understand resistance to dominant modes of subjectivity, production, and desire, especially as this resistance is connected somatically to the formation of will, agency, and the construction of meaning. A critical pedagogy needs to counter the tendency of some succulent bourgeois post-structuralists to dissolve agency, and their claim that we are always already produced and finalized as subjects within discourse. Here, desire has been encysted in tight polyester lingerie and has turned agency into whatever fantasies cannot be contained by the constraints of discourse. We must recognize that there also exist modes of resistant subjectivity which are often more closely tied to the means of cultural production than the means of economic production and which develop as oppositional engagements with the dominant cultural hegemony.

It is one thing to say that individuals do not exist independently, as body/subjects, from surrounding social structures. Yet it is quite another to claim that they are simply the product of a monolithic engagement or identification with social texts. To mistake ourselves as merely products rather than producers of subjectivity is, in Lichtman's words, "to reify our alienation by having absorbed the mere facticity to which we have reduced the world into the very conception of ourselves" (1982: 257). Furthermore, Litchman warns that "To hold that we do not deceive ourselves but that reality deceives us implies that we are absolved from struggling through the ambivalent vicissitudes of our own lived experience" (1982: 256). The body/subject is not simply the product of a homogenous totality of discourses but rather a site of struggle, conflict, and contradictions.

One of the central challenges of critical pedagogy is to reveal to students how conflictual social relations (society's social logic) are actively inscribed in human intentionality and agency without reducing individuals to simply the static outcomes of social determinations. While I agree with the post-structuralists who remorselessly decry an essentialist reading of the self and who claim that we cannot speak of the self as an essence or unmediated object of reflection, I disagree that the self is constituted only through background beliefs – both unconscious and conscious – engendered through enfleshment. That is why the important distinction must be made that human beings – bodies – *are self-conscious and not self-constituting*. That is, while individuals are constituted by background beliefs which are inaccessible to explicit self-understanding and knowledge (and which primarily lie outside of consciousness), their subjectivities are also informed by their self-consciousness. Self-consciousness and repression both play important roles in our subjective formation. Bodies cannot will their own subjective formation or determine their own significance by fiat. Unlike the self-conscious, self-present Cartesian body/subject, which claims the power to individuate consciousness by an act of will alone, individuals are not capable of intentional, transparent communication or unmediated actions in the world (Turner 1983). Yet it is necessary to acknowledge that the capacity of individuals to recognize at least partially the constitution of the self is what makes liberation possible. (This goes directly against Lacan's notion of the subject as a "vanishing point" which resists self-perception; see Larmore [1981].) It is also a precondition for *refleshment*, or forming a space of desire where we can assume self-consciously and critically new modes of subjectivity hospitable to a praxis of self- and social empowerment. We must not forget that *we can act in ways other than we do.*

The task of critical pedagogy is to increase our self-consciousness, to strip away distortion, to discover modes of subjectivity which cohere in the capitalist body/subject and to assist the subject in its historical remaking. The project of placing desire into critical and self-conscious circulation necessitates a language that speaks to the lived experiences and felt needs of students but also a critical language that can problematize social relations which we often take for granted. It needs a non-totalizing language that refuses to strip experience from its contingency and open-endedness, that refuses to textualize oppression, and that refuses to dehistoricize or desexualize or degender the body, or to smooth over the difference in the name of justice or equality (Giroux 1988b).

IDEOLOGICAL CONTRADICTIONS AND THE POLITICS OF PLEASURE

An important aspect of the production of pleasure within youth culture consists of what Grossberg terms *affective investment* – "the intensity or desire with which we invest the world and our relations to it" (1986b: 185) – in which different and often contradictory modes of desire and subjectivity are embraced which are generally absent in traditional school sites. Here, modes of desire may *consist of the very pleasure of participating in the act of desiring itself.* Bodies are produced which actively refuse the moral technologies, panoptic spaces, and modes of subjectivity produced in schools (Shumway 1989).

While it is important to stress that individuals as body/subjects – as embodied or enfleshed subjectivity – constitute precisely the contradictory logic of the social world, it is wrong to assume that individuals remain passive within such a process of subjective formation. Students are inserted into culture in ways which are often arrestingly different and contradictory. For instance, what is often mistaken as youth conservatism or youth indifference is, in actuality, an active refusal to politicize reality. Youth often accomplish this by *entering the present more fully* as part of an affective rather than merely intellectual investment. Grossberg notes that "Youth's power lies in their ability to appropriate any text, to undermine the distinction between production and consumption and, in this way, to deny the power of ideology, and of the commodity" (1988b: 140).

Consider the celebrated success of MTV. John Fiske writes that

> MTV is read by the body, experienced through the senses, and resists sense which is always theirs. MTV is experienced as pleasure. . . . The threat of the signifier is its resistance to ideology, its location in the sensations of the body, the physical senses rather than the mental senses. The plurality of meanings on video clips makes us talk of their senses, not of their sense.
>
> (Fiske 1986: 75)

The pure materiality and overvaluation of the signifier, unattached and autonomous, freed from any secured signified, forms a seamless cultural surface of the present that resists ideological investment. In fact, to be confronted by the inherent ambiguity of this particular form of image production constitutes a *refusal of ideology.* Yet at the same time, to embrace such politics of representation is to inhabit most fully the bourgeois mode of subjectivity which believes that such an ambiguity of meaning represents a space offered for exercising the liberal humanistic freedom to choose one's own meaning. True, individuals can accept, reject, or choose particular meanings associated with free-floating images. But there is always an overdeterminate or "preferred" reading of images within the dominant culture. To believe that one can escape this sovereign or imperial reading by an exercise of critical reflection alone also presupposes that people make choices only on the basis of semantic understanding, and not through either the mobilization of desire and affect or a form of deintensification of experience, what David J. Sholle calls the "spectacle stance of the audience" (1988: 33). In their engagement with forms of media-generated images, viewers become the most vulnerable to the political agenda behind such images precisely when they feel they can intellectually distance themselves from their discursive articulation and persuasive power.

The New Right has most often benefitted from the fact that the mass media communicates most effectively not to the faculties of logic but in mapping out our primary structures of affect. Consider the image of "Willy" Horton exploited by George Bush's ad men in the 1988 presidential election campaign. The Bush camp was able to compress its ideology on criminal justice into the negative image of Horton, an African–American man who committed murder while on a prison furlough in Massachusetts. While most viewers more than likely understood this to be another sleazy ideological ploy (not to mention another historical violation of the African–American body) and felt that they still had free choice in the matter of accepting or rejecting what appears to be the intended effect of such an image, among large numbers of whites, the picture of Willy Horton nevertheless resonated *affectively* with previous socially induced fears. Here, an affective as opposed to ideological alliance was created with Bush's reactionary views on criminal justice (which would supposedly prevent more wild-eyed and teeth-clenching Willy Hortons from running loose and terrorizing whites by the abolition of prison furloughs). The success of such an alliance appears to confirm one of Adorno's major insights (1974) that cultural products are often accepted even though their ideological messages are understood by those who engage them (Sholle 1988: 33). Despite the fact that many viewers resisted the ideological message in the image of Willy Horton on a semantic level, they were nevertheless seduced by the affective play of the surface of the image – what Schulte-Sasse calls "the relatively unstructured semantic homogeneity of the world of images" (1986/87: 46) – and the Bush campaign was able to further advance its war of position. What is putatively a conscious refusal of ideology inscribed in televisual images often means that images from both the political left and right are accepted in a spectatorial detachment, as a chain of equivalent signified. Further, it suggests that electronic images are always already inscribed by the logic of the medium and overdetermined by it. Ideology in this case is not so much a form of cognitive mapping as it is the production of structures of affect.

A critical pedagogy must focus on popular culture and develop curricular strategies based on how student subjectivity is informed within it (Giroux and Simon 1988). For if we do not work with students in this area of their lives we deny them the very modes of subjectivity which give flesh to the meaning of their lives. If we want to take seriously the emancipatory possibilities inscribed within student resistance, then we must attempt to answer the following questions: How are the subjectivities, dreams, desires, and needs of students forged by the media, by leisure activities, by institutions such as the family, and by cultural forms such as rock 'n roll and music videos? How for instance, are the practical ethics with which students engage everyday life inscribed within a contestatory politics of signification? How are images of male and female socially constructed? How do the politics of signification structure the problematization of experience? How are the subjectivities of students constituted by the effects of representations which penetrate the level of the body? It is imperative that as educators in the postmodern age we begin to examine issues such as the feminization and masculization of the body and the reification of the body politic. We need to study how our needs and desires as educators have been shaped in contradictory ways through dominant cultural forms, modes of subjectivity, and circuits of power. A critical pedagogy must grapple with the ways in which youth resist the dominant culture *at the level of their bodies* because in so doing the utopian moments to which such resistance points can be transformed pedagogically into strategies of empowerment. Jochen Schulte-Sasse writes that the empowerment of the imagination is inefficient as a culture-revolutionary project; what is more pressingly needed are "rhetorical strategies that break through the reign of the simulacrum and grasp, as adequately as possible, the linguistically and mentally receding structures of our id and of the global economy, and comprehend the inscriptions both leave on our bodies" (1986/87: 47–8).

A critical pedagogy must help us to distinguish our real needs and those of our students from predatory fantasies in pursuit of artificial needs and to enunciate the demand for a new ethics of compassion and solidarity. I am speaking here about a praxis in which the knowing subject is an acting body/subject, a praxis which can empower us to take responsibility for history and for developing a vision of the world which is not yet. This is not to deny the historicism of praxis but to embrace it more fully with a recognition that even in these postmodern times we are capable of seizing the stage of history in the unity of our thinking and doing, and bringing forth a new world at the command of our own voices and with the strength of our own hands. The prerequisite for such an enterprise lies in reclaiming the body and in formulating strategies of opposition whose primary referent consists of new ways of thematizing knowledge and subjectivity in relation to the body.

Such a project would culminate in a critical praxis of social transformation that works against the political and predatory horrors of our time. New communities of collective body/subjects must be shaped both by uncovering the subversive work of desire and by creating social and cultural forms in which new desires may be produced, and new modes of subjectivities formed based on compassion and reciprocity. We need to explore our self-constitutivity by using pedagogical strategies which allow us to bear witness to and enact the struggle of the oppressed rather than engage in strategies which demarginalize, decolor, degender, and aestheticize such suffering. Here, the unfixity and open-endedness which characterizes the postmodern condition can make possible "new enfoldings," what George Yudice describes as "unfixity delimited by the unboundedness of struggle" (1988: 229). In this way the guardians of the dominant culture can be deprived of the moral and political certainty they have taken as their refuge. Of course, in achieving such a goal we must never cease to retravel the road which runs from a negative dialectics to a critical hope. Nor must we ever abandon our theoretical vigilance on the basis of our claim to moral innocence. To claim immunity from our exercising domination over others on the basis that we have good intentions is to dodge euphemistically Michel Foucault's injunction that we judge truth by its effects and to deny our complicity in economies of oppression on the grounds of our theoretical ignorance or superiority.

CRITICAL PEDAGOGY AND THE POLITICS OF MEANING

A pedagogy of the postmodern body/subject can help educators better understand how the resistant body/subject attempts to signify beyond normative and available systems of signification, challenging and disrupting the discourses that create the space of subjectivity. Yet paradoxically, resistant body/subjects sign their own subjection by refusing to occupy the normative space of the body/subject – the socially encoded "proper" spaces of the "masculine," the "feminine," and the "citizen" – and by refusing to be semiotically engineered into the subjective mode of bourgeois "happiness." This is the case because it is difficult even for resistant students to escape reinscription as subjects into the consumer-driven codes of late capitalism. Within postmodernity it is more difficult to separate body/subjects from the languages which represent their desire. Lacking a language of resistance, resistant students simply become signs of themselves, and can only encode the anxiety of the present and apprehension of the future. Consequently, they remain in their resistance, dragged by images fleeing history, rather than forging symbols with the power to transform it. They enflesh the terror and not the promise of postmodernity. Fending off the fear of uncertainty, the horror of ambiguity, and the threat of difference requires body/subjects to construct a language that refuses its own limits, that is capable of locating gaps and fissures within the prevailing cultural hegemony. Such a language must enable its users to reflect on their own subjective formation and incorporation in the social relations of capital as well as participate in their own self-transformation.

Such a language must also help to transform critical pedagogy into a pedagogy of hope. It must move beyond the divisiveness of sectarian interest groups and beyond the various pluralisms of which Richard Bernstein (1988) is so eloquently critical: the "flabby pluralism" which constitutes a simple acceptance of the existence of a variety of perspectives and paradigms; a pluralism which regards different perspectives as virtually incommensurable; and the "decentered anarchistic pluralism" which celebrates uncertainty or lapses into a brooding and nihilistic retreat from life. We need to move beyond the general liberal Conversation and refuse to accept the constant deferral of meaning in any dialogue to the point where we choose only to speak to ourselves. The former position believes that by affirming difference unproblematically, liberation will ensue in a dance of pluralistic reverie. The latter believes that the tenuousness of all meaning inevitably places us in the thrall of discursive and ethical paralysis. At its least dangerous extreme, the Great Conversation lapses into a silly relativism while the post-structuralist position becomes merely political foolishness. At their worst extremes, both positions lead to political inertia and moral cowardice where educators remain frozen in the zone of "dead" practice in which it is assumed that all voices are those which silence or which contain the "other" by a higher act of violence, and all passionate ethical stances are those built upon the edifices of some form of tyranny or another. Unable to speak with any certainty, or with an absolute assurance that his or her pedagogy is untainted by any form of domination, the "post-critical" educator refuses to speak at all. This distressing position that has been assumed by some critical educators, reminds me of a form of philosophical detachment of some social critics who, by constantly criticizing and radicalizing themselves on their path to universality, often fail to form a concrete praxis based on their own principles (see Michael Walzer 1987).

For theorists like the ones I have been describing, pedagogy becomes a curse that can be abrogated only when all forms of persuasion, authority, rhetoric or self-assurance have been purged from the classroom discussion. In this view it is better to do nothing than engage in critical praxis because of the dominating interests that might lurk behind the lesson or the frames of reference with which the critical praxis takes as its ethical or conceptual starting point. It is one thing to ascertain in which ways the language of critical theory may be part of the oppressive unity of that which it attempts to liberate; it is quite another to banish such a language into the dustbin of history, as some "post-critical" groups are wont to do.

We have arrived now at a watershed in the development of critical pedagogy where we must ask the following: Are the various discourses of critical pedagogy capable of normatively grounding feminist and minority struggles for liberation? Only in an age which Cornel West (1989a: 256) characterizes as being "obsessed with articulations of particularities, e.g., gender, race, nation" could such a question be raised with such fervor. It is an important question which, of course, must be answered. But to answer "yes" invites some qualification. More specifically, to answer in the affirmative means to submit the various theoretical strands of critical pedagogy to both a constant ethical surveillance and self-monitoring and a rethinking of its conceptual edifice. This, of course, can be done without theoretical reductionism, and for the most part it has been the radical legacy of critical pedagogy, whose emancipatory project has always explored the preconditions of its own categorizations and assumptions. It is our responsibility to continue this legacy in our present and future theorizing. While much that currently passes for critical pedagogy bears the birthmark of a failed modernity, and while it may generate political contradictions and invite some confusion in the way it addresses questions of difference, it nevertheless provides an indispensable basis for a political and ethical revitalization of our schools as sites for self and social transformation.

Yet what is still not fully realized in the discourse of critical pedagogy is what I shall call a social–critical utopian praxis. This refers to critical action that is yet to be realized in history. Such a praxis is beginning to show promise in some of the ongoing critiques by critical educators of sexism, racism, economic exploitation, ecological violence, and militarism and in the ways revolutionary educators are forging a collaboration with Marxists, feminists, and social movements striving to uncover and confront the values and interests which are unknown but nevertheless are constantly operative in our pedagogies and liturgies of practical living – values which dehumanize and depersonalize. Social–critical utopian praxis calls for our unconditional withdrawal from inhumanity and for our movement towards what Agnes Heller (1988) calls the "common good," that is, towards a praxis which promotes the goodness of persons who prefer to suffer wrong than to commit wrong. In achieving the common good, we need to further develop a language of representation and a language of hope which together will allow the subaltern to speak outside the terms and frames of reference provided by the colonizer, whether or not the colonizer in this case happens to be the teacher, the researcher, or the administrator. We must acquire a language of analysis and hope that permits women to speak in words outside Name-of-the-Father vocabularies and does not prevent minorities and the excluded to speak their narratives of liberation and desire. Such a language must be able to uncover and transform the constructions of subjectivity. In so doing, the language of social–critical utopian praxis needs to de-authorize and rewrite the master narratives of liberal postindustrial democracy and the humanist, individualist, and patriarchal discourses which underwrite it, while at the same time undermining and reconstructing the idealized and romantic conception of the subject which is shaped by Eurocentric and androcentric discursive power relations. Such a pedagogical praxis refuses the class subjection of the proletarian body through its sterile aestheticization by bourgeois categories of the flesh. It also refuses the inscription of patriarchy upon the female body and the intextuation of masculinist ideologies. We need to provide the marginalized and the immiserated with power over the direction of their desiring. The project of critical pedagogy is positioned irreverently against a pedantic cult of singularity in which moral authority and theoretical assurance are arrived at unproblematically without regard to the repressed narratives and suffering of the historically disenfranchised.

We need to understand, as critical educators, that we are living in an epochal transition to an era of multiple feminisms, liberalisms, Marxisms which, on the one hand, hold the enabling promise of liberation, while on the other hand threaten to splinter the left irrevocably in a maze of often mutually antagonistic micro-politics. This calls for some form of totalizing vision – what I want to call an arch of social dreaming – that spans the current divisiveness we are witnessing within the field. This arch of social dreaming is meant to give shape, coherence, and protection to the unity of our collective struggles. It means the conquest of a vision of what the total transformation of society might mean. As Best remarks:

> If totality can signify a dystopian nightmare of coercion, closure, and endorsed identity, it can also signify the utopian dream of personal development and social and ecological harmony. . .
>
> (Best 1989: 359)

Of course, the realization of this vision means that critical pedagogy must not become a site of further divisiveness among the left but rather serve as a forum which can generate an ethos of solidarity that speaks to what educators as critical agents – Latinos, African–Americans, Anglos, feminists, gays, and others – share in the common struggle against domination and for freedom while preserving the specificity of difference. Attali catches the spirit of the creation of this new *groupe moteur* or "subject of history" to which I have been referring in his discussion of musical composition:

> [I]n composition, it is no longer, as in repetition, a question of marking the body; nor is it a question of producing it, as in repetition. It is a question of taking pleasure in it. That is what relationship tends toward.

> An exchange between bodies – through work, not through objects. This constitutes the most fundamental subversion . . . to create, in common, the code within which communication will take place.
>
> (Attali 1987: 143)

Those of us who work within the critical tradition in education would do well to look at what Cornel West (1989a) had formulated as "prophetic pragmatism" as a "form of American Left thought and action in our postmodern moment" (p. 239). Indebted to Marxism, structuralism, and post-structuralism, it also is an attempt to advance beyond "a Eurocentric and patriarchal discourse that not simply fails to theoretically consider racial and gender forms of subjugation, but also remains silent on the antiracist and feminist dimensions of concrete progressive political struggles" (p. 215). Rejecting the Enlightenment search for foundations and the quest for certainty, prophetic pragmatism situates human inquiry into truth and knowledge in the social and communal circumstances under which persons can communicate and cooperate in the process of gaining knowledge (p. 213). Prophetic pragmatism is a political mode of cultural criticism. It reflects Emerson's concepts of power, provocation and personality, Dewey's stress on historical consciousness, and DuBois's focus on the plight of the wretched of the earth. West recaptures Emerson's utopian vision, Dewey's conception of creative democracy, and DuBois's socio-structural analysis of the limits of capitalist democracy and links it all to the work of Niebuhr, C. W. Mills, and Gramsci. Prophetic pragmatism is not only an oppositional cultural criticism but "a material force for individuality and democracy" (p. 232). Like Gramsci's organic intellectual and Mills's activist intellectual, the prophetic pragmatist "puts a premium on educating and being educated by struggling peoples, organizing and being organized by resisting groups" (p. 234). West summarizes this position as follows:

> Prophetic pragmatism worships at no ideological altars. It condemns oppression anywhere and everywhere, be it the brutal butchery of third-world dictators, the regimentation and repression of peoples in the Soviet Union and Soviet-bloc countries, or the racism, patriarchy, homophobia, and economic injustice in the first-world capitalist nations. In this way, the precious ideals of individuality and democracy of prophetic pragmatism oppose all those power structures that lack public accountability, be they headed by military generals, bureaucratic party bosses, or corporate tycoons. Nor is prophetic pragmatism confined to any preordained historical agent, such as the working class, black people, or women. Rather, it invites all people of goodwill both here and abroad to fight for an Emersonian culture of creative democracy in which the plight of the wretched of the earth is alleviated.
>
> (West 1989a: 235)

Prophetic pragmatism is hardly unproblematic, but it does offer educators a Left philosophical approach that is tied to U.S. history and struggle and which speaks directly to the conditions for social transformation. It is, furthermore, an approach that avoids the paralysis of the will that plagues many current postmodern theoretical perspectives.

Given the conditions of contemporary social life, its unleashing of collective desire with an absent center – a vacant theatre of the self built out of impotent illusions and hallucinated certainties which are in danger of collapsing under their own irreducible excess of signifiers, and which render our identities self-interested, insatiable anarchic, and free-floating – prophetic pragmatism "gives prominence to the plight of those peoples who embody and enact the postmodern themes of degraded otherness, subjected alienness, and subaltern marginality, that is, the wretched of the earth (poor peoples of color, women, workers)" (West 1989a: 237).

A PEDAGOGY VOICED FROM THE MARGINS

Critical pedagogy in its many diverse incarnations has been, since its earliest developments, on a collision course with the empowerment of the student as *Werkindividualitat*, or autonomous individual. Empowerment of the self without regard to the transformation of those social structures which shape the very lineaments of the self is not empowerment at all but a *naif* sojourn into a version of humanistic therapy where catharsis is mistaken for liberation. Critical pedagogy is more than a de-sacralization of the grand narratives of modernity, but seeks to establish new moral and political frontiers of emancipatory and collective struggle, where both subjugated narratives and new narratives can be written and voiced in the arena of democracy. These new – sometimes outré – narratives are not unified by objective and regulative moral principles but by a common ethos of solidarity and struggle for the realization of a deeper democracy and civic participation. The critical pedagogy which I have been describing is more than the exercise of imaginative sympathy or creative compassion. It is more than the civic pity of the *optimates*, luxuriant empathy of the liberal humanist, or the formalized interest of the academic, an interest too often cleansed of history and struggle. Critical pedagogy does not refuse to take sides, balancing truth somewhere in an imaginary middle between silence and chaos. It does not domesticate indifference by ignoring the historical and cultural ruptures within Western industrial societies, or the imperial project of colonizing students' subjectivities in the interest of Western civility. Pedagogy for liberation works outside the inviolable boundaries of order, in the rift between a subversive praxis and a concrete utopia. It recalls history not as a surrogate for experience but as a means of providing those memories which have been policed into silence with a voice unmuted by the echoes of industry or the motors of progress.

The hope that is critical pedagogy rests with those educators who keep its languages and practices alive and *in corpore* while taking account of changing historical contexts and the specificity and limitations of difference. The hope is with those who refuse to allow oppression of the mind and the body to become oppression of the spirit and who resist the grotesque identification of education with the economic interests of the dominant class and the necropolis of tradition. As Dean MacCannell has noted in his discussion of California, we are all "potential soldiers in a fascist army" (1992: 204). This is because we live in an age "where a slick surface of correctness develops as a cover for absolute moral rot" (p. 209). In the over-dramatization of the ordinary, the aesthetization of politics, and the "crotch-drenching intensity" of love expressed as a sublime national duty to preserve "family values" America, we are vulnerable to a fascist seducation of our volatilized, hysterical bodies into cool, laid back, nonchalant bodies – perfect bodies. Perfect for what? For living out a soft-core fascist drama as a corporate warlord? Or an aerobics instructor in a G-string? Or a serial killer? At the end of history – which is right now – it really doesn't matter. They'll all receive equal media time. We desperately need an embodied hope, an informed hope as we face the dawn of a new century.

Left to be swallowed by the darkness that exists outside the concreteness of historical and collective struggle, desire transforms itself into fantasy, endlessly in pursuit of what it lacks. Yet critical reason can give desire wings, so that thought can be lifted beyond the limitations of the present moment in order to be transformed into dreams of possibility. And with dreams we can do wonderful things.

Part II

Critical agency, border narratives, and resistance multiculturalism

Chapter 3

Border disputes

Multicultural narrative, *Rasquachismo*,[1] and critical pedagogy in postmodern America

GRAND HOTEL ABYSS

We live in dangerous times. Not only are public schools under a massive and coordinated assault, but the very idea of public institutions is increasingly becoming threatened by the New Right's clarion call for privatization of the public sphere. It is an era of economic terror propped up by "enterprise culture" and the growing number of transnational corporations whose omnipotent sway in foreign policy brought us Grenada, Panama, and Desert Storm. International bankers have become the new "warrior-prophets" of predatory culture; their synthetically manufactured political mythology has ushered in a new global agenda of takeovers and buy-outs. On the one hand, the world has been bequeathed, to borrow a description by Vincent Pecora (1991: 130), "one grandly obfuscating vision of global harmony and interdependence policed by Conan the American – the 'new world order,' a phrase whose historical resonance alone demands the keenest suspicion of all that it attempts to name." On the other hand, post-Fordist capitalism has effectively transformed the relationship between subjectivity and the structures through which experiences become constituted such that subjectivity is now experienced as decentered and radically discontinuous. Our identities have been respatialized and reinvested in new forms of desire. Our agency has been dispersed on the predatory horizon of micro-politics with no common understanding of oppression or collective strategy to challenge it.

Historical reason mocks us as we allow it to linger in our educational thinking and policies; for one of the lessons of modernity has been that a teleological and totalizing view of scientific progress is antipathetic to liberation. Paradoxically, it has produced an intractable thralldom to the very logic of domination and malignant chaos which it has set out to both contain and contest and in doing so has reproduced part of the repression to which it so disdainfully pointed. The inevitability of alienation has been accepted and has fostered a growth in intellectual markets where fashion-prone theories of dissent and a voguish nihilism are being recuperated by academic establishments which have turned marginalization and alienation into a profitable business.

We have produced a culture modeled on a masculinist heroics, a reactive desire and a compulsive need to consume. As in the film by Wim Wenders, *Until the End of the World*, the flesh of our dreams has been soldered to the electronic circuitry of high-tech gadgets which reroute our desires in the service of profit and corporate advantage. What is significant about these "new times" is that we have become the wardens of our own souls through the global logic of "consumer sovereignty" and the thrilling self-indulgence that marks the ecocidal desire to endlessly consume. This new form of democracy asserts that consumers vote with their dollars in a free market where consumer demands determine the products, amount of goods produced, and the prices charged for these products. Of course, it doesn't matter that there exists only a select number of wealthy customers – a hypertrophic cult of the "rich and famous" – whose millions of dollars for luxury items considerably "outvote" masses of people who can barely afford to purchase food and shelter (McGovern 1981). Never mind that consumer sovereignty allots votes according to income and permits one person to be worth a thousand votes while another – as long as he or she manages to survive – is worth only one. This is a time when the gap between the wealthy and the poor is widening vertiginously, a time ironically termed "the age of democratic capitalism" (McGovern 1981: 317), a time of corporate partnership and the rationalized machinery of social power acting on behalf of the most privileged groups.

Felix Guattari and Toni Negri describe the structuring on a global scale of "capitalist voraciousness" as the production of poverty.

> To a certain extent, the poor find themselves produced twice by this system; by exploitation and by marginalization and death . . . there are only differences of degree between exploitation, destruction by industrial and urban pollution, welfare conceived as a separating out of zones of poverty, and the extermination of entire peoples, such as those which occur in the continents of Asia, Africa, and Latin America. . . . On all levels, on all scales, everything is permitted: speculation, extortion, provocations, destabilizations, blackmail, massive deportations, genocide. . . . In this virulent phase of decadence, the capitalist mode of production seems to rediscover, intact, the ferociousness of its origins.
>
> (1990: 59, 61)

These "new times" weigh heavily on the breast of history. The promotional dynamics and self-stagings of right-wing politicians, linked to the market imperative that drives our social universe, have instilled a vision of democracy in the American public that is a mixture of talk show mandarinism, game show enthusiasm, and the reckless effrontery of "new world order" jingoism: "We're number one!" In the distempered vision of moral apocalypse put forward by conservative political fundamentalists (as frighteningly revealed in the 1992 Republican National Convention), the reality of "democracy" has become continuous with the totalitarianism it seeks to displace. The elaborately staged self-celebrations of national identity now revolve around Euro-American strategies of, to borrow a phrase from Gayatri Chakravorty Spivak (1990b: 789), "[Making] the straight white Christian man of property the ethical universal."

These "new times" are also reflective of the narratives we live by. They mirror the stories we tell ourselves about ourselves, stories that shape both the ecstasy and the terror of our world, disease our values, misplace our absolutes, and yet strangely give us hope, inspiration, and framework for insights. We can't escape narratives but I believe we can resist and transform them.

Narratives form a cultural contract between individuals, groups, and our social universe. If narratives give our lives meaning we need to understand what those narratives are and how they have come to exert such an influence on us and our students. My position is that we need to be able to read critically the narratives *that are already reading us.* My general thesis is that all cultural identities presuppose a certain narrative intentionality and are informed by particular stories. Put another way, I want to argue that identities are partly the result of the narrativity of social life. Every claim to selfhood implies a narrative that recognizes temporal and ethical aspects of human knowing. It implies a politically, historically, and ethically meaningful succession of events. One issue, of course, is whether or not there can be "true" speakers of narratives. Do narratives speak us or are we spoken through narratives? We use different kinds of narratives to tell different kinds of stories, but we also sanction certain narratives and discount others for ideological and political reasons. To a large extent, our narrative identities determine our social action as agents of history and the constraints we place on the identities of others.

In other words, narratives can become politically enabling of social transformation or can serve as strategies of containment that locate "difference in close epistemological discourse." Homi K. Bhabha notes that, with respect to the former function,

> Narrative and the *cultural* politics of difference become the closed circle of interpretation. The "Other" loses its power to signify, to negate, to initiate its "desire," to split its "sign" of identity, to establish its own institutional and oppositional discourse. However impeccably the content of an other culture may be known, however anti-ethnocentrically it is represented, it is its *location* as the "closure" of grand theories, the demand that, in analytical terms, it be always the "good" object of knowledge, the docile body of difference, that reproduces a

> relation of domination and is the most serious indictment of the institutional powers of critical theory.
>
> (1988: 16)

This is not the time to present a full-dress account of narrative theory. Since I will frame my discussion of narrative quite specifically in the context of questions of domination and liberation, it is not my intention to discuss narrative in isolation from the material struggles over identity and dignity that are so integral a part of our increasingly terroristic social order. Consequently, I shall forgo a more semiotic and linguistic analysis of narrative; for instance, examining narrative as a scheme of predicates in a transformational-generative sense; nor is it my purpose to expand on the way, for example, linguistic narrative works – in either a proto-structuralist (e.g. Frye, Propp) or post-structuralist (e.g. Derrida, Barthes) sense (see Coste 1989). This is not to denigrate the importance of narrative grammar which has, over recent years, become an increasingly important field. Rather than explore the work of notable figures such as Eco, Propp, Greimas, Lévi-Strauss, Culler, Bremond, and others, and the world of specialized grammatical forms, such as the production and interpretation of sign-functives, I wish merely to bring narratology into the province of historical and textual practices. This more modest approach to narrative is designed to concentrate on what Coste (1989: 15) calls narratology's "overtly incestuous relationship with theories of action" and how narratology "lives in the shade of the concepts of history that prevail in our cultures and... impinge[s] on the strategic programs and games of various socioeconomic groups." In other words, I am more interested in approaching "the formative or enslaving exchanges that obtain between 'history' and its subjects and objects" (Coste 1989: 15) outside of a purely linguistic or metahistorical approach to narrative. To a large extent I follow Paul Richoeur's lead in establishing a relationship between narrative, identity, and ethics.

This chapter is not governed by a need to follow a single narrative order but rather to offer a series of commentaries about narrative's intersection with subjectivity, agency, and identity and the way it structures our theoretical approaches to these topics. My primary focus will be on narrative as the production of interested projects, as textual practices and social symbolic acts linked to the practice of theory and the theorizing of practice. I will be concentrating on what I call the "narrative economy of textual identities" and the development of "postcolonial" narratives that are able to unfix, unsettle, and subvert totalizing narratives of domination as well as engender an infinity of new contexts for destabilizing meaning. Further, I will draw attention to imperialist narrative as a form of epistemic violence, that is, as constituting dominative systems of knowledge and structures of intelligibility that construct forms of social life – textual practices that have distinct, though contradictory, social effects. Another purpose is to provisionally sketch out some new narrative practices in pedagogy – a new narrative economy of social texts of sorts. Such a pedagogy is grounded in what I call "critical narratology." Critical narratology means reading personal narrative (our own and those of our students) against society's treasured stock of imperial or magisterial narratives, since not all narratives share a similar status and there are those which exist, highly devalued, within society's rifts and margins.

While I am interested in examining narrativity in terms of teleological aspects of representational effects, I will not make fine-grained distinctions between narrative, plot, and story. Scholars who work in literary studies will possibly find my discussion of narrative much too general. In fact, I intend to employ a minimalist definition of narrative as a "discursive representation of a sequence of randomly connected events" (Rigney 1991: 591). Narratives, in other words, may be said to organize relationships of difference and such a process is socially determined and context specific. This general description of narrative and the more detailed accounts that follow are intended to serve as heuristic devices to enable teachers to grasp social life and the production of identity – and theorize about it – as various forms of story.

While I am interested in narratology as it has been employed in poetics, I am focusing here on narrativity and narratological discussion primarily as it has been linked to historiographical debates. Narratological reflection in poetics deals mainly with fiction whereas history writing focuses on the representation of "real" occurrences. While my concerns are both historiographical and poetical, the former will figure more prominently. The ideological character of narrative (as a tension between desire and the law) has been stressed in Hayden White's *The Content of the Form: Narrative Discourse and Historical Representation* (1987) where narrative is defined as:

> a particularly effective system of discursive meaning production by which individuals can be taught to live a distinctly "imaginary relation to their real conditions of existence," that is to say, an unreal but meaningful relation to the social formations in which they are indentured to live out their lives and realize their destines as social subject.
> (cited in Rigney 1991: 597)

Following this perspective, narratives may be said to be invested with imaginary coherence through the form of content and rhetorical persuasiveness (White 1987; Rigney 1991). Of particular interest is narrative's socializing function and the way narratives introduce individuals or groups into a particular way of life through their authorial voice and legitimating functions. Theories, ideologies, and social and institutional practices – and our relationship to them – are all informed by narratives. What gives these narratives structural, rhetorical, and discursive solvency? What secures their anchorage in our histories? How do narratives enable us to see cross-dimensionally? To cast and recast our identities spatio-temporally? To construct the boundaries of the self through forms of imaginary coherence? What is the specific rhetorical appeal of certain forms of narrativized morality? How do narratives occult our identities in the name of objectivity and truth? How are narratives implicated in the distribution of privilege within the larger capitalist society and why do the identities of certain groups often share a common narrative finality based on relations of race, gender, class, and sexual orientation? I can offer no definitive answers to these questions, but pose them as challenges for educators and cultural workers who wish to explore their implications for critical research and teaching.

THE POLITICS OF NARRATIVE

Narratives help us to represent the world. They also help us to remember and forget both its pleasures and its horror. Narratives structure our dreams, our myths, and our visions as much as they are dreamt, mythified and envisioned. They help share our social reality as much by what they exclude as what they include. They provide the discursive vehicles for transforming the burden of knowing to the act of telling. Translating an experience into a story is perhaps the most fundamental act of human understanding. Terry Eagleton (1981: 72) notes that "we cannot think, act or desire except in narrative; it is by narrative that the subject forges that 'sutured' chain of signifiers that grants its relative condition of division sufficient imaginary cohesion to enable it to act."

Narrative provides us with a framework that helps us hold our gaze, that brings an economy of movement to the way we survey our surroundings and the way we suture disparate images and readings of the world into a coherent story, one that partakes of continuity, of a fiction of stasis in a world that is always in motion.

Dwight Conquergood (1993) has delineated the concept of "narrative knowing," which follows Victor Turner's tracing of narrative's origin in the Latin *narrare*, to tell, and *gnarus*, knowing, both derived from the Indo-European root *gna*, to know. He writes:

> Narrative is a way of knowing, a search for meaning, that privileges experience, process, action, and peril. Knowledge is not stored in storytelling so much as it is enacted, reconfigured, tested and engaged by imaginative summonings and interpretive replays of past events in the light of present situations and struggles. Active and emergent, instead of abstract and inert, narrative knowing recalls and recasts experience into meaningful signposts and supports for ongoing action. The recountal is always an encounter, often full of risk.
>
> (p. 337)

There exists no preontological or pretextual reality that prevents narrative's refraction by rhetorical structures and tropes. That is, narrative neither precedes nor follows historical time because each presupposes the other. They are mutually constitutive, mutually informing, interanimated (Connerty 1990; Ricoeur 1984). Narrative is implicated not simply in our biographical accounts of ourselves and others, but also structures the basic forms of our thinking and theorizing. The narratives we live by are not only evident in the way we reflect upon and analyze the past, present, and future, but are ingrained in the very theoretical formulations, paradigms, and principles that constitute the models for such reflection and analysis. Anthony Appiah (1991: 74) has presciently remarked that the relation between structural explanation and the logic of the subject (theories of agency and structure) is not one of competition over causal space but rather for *narrative space.*

Theories are not just about seeing the world in different ways, some truer than others, but about *living in particular ways.* What Appiah is saying is that *all theories presuppose a narrative intentionality* as well as an empirical social outcome. That is, all theories have a story to tell about social life and an attitude towards it; theories reflect the theorist's situatedness in a particular way of life.

Peter T. Kemp (1989) observes a number of features that may be attributed to narrative. Narrative transforms the paradigmatic order of daily action into the syntactic order of literature or history. Narrative action is always already articulated as the fundamental "cultural codes" (signs, rules, and norms) of the society. Daily praxis orders the world temporally. If life (*Die Lebenswelt*) were not structured as narrative we would have no experience of time. Narratives possess a dialectical quality – they are "told in being lived and lived in being told" (1989: 72). Personal identity is linked to the coherence of one's life story. To take on the burden of being the storyteller of one's own life (after Heidegger) is not only to give life coherence, but to preserve one's identity. Action itself prefigures the world of narrative composition and without such narratives there can exist no ethics; however, a narrative structure is a necessary but not sufficient condition to constitute an ethical vision. Grand narratives which transcend individual biographies must not be turned into law of the sort which represses members of the community; however, the fact that some grand narratives serve absolutist and authoritarian roles should not suggest that all historical narratives are of destructive import.

Richard Harvey Brown makes similar observations to those of Kemp, placing perhaps a stronger emphasis on the act of predicting or naming reality as a way of guiding perception and constructing public spheres. The textual or narrative grammar of individuals, notes Brown (1987: 130), "constitute them as a polity." Brown (p. 143) defines narrative as "an account of an agent whose character or destiny unfolds through events in time." Plot is an essential ingredient of narrative and is taken by Brown to describe "the means by which essential features of human existence are expressed through specific event." Defined as such, the very existence of narratives presupposes for Brown "a social order of meaning in which significant action by moral agents is possible" (p. 144). As an "emblem of a larger social text," a narrative "requires a political economy and collective psychology in which a sense of lived connection between personal character and public conduct prevails."

Brown describes the postmodern text as having been ushered in by the disintegration of the human community which "bears witness to the problematic nature of contemporary meaning, identity, and experience" (p. 159). According to Brown, our lived experiences have become integrated with our moral existence through forms of technical rationality when what is really needed is a public narrative discourse. With the postmodern disintegration of community "has come a reintegration, not of community, but of the cybernetic state" (p. 160). Echoing Brown's insight, Felix Guattari and Toni Negri (1990: 58) write that at the heart of global capitalist integration "one finds the immense enterprise of the production of cybernetic subjectivity [*subjectivité informatisée*] which regulates the network of dependence and the process of marginalization."

Brown goes on to defend three central assertions:

> that narrative logic is universal and that hence other logics are derivative of it; that epistemological crises in the philosophic tradition of positivistic science are conflicts of narrative traditions; and that paradigm shifts in science itself are reformulations of cognitive traditions in terms of narrative logic.
>
> (Brown 1987: 164)

Brown's answer to the question of overcoming technical rationality and developing a narrative discourse of public life is to read social life from the perspective of a dialectical ironist – one who engages in a resistant social practice. His position very much resembles Adorno's concept of negative dialectics. Of course, I have no problem with teachers becoming ironists, even dialectical ones, as long as this does not mean that the master trope of political subversion for the decade ahead will be geared to turning out stand-up comedians or that revolutionary praxis will be reduced to academic forms of deconstructive playfulness which lead to a detachment that is disdainful of everyday life. After all, the world of electronically produced identity in the form of postmodern advertisements often flatters the ironist and strokes the skeptic as a marketing orientation. Irony can become a means of containing the political rather than challenging it.

NARRATIVE AND ORAL HISTORIES

Some very important observations of narrative based on the treatment of oral histories and life histories have been advanced by Allen Feldman in his brilliant ethnography of political terror in Northern Ireland, *Formations of Violence* (1991). Feldman's insights are germane to the critical post-structuralist focus of this chapter. According to Feldman, it is impossible for life histories to uncover that point where intention and discourse are essentially the same thing. Feldman correctly argues that subjective intention is not the archic site of truth since if "the self is the referential object of the life-history recitation, then it is interpellated by that discourse and cannot be prior to it" (p. 13). He understands that objects of discourse cannot exist outside of or prior to discursive formations. Here he follows Stuart Hall who similarly argues that "events, relations, structures do have conditions of existence and real effects, outside the sphere of the discursive, but that . . . only within the discursive, and subject to its specific conditions, limits, and modalities, do they have or can they be constructed with meaning" (1988: 27). The conception of identity that follows from these observations is instructive:

> The self is always the artifact of prior received and newly constructed narratives. It is engendered through narration and fulfills a syntactical function in the life history. The rules of narration may perform a stabilizing role in the cultural construction of truth, but then both self and truth are subordinate to the transindividual closures of narrative (spoken or written).
>
> (Feldman 1991: 13)

Following Lyotard's (1973) insight that the relations between events, agency, and narrative are not linear but rather achronic, and that altogether they form a narrative bloc, Feldman is able to describe the role of the self as someone who is both narrator and who has been narrated. He writes:

> In a political culture the self that narrates speaks from a position of having been narrated and edited by others – by political institutions, by concepts of historical causality, and possibly by violence. The narrator speaks because this agent is already the recipient of narratives in which he or she has been inserted as a political subject. The narrator writes himself into an oral history because the narrator has already been written and subjected to powerful inscriptions.
>
> (1991: 13)

Oral histories are *narratives of other narratives* which, in Feldman's terms, "fabricate temporalities and causalities such as linear time" (1991: 14). Following Ricoeur's (1984) notion of narration as emplotment, Feldman observes that "*The event is not what happens. The event is that which can be narrated.*" Consequently, making history and narrating history are really two sides of the same process with agency occurring "at the moment of enactment" (p. 15). The performance of a narrative can thus "exceed the social conditions of its production and thus exceed any particular ideological closure associated with its site of emergence" (p. 15). One of Feldman's most important insights is that the oral history of domination cannot completely codify the body – the site of living flesh – through violence and so oral histories emerge as the only narrative forms that can contain lived experience and resistance. Here, narratives emerge in symbiosis with the body through embodiment (what I have described in Chapter 2 as "enfleshment"). Narratives of domination that are produced in oral histories consequently serve to mediate "the dissonance between the instrumental imaginary of political rationality and the semantic excess of material violence" (p. 16). Narratives rooted in the body can accommodate semantic excess. They are the only narratives that can.

TOWARDS A POSTMODERN NARRATIVE ETHICS

Both Kemp and Brown make use of the work of Alistair MacIntyre and in doing so push the question of narrative into the realm of ethics. MacIntyre, to his credit, recognizes the essentially narrative character of the human condition – that subjectivities are enmeshed in a complex polymythic world of human narrativity. Narrative is, according to this view, the most appropriate form of unit for human life in that narratives render human actions both intelligible and accountable (Patton 1986). Paul Patton's criticism of MacIntyre pushes in the right direction, by addressing the concept of a postmodern narrative ethics. Patton (1986: 136) argues that MacIntyre's account of modern narrative leaves out certain dimensions of modern subjectivity, that is, it leaves out the idea that subjects are "fragmented and dispersed across the range of social categories and institutional sites: male, female; sick, healthy; school, workplace, and so on." According to Patton, MacIntyre's "undifferentiated and global notion of the modern self" leads him to call for essentially premodern forms of subjectivity.

While "recognizing that the unitary and socially embedded subjectivity implied by an Aristotelian concept of the virtues is only realizable within forms of community and social life incompatible with those of late capitalism" (p. 137), MacIntyre's diagnosis, argues Patton, contrasts the analysis of MacIntyre with that of Foucault. I believe the comparison to be very instructive. Patton notes that in exploring how power works in modern society, Foucault directs his analysis at the institutions of surveillance and domination and their micro-practices of power rather than, as in the case of MacIntyre, at the subjectivities which they effect. Foucault's particular starting point is consistent with my concern that narratives be situated ideologically, and not simply discursively. His notion of subjectivity is the antithesis of MacIntyre's modern self in that Foucault "presupposes an activist conception of the human subject" (p. 139). Patton is worth quoting at length on this observation:

> For Foucault, the human capacity for autonomous self-creation is not in doubt, but there are social and political limits to the exercise of that capacity. The political task which his work suggests is neither utopian nor nostalgic: it is the commitment to those movements in present society which are engaged in the attempt to push back those limits and to extend our sphere of freedom.
>
> (Patton 1986: 139)

Narratives are not unitary: they are better understood as assemblages created within "the different kinds of segmentarity which divide up modern social life" (Patton 1986: 143). Rather than lament the loss of premodern forms of narrative subjectivity, I believe that it makes more political sense to live in the narrative reality of the present, to encourage the subversion of stratified, hierarchized, and socially calcified forms of subjectivity and to struggle against present forms of subjectification which thwart our experimentation with new narrative forms of desire and modes of being-in-the-world.

NARRATIVES AND IDENTITY

Patrick Taylor (1989) maintains that narratives are fundamentally related to the organization of human experience. A narrative is, Taylor asserts,

> not merely a mental structure that can be imposed on reality; narrative is meaningful only to the extent that it captures the vitality and dynamic of social life. Narrative is transformed, its patterns are rearranged, its significance determined anew as the processes of history erupt into human experience.
>
> (p. xii)

As hegemonic inscriptions, narratives make legible lines of forces which criss-cross, cut through, freeze, trap, and repress power. As the product of discursive formations and social practices located in material interests, identities are located in historically continuous and pragmatically dispersed networks of social power. Stuart Hall (1987: 46) notes that "every identity is placed, positioned, in a culture, a language, a history."

Our subjectivities need to be inscribed or encoded through narrative in order for us to act. These may be counternarratives or narratives of resistance or else narratives forged out of the magisterial enterprise of empire and colonialism; the point is that our identities take shape with the discursive contingency of arbitrary yet incomplete closures of meaning in the larger text of historical memory. In fact, Hall (1987: 44) describes identity as "formed at the unstable point where the unspeakable stories of subjectivity meet the narratives of history, of a culture." He goes on to make the important observation that identity is possible only within unfinished closures of meaning. He writes:

> all identity is constructed across differences and begins to live with the politics of difference. But doesn't the acceptance of the fictional or narrative status of identity in relation to the world also require as a necessity, its opposite – the moment of arbitrary closure? Is it possible for there to be action or identity in the world without arbitrary closure – what one might call the necessity to meaning of the end of the sentence?
>
> (p. 45)

Hall notes correctly that new conceptions of identity as discursive contingency require us to redefine the meaning of political activity. For instance, we are alerted to "the politics of difference, the politics of self-reflexivity, a politics that is open to contingency but still able to act" (p. 45). He articulates a concept of identity that, in his own words, "isn't founded on the notion of some absolute, integral self and which clearly can't arise from some fully closed narrative of the self."

It is worth noting at this point the difference between Hall's concept of narrative and Jerome Bruner's (1991) account of *narrative accrual.* According to Bruner, this refers to "a 'local' capacity for accruing stories of happenings of the past into some sort of diachronic structure that permits a continuity into the present – in short, to construct a history, a tradition, a legal system, instruments assuring historical continuity if not legitimacy" (pp. 20–1). In this view, narrative is a type of "cultural tool kit" that enables humans to work together through "the process of joint narrative accrual" (p. 20). But we need to follow Hall in ensuring that what we locally and communally "accrue" is not monumentalized and sanctified simply because it has become part of a shared narrative archive. It is one thing to seek continuity as part of one's communal, civic, or national identity; it is quite another to fix identity in those narratives that will "read" us in a distinctly totalizing way. Contained in all cultural narratives is a preferred way of reading them. We don't only live particular narratives but we inhabit them (as they inhabit us). The degree to which we resist certain narratives depends upon how we are able to read them and rewrite them.

NARRATIVE AS TEXT

As texts, identities cannot be fixed within closed systems of meanings (i.e., a closed pattern of signifiers and signified); consequently, there are no *true* identities – only identities that are open to inscription, articulation, and interpretation. Richard Rorty (1991: 10) recently noted that " 'True' is not the name of a power which eventually wins through, it is just the nominalization of an approbative adjective." It is important to acknowledge that identities are never completed but always in the process of negotiation; they are continually struggled over within a polyvalent assemblage of discourses and through nomadic and atopic lines of flight. There is a compostability to identity formation, a malleability that is linked linguistically to the function of the signifier and the permutations of interpretive possibilities around which subjectivity pivots. The context of our identities does not determine how our identities are represented, but plays a part in their rhetorical inscription. For instance, we tend to view our identities in the context of romance, comedy, tragedy, satire, etc., or as conservative, liberal, or radical; but these contextual categories do not occur synchronically outside of history, but are in fact the result of struggles over meaning by various groups in the larger society.

Bhabha locates identity in symbolic consciousness – in "that iterative temporality of the signifier" (1987: 6) that occupies "the discursive and affective conditions of a *claim* to selfhood." In other words, the idea of a true, timeless self is a fiction of discourse – a "demand for identification" – that gives the sign a sense of autonomy. Bhabha asserts that the space of enunciation gives rise to the process of doubling (splitting the difference between Self and Other) – or fixing cultural differences in a confinable, visible object when, in fact, *difference is always uncertain and undecidable.* Identity cannot be identified as presence since there is always a principle of undecidability – the double inscription of the moment of enunciation – that can neither negate nor transcend difference.

While there is no clear-cut causal relationship between economic structures and psychological ones, I want to argue that new flexible forms of economic production, surveillance, and electronic strategies have produced dangerously "necessary" corresponding forms of subjectivity. The autonomous subject of liberal humanism lies in an unmarked grave, having been clubbed to death in the back alley of post-structuralist theory. So it is fairly safe now – if not commonplace – to make the statement that identities are not solely reflective of preconstituted social interests of which we are for the most part unaware. However, it is not so popular to share Terry Eagleton's observation that "the relation between certain social locations, and certain political forms, is a 'necessary' one – which is not, to repeat, to assert that it is inevitable, spontaneous, guaranteed or God-given" (1991: 218). Because this idea appears to have lost favor with an entire generation of post-Marxist social theorists (and I'm referring here to "ludic" and not "critical" strands of postmodern social theory), and because I feel we ignore it at our peril, I shall quote Eagleton extensively:

> Ideology is never the mere expressive effect of objective social interests; but neither are all ideological signifiers "free-floating" in respect of such interests. . . . Ideology is a matter of "discourse" rather than of "language" – of certain concrete discursive effects, rather than of signification as such. It represents the points where power impacts upon certain utterances and inscribes itself tacitly within them. But it is not therefore to be equated with just any form of discursive partisanship, "interested" speech or rhetorical bias; rather, the concept of ideology aims to disclose something of the relation between an utterance and its material conditions of possibility, when those conditions of possibility are viewed in the light of certain power-struggles central to the reproduction (or also, for some theories, contestation) of a whole form of social life.
>
> (1991: 223)

After Eagleton, I want to make the claim that within identity formation certain human interests "become masked, rationalized, naturalized, universalized, legitimated in the name of certain forms of political power" (1991: 202) and I believe that it is necessary for critical educators to focus on the *political effects* of discourses in the context of Western capitalist society.

I agree with post-structuralists on a number of crucial points: that language does not present us with a faded copy of some homogeneous and unchanging reality; that there exists "no privileged epistemological language which would allow us untroubled access to the real;" that "objects are internal to the discourses which constitute them" and that "language is not just some passive reflection of reality but actively constitutive of it." Nevertheless, I also believe, following Eagleton, that we need a concept of ideology to understand the relation between material situations and discursive formations because the Saussurean semiotic model used by some criticalists – a model that essentially argues that the signifier produces the signified – is largely inadequate.

Here, too, like Eagleton, I follow Charles Sanders Peirce's pragmatic phenomenology of the sign rather than Saussure's model in stressing the importance of the interpretant or *habit* which is embodied (received and lived). We can shift the meaning of the interpretant by critical self-reflexivity. This crucial aspect enables the historical agent to transcend arborescent spirals of endless semiosis in order to effect acts of political *transgression*. It acknowledges also that we can have direct experience of the world but that knowledge about it is only possible in a secondary sense through semiotic systems. It also helps to highlight the idea that material practices are legitimated through the essentially "ideological" workings of discourse. This means that there is an extra-discursive (material) reality and one's location in that reality can cause certain readings of and social practices within the material world to be overcoded.

I do not want to sound reductionist here by arguing that material location by, say, class or race *necessarily* furnishes an individual with some appropriate or iron-clad set of political beliefs and desires. Post-Marxists rightly assert there is no "internal relation between particular socio-economic conditions, and specific kinds of political or ideological positions" (Eagleton 1991: 210). Quite true. Nevertheless, what the "ludic" postmodernists describe as "pure contingency" or "undecidability" does not disconnect discourses from their political effects. Certain subjectivities are surely reinforced by the promotional culture of markets and merchandise in race-, class-, and gender-specific ways so that one could safely say that *there exist generic as well as idiosyncratic relationships between identities and social determinants.* The militant stress that some post-structuralists place on particularism cannot adequately explain the connections between forms of social consciousness and material conditions. Some relations are indeed "motivated" by narratives of class, race, ethnicity, and gender.

MARKET IDENTITIES IN THE "NEW TIMES"

I want to argue that there has occurred in these "new times" a particular zoning of subjective space, the segmentation and cleavage of identity, a retooling of subjective experience (personal genres of identification), many of which are reflective of a downgraded economy which exists in the twilight of modern Fordist production. These identities are partly the result of, partly constitutive of what Mayer (1991) calls "the eliminat[ion] of the achievements of the Fordist working class (social security, health insurance, and union representation,)" the growth of "part-time employment and short-term contracts" and "high levels of precarious and casualized jobs" which characterize shrinking local markets, the expansion of the urban informal sector, and the dynamics of "the advanced services and high-tech sector and the unregulated, labor-intensive informal sector." Advertisers and marketers can break society down into segments or subgroups, each characterized by certain attitudes and behaviors and lifestyles. These are the collective wills fashioned by market demands of the dominant culture – inevitable correlates of particular forms of economic power.

The current move towards a post-Fordist economy – services, automation, data processing – has not fundamentally changed the nature of work as "old style 'industrialization' has invaded the big firms in the non-industrial sectors, with rhythm of work and rates of output submitted to impersonal, mechanical control" (Castoriadis 1992: 14–15). Hence, modernity is finished as far as it can be linked to capitalism's project of social and individual autonomy. Yet modernity remains more alive than ever as far as it embodies "the unlimited expansion of (pseudo) rational (pseudo) mastery" (p. 23). Of course, there is a cultural dimension to this crisis of industrial labor and this is the "ethicization of labor" or the "degree to which employment determines individuals biographically and shapes them in a way characteristic for the particular labor situation" (Honneth 1992: 32). The labor sphere has been drastically marginalized in the biographies of individual workers in terms of permitting them to act as moral agents within roles of self-confirmation. As Axel Honneth (1992) notes, the decline of values associated with and constituted by industrial labor has also brought a chance for a greater pluralization of individual life forms. However, *these life forms are not grounded in the appropriate cultural and ethical preconditions.* Honneth writes that:

> Cultural everyday praxis is freed step by step from its received value commitments and traditions without them having already been replaced by encompassing orientation patterns, within which the individual subjects' attempts at self-realization could find intersubjective recognition.
>
> (1992: 32)

Market identities or prepackaged aesthetic substitutes for socially depleted biographies are being accepted by workers as a means of filling up the social vacuum created by the absence of postindustrial forms of ethical life (p. 32). The sphere of labor (including schooling) joins that of leisure in having become colonized by electronic modes of information. Postmodern information technologies have brought about the displacement of use-value by sign-value as information has replaced the demand for labor (McLuhan 1973; Baudrillard 1975). Manufactured consumer needs have taken precedence over labor power while the commodity form has subsumed subjectivity and identity under the laws of capital accumulation and the regime of productivity. Subjectivities and identities of citizens have been virtually reterritorialized by new postmodern electronic mediating devices of television, radio, film, and computers such that the stress on interpretation that was formerly linked to bourgeois individualism has given way to a simulated self that has become socially integrated though the politics of consumption with its surfeit of conservative ideologies. Identity in postmodern times mirrors opinion polls, and forms of organized resistance collapse into public apathy and mass inertia. The dominant strategy of resistance has become that of silence (Baudrillard 1975).

Marcy Darnovsky (1991) has made the important point that advertisers understand culture far better than do cultural critics. She has analyzed their "new traditionalist" ads which both articulate and respond to audiences' fears and desires "more clearly and sympathetically" than the discourse of leftist intellectuals. Stuart Hall has also touched on this theme recently, arguing that "If 'post-Fordism' exists, then it is as much a description of cultural as of economic change" (1990: 128). There exists a certain limited democratization of culture in the contradictory and commodified landscape of popular pleasures. These are reflected in the world of consumption and style. Hall writes that:

> Through marketing, layout and style, the "image" provides the mode of representation and fictional narrativisation of the body on which so much of modern consumption depends. Modern culture is relentlessly material in its practices and modes of production. And the material world of commodities and technologies is profoundly cultural. Young people, black and white, who can't even spell "postmodernism" but have grown up in the age of computer technology, rock-video and electronic music, already inhabit such a universe in their heads.
>
> (1990: 128)

Of course, market identities are exactly the kind of identities that fit comfortably with the corporate vision that conservative educators have of citizenship and schooling with its emphasis on free market enterprise and consumer logic. This could be seen in President Bush's Education 2000 program and Chris Whittle's plan for profit-making schools. The conservative educational agenda scorns the ideals of collective empowerment and social responsibility in the name of economic realism. Narratives of identity produced through an emphasis on private education based on market imperatives are aimed at producing compliant workers and loyal consumers. This master narrative takes many forms and is largely a result of the political conservatism of the 1980s in which the "New Right constructed conceptions of who its ideal subjects were, and how they personify the sacred values of religion, hard work, health, and self-reliance" (Denzin 1991: 150). Norman K. Denzin describes the condition of late capitalism as one that perpetuates the "ancient narratives" and myths of the nuclear family, imperialism and rugged individualism in which "capitalism needs and uses anything and everything to perpetuate its hegemonic control over popular culture" (p. 151).

> Late capitalism's "both-and" logic constantly expands, like a rubber band, to fit all that has come before, turning everything, including lived experience, into a commodity that is bought and sold on the contemporary marketplace. This logic requires a positive nostalgia which infuses the past with high value; for if the past were worthless, it could not be sold in the present. Old is good. New is good. Old and

new together are best. *This popular ideology scripts a politics which keeps ancient narratives alive.*

(1991: 151, emphasis supplied)

The New Right perpetuates its attack on difference, labor militancy, and the entire idea of a national school system by waging war on the very idea of the "public" as the enemy of profit-making private institutions, but in doing so it mistakes its own quest for power for a defense of freedom and misrepresents its reactionary power as democratic populism. As conservative spokespersons for the educational New Right such as Diane Ravitch and Chester Finn rail against entrenched self-interest in patriotic hyperbole that is as self-congratulatory, self-indulgent, and self-glorifying as it is obscenely lacking in insight, they in fact are serving the interests of corporate capital and the status-quo distribution of power and wealth which, let's face it, is the central narrative undergirding conservative policy.

POSTCOLONIAL NARRATIVES OF LIBERATION: BEYOND MARKETPLACE IDENTITY

We can, I believe, free ourselves from the dead weight of dominant corporate consumer narratives. We can do this by crossing cultural boundaries and negotiating new, hybrid identities. As an initial step towards creating emancipatory social practices in both private and public spheres, we can help our students bring a halt to the immutable constancy of imperial identities of the patriarchal family, the authoritarian state, and the narrative of the happy, compulsive consumer.

The construction of narrative identities of liberation must place a central emphasis on the meaning of difference. Angela Harris uses the term "multiple consciousness" to capture "a world in which people are not oppressed only on the basis of gender, but on the bases of race, class, sexual orientation, and other categories in inextricable webs" (1990: 587). The complexity of such oppression suggests that experience needs to be explored as multivocal – as that which cannot be described independently of other facets of experience. Consequently, as teachers and students we need to envision identity as a subjective formation which avoids assuming narrative forms based on race and gender essentialism (voices that monolithically claim to speak for all) – an essentialism which "forcibly" fragments experience in the name of a commonality, that is, in the name of that which masquerades as normative experience. There is no essential "female" identity, or "male" identity, or "American" identity. There is no universal narrative of citizenship that cannot or should not be open to contestation among students.

In understanding how narratives of the self become constituted in contexts of colonialism, postcolonialism, and neocolonialism, teachers can develop a new politics of difference and identity and bring about a new subject-space of meaning construction and praxis. To reveal the fissures in the continuity of the narrative self is to contest claims to domination by groups on the basis of race, class privilege, gender and other interests. For teachers, the classroom can be transformed into a hybrid pedagogical space where permission is not denied students who wish to narrate their own identities outside of marketplace identities and the politics of consumerism, a space where individual identities find meaning in collective expression and solidarity with cultural others, where mimetic, Eurocentric time recedes into the lived historical moment of contemporary struggles for identity. Here the imperatives of consumer culture and the hegemony of market identities are challenged by narratives of identity that are underwritten by a concern for liberation and social justice.

A pedagogy informed by a postcolonial narratology shifts the relation of the social actor to the object of his or her knowledge and the problematic in which identity is defined and struggled over. In this respect, a postcolonial narratology encourages the oppressed to contest the stories fabricated for them by "outsiders" and to construct counterstories that give shape and direction to the practice of hope and the struggle for an emancipatory politics of everyday life. It is a pedagogy that attempts to exorcise from the social body the invading pathologies of racism, sexism, and class privilege (Giroux and McLaren 1986a). It is a pedagogy that is able to rupture the dominant narratives of citizenship and destabilize the pretensions to monologic identity that this narrative exhibits. A postcolonial narratology must trouble the surface of the Western texts of identity such that the gaps and faults (*failles*) produced can create an historically discontinuous subject and thus can help to inhibit the resurfacing of colonialist discourses of the self. In this sense, a postcolonial narratology bears some affinity to what Linda Hutcheon refers to as "narcissistic narrative" or "metafiction" in that the text of liberation is explicitly recognized as socially constructed and demands that the social actor be engaged "intellectually, imaginatively, and *effectively* in its co-creation" (1980: 7, emphasis mine).

For postcolonial educators, this means raising the following questions about their pedagogies as part of a "critical narratology:" What is the narrative schematization that orders their own lives and the lives of their students? Is it populated by bourgeois individualism and by the assumptions of capitalist social life and their social and cultural correlates? How may the practice of a pedagogy of liberation be constructed so that it is not recuperable within a scenario of white supremacist colonial desire? Following De Lauretis (1990: 144), we need to begin to rethink the identity of liberation as becoming "the subject of an 'unusual knowing', a cognitive practice, a form of consciousness that is not primordial, universal or coextensive with human thought . . . but historically determined and yet subjectively and politically assumed." Postcolonial educators need to help in the development of what Cornel West (1990: 93) calls "a new kind of cultural worker" capable of exercising a "politics of difference" that will enable students to "interrogate the ways in which they are bound by certain conventions and to learn from and build on these very norms and models" (p. 107). We need to situate pedagogy within a narratology *that creates histories of our own making, which fractures the philosophical time of Western concepts and which can surmount the categorical oppositions of philosophical logic* (Godzich 1990). In other words, Western cultural authority is not a stable system of reference since cultural difference (as distinct from cultural diversity) is always about how culture is enunciated – how culture is constructed in terms of a politics of signification. Any cultural identity must acknowledge its discursive embeddedness and address as well as its politics of location and place. The way identities are enunciated is always ambivalent and they have no primordial origins that "fix" them as Latino, as African–American, or as Anglo. This does not mean identities as ethnicities are unimportant. But it does suggest that they do not guarantee one's politics.

THE PRODUCTION OF BORDER IDENTITIES

Border identities are narratives and counternarratives which we choose to enact (but as Marx reminds us, not in conditions of our own making) in the context of our everyday, mundane practical existence. Border identities are anchored in and are the outcome of those social practices that configure experience and shape affective investment in such experience *in relation to narratives of liberation* which challenge the market identities produced by the New Right's narratives of consumer citizenship. This form of auto-praxis follows authorizing strategies which consist of naming oppression and forging identity through positive forms of subjectivity *signified by one's active participation in making one's own history*; similarly, the construction of border identities consists of renaming and reconstructing reality rather than engaging reality through the production of a negative subjectivity (in which case identity is constructed out of signifiers of lack and omission). Border identities are created out of empathy for others by means of a passionate connection through difference. Such a connection is furthered by a narrative imagination which enables critical linkages to be made between our own stories and the stories of cultural others (Darder 1992).

While it is important to recognize that subjectivities are culturally constructed and discursively interpreted, this observation is not meant to defend the cultural relativism surrounding the claim that any one identity is as important as any other. This is not the meaning of border identity.

Nor is it simply a means of meeting the radical requirements of constructing one's identity in opposition to the *doxa* (the *déjà-dit* or "already said" of public consumer conventions) in order to form a narrative identity that is more enabling of social transformation. Rather, it is to fight against the foreshortening of the possibility of self- and social transformation as co-implicated in the dialectic of freedom. That is, it is to fight against our failure to see our own reflection in the eyes of others. Border identity requires what Ramon Saldivar (1990: 175) calls a "dialectics of difference" which refers to the formation of subjectivities of resistance, that is, subjectivities that are able to resist "the absolutizing tendencies of a racist, classist, patriarchal bourgeois world that founds itself on the notion of a fixed and positive identity and on specified gender roles based on this positive fixation."

The work of D. Emily Hicks (1988) on "border writing" and Henry A. Giroux's (1992) concept of "border pedagogy" are suggestive of what I mean when I discuss the concept of "border identity." Hicks describes border writing as an "anti-centering strategy" in which border narratives are decentered so that "there is no identity between the reader and individual character, but rather, an invitation to listen to a Voice of the Person which arises from an overlay of codes out of which characters and events emerge" (p. 51). She bases her concept of border writing on what she refers to as the heterogeneous border cultures of Latin America and their relationship to contemporary Latin American literature. She is also interested in exploring how the dominant cultures of Europe and the United States "are presented in their inter-action with Latin American culture" (p. 48). Her discussion of border writing draws upon writers whom she contends have actually prefigured recent forms of European postmodernism such as decentering the subject and appropriating images. She refers to, among others, the work of the Brazilian concrete poets and the artists of the *neo-gráfica* movement in Mexico. According to Hicks, border writing:

> emphasizes the differences in reference codes between two or more cultures and depicts, therefore, a kind of realism that approaches the experience of border crossers, those who live in a bilingual, bicultural, biconceptual reality. I am speaking of cultural, not physical, borders: the sensibility which informs border literature can exist among guest workers anywhere, including European countries in which the country of origin does not share a physical border with the host country.
> (1988: 49)

The attributes that Hicks applies to border writing, I am applying to the concept of identity formation. Similarly, what Giroux (1992) has called border pedagogy can be utilized suggestively in the project of remaking identities. To engage in the project of creating border identities is a means of deconstructing and taking control of narratives of the self, while recognizing the multiplicity of languages or codes within a single language – i.e., the polylingualism in one's own language – as well as appreciating the meaning-tropes in other languages. In effect, it is a dialogue with oneself and the Other, one that contests and ruptures the one-dimensional monotopic narrative structure of dominant social texts based on market incentives and consumer logic and their relationships to readers. Border identities are identities in which readers and narrators are both one and the Other in the sense that the "border crosser is both 'self' and 'other' " (Hicks 1988: 52). In other words, "The border crosser 'subject' emerges from double strings of signifiers of two sets of reference codes, from both sides of the border" (p. 52).

I am suggesting that teachers and students learn to re-present themselves through a form of border writing in which the narratives they construct for themselves in relation to the Other are effectively deterritorialized politically, culturally, and linguistically, so that the meaning-tropes through which subjectivity becomes constructed fail to dominate the Other. To construct border identities is to refuse to adopt a single perspective linked to cultural domination. Refusing "the metonymic reduction of reality to the instrumental logic of Western thought" (p. 56) is to reterritorialize identity in a way that holds out the possibility of "subverting the rationality of collective suicide" (p. 57).

A serious problem with forging an emancipatory pedagogy of border identity needs to be identified here. It stems from the failure of male critics to extricate themselves from their entrenchment in phallocentric discourses. Male critics are often reluctant to narrate the contingency of their own enunciative positions as masculine. Theorists need to specify their sexual locations and other sites of textual enunciation so that they do not mistakenly speak for others. Similarly, in the case of African–American communities, Cornel West notes that

> The modern Black diaspora problematic of invisibility and namelessness can be understood as the condition of *relative lack of Black power to present themselves to themselves and others as complex human beings, and thereby to contest the bombardment of negative, degrading stereotypes put forward by White supremacist ideologies.*
>
> (1990: 27; emphasis in original)

It is important that a project of liberation not constitute subaltern voices as simply the mirror image of the white, Western male sovereign subject. Euro-American liturgical calls for a common identity are camouflaged attempts to reclaim the past from those who threaten the image of what Americans currently represent and what they have been. Subaltern groups should not be turned into living allegories of menace by naturalizing the difference between "us" and "them" but must speak through the codes of their race-, class-, and gender-specific struggles for voice and freedom. All groups require a narrative that recognizes, in the words of Stuart Hall, "that we all speak from a particular place, out of a particular history, out of a particular experience, a particular culture, without being contained by that position" (1988: 29). However, rather than searching for the origins of our identities as historical agents in struggle, we need to focus more on what we can achieve together. What we might become together takes precedence over who we are. In other words, before I speak in solidarity I should not demand that others present to me their identity papers. To do so is to become the border guard, not the border crosser. Identities constructed in the act of solidarity will be provisional, and the alliances formed will be contingent on the strategies, negotiations, and translations that occur *in the act of struggle* for both a common ground of alliance-building (rather than a common culture) and a radical and transformative politics. It is more important to create identities out of strategies of resistance and the passion of struggle than out of a search for some primordial ground of being that will forever suture subjects to a narrative inevitability – to re-run identities in which subjectivity is primarily constituted through nostalgia and familiarity (cf. Grossberg 1992).

Identity formation needs to occur in what Homi Bhabha calls the "third space of translation." Translation requires that identities – especially cultural identities – be seen as "decentered structures" that are constituted only in relation to otherness. Through a displacement of origins, a creative liminality "opens up the possibility of articulating *different*, even incommensurable cultural practices and priorities" (1990a: 210–11). The "third space" refers to a condition of hybridity in which the essentialism of origins and the discourse of authenticity are challenged. Otherness always intervenes to prevent the subject from "fixing" itself in a closed system of meaning and keeps open "a new area of negotiation of meaning and representation" (p. 211). This enables "new structures of authority, new political initiatives, which are inadequately understood through received wisdom."

The construction of border identities follows Joel Kovel's "philosophy of becoming." To identify with the processual social and material event of "becoming" is to align oneself explicitly with a narrative of freedom. In Kovel's words, it is "to speak of a practical wish to be free" and to commit to a philosophy "in which the self can become Other to itself, and from that position either remain alienated or transcend itself" (1991: 108). Kovel expands on this idea by proclaiming:

> I am a subject, not merely an object; and I am not a Cartesian subject, whose subjectivity is pure inwardness, but rather an expressive subject, a transformative subject; I am a subject, therefore, who needs to

> project my being into the world, and transform the world as an expression of my being; and finally, I will appropriate my being rather than have it expropriated.
>
> (p. 108)

The production of border identities has less to do with the search for self-knowledge than it has to do with what Foucault saw as "a method of self care." From the perspective of a postcolonial narratology, the question is whether or not we can forge border identities that can resist reinscription or re-enthronement in the hegemonic mapping of nationalist, consumer-oriented culture. Will border identities simply become supplemental – an efflux of counterhegemonic discourses consumed rather than counterposed – conditional upon rather than resistant to the machineries of hegemonic state power? This question of incorporation – of reintegrating the oppressed into the world of unequal power relations – is a nagging one; yet it needs to be addressed. Capitalism thrives on the regulation and eventual assimilation of difference, after all. Difference becomes chartered in the service of capital so that the subjectivities of the citizenry can be emptied out as part of the rite of passage of becoming American. So the question remains, has the periphery become imperialist and if this is the case, what does it mean, in Giroux's (1992) important sense, to be a "border crosser?" Do border identities in this context mean simply a retooling of a consumerist ethics in the form of an aggressive individualism, a cult of hypermasculinity, of sales-motivated cultural ethics purveyed by an economy of "flexible specialization," of warrior-citizens bent on global domination? Or is it possible to dethrone mainstream pedagogical method in order to create cultural sites where counter-hegemonic subjectivities can be constructed that effectively destabilize the production of market identities?

Another issue is how to construct border identities that speak to the lived experiences of oppressed people – people who possess a natural suspicion of academics writing from the high-altitude vistas of Mount Olympus. The imperious call for a transcultural narrative identity that traverses particular identities constituted perhaps by a universal law of the unconscious parallels the corrosive call for a common culture and the collective de-ethnicization of the population. It is a vision snatched from the Eurocentric Archives and dipped in the blood of imperialism, a vision sharing the conspiracy of civilization (McLaren and Leonard 1993). It is a vision both academics and activists must abandon.

Majority discourses narrativized under the auspices of whiteness monologically locate and contain minority subjects as "ethnic" whereas white people are rarely accorded this status (hooks 1992). By masking their own situatedness in forms of white ethnicity, white people universalize the Other as ethnic and themselves as existing metaphysically beyond all forms of ethnic signification. They thus remove themselves from the negative connotations of the term "ethnic" that they themselves created. White culture unifies itself in its invisibility and avoids negative equivalences. White culture is thus able to occupy the position of the privileging signifier and its location in a fixed relation of binary opposition to people of color. One insidious irony is that white culture attempts to de-ethnicize America through its melting-pot ideology and yet is camouflaging a form of re-ethnicizing the citizenry into the flat and barren identity of white middle-class "family values" America.

Critical pedagogy needs to construct a praxis of border identity in which binary systems of thought (e.g. White vs. Black) no longer organize one's politics. The challenge is to create what Trinh T. Minh-ha calls a "shifting multi-place of resistance" that "no longer simply thrives on alternate, homogenized strategies of rejection, affirmation, confrontation, and opposition well-rooted in a tradition of contestation" (1991: 229). She asserts that this "challenge has to be taken up every time a positioning occurs: for just as one must situate oneself (in terms of ethnicity, class, gender, difference), one also refuses to be confined to that location" (pp. 229–30). Trinh's concept of multiculturalism is one that I have been attempting to chart throughout this chapter, one that neither endorses the idea of a juxtaposition of cultures nor "subscribes to a bland 'melting-pot' type of attitude that would level all differences" (p. 232). Instead, Trinh locates multiculturalism "in the intercultural acceptance of risks, unexpected detours, and complexities of relation between break and closure" (p. 232). The idea here is to develop a strategy of identity that Marcos Sanchez-Tranquilino and John Tagg (referring to Chicano art) describe as "not of fixed difference, but of the transformation of languages and spaces of operation to evade both invisibility and assimilation" (1991: 104).

Gloria Anzaldúa has described the identity of *la mestiza* within *la cultura chicana* that captures this sense of ambiguity and transformation associated with border identity. She writes that *la mestiza*

> can't hold concepts or ideas in rigid boundaries. The borders and walls that are supposed to keep the undesirable ideas out are entrenched habits and patterns of behavior; these habits and patterns are the enemy within. Rigidity means death. Only by remaining flexible is she able to stretch the psyche horizontally and vertically. *La mestiza* constantly has to shift out of habitual formations; from convergent thinking, analytical reasoning that tends to use rationality to move towards a single goal (a Western mode), to divergent thinking, characterized by movement away from set patterns and goals and toward a more whole perspective, one that includes rather than excludes.
>
> The new *mestiza* copes by developing a tolerance for contradictions,

> a tolerance for ambiguity. She learns to be an Indian in Mexican culture, to be Mexican from an Anglo point of view. She learns to juggle cultures. She has a plural personality, she operates in a pluralistic mode – nothing is thrust out, the good, the bad and the ugly, nothing rejected, nothing abandoned. Not only does she sustain contradictions, she turns the ambivalence into something else.
>
> (Anzaldúa 1987: 79)

Anzaldúa's project is a laudatory one, for she is genuinely trying to connect subaltern communities and critical theory. This is important because Western theories of identity are linked to the culture of whiteness in disabling ways. For instance, official Western discourses of identity exclude from the concept of "citizen" everything which challenges its determination as an empty signifier, a marker of "American" in which anything can be articulated with it that has sufficient authoritative exegesis. But before identities can be sutured to conventional meanings, they must first be cleansed of "ethnic" significations. Anzaldúa's task is to unmask the pretensions of Western identity formations and to cut them at their joints. She accomplishes this by dismantling false images – "rechazamos esas falsas imágenes" (1990: xxvii) and formulating marginal theories. For Anzaldúa, marginal theories:

> are partially outside and partially inside the Western frame of reference (if that is possible), theories that overlap many "worlds." We are articulating new positions in these "in-between," Borderland worlds of ethnic communities and academies, feminist and job worlds. . . . In our *mestizaje* theories we create new categories for those of us left out or pushed out of the existing ones. We recover and examine non-Western aesthetics while critiquing Western aesthetics; recover and examine non-rational modes and "blanked-out" realities while critiquing rational, consensual reality; recover and examine indigenous languages while critiquing the "languages" of the dominant culture. . . . If we have been gagged and disempowered by theories, we can also be loosened and empowered by theories.
>
> (1990: xxvi)

What Hall, hooks, Trinh, Giroux, Hicks, Anzaldúa and others are calling for is a borderization of identity, a rupturing of the unitary cohesiveness of the culture of terror we know as the politics of whiteness. It is an identity described with forceful elegance by Sanchez-Tranquilino and Tagg:

> What we begin to make out is another narration of identity, another resistance. One that asserts a difference, yet cannot be absorbed into the pleasures of a global marketing culture. One that locates its different voice, yet will not take a stand on the unmoving ground of a

> defensive fundamentalism. One that speaks its location as more than local, yet makes no claim to universality for its viewpoint or language. One that knows the border and crosses the line.
>
> (1991: 105)

Guillermo Gómez-Peña echoes Anzaldúa in capturing the "multiple repertoires" of identity in a response to questions about his own nationality:

> Today, eight years after my departure [from Mexico], when they ask me for my nationality or ethnic identity, I can't respond with one word, since my "identity" now possesses multiple repertoires: I am Mexican but I am also Chicano and Latin American. At the border they call me *chilango* or *mexiquillo*; in Mexico City it's *pocho* or *norteño*; and in Europe it's *sudaca*. the Anglos call me "Hispanic" or "Latino," and the Germans have, on more than one occasion, confused me with Turks or Italians. My wife Emilia is Anglo, but speaks Spanish with an Argentine accent, and together we walk amid the rubble of the Tower of Babel of our American postmodernity.
>
> (Gómez-Peña, cited in Yudice 1992: 214–15)

However, as George Yudice points out, multiculturalism must move beyond a mere ethnocentric celebration of cultural transformism and the crossing of linguistic, political and ethnic borders. He cites remarks made by Néstor García Canclini in response to interviews he conducted with residents of Tijuana, Mexico: "Other Tijuana artists and writers challenge the euphemistic treatment of the contradictions and uprooting. . . . They reject the celebration of migrations caused by poverty in the homeland and in the United States" (cited in Yudice 1992: 215). Yudice sounds a telling warning to U.S. critical multiculturalists when he suggests that we incur our own brand of imperialism when we unwittingly "become a 'front' for our own integration into a global market in which the image – the politics of representation – supplants resources and services, shrinking at an ever faster pace" (1992: 213). We do this when we assume that we can show the rest of the world how to discover itself. When we suggest that multiple subject positions should be celebrated as the apogee of a new postmodern hybridity that escapes the fascist tendencies of militant particularisms, we need to be careful. Some people cross borders willingly, some people are forced to cross them, and others are literally shot in their attempts at crossing. Yet at the same time there is a wonderful fecundity in the concept of the border crosser, as Hicks and Giroux have singularly illustrated. It is an edifying metaphor for a critical multiculturalism that needs to be taken seriously. That is why we need to exercise caution in defining for cultural others what the mestiza identity should look like. For instance, it will be different for the exile, for the metropolitan "professional" intellectual, and for the tourist. We need to map the different identifications constituted by border identities and appropriate the most critical elements and potentialities for both local and global struggles for liberation.

A critical narratology needs to be grounded in a politics of difference that is more than a salutary derangement of our enslavement to the habitual and the mundane. Critical narratology is a justificatory, defamiliarizing strategy but also a practice of hope. In Stuart Hall's terms (1990), I am speaking of fashioning a new collective will; of producing what Darnovsky (1991: 88) refers to as "self representations, forged self-consciously through confrontation . . . and negotiation." This has connections with Foucault's imperative of the practice of the self. We need new practices of identity that stem from new forms of subjectivity and historical agency. I want to emphasize a particular claim here by Paul Raymond Harrison that the rationalist narrative be contested by "multiple voices of reason through story-telling" (1989: 64). Critical narratology must be made compatible with a nonreductionist and nonrationalist concept of culture. Like Mexican artist Frida Kahlo, who "saw herself literally on the borderline – between nature and culture, between the ancient earth of pre-Columbian American and 'Gringolandia' – a distastefully technological USA" (Lippard 1987: 221), educators need to move between and within different zones of cultural semiosis. The absolutization of narrative through reductive notions of culture forecloses an exploration of "the complex and divergent character of our narrative condition in modernity, where we do not simply live in a narrated world, but many narrated worlds" (Harrison 1989: 76).

Richard Harvey Brown echoes the concerns of these authors when he advises us to write our narratives of liberation, of disidentification, by authorizing "a new vision of ourselves and our world" (1987: 147). It is important that we [summon] forth an alternative definition of the world and thereby [authorize] a new form of social existence." In Pêcheux's (1975/1982) terms, we need to displace and transform the subject form of our narratives, and not just abolish it. Harold Rosen makes the persuasive point that all narratives *need to be retold*. He writes that "In some cultures there are privileged tales . . . which must be retold; but every authentic teller must turn them into internally persuasive discourse or be reduced to a mere reciter, an inflexible mimic" (1986: 235). According to Rosen, students need to liberate themselves from the authority of another's discourse while not necessarily rejecting the discourse itself. The retelling of stories is what gives us our voice. While all stories – even or perhaps especially those that are retold – recruit the desires of the Other in order to maintain narrative authority and contain their own "surreptitious menace" (p. 235), they can also counter "magisterial" narratives. Teachers and students need access to insurgent narratives that challenge phallocentric self-stories that leave out that which is contingent, irrational, or ambiguous. They need a language of narrative refusal that contests the conventional rules of self-fashioning within autobiographical identities encouraged and legitimated within patriarchy (Smith 1987).

Teachers have a particular responsibility in constructing their narrative voice in the practice of pedagogy. They need to be aware of how history is represented or "inscribed" not only in their own voices, but the voices of their students. Of course, the question is whether these voices serve to expedite the process of the legitimation of the hegemonic culture or contest it. Here the question of narrative closure becomes important. According to Kalogeras (1991: 31) narrative closure "predicates a central consciousness that represents the structures and processes of 'reality' as if they naturally wield a specific meaning. Hence, this meaning is promoted as 'found' rather than as 'constructed'." The issue here, of course, especially in the case of the representation of ethnic history, is to what extent the process of narrativization "entails a totalization that suppresses the discontinuities, gaps, and silences that constitute not only one's life but also one's ethnic history" (p. 32). If teachers enacting their pedagogical duties serve to mediate between the host society and the ethnic cultures of their students, to what extent are the narratives that teachers use to mediate between dominant narratives and counternarratives, or narratives of difference, populated by imperial and corporate discourses of the host culture?

This question underscores the importance of inviting students themselves to become the mediators of their own narratives and assume narrative authority for their own lives by adopting a metacultural perspective in which they can become a critic of both cultures (cf. Kalogeras 1991). Of course, the underlying narrative and insurgent imagination that invites them to assume the role of metacultural mediator is one that speaks the story of hope and liberation. Such a narrative must not invite premature closure of the meaning of emancipation or simply annex the ongoing struggle for liberty to an outworn radical tradition. It can be employed to meet such an objective by encouraging students to remain ruthlessly self-critical in examining their own assumptions and recognizing when a praxis of liberation unwittingly serves to re-contain oppression. A narrative of hope and liberation must additionally be analyzed in relation to the historical and cultural specificity of its production in the context of classroom relations and the larger social order so as to reveal both its enabling and disabling effects. What needs to be secured within this process is a narrative identity that is restless and not merely reactive, one that does not simply run counter to a Eurocentric identity as a type of endless return, because this would be tantamount to turning the act of resistance into a millenarianism in reverse that tries to invert the subject of modernity produced by the logic of possessive individualism (Saénz 1991). Required, too, is a loyalty to possibility, to forging alternative identities that are contemporaneous with modernity but that do not simply invert its normative truths (Saénz 1991).

The struggle is a proleptic one against the archival knowledge of Western colonialism, the inherited vocabulary of mainstream pedagogy, and a narratology populated by identity formations whose overall trajectory is a logocentric orientation of consciousness – one which history has shaped within particular economies of desire. We need to introduce to teachers narratives that are contrary politically to those prescribed by the dominant regime of truth, counternarratives underwritten by a politically inspired teleology whose narrative closures are always contingent and therefore always open to the creative and the new. As teachers, we need to become theorists of a resistance postmodernism that can help students make the necessary connections among their desires, their frustrations, and the cultural forms and social practices which inform them. Norman K. Denzin notes that theorists of postmodernism are inevitably *storytellers* who enable us to understand social life as a cultural plot. He reports that "our most powerful effects as storytellers come when we expose the cultural ploy and the cultural practices that guide our writing hands" (1991: 156). Dwight Conquergood confronts us with a performance theory of pedagogy grounded in storytelling as narrative enactment, a pedagogy of "embodied objectivity" (Haraway 1991), creating what Bakhtin (1986) calls "bodies of meaning" (embodied experience). Here, notes Conquergood, participants speak *from* and not *about* a particular location, and create a situation in which they are more open to dialogue with other perspectives. Dialogue is understood in Bakhtin's sense, as removed from "sappy pluralism [and] gutless relativism" and focused instead on "facing up to other positions that might challenge and interrogate one's own location" (Conquergood 1992: 343). In other words, it "pivots on argument as much as agreement." In the final analysis we need to remember that the narratives we tell and retell in our classrooms are both reflective and constitutive of who we are and what we will become.

Chapter 4

White terror and oppositional agency

Towards a critical multiculturalism

> Nothing can be denounced if the denouncing is done within the system that belongs to the thing denounced.
>
> (Julio Cortázar, *Hopscotch*, Chapter 99)

As we approach the year 2000, we are increasingly living simulated identities that help us adjust our dreams and desires according to the terms of our imprisonment as schizo-subjects in an artificially generated world. These facsimile or imitative identities are negotiated for us by financial planners, corporate sponsors, and marketing strategists through the initiatives of transnational corporations, enabling a privileged elite of white Euro-Americans to control the information banks and terrorize the majority of the population into a state of intellectual and material impoverishment. With few, if any, ethically convincing prospects for transformation – or even survival – we have become cyber-nomads whose temporary homes become whatever electronic circuitry (if any) is available to us. In our hyper-fragmented and predatory postmodern culture, democracy is secured through the power to control consciousness and semioticize and discipline bodies by mapping and manipulating sounds, images and information and forcing identity to take refuge in forms of subjectivity increasingly experienced as isolated and separate from larger social contexts. The idea of democratic citizenship has now become synonymous with the private, consuming citizen and the increasing subalternization of the "Other." The representation of reality through corporate sponsorship and promotional culture has impeded the struggle to establish democratic public spheres and furthered the dissolution of historical solidarities and forms of community, accelerating the experience of circular narrative time and the postindustrial disintegration of public space. The proliferation and phantasmagoria of the image has hastened the death of modernist identity structures and has interpellated individuals and groups into a world of cyborg citizenry in which "other" individuals are reconstituted through market imperatives as a collective assemblage of "them" read against our "us."

THE DEBATE OVER MULTICULTURALISM

It is no secret, especially after the Los Angeles uprising – or what Mike Davis calls the "L.A. Intifada" (Katz and Smith 1992) – that the white-controlled media (often backed by victim-blaming white social scientists) have ignored the economic and social conditions responsible for bringing about in African-American communities what Cornel West has called a "*walking nihilism* of pervasive drug addiction, pervasive alcoholism, pervasive homicide, and an exponential rise in suicide" (cited in Stephanson 1988b: 276, emphasis in original). They have additionally ignored or sensationalized social conditions in Latin and Asian communities, polemicizing against their value systems and representing them as teleologically poised to explode into a welter of rioting and destruction. Such communities have been described as full of individuals who lash out at the dominant culture in an anarcho-voluntaristic frenzy in a country where there are more legal gun dealers than gas stations. In this view, agency seems to operate outside of forces and structures of oppression and policing discourses of domination and social practices. Subalternized individuals appear politically constituted outside of discursive formations, are essentialized as the products of their pathological "nature" as drug or alcohol users and as participants in crime, and forced to take early retirement from cultural worth and historical agency.

Furthermore, the white media have generated the racially pornographic term, "wilding," to account for recent acts of violence in urban centers by groups of young African-Americans (Cooper 1989). Apparently the term "wilding," first reported by New York City newspapers in relation to a group of Central Park rapists, was relevant only to violence committed by black male youth since the term was conspicuously absent in press reports of the attack by white male youths on Yusef Hawkins in Bensonhurst (Wallace 1991). In *Race, Culture and the City: A Pedagogy for Black Urban Struggle* (forthcoming b), Stephen Haymes surveys the ruins of black civil society in the aftermath of its shattering by both the white supremacist imagination and the social and cultural practices of flexible specialization that together advocate the constitution of both black and white identity around the notion of bureaucratically controlled consumption. Haymes is concerned, first and foremost, with the racializing of urban space from the standpoint of white supremacist ideologies that primitivize and pathologize black bodies, that discursively constitute black urban populations through jungle metaphors and racist myths surrounding the exotic black subject, and that lead to forms of black self-contempt. Of particular interest to Haymes is the means by which black subjectivities are produced within texts and subtexts of urban cultural myths, material development and social practices within urban "postmodernized" spaces. With an impressive sweep of scholarship ranging from neo-Marxist analysis to post-structuralist accounts of self and social formation, Haymes is able to capture the pain suffered and the struggle and hope exercised by African-Americans in contemporary urban settings where African-American communities serve as zones of contest between dominant discursive practices that locate black people as dangerous Others and the survival strategies of black people against the still prevalent practices of white racism, hatred and terror.

Haymes's analysis attempts to explain the impact of consumer-oriented capitalism on black identity politics and the devastating effects of the binary logic of the white racist imagination on the production of black culture and the biologization of black identity in postmodern "spacialized" urban arenas where Euro-Americans are disproportionately privileged. Haymes also addresses the implication of white consumer culture in the construction of black subjectivity, especially in terms of the way in which the consumer culture of the white middle class constructs an urban spatial arrangement that transforms the "black ghetto" into pleasure spaces for white middle-class consumption. These spaces of pleasure are tied inexorably to the ideology of the free market and amount to the production of gentrified neighborhoods in which whites consume black music, sports and fashion with the aid of their private security systems, forms of electronic surveillance, and the support of the police. Regrettably, the postmodern image which many white people now entertain in relation to the African-American underclass is one constructed upon violence and grotesquerie – a population spawning mutant youths who, in the throes of bloodlust, roam the perimeter of the urban landscape high on angel dust, randomly hunting whites with steel pipes. In addition to helping to justify police "attitude adjustments" inflicted upon black people in places such as L.A., Detroit, and Sabine County, Texas, this image of minorities has engendered hostility to their efforts to articulate their own understanding of race relations and to advance a conception of democracy in a way that is compatible with a critical multiculturalism.

FORMS OF MULTICULTURALISM

This chapter advances a conception of "critical multiculturalism" distinct from conservative or corporate multiculturalism, liberal multiculturalism and left–liberal multiculturalism. These are, to be sure, ideal-typical labels meant to serve only as a "heuristic" device. In reality the characteristics of each position tend to blend into each other within the general horizon of our social lifeworld. As with all typologies and criteriologies, one must risk monolithically projecting them onto all spheres of cultural production and instantiating an overly abstract totality that dangerously reduces the complexity of the issues at stake. My effort should be understood only as an initial attempt at transcoding and mapping the cultural field of race and ethnicity so as to formulate a tentative theoretical grid that can help discern the multiple ways in which difference is both constructed and engaged.

Conservative multiculturalism

Conservative multiculturalism can be traced to colonial views of African-Americans as slaves, servants, and entertainers, views which were embedded in the self-serving, self-congratulatory and profoundly imperialist attitude of Europe and North America. Such an attitude depicted Africa as a savage and barbaric continent populated by the most lowly of creatures who were deprived of the saving graces of Western civilization.[1] It can also be located in evolutionary theories which supported U.S. Manifest Destiny, imperial largesse, and Christian imperialism. And it can further be seen as a direct result of the legacy of doctrines of white supremacy which biologized Africans as "creatures" by equating them with the earliest stages of human development. Africans were likened by whites to savage beasts or merry-hearted singing and dancing children. The former stereotype led a 10-year-old black boy – Joseph Moller – to be exhibited at the Antwerp Zoo at the turn of the century. Closer to home and less remote in time is the case of Ota Benga, a "pygmy" boy exhibited in 1906 at the Monkey House in the Bronx Zoo as an "African homunculus" and as the "missing link" and encouraged by zoo keepers to charge the bars of his cage with his mouth open and teeth bared (Bradford and Blume 1992). In less sensational guise, this attitude continues right up to the present time. For instance, in 1992, the Secretary of Health and Human Services in the Bush Administration appointed Frederick A. Goodwin, a research psychiatrist and career federal scientist, as Director of the National Institute for Mental Health. Goodwin used animal research findings to compare youth gangs to groups of "hyperaggressive" and "hypersexual" monkeys and commented that "maybe it isn't just the careless use of the word when people call certain areas of certain cities, 'jungles' " (*Observer*, p. 20).

Whether conceived as the return of the repressed of Victorian puritanism, a leftover from Aristotelian hierarchical discourse or colonial and imperialist ideology, it remains the terrible truth of history that Africans have been forcibly placed at the foot of the human ladder of civilization (Pieterse 1992). As Jan Nederveen Pieterse notes, America historically has been "the 'white man's country', in which institutional and ideological patterns of the supremacy of white over black, and of men over women, supplemented and reinforced one another" (1992: 220).

While I do not wish to lapse into either an essentialized nativism which sees non-Western indigenous cultures as homogeneous or a view of the West that sees it as all of one piece – a monolithic block – and unaffected by its colonized subjects, or solely as an engine of imperialism, I need to affirm the fact that many conservative multiculturalists have scarcely removed themselves from the colonist legacy of white supremacy. Although they would distance themselves from racist ideologies, conservative multiculturalists pay only lip-service to the cognitive equality of all races and charge unsuccessful minorities with having "culturally deprived backgrounds" and a "lack of strong family-oriented values." This "environmentalist" position still accepts Black cognitive inferiority to whites as a general premise and provides conservative multiculturalists with a means of rationalizing why some minority groups are successful while others are not. This also gives the white cultural elite the excuse they need for unreflectively and disproportionately occupying positions of power. They are not unlike the *inscripti* of the right-wing Roman Catholic organization, *Opus Dei*, who attempt to intellectually and culturally sequester or barricade their members from the tools for critical analyses of social life in order to shore up their own power to manipulate and propagandize.

One particularly invidious project of conservative or corporate multiculturalism is to construct a common culture – a seamless web of textuality – bent on annulling the concept of the border through the delegitimization of foreign languages and regional and ethnic dialects, a persistent attack on non-standard English, and the undermining of bilingual education (Macedo, in press). Gramsci's understanding of this process is instructive, and is cogently articulated by Michael Gardiner:

> For Gramsci, the political character of language was most apparent in the attempt by the dominant class to create a common cultural "climate" and to "transform the popular mentality" through the imposition of a national language. Therefore, he felt that linguistic hegemony involved the articulation of signs and symbols which tended to codify and reinforce the dominant viewpoint. Thus, Gramsci argued that there existed a close relationship between linguistic stratification and social hierarchization, in that the various dialects and accents found within a given society are always rank-ordered as to their perceived legitimacy, appropriateness, and so on. Accordingly, concrete language usage reflects underlying, asymmetrical power relations, and it registers profound changes which occur in the cultural, moral, and political worlds. Such changes were primarily expressed through what Gramsci termed "normative grammar"; roughly, the system of norms whereby particular utterances could be evaluated and mutually understood . . . which was an important aspect of the state's attempt to establish linguistic conformity. Gramsci also felt that the maintenance of regional dialects helped peasants and workers partially to resist the forces of political and cultural hegemony.
>
> (Gardiner 1992: 186)

In addition to its position on common culture and bilingual education, there are further reasons why corporate multiculturalism must be rejected. First, it refuses to treat whiteness as a form of ethnicity and in doing so posits whiteness as an invisible norm by which other ethnicities are judged. Second, conservative multiculturalism – as espoused by Diane Ravitch, Arthur Schlesinger, Jr., Lynne V. B. Cheney, Chester Finn, and others – uses the term "diversity" to cover up the ideology of assimilation that undergirds its position. In this view, ethnic groups are reduced to "add-ons" to the dominant culture. Before you can be "added on" to the dominant U.S. culture you must first adopt a consensual view of culture and learn to accept the essentially Euro-American patriarchal norms of the "host" country. Third, as I mentioned earlier, conservative multiculturalism is essentially monolingual and adopts the position that English should be the only official language. It is often virulently opposed to bilingual education programs. Fourth, conservative multiculturalists posit standards of achievement for all youth that are premised on the cultural capital of the Anglo middle class. Fifth, conservative multiculturalism fails to interrogate the high-status knowledge – knowledge that is deemed of most value in white, middle-class America – to which the educational system is geared. It fails, in other words, to interrogate dominant regimes of discourse and social and cultural practices that are implicated in global dominance and are inscribed in racist, classist, sexist and homophobic assumptions. Conservative multiculturalism wants to assimilate students to an unjust social order by arguing that every member of every ethnic group can reap the economic benefits of neocolonialist ideologies and corresponding social and economic practices. But a prerequisite to "joining the club" is to become denuded, deracinated, and culturally stripped.

Recent popular conservative texts set firmly against liberal, left–liberal, and critical strands of multiculturalism include Richard Brookhiser's *The Way of the Wasp: How it Made America, and How it Can Save it, So to Speak*, Arthur Schlesinger, Jr.'s *The Disuniting of America: Reflections on a Multicultural Society*, and Laurence Auster's *The Path to National Suicide: An Essay on Immigration and Multiculturalism*. According to Stanley Fish (1992), these texts, which appeal to national unity and a harmonious citizenry, can readily be traced to earlier currents of Christianity (proclamations that it was God's wish that the future of civilization be secured in the United States) and social Darwinism (U.S. Anglo-Saxon stock is used to confirm the theory of natural selection). Reflecting and enforcing the assumptions made by the authors (whom Fish describes as racist not in the sense that they actively seek the subjugation of groups but in that they perpetuate racial stereotypes and support the institutions that promote them) is the SAT exam used in high school for college admission. Fish notes that one of the authors of this test, Carl Campbell Brigham, championed in his *A Study of American Intelligence* a classification of races which identified the Nordic as the superior race and, in descending order, located the less superior races as Alpine, Mediterranean, Eastern, New Eastern, and Negro. This hierarchy was first expounded by Madison Grant in *The Passing of the Great Race* (Fish 1992) and reflected in earlier European works such as *Essai sur l'inégalité des races humaines*, a four-volume testament to the racial superiority of the Germanic race by Joseph Arthur (Comte de Govineau) and Edward Gibbon's *Decline and Fall of the Roman Empire*, a work which blamed miscegination for the decline of civilization (Pieterse 1992). Not surprisingly, this hierarchy is confirmed in Brigham's later comparative analysis of intelligence. The library at the Educational Testing Service compound still bears Brigham's name (Fish 1992). Also problematic, as Mike Dyson points out, are theories linking white racism to biological determinism, such as recent discussions of "melanin theory" in which black researchers view whiteness as a genetic deficiency state that leads whites to act violently against Blacks because of white feelings of color inferiority (Dyson 1993).

When we contrast Brookhiser's key WASP virtues with non-WASP virtues (those of the Asians, or African-Americans or Latinos) we see the Western virtues of the former – Conscience, Anti-sensuality, Industry, Use, Success, and Civic Mindedness – being distinguished as more American than the lesser virtues of the latter – Self, Creativity, Ambition, Diffidence, Gratification and Group Mindedness. This also reflects a privileging of Western languages (English, French, German, and ancient Greek) over non-Western languages (see Fish 1992). Supposedly, Western European languages are the only ones sophisticated enough to grasp truth as an "essence." The search for the "truth" of the Western canon of "Great Works" is actually based on an epistemological error that presumes there exists a language of primordial Being and Truth. This error is linked to the phenomenalist reduction of linguistic meaning which endows language (through analogy) with sense perceptions and thereby reduces the act of interpretation to uncovering the "true understanding" that reciprocally binds the truth of the text to the pre-understanding, tacit knowledge, or foreknowledge of the reader (Norris 1990). From this view of the mimetic transparency of language, aesthetic judgments are seen as linked directly to ethics or politics through a type of direct correspondence (Norris 1990). Language, therefore, becomes elevated to a "truth-telling status" which remains exempt from its ethico-political situatedness or embeddedness. It is this epistemological error that permits conservatives to denounce totalitarianism in the name of its own truth and serves as a ruse for expanding present forms of domination. It is not hard to see how racism can become a precondition for this form of conservative multiculturalism in so far as Western virtues (which can be traced back as far as Aristotle's Great Chain of Being) become the national-aesthetic-ist ground for the conservative multiculturalist's view of civilization and citizenship. The power of conservative multiculturalism lays claim to its constituents by conferring a space for the reception of its discourses that is safe and sovereignly secure. It does this by sanctioning empiricism as the fulcrum for weighing the "truth" of culture. What discursively thrives in this perspective is an epistemology which privileges the logic of cause-and-effect narrative construction (see Norris 1990). In this case, intelligence quotients and test scores become the primary repository of authoritative exegesis in what constitutes successful school citizenship. Fortunately, as Foucault points out, subjectivity is not simply constituted through discourses and social practices of subjugation. Liberal, left–liberal, and critical forms of multiculturalism envisage a different "practice of the self" and new forms of self-fashioning and subjectivity based on more progressive conceptions of freedom and justice.

Liberal multiculturalism

Liberal multiculturalism argues that a natural equality exists among whites, African-Americans, Latinos, Asians and other racial populations. This perspective is based on the intellectual "sameness" among the races, on their cognitive equivalence or the rationality imminent in all races that permits them to compete equally in a capitalist society. However, from the point of view of liberal multiculturalism, equality is absent in U.S. society not because of black or Latino cultural deprivation but because social and educational opportunities do not exist that permit everyone to compete equally in the capitalist marketplace. Unlike their critical counterparts, they believe that existing cultural social and economic constraints can be modified or reformed in order for relative equality to be realized. This view often collapses into an ethnocentric and oppressively universalistic humanism in which the legitimating norms governing the substance of citizenship are identified most strongly with Anglo-American cultural–political communities.

Left–liberal multiculturalism

Left–liberal multiculturalism emphasizes cultural differences and suggests that the stress on the equality of races smothers those important cultural differences between races that are responsible for different behaviors, values, attitudes, cognitive styles, and social practices. Left–liberal multiculturalists feel that mainstream approaches to multiculturalism occlude characteristics and differences related to race, class, gender, and sexuality. Those who work within this perspective have a tendency to essentialize cultural differences, however, and ignore the historical and cultural situatedness of difference, which is understood as a form of signification removed from social and historical constraints. That is, there is a tendency to ignore difference as a social and historical construction that is constitutive of the power to represent meanings. It is often assumed that there exists an authentic "female" or "African-American" or "Latino" experience or way of being-in-the-world. Left–liberal multiculturalism treats difference as an "essence" that exists independently of history, culture, and power. Often one is asked to show one's identity papers before dialogue can begin.

This perspective often locates meaning through the conduit of "authentic" experience in the mistaken belief that one's own politics of location somehow guarantees "political correctness" in advance. Either a person's physical proximity to the oppressed or their own location as an oppressed person is supposed to offer a special authority from which to speak. What often happens is that a populist elitism gets constructed as inner-city teachers or trade unionists or those engaged in activist politics establish a pedigree of voice based on personal history, class, race, gender, and experience. Here the political is often reduced only to the personal where theory is dismissed in favor of one's own personal and cultural identity. Of course, a person's lived experience, race, class, gender, and history are important in the formation of his or her political identity, but we must be willing to examine our personal experiences and speaking voices in terms of the ideological and discursive complexity of their formation.

Of course, when a person speaks it is always from somewhere (Hall 1991) but this process of meaning production needs to be interrogated in order to understand how identity is constantly being produced through a play of difference linked to and reflected by shifting and conflicting discursive and ideological relations, formations and articulations (see Giroux 1992; Scott 1992). Experience needs to be recognized as a site of ideological production and the mobilization of affect and can be examined largely through its imbrication in our universal and local knowledges and modes of intelligibility and its relationship to language, desire, and the body. As Joan Scott notes, "experience is a subject's history. Language is the site of history's enactment" (1992: 34). Of course, I am not arguing against the importance of experience in the formation of political identity, but rather pointing out that it has become the new imprimatur for legitimating the political currency and uncontestable validity of one's arguments. This has often resulted in a reverse form of academic elitism. Not only is the authority of the academic under assault (and rightly so, in many cases) but it has been replaced by a populist elitism based on one's own identity papers.

CRITICAL AND RESISTANCE MULTICULTURALISM

Multiculturalism without a transformative political agenda can just be another form of accommodation to the larger social order. I believe that because they are immersed in the discourse of "reform," liberal and left–liberal positions on multiculturalism do not go nearly far enough in advancing a project of social transformation. With this concern in mind, I am developing the idea of critical multiculturalism from the perspective of a resistance post-structuralist approach to meaning, and emphasizing the role that language and representation play in the construction of meaning and identity. The post-structuralist insight that I am relying on is located within the larger context of postmodern theory – that disciplinary archipelago that is scattered through the sea of social theory – and asserts that signs and significations are essentially unstable and shifting and can only be temporarily fixed, depending on how they are articulated within particular discursive and historical struggles. The perspective of what I am calling critical multiculturalism understands representations of race, class, and gender as the result of larger social struggles over signs and meanings, and in this way emphasizes not simply textual play or metaphorical displacement as a form of resistance (as in the case of left–liberal multiculturalism) but stresses the central task of transforming the social, cultural, and institutional relations in which meanings are generated.

From the perspective of critical multiculturalism, the conservative/liberal stress on sameness and the left–liberal emphasis on difference form a false opposition. Both identity based on "sameness" and identity based on "difference" are forms of essentialist logic: in both, individual identities are presumed to be autonomous, self-contained and self-directed. Resistance multiculturalism also refuses to see culture as non-conflictual, harmonious and consensual. Democracy is understood from this perspective as busy – not a seamless, smooth or always harmonious political and cultural state of affairs. Resistance multiculturalism doesn't see diversity itself as a goal but rather argues that diversity must be affirmed within a politics of cultural criticism and a commitment to social justice. It must be attentive to the notion of "difference." Difference is always a product of history, culture, power, and ideology. Differences occur *between* and *among* groups and must be understood in terms of the specificity of their production. Critical multiculturalism interrogates the construction of difference and identity in relation to a radical politics. It is positioned against the neo-imperial romance with monoglot ethnicity grounded in a shared or "common" experience of "America" that is associated with conservative and liberal strands of multiculturalism.

Viewed from the perspective of a critical multiculturalism, conservative attacks on multiculturalism as separatist and ethnocentric carry with them the erroneous assumption by white Anglo constituencies that North

American society fundamentally constitutes social relations of uninterrupted accord. The liberal view is seen to underscore the idea that North American society is simply a forum of consensus with different minority viewpoints accretively added on. We are faced here with a politics of pluralism which largely ignores the workings of power and privilege. More specifically, the liberal perspective "involves a very insidious exclusion as far as any structural politics of change is concerned: it excludes and occludes global or structural relations of power as 'ideological' and 'totalizing' " (Ebert, in press a). In addition, it presupposes harmony and agreement – an undisturbed space in which differences can coexist. Within such a space, individuals are invited to shed their positive characteristics in order to become disembodied and transparent American citizens (Copjec 1991; Rosaldo 1989), a cultural practice that creates what David Lloyd (1991: 70) calls a "subject without properties." In this instance, citizens are able to occupy a place of "pure exchangeability." This accords the universalized white subject a privileged status. Such a proposition is dangerously problematic. Chandra Mohanty (1989/90) notes that difference cannot be formulated as negotiation among culturally diverse groups against a backdrop of benign variation or presumed cultural homogeneity. Difference is the recognition that knowledges are forged in histories that are riven with differentially constituted relations of power; that is, knowledges, subjectivities, and social practices are forged within "asymmetrical and incommensurate cultural spheres" (1989/90: 181).

Homi K. Bhabha makes the lucid observation that in attributing the racism and sexism of the common culture solely to "the underlying logic of late capitalism and its patriarchal overlay," leftists are actually providing an alibi for the common culture argument. The common culture is transformed in this instance into a form of ethical critique of the political system that supposedly fosters unity within a system of differences. The concept of cultural otherness is taken up superficially to celebrate a "range of 'nation-centred' cultural discourses (on a wide axis from right to left)" (1992: 235). It is worth quoting at length Bhabha's notion of common culture as the regulation and normalization of difference:

> Like all myths of the nation's "unity," the common culture is a profoundly conflicted ideological strategy. It is a declaration of democratic faith in a plural, diverse society and, at the same time, a defense against the real, subversive demands that the articulation of cultural difference – the empowering of minorities – makes upon democratic pluralism. Simply saying that the "nation's cement" is inherently sexist or racist – because of the underlying logic of late capitalism and its patriarchal overlay – ironically provides the "common culture" argument with the alibi it needs. The vision of a common culture is

> perceived to be an ethical mission whose value lies in revealing, prophylactically, the imperfections and exclusions of the political system as it exists. The healing grace of a culture of commonality is supposedly the coevality it establishes between social differences – ethnicities, ideologies, sexualities – "an intimation of simultaneity across homogeneous empty time" that welds these different voices into a "unisonance" that is expressive of the "contemporaneous community of the national culture".
>
> (Bhabha 1992: 234–5)

Too often liberal and conservative positions on diversity constitute an attempt to view culture as a soothing balm – the aftermath of historical disagreement – some mythical present where the irrationalities of historical conflict have been smoothed out. This is not only a disingenuous view of culture, it is profoundly dishonest. It overlooks the importance of engaging in some instances in dissensus in order to contest hegemonic forms of domination, and to affirm differences. The liberal and conservative positions on culture also assume that justice already exists and needs only to be evenly apportioned. However, both teachers and students need to realize that justice does not already exist simply because laws exist. Justice needs to be continually created and constantly struggled for (Darder 1992). The question that I want to pose to teachers is this: Do teachers and cultural workers have access to a language that allows them sufficiently to critique and transform existing social and cultural practices that are defended by liberals and conservatives as unifyingly democratic?

CRITICAL MULTICULTURALISM AND THE POLITICS OF SIGNIFICATION

Since all experience is the experience of meaning, we need to recognize the role that language plays in the production of experience. You don't have an experience and then search for a word to describe that experience. Rather, language helps to constitute experience by providing a structure of intelligibility or mediating device through which experiences can be understood. Rather than talking about experience, it is more accurate to talk about "experience effects" (Zavarzadeh and Morton 1990).

Western language and thought are constructed as a system of differences organized de facto and de jure as binary oppositions – white/black, good/bad, normal/deviant, etc. – with the primary term being privileged and designated as the defining term or the norm of cultural meaning, creating a dependent hierarchy. Yet the secondary term does not really exist outside the first, but in effect exists inside it, even though the phallogocentric logic of white supremacist ideology makes you think it exists outside and in opposition to the first term. The critical multiculturalist critique argues that the relationship between signifier and signified is *insecure* and *unstable.* Signs are part of an ideological struggle which creates a particular regime of representation serving to legitimate a certain cultural reality. For instance, we have witnessed a struggle in our society over the meaning of terms such as "negro," "black," and "African-American."

According to Teresa Ebert (1991b), our current ways of seeing and acting are being disciplined for us through forms of signification, that is, through modes of intelligibility and ideological frames of sense-making. Rejecting the Saussurian semiotics of signifying practices (and its continuing use in contemporary post-structuralism) as "historical operations of language and tropes," Ebert characterizes signifying practices as "an ensemble of material operations involved in economic and political relations" (p. 117). She maintains, rightly in my view, that socio-economic relations of power require distinctions to be made among groups through forms of signification in order to organize subjects according to the unequal distribution of privilege and power.

To illustrate the politics of signification at work in the construction and formation of racist subjects, Ebert offers the example of the way in which the terms "negro" and "black" have been employed within the racial politics of the United States. Just as the term "negro" became an immutable mark of difference and naturalized the political arrangements of racism in the 1960s, so too is the term "black" being refigured in the white dominant culture to mean criminality, violence, and social degeneracy. This was made clear in the "Willie" Horton campaign ads of George Bush and was also evident in the verdict of the Rodney King case in Los Angeles. It is also evident in media coverage of the O. J. Simpson trial.

Carlos Muñoz, Jr. (1989) has revealed how the term "Hispanic" in the mid-1970s became a "politics of white ethnic identity" that de-emphasized and in some cases rejected the Mexican cultural base of Mexican Americans. Muñoz writes that the term "Hispanic" is derived from "Hispania" which was the name the Romans gave to the Iberian peninsula, most of which became Spain, and "implicitly emphasizes the white European culture of Spain at the expense of the nonwhite cultures that have profoundly shaped the experiences of all Latin Americans" (p. 11). Not only is this term blind to the multiracial reality of Mexican Americans through its refusal to acknowledge "the nonwhite indigenous cultures of the Americas, Africa, and Asia, which historically have produced multicultural and multiracial peoples in Latin America and the United States" (p. 11), it is a term that ignores the complexities within these various cultural groups. Here is another example of the melting pot theory of assimilation fostered through a politics of signification. So we might ask ourselves what meanings will be attached to certain terms such as "welfare mothers?" Most of us know what government officials mean when they refer derisively to "welfare mothers." They mean black and Latino mothers.

Kobena Mercer has recently described what he calls "black struggles over the sign" (1992: 428). Mercer, following Volosinov, argues that every sign has a "social multi-accentuality" and it is this polyvocal character that can rearticulate the sign through the inscription of different connotations surrounding it. The dominant ideology always tries to stabilize certain meanings of the term. Mercer writes that for over four centuries of Western civilization, the sign "black" was "structured by the closure of an absolute symbolic division of what was white and what was non-white" (1992: 428) through the "morphological equation" of racial superiority. This equation accorded whiteness with civility and rationality and blackness with savagery and irrationality. Subaltern subjects themselves brought about a reappropriation and rearticulation of the "proper name" – Negro, Colored, Black, Afro-American – in which a collective subjectivity was renamed. Mercer notes that in the 1960s and 1970s, the term "ethnic minorities" likened the black subject to "a minor, an abject childlike figure necessary for the legitimation of paternalistic ideologies of assimilation and integration that underpinned the strategy of multiculturalism" (p. 429). The term "black community" arose out of a reappropriation of the term "community relations." The state had tried to colonize a definition of social democratic consensus designed to "manage" race relations through the use of "community relations."

The examples discussed above underscore the central theoretical position of critical multiculturalism: that differences are produced according to the ideological production and reception of cultural signs. As Mas'ud Zavarzadeh and Donald Morton point out, "Signs are neither eternally predetermined nor pan-historically undecidable: they are rather 'decided' or rendered as 'undecidable' in the moment of social conflicts" (1990: 156). Difference is not "cultural obviousness" such as black versus white or Latino versus European or Anglo-American; rather, differences are historical and cultural constructions (Ebert 1991a).

Just as we can see the politics of signification at work in instances of police brutality, or in the way Blacks and Latinos are portrayed as drug pushers, gang members, or the minority sidekick to the white cop in movies and television, we can see it in special education placement where a greater proportion of Black and Latino students are considered for "behavioral" placements whereas white, middle-class students are provided for the most part with the more comforting and comfortable label of "learning disabled" (McLaren 1989b). Here, a critical multiculturalist curriculum can help teachers explore the ways in which students are differentially subjected to ideological inscriptions and multiply-organized discourses of desire through a politics of signification.

A critical multiculturalism suggests that teachers and cultural workers need to take up the issue of "difference" in ways that do not replay the monocultural essentialism of the "centrisms" – Anglocentrism, Eurocentrism, phallocentrism, androcentrism, and the like. They need to build a politics of alliance-building, of dreaming together, of solidarity that moves beyond the condescension of, say, "race awareness week" that actually serves to keep forms of institutionalized racism intact. We must struggle for a solidarity that is not centered around market imperatives, and which develops out of the imperatives of freedom, liberation, democracy, and critical citizenship.

The notion of the citizen has been pluralized and hybridized, as Kobena Mercer notes, by the presence of a diversity of social subjects. Mercer is instructive in pointing out that "solidarity does not mean that everyone thinks the same way, it begins when people have the confidence to disagree over issues because they 'care' about constructing a common ground" (1990: 68). Solidarity is not impermeably solid but depends to a certain degree on antagonism and uncertainty. Timothy Maliqualim Simone calls this type of multiracial solidarity "geared to maximizing points of interaction rather than harmonizing, balancing, or equilibrating the distribution of bodies, resources, and territories" (Simone 1989: 191).

Whereas left–liberal multiculturalism equates resistance with destabilizing dominant systems of representation, critical multiculturalism goes one step further by asserting that all representations are the result of social struggles over signifiers and their signifieds. This suggests that resistance must take into account an intervention into social struggle in order "to provide equal access to social resources and to transform the dominant power relations which limit this access according to class privilege, race, and gender' (Ebert 1991a: 294). Differences *within* culture must be defined as political difference and not just formal, textual, or linguistic difference. Global or structural relations of power must not be ignored. The concept of totality must not be abandoned but rather seen as an *overdetermined structure of difference.* Differences are always *differences in relation*, they are never simply free-floating. Differences are not seen as absolute, irreducible or intractable, but rather as undecidable and socially and culturally relational (see Ebert 1991a).

Resistance or critical multiculturalism does not agree with those left–liberal multiculturalists who argue that difference needs only to be interrogated as a form of rhetoric, thereby reducing politics to signifying structures and history to textuality (Ebert 1991a). We need to go beyond destabilizing meaning, by transforming the social and historical conditions in which meaning-making occurs. Rather than remaining satisfied with erasing the privilege of oppressive ideologies that have been naturalized within the dominant culture, or with restating dangerous memories that have been repressed within the political unconscious of the state, critical multiculturalist praxis attempts to revise existing hegemonic arrangements. A critical multiculturalist praxis does not simply reject the bourgeois decorum that has consigned the imperialized other to the realm of the grotesque, but effectively attempts to remap desire by fighting for a linguistically multivalenced culture and new structures of experience in which individuals refuse the role of the omniscient narrator and conceive of identity as a polyvalent assemblage of (contradictory and overdetermined) subject positions. Existing systems of difference which organize social life into patterns of domination and subordination must be reconstructed. We need to do more than unflaggingly problematize difference as a condition of rhetoric, or unceasingly interrogate the status of all knowledge as discursive inscription, because, as Ebert notes, this annuls the grounds of both reactionary and revolutionary politics. Rather, we need a rewriting of difference as *difference-in-relation* followed by attempts to change dramatically the material conditions that allow relations of domination to prevail over relations of equality and social justice. This is a different cultural politics than one of simply re-establishing an inverse hierarchical order of blacks or Latinos *over* whites. Rather it is an attempt to transform the very value of hierarchy itself, followed by a challenge to the material structures that are responsible for the overdetermination of structures of difference in the direction of oppression, injustice, and human suffering. However, this is not to claim that all individuals are oppressed in the same ways, since groups are oppressed non-synchronously in conjunction with systems such as class, race, gender, age, ethnicity, sexuality, etc. (McCarthy 1988). People can be situated very differently in the *same totalizing structures of oppression.* We need to analyze and challenge both the specific enunciations of micro-differences within difference and the macro-structure of difference-in-relation (Ebert 1991b). We need to refocus on "structural" oppression in the forms of patriarchy, capitalism, and white supremacy – structures that tend to get ignored by liberal multiculturalists in their veneration of difference as identity. As educators and cultural workers, we must critically intervene in those power relations that organize difference.

WHITENESS: THE INVISIBLE CULTURE OF TERROR

Educators need to examine critically the development of pedagogical discourses and practices that demonize Others who are different (through transforming them into absence or deviance). Critical multiculturalism calls serious attention to the dominant meaning systems readily available to students and teachers, most of which are ideologically stitched into the fabric of Western imperialism and patriarchy. It challenges meaning systems that impose attributes on the Other under the direction of sovereign signifiers and tropes. And this means directing all our efforts not at understanding ethnicity as "other than white," but at interrogating the culture of whiteness itself. This is crucial because unless we do this – unless we give white students a sense of their own identity as an emergent ethnicity – we naturalize whiteness as a cultural marker against which Otherness is defined. Coco Fusco warns that "To ignore white ethnicity is to redouble its hegemony by naturalizing it. Without specifically addressing white ethnicity there can be no critical evaluation of the construction of the other" (cited in Wallace 1991: 7). White groups need to examine their own ethnic histories so that they are less likely to judge their own cultural norms as neutral and universal. The supposed neutrality of white culture enables it to commodify blackness to its own advantage and ends. It allows it to manipulate the "other" but not see this "otherness" as a white tool of exploitation. "Whiteness" does not exist outside of culture but constitutes the prevailing social texts in which social norms are made and remade. As part of a politics of signification that passes unobserved into the rhythms of daily life, and a "politically constructed category parasitic on 'Blackness' " (West 1990: 29), "whiteness" has become the invisible norm, the standard against which the dominant culture measures its own worth.

Using an ethnosemiotic approach as a means of interrogating the culture of whiteness and understanding ethnicity as a rhetorical form, Dean MacCannell raises the question:

> In their interactions with others, how can groups in power manage to convey the impression that they are less ethnic than those over whom they exercise their power; in other words, how can they foster the impression that their own traits and qualities are merely correct, while the corresponding qualities of others are "ethnic?"
>
> (1992: 121–2)

Furthermore, asks MacCannell, how does the consensus that is achieved in this matter structure our institutions? His answer leads us to explore the secret of power in discourse – that simply because language is essentially rhetorical (i.e., free of all bias because it is pure bias) we cannot escape the fact that rhetoric and grammar always intersect in particular ideological formations, which makes language unavoidably a *social relation*. And every social relation is a structurally located one that can never be situated outside of relations of power. MacCannell locates this power in the ability of the speaking subject to move into the position of "he" without seeming to leave the position of "I" or "you" (which are empty or "floating" signifiers that have no referent outside the immediate situation). The personal pronoun "he" refers to an objective situation outside of the immediate subjectively apprehended situation. MacCannell asserts that whites have mastered interactional forms that permit them to operate as *interactants* while seeming to be detached from the situation, to be both an "I" or a "you" and a "he" at the same time – to operate within the situation *and* to judge it. Dominant groups will always want to occupy the grammatical power position; that is, assume the external objective and judgmental role of the "he" by suggesting that their use of language is free of bias. White culture, according to MacCannell, is an enormous totalization that arrogates to itself the right to represent all other ethnic groups. For instance, binary oppositions such as "white opposed to non-white" always occupy the grammatical position of "him", never "I" or "you," and we know that in white culture, "whiteness" will prevail and continue to be parasitic on the meaning of "blackness."

Cornel West (1990: 29) remarks that " 'Whiteness' is a politically constructed category parasitic on 'blackness.' " He further asserts that "One cannot deconstruct the binary oppositional logic of images of Blackness without extending it to the contrary condition of Blackness/Whiteness itself." According to Jim Rutherford,

> binarism operates in the same way as splitting and projection: the center expels its anxieties, contradictions and irrationalities onto the subordinate term, filling it with the antithesis of its own identity; the Other, in its very alienness, simply mirrors and represents what is deeply familiar to the center, but projected outside of itself. It is in these very processes and representations of marginality that the violence, antagonisms, and aversions which are at the core of the dominant discourses and identities become manifest – racism, homophobia, misogyny, and class contempt are the products of this frontier.
>
> (1990: 22)

Of course, when binarisms become racially and culturally marked, *white* occupies the grammatical position of *him*, never *I* or *you* and, notes MacCannell, "always operates *as if* not dependent on rhetoric to maintain its position" (p. 131). Rhetoric is aligned with *non-truth* and whiteness is perceived as neutral and devoid of interest. Of course, "whiteness" projects onto the term "blackness" an array of specific qualities and characteristics such as wild, exotic, uncontrolled, deviant, and savage. Whiteness is founded on the principle of the depersonalization of all human relationships and the idealization of objective judgement and duty.

> To say that White Culture is impersonal is not the same thing as saying that it does not function like a subject or subjectivity. But it is the kind that is cold, the kind that laughs at feelings while demanding that all surplus libido, energy and capital be handed over to it. . . . White culture begins with the pretense that it, above all, does not express itself rhetorically. Rather, the form of its expression is always represented as only incidental to the "truth". And its totalizing power

> radiates from this pretense which is maintained by interpreting all ethnic expression as "representative," and therefore, *merely* rhetorical.
> (MacCannell 1992: 130)

When people of color attack white ground rules for handling disputes, or bureaucratic procedures, or specific policies of institutionalized racism, these are necessary oppositional acts, but insufficient to bring about structural change because, as MacCannell notes, this work is "framed by the assumption of the dominance of white culture" (p. 131). This is because white culture is predicated upon the universalization of the concept of "exchange-values" – systems of equivalences, the transcribability of all languages, the translatability of any language into any other language, and the division of the earth into real-estate holdings in which it is possible to calculate and calibrate with precision the worth of every person. Within such a totalization brought about by white culture, indigenous groups can only belong as an "ethnicity." As long as white culture, as the defining cultural frame for white–ethnic transactions, sets the limits on all thought about human relations, there can be no prospect for human equality.

Richard Dyer (1988) has made some useful observations about the culture of whiteness, claiming that its property of being both "everything" and "nothing" is the source of its representational power in the sense that white culture possesses the power to colonize the definition of the normal with respect to class, gender, sexuality, and nationality. Perhaps white culture's most formidable attribute is its ability to mask itself as a category. Whites will often think of their Scottishness, Irishness, Jewishness, and so on, before they think of their whiteness. Michael Goldfield (1992) argues that white supremacy has been responsible for holding back working-class struggle in the United States, as labor groups tragically failed to grasp the strategic importance for labor in fighting the system of white supremacy, missing an opportunity – especially during the Reconstruction – for changing the face of U.S. politics.

In her recent book, *Black Looks*, bell hooks notes that white people are often shocked when black people "critically assess white people from a standpoint where 'whiteness' is the privileged signifier". She remarks that:

> Their [white people's] amazement that black people match white people with a critical "ethnographic" gaze, is itself an expression of racism. Often their rage errupts because they believe that all ways of looking that highlight difference subvert the liberal belief in a universal subjectivity (we are all just people) that they think will make racism disappear. They have a deep emotional investment in the myth of "sameness," even as their actions reflect the primacy of whiteness as a sign informing who they are and how they think. Many of them are shocked that black people think critically about whiteness because racist thinking perpetuates the fantasy that the Other who is subju-

> gated, who is subhuman, lacks the ability to comprehend, to understand, to see the working of the powerful. Even though the majority of those students politically consider themselves liberals and anti-racist, they too unwittingly invest in the sense of whiteness as mystery.
>
> (hooks 1992: 167–8)

hooks discusses the representation of whiteness as a form of terror within black communities and is careful not simply to invert the stereotypical racist association of whiteness as goodness and blackness as evil. The depiction of whiteness as "terrorizing" emerges in hooks's discussion not as a reaction to stereotypes but, as she puts it, "as a response to the traumatic pain and anguish that remains a consequence of white racist domination, a psychic state that informs and shapes the way black folks 'see' whiteness" (p. 169).

Discussing whiteness in the context of the literary imagination, Toni Morrison comments that since we live in a "wholly racialized society" (1993: 12–13) we cannot escape from "racially inflected language" (p. 13). Consequently, it stands to reason, according to Morrison, that language and literature are always political. She remarks that "A criticism that needs to insist that literature is not only 'universal' but also 'race-free' risks lobotomizing that literature, and diminishes both the art and the artist" (p. 12). Morrison condemns the paucity of critical material on race in literature and the construction of literary "whiteness." In such a context, to enforce the "invisibility" of race "through silence is to allow the black body a shadowless participation in the dominant cultural body" (p. 10). American identity as it has been cobbled in its literary history "is made possible by, shaped by, activated by a complex awareness and employment of a constituted Africanism. It was this Africanism, deployed as rawness and savagery, that provided the staging ground and arena for the elaboration of the quintessential American identity" (p. 44). Not only do American writers need the "racial other" for self-definition, but so do everyday so-called enlightened citizens.

THE POLITICS OF MULTICULTURAL RESISTANCE

Critical pedagogy needs to hold a non-reductionist view of the social order: to see society as an irreducible indeterminacy. The social field is always open and we must explore its fissures, fault-lines, gaps, and silences. Power relations may not always have a conscious design, but they have unintended consequences which define deep structural aspects of oppression, even though every ideological totalization of the social is designed to fail. This is not to affirm Schopenhauer's unwilled patterns of history but rather to assert that while domination has a logic without design in its sign systems and social practices, it does operate through overdetermined structures of race, class, and gender difference. Resistance to such domination means deconstructing the social by means of a reflexive intersubjective consciousness – what Freire terms *conscientização*. With this comes a recognition that ideology is not just an epistemological concern about the status of certain facts, but the way in which discourse and discursive systems generate particular social relations as well as reflect them. A reflexive intersubjective consciousness is the beginning – but only the beginning – of revolutionary praxis.

We also need to construct new narratives – new "border narratives" – in order to re-author the discourses of oppression in politically subversive ways, as well as create sites of possibility and enablement. For instance, we need to ask: How are our identities bound up with historical forms of discursive practices? It is one thing to argue against attacks on polyvocal and unassimilable difference and on narrative closure or to stress the heterogeneity of contemporary culture. But in doing so we must remember that dominant discourses are sites of struggle and their meanings are linked to social antagonisms and labor/economic relations, and naturalized in particular textual/linguistic referents. Consequently, self-reflection alone – even if it is inimicably opposed to all forms of domination and oppression – is only a necessary but not nearly sufficient condition for emancipation. This must go hand in hand with changes in material and social conditions through counterhegemonic action (Hammer and McLaren 1991). The socio-historical dynamics of race, clan, and gender domination must never be left out of the equation of social struggle or take a back seat to the sociology seminar room. Commonsense consciousness is not enough. We need a language of criticism as an antidote to the atheoretical use of "personal experience" in advancing claims for emancipatory action. However, this needs to be followed by the development of truly counterhegemonic public spheres. More than rhetorical displacements of oppression, we must have co-ordinated resistance to racist patriarchal capitalism and gender-divided labor relations. According to Teresa Ebert (in press a), what is needed is an intervention into the system of patriarchal oppression at both the macro-political level of the structural organization of domination (a transformative politics of labor relations) and the micro-political level of different and contradictory manifestations of oppression (cultural politics).

Those of us working in the area of curriculum reform need to move beyond the tabloid reportage surrounding the political correctness debate, take the issue of difference seriously, and challenge the dismissive undercutting of difference by the conservative multiculturalists. First we need to move beyond admitting one or two Latin American or African-American books into the canon of great works. Rather, *we need to legitimize multiple traditions of knowledge*. By focusing merely on "diversity" we are actually reinforcing the power of the discourses from the Western traditions that occupy the contexts of social privilege. Second, curriculum reform requires teachers to interrogate the discursive presuppositions that inform their curriculum practices with respect to race, class, gender, and sexual orientation. In addition, curricularists need to unsettle their complacency with respect to Eurocentrism. Third, what is perceived as the inherent superiority of whiteness and Western rationality needs to be displaced. The very notion of "the West" is something that critical educators find highly problematic. Why is Toni Morrison, for instance, denounced as non-Western simply because she is African-American? (This is complicated by the fact that conservative multiculturalists often retort with the insinuation that any attack on Western culture is an attack against being American.) Fourth, curriculum reform means recognizing that groups are differentially situated in the production of Western high-status knowledge. How are certain groups represented in the official knowledge that makes up the curriculum? Are they stigmatized because they are associated with the Third World? Are we, as teachers, complicitous with the oppression of these people when we refuse to interrogate popular films and T.V. shows that reinforce their subaltern status? Educators would do well to follow hooks in dehegemonizing racist discourses such that "progressive white people who are anti-racist might be able to understand the way in which their cultural practice reinscribes white supremacy without promoting paralyzing guilt or denial" (hooks 1992: 177). In addition, curriculum reform means affirming the voices of the oppressed: teachers need to give the marginalized and the powerless a preferential option. Similarly, students must be encouraged to produce their own oppositional readings of curriculum content. And lastly, curriculum reform must recognize the importance of encouraging spaces for the multiplicity of voices in our classrooms, and creating a dialogical pedagogy in which subjects see others as subjects and not as objects. When this happens, students are more likely to participate in history than become its victims.

In taking seriously the irreducible social materiality of discourse and the fact that the very semantics of discourse is always organized and interested, critical pedagogy has revealed how student identities are differentially constructed through social relations of schooling that promote and sustain asymmetrical relations of power and privilege. It has shown that this construction follows a normative profile of citizenship and an epistemology that attempts to reconcile the discourse of ideals with the discourse of needs. Discourses have been revealed to possess the power to nominate others as deviant or normal. Dominant discourses of schooling are not laws. Rather, they are strategies – disciplined mobilizations for normative performances. Ian Hunter (1992) has shown that the concept of citizenship taught in schools has less to do with ethical ideals than disciplinary practices and techniques of reading and writing and the way students are distributed into political and aesthetic spaces. We are being aesthetically and morally reconciled with the governing norms of a civic unconscious. The "unconscious" is not a semiotic puzzle to be opened through the discovery of some universal grammar but is rather an ethical technology designed to "complete" students as citizens. Pedagogically, this process is deceptive because it uses liberal humanism and progressive education to complete the circuit of hegemony. The liberal position on pedagogy is to use it to open social texts to a plurality of readings. Because we live in an age of cynical reason, this pedagogy provides a "knowing wink" to students which effectively says: "We know there are multiple ways to make sense of the world and we know that you know, too. So let's knowingly enter this world of multiple interpretations together and take pleasure in rejecting the dominant codes." Consequently, teachers and students engage in a tropological displacement and unsettling of normative discourses and revel in the semantic excess that prevents any meaning from becoming transcendentally fixed. The result of this practice of turning knowledge into floating signifiers circulating in an avant-garde text (whose discursive trajectory is everywhere and nowhere and whose meaning is ultimately undecidable) is simply a re-containment of the political. By positing undecidability in advance, identity is reduced to a form of self-indexing or academic "vogue-ing." Liberation becomes transformed into a form of discursive "cleverness," of postmodern transgressive-chic grounded in playfully high vogue decodings of always already constructed texts.

I would also like to rehearse some ideas that I introduced in Chapter 3 on the topic of border identities. Border identities are intersubjective spaces of cultural translation – linguistically multivalenced spaces of intercultural dialogue, spaces where one can find an overlay of codes, a multiplicity of culturally inscribed subject positions, a displacement of normative reference codes, and a polyvalent assemblage of new cultural meanings (see Giroux 1992).

Border identities are produced in sites of "occult instability" and result in "un laberinto de significados." Here, knowledge is produced by a transrepresentational access to the real – through reflexive, relational understanding amidst the connotative matrixes of numerous cultural codes. It is a world where identity and critical subjectivity depend upon the process of translating a profusion of intersecting cultural meanings (Hicks 1988; Giroux 1992). We need to remember that we live in a repressive regime in which identities are teleologically inscribed towards a standard end – the informed, employed citizen. There is a tension between this narrative which schools have attempted to install in students through normative pedagogical practices and the non-linear narratives that they "play out" in the world outside of the school. But students and even their often well-intentioned teachers are frequently incapable of intervening.

Especially in inner-city schools, students can be seen inhabiting what I call "border cultures." These are cultures in which, though there is a repetition of certain normative structures and codes, these often "collide" with other codes and structures whose referential status is often unknown or only partially known. In Los Angeles, for instance, it is possible that an inner-city neighborhood will contain Latino cultures, Asian cultures, and Anglo cultures and students live interculturally as they cross the borderlines of linguistic, cultural and conceptual realities. Students, in other words, have the opportunity to live multidimensionally. Living in border cultures is an anticentering experience, as school time and space are constantly deformed, and often a carnivalesque liminal space emerges as bourgeois linear time is displaced. Because the dominant model of multiculturalism in mainstream pedagogy is of the corporate or conservative variety, the notion of sameness is enforced and cultural differences that challenge white Anglo cultures are considered deviant and in need of enforced homogenization into the dominant referential codes and structures of Euro-American discourse.

I am in agreement with critics who assert that border identity cannot be subsumed under either dialectical or analytic logic (Hicks 1991). It is, rather, to experience a deterritorialization of signification (Larsen 1991) in a postnationalist cultural space – that is, in a postcolonial, postnational space. It is an identity structure that occurs in a postimperial space of cultural possibility. The postcolonial subject that arises out of the construction of border identity is non-identical with itself. It acquires a new form of agency outside of Euro-American Cartesian discourses. It is not simply an inverted Eurocentrism but one that salvages the modernist referent of liberation from oppression for all suffering peoples. I am here stressing the universality of human rights but at the same time criticizing essentialist universality as a site of transcendental meaning. In other words, I am emphasizing the universality of rights as historically produced. Social justice is a goal that needs to be situated historically, contextually, and contingently as the product of material struggles over modes of intelligibility as well as institutional and social practices. I need to be clear about what I mean by a referent for social justice and human freedom. The project underlying multicultural education needs to be situated from the standpoint not only of the *concrete other* but also the *generalized other*. All universal rights in this view must recognize the specific needs and desires of the concrete other without sacrificing the standpoint of a generalized other, without which it is impossible to speak of a radical ethics at all. Seyla Benhabib distinguishes between this perspective – what she refers to as an "interactive universalism" – and a "substitutionalist universalism:" "Substitutionalist universalism dismisses the concrete other behind the facade of a definitional identity of all as rational beings, while interactive universalism acknowledges that every generalized other is also a concrete other" (1992:165). This position speaks exclusively to neither a liberal humanist ethics of empathy and benevolence nor a ludic post-modernist ethics of local narratives or "les petits recits," but to one based on engagement, confrontation and dialogue, and collective moral argumentation between and across borders. It takes into account both macro- and micro-theory (Best and Kellner 1991) and some degree of normative justification and adjudication of choices. As Best and Kellner note, "one needs new critical theories to conceptualize, describe, and interpret macro social processes, just as one needs political theories able to articulate common or general interests that cut across divisions of sex, race, and class" (1991:301). In this sense I take issue with "ludic" voices of postmodernism that proclaim an end both to self-reflective agenthood and the importance of engaging historical narratives and which proclaim the impossibility of legitimizing institutions outside of "an immanent appeal to the self-legitimation of 'small narratives' " (Benhabib 1992: 220). Rather, a critical multiculturalism must take into account the "methodological assumptions guiding one's choice of narratives, and a clarification of those principles in the name of which one speaks" (p. 226).

A border identity is not simply an identity that is anti-capitalist and counterhegemonic but is also critically utopian. It is an identity that transforms the burden of knowledge into a scandal of hope. The destructive extremes of Eurocentrism and national–cultural identities are evident in the wreckage of Yugoslavia. We need to occupy locations between our political unconscious and everyday praxis and struggle but at the same time guided by a universalist emancipatory world-view in the form of a provisional utopia or contingent foundationalism (see Butler 1991). A provisional utopia is not a categorical blueprint for social change (as in fascism) but an anticipation of the future through practices of solidarity and community. Such a utopian vision demands that we gain control of the production of meaning, but in a post-nationalist sense. We can achieve this by negotiating with the borders of our identity – those unstable constellations of discursive structures – in our search for a radical otherness that can empower us to reach beyond them.

Border identities constitute a bold infringement on normalcy, a violation of the canons of bourgeois decorum, a space where we can cannibalize the traces of our narrative repression or engage them critically through the practice of cultural translation – a translation of one level of reality into another, creating a multidimensional reality that I call the *cultural imaginary*, a space of cultural articulation resulting from the collision of multiple strands of referential codes and sign systems. Such collisions can create hybrid significations through a hemorrhage of signifiers whose meanings endlessly bleed into each other or else take on the force of historical agency as a new *mestizaje* consciousness (Anzaldúa 1987). This is not simply a doctrine of identity based on cultural bricolage or a form of bric-a-brac subjectivity but a critical practice of cultural negotiation and translation that attempts to transcend the contradictions of Western dualistic thinking. As Chandra Talpade Mohanty remarks:

> A mestiza consciousness is a consciousness of the borderlands, a consciousness born of the historical collusion of Anglo and Mexican cultures and frames of reference. It is a plural consciousness in that it requires understanding multiple, often opposing ideas and knowledges, and negotiating these knowledges, not just taking a simple counter-stance.
>
> (1991: 36)

Anzaldúa speaks of a notion of agency that moves beyond the postmodernist concept of "split subject" by situating agency in its historical and geopolitical specificity (Mohanty 1991: 37). Borders cannot simply be evoked in an abstract transcendental sense but need to be identified specifically. Borders can be linguistic, spacial, ideological and geographical. They not only demarcate otherness but stipulate the manner in which otherness is maintained and reproduced. A *mestizaje* consciousness is linked, therefore, to the specificity of historical struggles (Mohanty 1991: 38).

A critical multiculturalism needs to testify not only to the pain, suffering, and "walking nihilism" of oppressed peoples, but also to the intermittent, epiphanic ruptures and moments of *jouissance* that occur when solidarity is established around struggles for liberation. As I have tried to argue, with others, elsewhere (McLaren and Hammer 1989; Estrada and McLaren, in press), we need to abandon our pedagogies of protest (which, as Houston Baker reminds us, simply reinforce the dualism of "self" and "other" and reinstate the basis of dominant racist evaluations, and preserve the "always already" arrangements of white male hegemony; see Baker 1985) in favor of a politics of transformation. Those of us who are white need also to avoid the "white male confessional" that Baker describes as the "confessional *manqué* of the colonial subject" (Baker 1985: 388).

White male confessionals simply "induce shame" rather than convince people to change their axiology, yet still employ the language and "shrewd methods of the overseers." It is the type of confessional that proclaims oppressed people of color are "as good as" white people. It simply asserts that subaltern voices measure up to dominant voices and that African–Americans are merely "different" and not deviant. In contrast, Baker calls for a form of "supraliteracy" or "guerrilla action" carried out *within* linguistic territories. This constitutes an invasion of the dominant linguistic terrain of the traditional academic disciplines – an invasion that he describes as a "deformation of mastery." From this perspective, critical pedagogy needs to be more attentive to the dimension of the vernacular – "to sound racial poetry in the courts of the civilized" (p. 395). Teachers need to include non-literary cultural forms in our classrooms – such as video, film, popular fiction, and radio – and a critical means of understanding their role in the production of subjectivity and agency.

Concentrating on the reflexive modalities of the intellect or returning to some pre-theoretical empirical experience are both bad strategies for challenging the politics of the white confessional. The former is advocated mostly by academics while the latter is exercised by educational activists suspicious of the new languages of deconstruction and the fashionable apostasy of the post-structuralists whose intellectual home is in the margins. Academic theorists tend to textualize and displace experience to the abstract equivalence of the signified, whilst activists view "commonsense" experience as essentially devoid of ideology or interest. We need to avoid approaches that disconnect us from the lives of real people who suffer and from issues of power and justice that directly affect the oppressed.

Critical social theory as a form of multicultural resistance must be wary of locating liberatory praxis in the realm of diachrony – as something to be resolved dialectically in some higher unity outside of the historical struggle and pain and suffering to which we must serve as pedagogical witnesses and agents of radical hope. Yet at the same time, critical pedagogy needs to be wary of forms of populist elitism that privilege only the reform efforts of those who have direct experience with the oppressed. After all, no single unsurpassable and "authentic" reality can be reached through "experience" since no experience is pre-ontologically available outside of a politics of representation.

As multicultural educators informed by critical and feminist pedagogies, we need to keep students connected to the power of the unacceptable and comfortable with the unthinkable by producing critical forms of policy analysis and pedagogy. In tandem with this, we must actively help students to challenge sites of discursive hierarchy rather than delocalizing and dehistoricizing them, and to contest the ways that their desires and pleasures are being policed in relationship to them. It is important that as critical educators, we do not simply manipulate students to accept our intellectual positions nor presume at the same time to speak *for* them. Nor should our critical theorizing be simply a service to the culture of domination by extending student insights into the present system without at the same time challenging the very assumptions of the system. We cannot afford only to temporarily disengage students from the *doxa* – the language of common sense. If we want to recruit students to a transformative praxis, students must not only be encouraged to choose a language of analysis that is undergirded by a project of liberation, but must affectively invest in it.

If we are to be redeemed from our finitude as passive supplicants of history, we must, as students and teachers, adopt more directly oppositional and politically combative social and cultural practices. The destructive fanaticism of present-day xenophobia is only exacerbated by the current ethical motionlessness among many left constituencies. Insurgent intellectuals and theorists must steer a course between the monumentalization of judgment and taste, and a ride on the postmodern currents of despair in a free-fall exhilaration of political impotence.

The present historical moment is populated by memories that are surfacing at the margins of our culture, alòng the fault-lines of our logocentric consciousness. Decolonized spaces are forming in the borderlands – linguistic, epistemological, intersubjective – and these will affect the classrooms of the future. Here saints and Iwa walk together and the Orishas speak to us through the rhythms of the earth and the pulse of the body. The sounds produced in the borderlands are quite different from the convulsive monotones voiced in "Waspano" or "gringoñol" that echo from the schizophrenic boundaries of Weber's iron cage. Here it is in the hybrid polyrhythms of the drum that the new pulse of freedom can be felt. Within such borderlands our pedagogies of liberation can be invested once again with the passion of mystery and the reason of commitment. This is neither a Dionysian rejection of rationality nor a blind, pre-rational plunge into myth but rather an attempt to embrace and reclaim the memories of those pulsating, sinewed bodies that have been forgotten in our modernist assault on difference and uncertainty.

Chapter 5

Pedagogies of dissent and transformation:

A dialogue with Kris Gutierrez

Kris Gutierrez: Your work on schooling, identity, and critical pedagogy is noted for its attempt to locate itself in a discussion of larger social contexts of consumer capitalism and identity formation. You are noted for discussing social and cultural issues related to power that exist outside of the classroom as much as you are for dealing with these issues as they inscribe social relations inside the classroom. This is one of the reasons that I find your work interesting and important. The language that you use is often quite literary and is situated in transdisciplinary theoretical terminology where post-structuralism and theories of post colonialism, among other theoretical perspectives, play a significant role. I think, however, that this mixture of the theoretical and, if you will, poetical, has both advantages and disadvantages. While it gives you new angles and perspectives on the production of subjectivity within capitalist social formations, don't you think it tends to restrict your audience to specialists in the critical social sciences and is less likely to find its way in teacher education courses where I would think that you would want your work to be taken up? Your view of contemporary culture is sometimes considered to be quite pessimistic – although far from nihilistic – and I wonder if your criticisms of everyday life in the United States are perhaps deliberate attempts at overstatement for the sake of shocking your readers into an awareness of the very serious social problems that face us? For instance, I read some comments by you recently in which you talked about the "structural unconscious" of the United States resembling the minds of serial killers such as Ted Bundy. You write in *Thirteen Questions*: "Serial killer Ted Bundy has donated his multiple texts of identity to our structural unconscious and *we are living them*."[1] Is this a motivated exaggeration, a form of theoretical hyperbole for the sake of making a point about the violence that pervades everyday life?

Peter McLaren: Yes and no, Kris. I consider my writing to be simultaneously cynical and utopian. I think it was Adorno who once said something to the effect that in every exaggeration there exists some truth.

And, of course, as somebody who lives in Los Angeles, you don't need to be reminded about violence. Perhaps I focus on the more violent effects of capitalism on social formations because I really do believe that violence exists at the very heart of postindustrial capitalism as a structural precondition for it, that capitalism, in fact, is steadfastly predatory on violence and that it fundamentally constitutes what could be called a "necessary contingency" within what has come to be called "the cultural logic of late capitalism." This is perhaps part of what Arthur Kroker refers to as "the contemporary human situation of living at the violent edge of primitivism and simulation, of an infinite reversibility in the order of things wherein only the excessive cancellation of difference through violence reenergizes the process."[2]

Kris: What about Los Angeles? In his book, *City of Quartz*, Mike Davis has described Los Angeles as existing "on the bad edge of postmodernity."[3] Can you give us a cultural autopsy report?

Peter: Los Angeles is hemorrhaging from its social wounds. The steel fist of despotic capitalism has pulverized the soul of this city. The cowardly federal retreat from the big cities is certainly not going to help stop the bleeding of Los Angeles, a city now referred to by some as the new capital of the Third World. In fact, Los Angeles is facing at the present moment the worst economic crisis since 1938. People seem to forget that after the Watts rebellion in 1965 there were 164 major riots that spread through urban ghettoes across the United States – a period sometimes referred to as the "Second Civil War." This provoked Lyndon Johnson's administration to push its Model Cities Bill through Congress. Yet this historical fact and the recent Los Angeles rebellion have not provoked any serious action on the part of the federal government. You mentioned Mike Davis, whose work I admire very much. Davis has chronicled the crisis of Los Angeles very thoroughly and my comments simply rehearse what he has said on a number of occasions. The current crisis of Los Angeles has to be seen in the context of the combination of international finance capital and low-wage immigrant labor and what some have called the 'Third Worlding" of the city (although I have problems with the way this term is frequently used). There is little cause for optimism about the future of Los Angeles when the Czar of the 1984 Olympics, Peter Ueberroth, is given the task of rebuilding Los Angeles through corporate coalition building and voluntarism. Current government responses that center around the creation of micro-enterprise zones and "infrastructure" are not a great improvement on the former Bush administration's efforts to repackage existing programs under the banner of new while at the same time preventing small business loans and food stamps from reaching needy neighborhoods. Not to mention Dan Quayle's advice to sell the

Los Angeles Airport to help rebuild the city after the uprising. Mike Davis discussed this at length.

Kris: Federal disinvestment policies have had a devastating effect on the city. But the problem is more widespread than California. Key industrial states are reducing welfare and educational entitlements. It's shameful that this could happen in a country which poured so much money into the Gulf War and the S&L bailout.

Peter: Mike Davis describes current government initiatives directed at rebuilding Los Angeles as "shoe string local efforts and corporate charity." He refers to government aid after the rapid deployment of federal combat troops to South Central as little more than an "urban fire sale." I agree with Davis's criticism of the Republican war on big cities. During the Reagan–Bush era, big cities became what Davis describes as "the domestic equivalent of an insolvent, criminalized Third World whose only road to redemption is a combination of militarization and privatization." So now we're faced with what Davis sees as white flight to "edge cities" along beltways and intercity corridors, the Latinization of manual labor, deficits in the jobs-to-housing ratios among blacks, and the new segregation in cities which Davis refers to as "spacial apartheid."

Kris: So how does this affect the average youth? I am the mother of a bi-racial 12-year-old. Despite the fact that he has had access to and participation in academic, cultural, social, and political activities and experiences that privilege him in so many ways, his "Blackness/Latinoness," accentuated by his large frame and his ability and willingness to articulate elaborated sociopolitical analyses of his own life and the world around him, position him at the very margins, the borderlands, of most of his classroom communities. His strong literacy skills are not valued when they are used to write poems about the L.A. uprising or to critique or challenge the content of the classroom curriculum. For example, his Honors History class was recently studying about Mecca. In an attempt to provide the students with a visual portrait of Mecca, the teacher brought in the videotape of the movie "X." The teacher played a segment of the movie, the scene which shows Malcolm arriving in Mecca. After viewing this particular scene, the teacher asked the children to identify what was important. My son's hand shot up as he offered his response, "Well, I think that the fact that Malcolm is being followed by two white C.I.A. agents as he goes to worship in Mecca is very interesting." He was publicly chastised for being off-topic, for not being focused, "we're studying Mecca not Malcolm" quipped his teacher. "But can't we study history when we're studying geography?" asked my son. The teacher simply did not get it. His is not so much the "spacial apartheid" about which Davis writes. Instead, his is an "intellectual apartheid" that silences and marginalizes young adults in schools, particularly Black/Latino males, who take up various forms of resistance and contestation to demand the affirmation of their particular existences. But as Cornel West has asked, "How does one affirm oneself without reenacting negative black stereotypes or overreacting to white supremacist ideals?" How does this discourse of contestation not become what Foucault calls "reverse discourse?"[4] As Henry Louis Gates, Jr. has written, this discourse "remains entrapped within the presuppositions of the discourse it means to oppose, enacts a conflict internal to that 'master discourse'; but when the terms of argument have already been defined, it may look like the only form of contestation possible."[5] How are these factors lived out in the everyday existence of today's urban students?

Peter: That's the key issue for me, Kris. I think we need to look beyond the transgressive desire of graffiti artists and taggers, P.T.A. groups, and anti-crime community activists to find the seedbeds of a new cultural politics. We need to begin the fight against racism and social injustice in the school. In doing so, educators need to ask themselves how students' identities are organized macro-spatially and geopolitically as well as within the micro-politics of the classroom. How are students specifically positioned (in terms of race, class, gender, sexuality) within the grid of late capitalist economic containment and sociopolitical control? How are their structures of affect (what Larry Grossberg calls "mattering maps") organized? How are students situated in both libidinal economies as well as conceptual ones? These are pressing issues, many of which have been addressed by people such as Henry Giroux, Chandra Mohanty, Larry Grossberg, bell hooks, Michele Wallace, and others. It's hard today to draw clear boundaries around the affective and cognitive modes of existence or even to identify ontological categories. This is partly due to the allegorical effects of technology, to what some writers refer to as hyperreality or the imploded regions of cyberspace created by the new rhetoricity of our media-saturated lives. Identity has become fluid, reduced to an abstract code not simply of difference but also indifference. Today it is difficult to have an identity, let alone pursue one. We are, in a very grave sense, always traveling incognito in hyperreality. Students in classrooms are attempting to construct their identity through transgressive acts, through resisting those normalizing laws that render subversive, obscene and unthinkable contestatory possibilities and a pragmatics of hope.

Kris: Fear has taken on a new meaning, it seems. It has become intensified in new ways.

Peter: Kris, I believe that we are witnessing the hyperreal formation of an entirely new species of fear. I live not far from the U.C.L.A. campus in Westwood and nearly every night I hear the wailing cries of drunken students, cries which at once evoke the empty humor of Hee-Haw and the more serious, reflective pain of youthful bodies responding to the slow commodification of their will under late capitalism. Their wails remind me of a desperate attempt to fill in the empty spaces of their souls with a presence-effect of pure intensity. I think that as teachers we need to ask ourselves: What does it mean to live in this fear in an arena of shifting forms of global capitalism? How does such fear direct urban policy and school policy? How is everyday life saturated by such fear and what role does this fear play in student learning? What kinds of learning need to take place in order to resist or overcome the fear of participating in the construction of terminal identities? What politics of liberation must be engaged in as part of a struggle for a better future for our schools and our youth who attend them? Brian Massumi has done a brilliant job in discussing the breaking down of the "humanistic" integrative strategy of Keynesian economics and the advent of "unapologetically ruthless strategies of displacement, fluidification, and intensification."[6] We're talking here about the utilitarian and socially repugnant dismantling of the welfare state and the restructuring and dissolution of identities and entire lives that follow such a dismantling. Briefly put, Kris, displacement refers to exporting industrial production to the "Third World" where the growing middle class there can provide an important market outlet for consumer durables. In the U.S. economies of the center this means producing more information and communication services in new and mostly non-unionized domains, leaving youth to their "McJobs" (to coin a term by Canadian novelist, Douglas Coupland in his book, *Generation X*).[7] Massumi uses the term "fluidification" to mean the increasing fluidity of capital and the workforce as well as creating rapid product turnovers. Use-value in this case is increasingly replaced by image-value. Massumi uses the term "intensification" to refer to basically the merging of production and consumption which is accompanied by the disappearance of leisure and a focus on self-improvement in the service of gaining a competitive edge in the marketplace. Massumi notes that the very contours of postmodern existence have become a form of surplus value as the wage relation virtually collapses into the commodity relation. Capitalism has colonized all geographical and social space and schools have not been immune. In fact, they are perhaps one of the most vulnerable social sites for this kind of colonization as we can see in the example of Channel One and the powerful forces that are being put in place by corporate logic to ensure the privatization of education. Massumi argues that capitalism is co-extensive with its own inside such that it has now become both a field of immanence and exteriority. There is no escape. There is only fear. Fear, reports Massumi, is now the objective condition of subjectivity in the era of late capitalism. In this sense it means something more than a fear of downward mobility but rather the constitution of the self within a market culture and market morality. When non-market values disappear from everyday life – such as love and compassion – nihilism sets in. Cornel West speaks eloquently about this dilemma, especially in relation to urban settings.

I agree with Anthony Appiah when he says that Weber mistook the Enlightenment universalization of the secular for the triumph of instrumental reason. I believe, as does Appiah, that the Enlightenment has more to do with the transformation of the real into sign value than it does with the incursion of instrumental rationality into the multiple spheres of the social. What Weber missed was the incorporation of all areas of public and private life into the money economy. There exists no autochthonous and monolithic space of pure culture or uncontaminated identity – everything has been commodified. Use-value is now supported by what Massumi calls "fulfillment-effect" or "image-value." We are, all of us, the subjects of capital – the *point d'appui* between wage relations and commodity relations, with commodification representing the hinge between the future and the past. According to Massumi, consummation and consumption are continually conflated under late capitalism, as we increasingly come to live in the time-form of the future perfect or future anterior which can be expressed in the existential equation "will have bought = will have been." Surplus value has become, in effect, a metonym for everyday existence. Of course, all of this points to the urgency of understanding how students invest in their lives and bring meaning to everyday life. It suggests students need to understand more about the structural and more fluid contexts that produce their everyday lives and how their identities are constructed out of the vectors and circuits of capital, social relations, cultural forms, and relations of power. It means understanding more than simply how the media and dominant school curricula control the representation of the racialized other and influence our attitudes and desires.

I will be the first to emphasize the importance of understanding the politics of representation and the ways in which our subjectivities are constructed through the economies of signs in our media-saturated world. But as Giroux and others have emphasized, we need to go further than this. We need to understand how identities are produced through structural relations and constraints and the systems of intelligibility we have historically inherited and invented and which produce us on a daily basis. It means understanding the causes of oppression and exploitation and the material effects of economic practices and capitalist logics. Something that has struck me for quite some time has recently been articulated in a brilliant book by Rey Chow, *Writing Diaspora*.[8] Global capitalism and its technological apparatuses of domination have ushered in what Chow refers to as "a universal speed culture." Here she is referring, after Virilio, to the mediatization of information. Such mediatization and human life, while incompatible, are now interchangeable. Electronic communication makes this possible. She notes that human labor is "finally exchangeable in digitalized form, without going through the stage of the concrete commodity whose mysteriousness Marx so memorably describes" [p. 180]. We now live in a world of what Chow calls "electronic immigrants" who work in countries such as India and Russia where well-trained but jobless technical professionals sell their labor for low wages to U.S. computer companies. They work through the phone lines (where there are no import duties) as cheap data processors. This digitalized form of labor has implications for the potential of developing critical forms of literacy in school. Moving now to the question of schooling, you have been developing a politics of literacy that I think is extremely important in helping educators to understand how knowledge is constructed within a variety of social contexts. Can you talk about the role social context plays in your own work with immigrant Latino children?

Kris: As you know, Peter, the focus of my work involves communities and schools here in Los Angeles and concerns itself primarily with how contexts of learning in schools influence the nature of the teaching and learning of literacy for linguistically and culturally diverse student populations. This means doing intensive ethnographic fieldwork in both the schools and the communities. In the course of doing this ethnographic work, we[9] have examined how certain contexts provide or deny access to particular forms of learning and literacy learning in particular. I believe this kind of work helps make visible the ways in which literacy instruction continues to function as a way of socializing historically marginalized students into particular forms of knowing and being that make access to critical forms and practices of literacy in either their first or second language difficult. What becomes evident in this work is how this socialization process cannot be understood apart from the sociohistorical context in which it occurs and implicates how teachers' beliefs influence who gets to learn and how.

Peter: It seems to me, Kris, that teachers have a mandate to understand their own process of identity formation as well as those of their students. And in order to do this they need to at least have a rudimentary understanding of how their subjectivities are produced. They need to break free from the time-encrusted conceptions of identity, which, throughout the history of liberal humanism, have given credibility to the idea of the transparent ego, the autonomous will or the metaphysical illusion of self-identity. They need to escape from the hallucinatory idea of the boundaried, self-sufficient agent of history and see how anonymous political and economic structures colonize their lifeworlds, instrumentalize forms of human agency, and sediment forms of desire. And then they need to engage such practices of colonization with some normative and regulative idea of justice and human freedom. Which is not to suggest teachers develop some metaphysical or transcendental platform of ethico-political judgement.

Kris: That's true. However, this country has found itself completely unprepared and, in some cases, unwilling to address the educational and social needs of its multicultural student population. As a result of the shortage of multicultural, multilingual teachers, teachers are given emergency credentials to teach. These teachers have little opportunity to develop an understanding of what it means to teach in a multilingual and multicultural society. Moreover, teacher preparation programs continue to focus on the teaching and learning of monocultural and acontextual "models" of instruction such as the seven-step lesson plan. Who needs to be critical and reflective if the continued use of decontextualized "teacher proofed" methods, materials, and curricula is the normative practice in schools?

Peter: How do your studies help teachers in this task?

Kris: I would argue that these long-term, classroom-based studies help us understand how teachers themselves, through their own experiences as students and through their preservice and inservice experience, have been socialized to particular understandings of "knowing" and "doing." Further constrained by deplorable working conditions and inadequate preparation, these teachers have little opportunity for reflective, critical practice. Understanding how these cycles of socialization influence classroom culture helps explain how the structures, that is, the social and discursive practices of many classrooms, reflect the relations of power and systems of knowledge distribution in the larger society. Critical theorists such as yourself, Michael Apple and Henry Giroux provide the needed meta-analysis of the function of schools in corporate capitalistic societies and the effects of its pedagogies on multicultural student populations. However, to truly transform the nature of teaching and learning requires work at multiple levels and requires the development of situated understandings of what counts as teaching and learning in classrooms and the larger social context.

Peter: I agree with you. Your attentiveness to multiple levels of analysis is what I admire so much about your work. Of course, social life would be impossible without some form of discursive and non-discursive domestication. All forms of nomination – of naming – are in some ways violent in that the world is reduced to objects of knowledge. I'm not opposed to naming social life but I am opposed to certain values that are embodied in the formation of the social at the level of micro-politics as well as macro-politics, whose persistent and motivated unnaming further reproduces existing relations of power and privilege.

Kris: I know that some critical theorists are critical of micro-analytic educational research and I certainly agree with much of the criticism, of the failure to locate the dynamics of classrooms and school life in larger sociopolitical contexts. I also believe that much of educational research does not discuss the ways in which hegemonic classroom practices are both the co-construction of particular sets of individuals, as well as the reinstantiation of larger sociohistorical processes and practices; however, I think that some critics of classroom based, action-oriented research have not spent enough time in schools and, thus, do not understand that unless we can also unpackage the construction of these hegemonic practices at the micro-level we will not be able to assist teachers in their attempts to transform the contexts for learning and their roles in that process.

Peter: Yes Kris. I agree. But we need to be wary of researchers who supply us with specific contextual data in ways that enable such data to become unwittingly recoded and reconverted in teaching practices professing to be liberatory so that it becomes complicitous with the dominant ideology of colonialism.

Kris: That's always an important issue. As Gramsci reminded us, intellectuals are experts in legitimation and in defining what counts as knowledge. I'm reminded of linguistic anthropologist, Charles Goodwin's analysis of the first Rodney King case.[10] In his essay, he demonstrated how the prosecution recodified the data frame by frame, created new schemas and provided an institutionalized scientific language to redefine Rodney King as the violent, crazed aggressor and the police behavior as the appropriate and measured response to imminent danger. The data were recodified and, thus, redefined, the obvious brutality. A good lesson here. The fact that a researcher is engaged in an anti-imperialist ethnographic study is no guarantee that a transformative politics and pedagogy will always emerge; it does not prevent at some level the recuperation of some of the very colonialist discourses one is contesting. That's what makes our work so difficult. I'm sure you noticed the reaction to Willis's *Learning to Labor* by feminist researchers and to your early ethnographic work. I believe some of the engagements you had in your formative years as an ethnographic researcher with your critics has helped deepen and extend your own methods of analysis.

Peter: I try to be ruthlessly self-critical about my own work. When you are engaged in a collective struggle, the stakes are always high.

Kris: The task for transforming instruction is an urgent one and, as you know, action-oriented, ethnographic research is one way of advancing this struggle. I believe that many teachers recognize the need for radical change. But teachers also need assistance in re-imagining instructional contexts in which a problem-posing curriculum, an organic curriculum, emerges from the sociocultural and linguistic experiences of the participants; contexts in which the teaching and learning of literacy leads to critical, reflective practice.

Peter: Kris, elaborate if you would on the kind of ethnographic work that you feel is central to the emancipatory agenda of criticalists in the field.

Kris: I'm interested in ethnographic research that is informed by transdisciplinary work – cross-cultural, sociocultural, sociopolitical, and sociohistorical perspectives concerning the relationships among language, development, culture, and power. The work of Jean Lave, Barbara Rogoff, Elinor Ochs, and Marjorie Goodwin comes to mind. It is these kinds of studies that I believe are extremely useful in helping us understand the sociohistorical and sociocultural nature of development and in producing contextualized or situated understandings of the effects of current schooling practices on particular groups of students. But such work has to also have a social and political agenda to be transformative.

Peter: When you talk about effects on "particular groups of students" I take it that you mean the contextual specificity of schooling practices in relation to the construction of gendered, classed, and racialized subjects.

Kris: Precisely. Classroom-based research that identifies what counts as knowledge in classrooms, and that describes how that knowledge is constructed, as well as whose knowledge gets constructed, is essential to transforming schools from the bottom up and for understanding the social construction of classroom culture, of how gendered, classed and racialized subjects are constructed. The hegemonic practices that structure the teacher-centered pedagogy of so many of the classrooms of bicultural students, for example, must be unpackaged at the micro-level, that is, in the moment-to-moment interactions of teacher and students as they participate in everyday classroom routines. I have found that this kind of research provides teachers with both the theoretical and analytical tools, as well as a language for transforming their own pedagogies. This process of becoming a critical teacher/researcher, however, requires a redefinition of the hierarchical social relationships between researcher and classroom teacher; it requires movement away from the traditional objectification of those studied to action-oriented research in which both teacher-researcher and researcher are brought together to define the research agenda, as well as their own positions in those processes. In short, these research agendas have social and political consequences.

Peter: What concerns me about the hegemonic articulations of dominant schooling practices is the way in which teachers participate in institutionalized structures, practices, and discourses that set up forms of racial differentiation and differential exclusion. It is the "whiteness" of the dominant ideology that metonymizes the standard curricula and constructs the legitimating norms for our pedagogies. I'm talking here about what David Theo Goldberg refers to as "the constitution of alterity."[11] Goldberg is referring here to the hold of racialized discourses and racist exclusions over subject formation and expression. I don't think that, as educators, we have carefully thought through this issue in our day-to-day teaching practices, especially the way in which racist discourses become conjoined with the discourses of class, gender, nation, and capitalism. As Goldberg notes, all racisms have to do with exclusions on the basis of belonging to particular racial groups, even though there is not a single transhistorical meaning of the word "race." I think we need to do more ethnographic work on how racial groups are constituted discursively and how race is inscribed by the interests of different groups and institutions and how racial preferences are assigned. Some of my recent visits to Brazil have been very illuminating in terms of understanding the discursive constitution of racialized subjects. For instance, racialized descriptions of individuals based on morphology and skin color are much more nuanced there. Some of the descriptive categories include the *mulato escuro* (dark skin) and the *mulato claro* (light skin) which refer to persons of mixed racial groups (Caucasian and Afro-Brazilian). One of my African-American students reminded me that the term *mulato* is derived from the term "mule" – a cross between a donkey and a horse and which is often born sterile. The demonizing of the African can be seen in this choice of term, as well as the fear of miscegenation. The *sarara* has light skin with blonde or red kinky hair and varied facial features while the *moreno* has dark curly hair but light skin that is not white. The *cabo verde* has thin lips and a narrow straight nose whereas the *preto retinto* has black skin and a broad nose and kinky hair. The *cabra* and *cabrocha* are lighter than the *preto* but darker than the *cabo verde*. Whites are also subclassified according to skin color, hair, and facial attributes. Here in the U.S. our system of classification is in terms of binary oppositions – black versus white – whereas in Brazil there is a complex system of differences based on distinctions. But these distinctions are still made on the basis of privileging whiteness. Whiteness is still a marker of special distinction and one has to see this historically and link it to the capitalist elites who have the power to suture ideological discourses to material relations of political, social, and economic advantage. How will global capitalism continue to reinforce such distinctions? That, to me, is an important issue. Howard Winant's work has been helpful to me to understand racism in Brazil and elsewhere.

Kris: But these distinctions are also made here in the U.S. For example, Chicano sociologists, Eddie Telles and Ed Murguia, have identified how phenotype influences which Chicanos have access to particular academic and economic opportunities.[12] Still, I agree that we need more qualitative work that allows us to see how privileging on the basis of whiteness, language and class is instantiated in the classroom. I also believe that qualitative work that is informed by a very different epistemology allows us to see the effects of unidirectional socialization processes of schools. For example, the socializing nature of institutional contexts is made evident in the institutional nature of the classroom discourse and interaction among participants and in the instantiation of teacher beliefs in the contexts for learning. For example, we have observed how the uniform turn-taking pattern of speech in the many classrooms we have studied exhibits overwhelming adherence to institutionally appropriate procedures – procedures that are both historically and socially situated. In particular, a differential and restricted system of knowledge distribution and access to meaningful conversation and participation characterize the normative teaching and learning practices of many classrooms of linguistically and culturally diverse children. In these contexts, we found that the rules and rights of participation were set by the teacher, that is, the teacher determined who was allowed to speak, how often, for how long, when, to whom, and for what purpose. Thus, the social hierarchy and the asymmetrical social relationships among participants and their roles in the learning process privileged teachers' knowledge in the knowledge exchange system. Consequently, the linguistic and sociocultural experiences of these Latino children rarely became incorporated into the classroom narratives, as they were routinely denied access to meaningful and legitimate participation, that is, access to practice as a means of learning. Moreover, access to the means and forms of learning for Latino children is restricted at several levels of instruction. For example, these students are provided with limited opportunities to develop comprehensive literacy skills (i.e., reading, writing, talking, critical thinking, as well as the sociocultural knowledge needed for successful participation in this discourse community) in both their native and second language, that is, few opportunities to become biliterate. Further, the classroom discourse which serves as the medium of instruction is itself restrictive and, thus, limits opportunities for students to engage in and produce the very discourse they are expected to learn. Even when they are encouraged to produce written and oral text, they are not encouraged to use literacy in ways that allow them to narrate their own experiences, much less to critique the sociopolitical and economic realities in their everyday lives. In this way, both the language of instruction and the form of discourse both reconstruct and preserve the traditional forms of language use, interaction and the traditional knowledge exchange system constitutive of teacher-centered instruction – instruction that is centered around a decontextualized and uncritical curriculum. Thus, the relationships between discourse, power and forms of knowledge are made evident in everyday practices of literacy instruction.[13]

Current language practices in schools, despite attempts to incorporate bilingual instruction, provide the most effective means of denying access to both knowledge and practice. Richard Ruiz's research on language policies and practices, for example, points out that particular language policies are, in fact, responses to the presence of particular language communities rather than a need or desire to improve or expand language practices.[14] Current language policies aimed at quickly moving children from native language usage to English are no different.

Such language programs are historically rooted in the policies and practices of a monocultural and monolingual society in which assimilation is highly valued and necessary. Multiculturalism and multilingualism are seen as threats to the social, political and cultural stability of this country. In these times of economic crisis, as support for the wave of anti-immigrant legislation increases, it becomes even more critical to understand how these sentiments manifest themselves in school policies and practices, in classroom instruction.

In our literacy studies, we find that the linguistic, economic, educational and sociocultural needs of immigrant Latino children, particularly the Mexican immigrant, are still defined by the same Eurocentric lens used to define earlier immigrant experiences. However, these children are not monocultural, monolingual; they, and their families, transmigrate from Los Angeles to Mexico, for example, at least several times each year. The sociocultural, political and linguistic realities of their everyday lives require them to draw on their bicultural experiences and their various languages and discourses. If we continue to define these students' experience as being similar to the immigrant experience of European-American and even of other linguistically and culturally different immigrants, we simply will not be able to understand the educational and larger social needs of this immigrant student population. In defining them as traditional immigrants, we fail to understand how transmigration better explains their existence; to understand how these students are not monocultural but bicultural children in a multicultural society. From this perspective, the linguistic and cultural characteristics of this student population are not the same as those of children who have previously immigrated to this country. Thus, a more appropriate response to the linguistic needs of these students would be to create language policies that move beyond monolingualism and bilingualism to policies that promote biliteracy: that is, language practices that focus on the acquisition of a more comprehensive set of literacy skills, including writing, in both the native and second language.

Such policies and practices acknowledge the complex linguistic and social needs of a multicultural society. Further, this recognition is an important first step in redefining bicultural children as a tremendously valuable national resource. This redefinition, however, will necessarily challenge the folk knowledge that currently informs so much of school practice and will also challenge current attitudes that underlie the growing anti-immigrant sentiment in our country.

Peter: One of the crucial issues for criticalists working in the field of literacy is to rethink the conditions of possibility for the subaltern to speak, to escape the labyrinth of subjugation, to make critical counter-statements against the logic of domination that informs the dominant white supremacist ideology of patriarchal capitalism and to transform the ideological precepts that make up the "imponderability" of everyday life where social relations of power and privilege are naturalized throughout the curriculum. As Brackette Williams has pointed out,[15] if you use the term "American" without a hyphen you are taken to be white and if you do hyphenate the term, then you are not only categorized as non-white but also as "ethnic." Non-white groups are defined in our schools as "problems," a status which Vine Deloria argues "relegates minority existence into an adjectival status within the homogeneity of American life."[16] The conservative multiculturalists writing under the sign of whiteness are trying to protect the unitary cohesiveness of cultural life, making culture isomorphic with the logic of assimilation and homogenization and a unified racio-national configuration. Even the difference-in-unity of the liberals and left-liberals attempts a cultural balancing act in which harmony and consensus is sought while minorities continue to be excluded and oppressed. Interestingly, David Theo Goldberg suggests that capitalism's new demands for flexible accumulation loosens the sociocultural and spacial boundaries that help to promote racialized antagonisms. There is a greater opportunity for transgressing "the established racialized limits of spatial confines and political imagination." At the same time Goldberg notes that diversity in the public domain is challenged and delimited by the privatization of "univocality, exclusion, and exclusivity." In other words, diversity itself has become commodified in the interests of corporate capitalism. Multiculturalism is one of the hottest commodities presently circulating in the global marketplace. I want to know more about the direction of your work in relation to multiculturalism.

Kris: In our work, we attempt to redirect the discourse on multiculturalism from an exclusively sociopolitical discussion to one that is also informed by theories and research that help us better understand the relationship between language, culture, development, and power. To make the shift to include sociocultural frames, however, requires an understanding of how socioeconomic and sociopolitical forces gave rise to the emergence of multiculturalism. Although multiculturalism is most often identified with educational reform movements, the roots of multiculturalism are grounded in economic and sociopolitical processes. From a world systems perspective, for example, multiculturalism is the ideological reflection of two medium-term processes that have unfolded in the core area of the world system (e.g. Europe and the U.S. and the other rich countries of the advanced capitalist societies). The first process is a structural response produced by the workings of global capital in the post-World War II era. These world processes are eroding and recreating national boundaries and are diffusing the notion and practice of nation stateness. Thus, global production and simultaneous widespread global migration are challenging the notion of monoculturalism – a concept inextricably linked to the concept of nation building. From this perspective, multiculturalism has emerged as a consequence of global capitalism and its accompanying great migration has thrown monoculturalism into a crisis; multiculturalism in part, then, has emerged as an unintended consequence of these worldwide socioeconomic processes.

Peter: But we need to be reminded of the specificity of these processes, especially in light of the growing nationalisms in places like the former Soviet Union and Yugoslavia.

Kris: Of course. It's also important to understand that the need for multiculturalism has also been created by sociopolitical forces. For example, multiculturalism is also the sociopolitical challenge of the subordinated peoples both in the peripheral areas of the global world system and in the racialized areas of the core countries, the people participating in national liberation struggles in the Third World and those struggling for human and civil rights in the first world.

Multiculturalism is a new paradigm of race relations; a new concept of the proper relations between ethnic groups and races and is a reflection of the post-World War II challenge by people who have been marginalized and colonized. The ethnic and discriminated races have challenged the assumption of the inherent superiority of European cultures and have demanded the elevation of their cultures to equal those of Europe or white America. This particular sociological analysis attributes the emergence of multiculturalist movements to the inability of the monocultural systems to control the processes of globalizing capital and to enforce the sustained subordination of a racialized strata of its working people. However, until an overarching concept of nationhood is created – a concept that accommodates the globalizing tendencies of postindustrial capitalism and the inherent instability it creates – multiculturalism itself cannot serve to resolve the crisis, as you point out in the examples of the former Soviet Union and Yugoslavia.

Thus, despite its limited impact, multiculturalism has already begun to challenge monocultural beliefs and practices and has begun to destabilize Eurocultural strongholds. Yet, we need to recognize that we are in a period of transition for which the social order has yet to be established. We need to understand that monoculturalism requires a hierarchy of cultures and particular power relations. Multiculturalism requires a transformation of these hierarchies and the accompanying social relationships among diverse populations.

In an educational context, however, few who are doing work in multicultural education address the necessity of transforming traditional hierarchical relationships and redefining the purposes of education. Some forms of multicultural education have emerged as a means for celebrating difference. But these are additive models that do not challenge existing paradigms and frames of reference. Educators, then, have come to terms in limited ways with addressing some issues of ethnicity but still have difficulty understanding how to deal with culturally and linguistically diverse communities. The discourse around the education of bicultural children still defines the educational and social needs of these African-American, Latino, Native American and Asian children as problems that need to be addressed. Cornel West underscores this point: ". . . we confine discussions about race in American to the 'problems' black people pose for whites rather than consider what this way of viewing black people reveals about us as a nation." That's why you and others are using the term "critical multiculturalism" to distinguish the criticalist multiculturalist agenda from those of conservatives and liberals.

Thus, to fully understand the difficulty in reforming practices that promote inequity, we must recognize that such practices, as David Theo Goldberg suggests, are deeply and historically rooted in beliefs about racial hierarchies and capacities; beliefs that are an inherent part of monocultural/monolingual societies. So part of the resistance to the implementation of radical pedagogies that call for transformative practice, such as language programs that promote biliteracy, for example, is a resistance to multiculturalism and multilingualism and other changes that disrupt the maintenance of racialized ways of life.

Peter: I'm wondering if we can discuss some of the possibilities that are emerging from criticalist work such as yours.

Kris: While I recognize that only limited change can occur without major reform on a wider scale, critical educators, in collaboration with classroom teachers, must begin the process of rethinking teaching and learning in a multicultural society. I'm very hopeful about the possibility of transforming classrooms into very different kinds of communities in which dialogic rather than monologic forms of instruction are evident – heteroglossic communities in which the social relationships and discourses are dramatically transformed. In our studies of the social contexts of literacy, so many of the classrooms we studied reinstantiated traditional social relationships of teacher as information giver and student as receiver of knowledge and, thus, created very restricted forms of learning and limited opportunity for the linguistic, social and cultural experiences of the children to become organically constitutive of classroom life. However, we did identify some classrooms in which very different contexts for literacy learning existed. In these classrooms, the co-construction of discourse, activity and knowledge were the normative practices for both teacher and student. Instruction was not driven by what Stanley Aronowitz calls methodologically oriented practice; instead, in these more interactive contexts for learning, or what we call "responsive/collaborative" classrooms, the nature of participation for both students and teachers was transformed and created new, as well as more, opportunity spaces for students to function as apprentices and as experts in the literacy learning process. In these communities of practice, the socialization process was bi-directional and students with varying levels of experience and expertise were full participants in legitimate and meaningful praxis. They were not relegated to skill-drill-and-kill work; instead meaningful discourse and practice were both the means and the ends to critical literacy.[17]

In these more democratic classrooms, there were zones of possibility for both teachers and students to dialogue, to pose critical questions, to co-construct both process and product. They were critical ethnographers in both their classrooms and surrounding communities. In this way, the curriculum of the classroom relied on "funds of knowledge" that existed in children's families, social networks and communities.[18] Literacy learning, then, necessarily addressed the lived experiences of children. While it's true that these classrooms had not resolved issues of power relations, racism and sexism, these were themes that informed many of the classroom narratives. In this way, I believe that responsive/collaborative classrooms set up the conditions for problem-posing pedagogy and increase the potential for radical pedagogy, for different representations of and stances toward knowledge and different ways of "doing and being student and teacher." It's an encouraging beginning.[19]

As we develop new pedagogies for teaching the new student population there is much to be learned from the struggles in ethnic, woman, and cultural studies. For example, cultural studies programs have brought together transdisciplinary perspectives and methods of inquiry to more comprehensively examine the social, economic, political, cultural, and historical dimensions that shape the lives of America's ethnic and racial groups. Thus, cultural studies reflect the intersection of issues of race, ethnicity, class, gender, culture, and power.

One of the central aims of ethnic studies, for example, has been to make visible the essential philosophies, cultures, and histories of ethnic peoples and, thus, to produce a complete scholarship that necessarily challenges prevailing Euro-centric thought and methods. From this perspective, then, ethnic studies is not the inclusion or integration of new themes or experiences into the existing curriculum; that would simply require studying new subjects through the same Eurocentric lens, rather than a process by which students, teachers, and researchers develop new forms of agency. Instead, ethnic studies seeks to locate itself in a much broader sociocultural terrain in which groups of color and women of color are integral to the understanding of everyday life in an American context.

Because ethnic studies was not conceptualized as an addition or an appendage of existing curricula, the development of ethnic studies provided the occasion not only to create a new epistemology but necessarily became an occasion to substantively transform both pedagogy and curricula, to develop a very different stance towards the production of knowledge. Curricular transformation, then, was not an inadvertent by-product of ethnic studies. Rather, the epistemological roots of ethnic studies were reflected in the interdisciplinary and cross-disciplinary nature of its methodology, in the content of the curriculum and its pedagogy. In this way, ethnic studies was constitutive of a coherent content, methodology and pedagogy which allowed the development of a curricula that focused on an examination of the interactions among particular groups of people and others and on the explication of these experiences within and across the total population. Transforming the general curricula for a multicultural student population requires the same processes. I would argue, however, for a pedagogy that does not promote an essentialist agenda.

I spend a great deal of time working with teachers and working in the teacher education programs. There's so much to be done. This transformation is not about using the right materials, reform-oriented pedagogies or celebrating ethnic life in the form of food, fun and fiestas, or simply "retraining" teachers so that they become tolerant or sympathetic to difference. It's about developing a very different space for teachers, students and parents in the educational process.

Peter: I think one of the biggest problems in establishing a criticalist movement in pedagogy on a wider scale than it presently exists has been the pervasiveness of the way experience is understood and employed by bourgeois educators. There has been a strong tendency to essentialize experience, to view experience as self-evident. Some groups argue that there is an essential Chicano or Chicana experience, or Anglo experience, or African-American experience or gay experience. Personal history is spoken about as if it somehow affords transparent access to the real, as though it were removed from the effects of larger structures of mediation. This is to hold to the mistaken belief that experiences constitute some originary or foundational event. Identity is therefore conceived as an original authorship, as possessing the means to foreclose contingency and stabilize or impose a unity on the process of signification. It's my contention that in such cases the employment of experience as a referent for a transformative pedagogy needs to be rethought because too often it leads to the reproduction of those strategies of containment, regulation, and normalization that one is trying to contest. I've been in classes where students demand to speak from their own experiences and where the voice of experience becomes for them a license to render as the ultimate authority whatever they happen to "feel" about an event. Classes based on the privileging of personal experience and a fear of theory tend to degenerate into a forum for telling personal anecdotes or stories. Now I believe stories are extremely important since they narrativize our cultural world in important ways. And life experiences are absolutely crucial to identity formation and historical agency. But, as I have argued elsewhere (along with Henry Giroux, Joan Scott, and others), experience is fundamentally discursive. That is, we cannot separate experience from language and the conflict among and contradictions within systems of signification. Experience permits us to establish a system of similarities and differences. But we can never "have" an experience and then simply attach a word or concept to that experience. Because experience is always a form of languaging – it is always an event. A material event in the sense that language always reflects and dialectically re-initiates social relations, structural relationships to otherness, and the world of objects and events. But it is always an after-effect, too, since it is always housed within particular conceptual frameworks and can never exist in a pure state unsullied by ideology or interest. Experience, in other words, never occurs outside of its specific forms of intelligibility or signification. It always occurs in relationship to the normativizing power of social life and the exclusionary logics of dominant subject positions. All experiences occur within more or less established regimes of signification or meanings. We need a theoretical language if we want to be able to interrogate the manner in which we enable our experiences to be understood and acted upon. Joan Scott notes that since experience is discursive it "is at once always already an interpretation *and* is in need of interpretation." She adds something very insightful when she says: "Experience is a subject's history. Language is the site of history's enactment."[20] We cannot separate experience from language. After all, experience is produced by systems of intelligibility that help to recognize it *as experience*. When we acquire a new language of analysis we reinvent experience retroactively. For instance, when my students discover feminist theory, some of them are motivated to return to their prior experiences and relive them through the conceptual frameworks of this new language and their experiences become transformed as a result. Confronting the often suffocating and periphrastic values of the controlling patriarchal and white supremacist hegemonic formations often leads these students to new ways of understanding, of acting *in and on* the world. Students acquire a new form of agency. While experience is a linguistic event, Scott emphasizes that it is not confined to a fixed order of meaning. We read texts but are also read by them. But because texts read us, that is, install us as readers within particular discursive communities, this doesn't mean we are simply the dupes of our language use. Experiences don't determine our agency in the world but certainly help constitute it. Of course, to a certain extent our experiences are overdetermined by larger social, cultural and economic structures. They are installed and constituted by a signifying chain of prior meanings and usages. Yet they don't determine our identities but often create the conditions of possibility for our ability to understand them and recreate them. In order to make the experiences of the oppressed more visible and more central to our way of understanding the world, we need to be able to understand the discursive processes and practices that constitute our experiences and subjectivities. We need to be careful that our denaturalizing strategies (making the familiar strange and the strange familiar) do not recuperate whiteness as a foundational reference against which alterity and abjectness is constructed. Kris, I'm growing weary of the banner flown by the liberals which announces that we must be merely tolerant of difference. This suggests to me that the "other" to whom they hope to show tolerance is considered to be quite repugnant. Of course, liberal multiculturalism sees racism as some personal lifestyle problem and not a serious social and historical problem in which teachers must be called upon to interrogate the linkage of epistemological and social history as well as education and political culture. We don't need a pedagogy of lifestyle tolerance. Nor do we need a pedagogy of attitude adjustments – the police carry that out successfully with batons and tear gas. We need to understand racialized discourse as complexly linked to the totality of discourses that make up our "empire of signs." We also need to understand how this linkage is reproductive of social relations of domination and oppression. In other words, our experiences are always constrained by conditions of possibility – systems of power that give significance to particular experiences. We need to transform these systems of power when they unwittingly give legitimacy to racist and homophobic social and pedagogical practices. Critical pedagogy tries to contest the sovereign and imperial discourses of the controlling hegemonic formations. It is a disintegrative stance, refusing to allow the marginalized, the immiserated and the powerless to be absorbed into the cultural dominant. It works against the incrementalist position of slowly "adding on" minorities to the mainstream in order to give minorities a stronger voice *here and now.* It renegotiates sociopolitical space. It moves towards the direction of Goldberg's "transformative incorporation" by following an "antiracist insistence upon incorporative politics over some exclusionary social standard." Critical pedagogy strikes at the practices of oppression in their many guises, limiting and where possible, eliminating, the conditions of possibility for their ongoing production. Let me uncoil a particular concern I have at this moment.

Part of the problem with theorizing about multiculturalism can be attributed to the turn taken by some postmodern theorists who virtually ignore, and thereby deny, the legitimacy of non-Western articulations and theorizations of the postmodern condition with respect to issues of difference. Political efforts by Latin American theorists to de-hegemonize the West both in terms of theory and direct political intervention need to be engaged by Euro-American postmodern theorists. This is important so that we not only understand more deeply cultural hybridization and the mestizajae identities of, say, Mexican and Peruvian groups but also the identity formation of groups within the United States. I call this a politics of border identity or a pedagogy of border identity. By this I mean, broadly put, reinventing Euro-American identities by locating ourselves Otherwise. We achieve this, at least in part, by listening loudly to the discourses of liberation sounded from the South, to voices populated by the traces of counter-hegemonic struggles for liberation, voices inscribed by the suffering and strength of subjugated peoples. We are then in a better politico-conceptual position from which to understand and exercise judgment. We are then enabled to inhabit other standpoint epistemologies from which to resituate ourselves within, between, and across borders simultaneously. We come to know in a more multivalenced way the formation of our own subjectivities as well as those created south of the physical border that defines the nation states of Latin America. I am talking about occupying new linguistic, cultural, and epistemological zones, occult sites which are always in flux, surrounded by culturally webbed membranes of meaning that are always already fissured and pockmarked by class, race, gender, and sexual antagonisms. We need the Third World to better understand ourselves, but we need not keep on draining their historically ravaged veins. The United States is a nation of imperialist gluttons, identity addicts, predators who feel metaphysically and mythically privileged to drain material resources across borders and then we excrete our cultural excess back to our victims and they are supposed to feel grateful that we offer to let them eat our shit. The point is that the Third World may be the site from which we can begin to rethink our own revolutionary struggle in the United States. It may surprise some that the politicalization of Foucault in 1968 was not due to his involvement in the May student rebellion in France in 1968 but, as he notes, was influenced by his involvement in the Third World, specifically the March 1968 rebellions in Tunisia (Foucault 1991). Western society is now indifferent to virtue and bored with integrity and for the most part has postponed history altogether. While I don't want to romanticize the Third World – goodness, this was part of our problem with Cuba, especially – I do believe we need to create a ground of struggle from which we can contest the very logic of capital, especially its hyperindustrial incarnations which have produced among the uncommon common people and bourgeoisie alike, a type of entropy of the will. We need to listen to Marcos and other leaders of the Zapatista resistance who are offering us a political wake-up call. Rather than locating such resistance as a retro-chic narrative of incitement, and trend-setting posture of antagonism, a geopolitical pocket of decadent rebelliousness; rather than situating resistance and struggle from the scorched, decimated debris of Euro-American liberalism, in which efforts at political struggle become artifactualized, museumified, and transformed into standard canonizations and curatorial texts, into officially salvaged, sovereign and denunciated objects, it would serve as well both to reclaim and reinvent not only the narrative order and cultural logic of resistance but its instantiation in acts of physical, cultural, and political rebellion – one that takes seriously everyday praxis in the interest of social justice as something more than simply an "event status" for the posturing intellectual. We need more than the experiential essentialism of liberals to do this.

Kris: Peter, I agree with your analysis of how experience has been essentialized by liberal educators. What we're arguing for is not a liberal "I'm Okay. You're Okay" pedagogy. Instead, like Lisa Delpit,[21] we also expose the effects of liberal pedagogy on bicultural students. In our research, for example, we have identified the consequences that some forms of liberal reform pedagogies, such as the teaching of "the writing process" to second language learners, have on the development of literacy and biliteracy. As I previously stated, despite vigorous attempts to reform the curriculum, there were almost no opportunities in many of the classrooms we studied, neither in the curriculum nor in the participation structures of the classroom, for students' voices and experiences, in either written and oral form, to be affirmed and to become constitutive of classroom knowledge. There was little opportunity to build on prior knowledge and experience and, thus, to expand, revise, or challenge prior understandings of both the local and larger society. Such practices are fundamental to development.

In our work, we too insist that teachers be theoretically grounded so that they can examine the local and folk knowledge that informs their assumptions about how children learn and who can learn. Simultaneously, we, along with other educators and classroom teachers, are developing a theory and a language to help us describe and critique the processes we observe in schools that affect both teachers and students. For example, in a qualitative study with nineteen novice teachers last year, I gathered empirical data that substantiated what I already knew from my experience as a classroom teacher and my continued experience with teachers. When teachers are treated as intellectuals, are provided occasions for reflective and informed practice, and are assisted in developing informed ways of "knowing and doing teacher," they begin to understand the political, social and cognitive consequences of schooling. They develop new understanding of how classroom culture is constructed, of how certain contexts for learning deny or increase access to particular forms of literacy, and new understandings of the importance of developing agency and new frames of reference for both students and teachers. These teachers are not intimidated by research and theory; instead, they co-construct the discourse of theory and practice. In this way, we are attempting to conduct research that has multiple agendas, that is, research that has academic, social, and political consequences.

Peter: What you've told me sounds crucial and suggests that we need a radical new approach to teacher education in this country. I'm especially concerned with the Los Angeles context, naturally. What kind of proto-fascist citizenry are we producing here? Dean MacCannell has described the social contract of fascism here in California, the state that has nurtured new postmodern forms of violence hitherto unimaginable – forms that bring to mind Jim Jones, the Zodiac killer, Charles Manson, the Hillside Strangler, Bobby Kennedy, Harvey Milk, Sharon Tate, Nicole Brown Simpson, and Ronald Goldman. We're reminded of White Workers' Day in San Francisco and the all-volunteer Mexican border patrol known as "The Iron Guard". All these murders, these proto-fascists, and their victims were once students who became lost in the hypercrowds of our postmodern cities. MacCannell warns against a society such as ours which glosses over horror in the name of the ordinary, which coolly reinscribes at the level of everyday life absolute unreason, absolute self-delusion. We need to teach our students to be outraged, to reject the naturalization of nationalism and racism into the quotidian soft-core forms of fascism that surround us today. We need to reject postmodern ideologies of fulfillment in favour of a politics of transformation that can reclaim human dignity, that can cohere around a politics of compassion and a preferential option for the oppressed, for those whose needs are real. We need a radical materialist pedagogy of dissent.

Part III

Postcolonial pedagogies and the politics of difference

Chapter 6

Postmodernism, postcolonialism, and pedagogy

In *Pedagogy of the Oppressed*, Paulo Freire emphasizes the importance of dialogue and connects it to the struggle of the oppressed to become subjects. He stresses that, "Love is at the same time the foundation of dialogue and dialogical itself. It is thus necessarily the task of responsible Subjects and cannot exist in a relation of domination." Freire comments further, "I am more and more convinced that true revolutionaries must perceive the revolution, because of its creative and liberating nature, as an act of love. . . . The distortion imposed on the word *love* by the capitalist world cannot prevent the revolution from being essentially loving in character. . . ." Significantly, male domination suppresses this dialogue that is essential to love, so that women and men cannot hear themselves talking to one another as they go about their daily lives. As feminists speak more to women and men about patriarchy, it is important that we address the truth that circumstances of male domination make authentic, loving relationships between most women and men impossible. We must distinguish between the bonds of care and commitment that develop in a dominant–submissive, subject–object encounter and that care and commitment which emerges in a context of non-domination, of reciprocity, of mutuality. It is this bonding that enables sustained love, that enables men and women to nurture one another, to grow fully and freely.

(hooks 1989: 131)

I was walking about one night at the University of Texas, Austin, where they have a good large business school, and I happened to go past a classroom where a take-home exam was put on the blackboard. This was just before Grenada. There was a little exercise: "Suppose a communist country has just taken over a small island in such-and-such a place. What kinds of modifications would you make in your development program in terms of project maximization and cost efficiency?" Capitalism, racism, and sexism are examples of correct theoretical practice. Axiology is getting taught in a much more implicit way.

(Spivak 1990a: 140)

IDEOLOGICAL INITIATIVE AND THE ASCENDANCY OF THE NEW RIGHT

It used to be the case that the United States took pains to resuscitate its vanquished history. Just a few years ago Oliver North and his gap-toothed grin became emblematic of the naturalized and universalized American "we" at a time when to be an "American" demanded a fixed meaning in a sea of differences. Those days are certainly not over but they could be soon. Now we are living in the future anterior in which we are discovering that we have a profound nostalgia for a moment that has yet to take place, even in the imagination. We have arrived at the cusp of an absent present era of unspeakable horrors and unnameable pleasures. Democracy is becoming less the motor force of our daily lives, its pedigree of innocence having long been exposed as the posture of the shameless knave. We have given up the search for an all-embracing, undifferentiated and transcendental conception of democratic justice. We now desire not justice but accessibility. We demand that everything to be made accessible to us – including the past, present, and future – at a single moment's notice. Humanism has failed to restrict the bourgeois citizen's desire for power. Power disguised as liberation has become deputized by the logic of exploitation that drives market forces. Imperialism is the name of this power. It used to be dressed in a military uniform. Now it can be clothed in the kinder whore fashion of Courtney Love.

Oppositional social movements are currently witnessing the dissolution of their public and collective voice; their capacity to engage in a counter-hegemonic war of position is rapidly diminishing. On the academic front, new discursive strategies of transgression brought on by the current revolution in social theory have largely remained marginal appurtenances stuck in the fissures of transformative possibility. For the most part, these emergent discourses of post-Enlightenment and postcolonial thinking have been unable to subvert their host discourses of logocentrism, Eurocentrism, and patriarchy. Even leftist critics have found their own work held captive in the discursive grip of a neocolonialist politics. Regrettably, many of their attempts to sustain an adversarial politics have only unwittingly rearticulated the non-synchronous experiences of marginalized groups into a unilinear narrative of Enlightenment politics – a condition Benita Parry (1987: 51) calls the "Eurovision of the metropolitan left."

The obdurate conditions of modernity leading to a failure of the Left to compel Western discourses and social practices to reflect upon their colonialist presuppositions, have advanced well beyond what Ferdinand

Toennies could have envisioned through his *Gemeinschaft* and *Gesellschaft* distinction, what Emile Durkheim could have imagined through his concepts of mechanical and organic solidarity, or what Talcott Parsons could have foreseen by employing his concept of differentiation. Following the imperatives of the Enlightenment tradition, twentieth-century social theory has failed to rescue civilization from the carnage of false promises and shattered dreams engendered by the struggle for empire. The feudalization of consciousness – the "we happy few" of Shakespeare's *Henry V* – has infected not only Durkheim's anomie-ridden "children of the Enlightenment," but forms of individual and social pathology brought on by the construction of new modes of colonialist discourses linked to the sovereignty of the Eurocentric subject of modernism. Gayatri Chakravorty Spivak has termed such a condition "epistemic violence" (1990a: 126).

Homi Bhabha (1984: 126) describes the present condition of post-Enlightenment as a form of colonial mimicry which he defines as "the desire for a reformed, recognizable Other, as a *subject of a difference that is almost the same, but not quite*" (emphasis in original). Bhabha stresses that the world of colonial domination is always partial, always ambivalent, always produced at a site of interdiction. He remarks that "In the ambivalent world of the 'not quite/not white,' on the margins of metropolitan desire, the *founding objects* of the Western world become the erratic, eccentric, accidental *objets trouvés* of the colonial discourse – the part-objects of presence" (p. 132).

Describing the conditions through which such colonial violence becomes universalized and naturalized as a form of natural law, Sol Yurick writes:

> As modern "empire's" dominion, the meta-state, is extended and becomes internationalized, universal, the lessons of the source-pasts, over which most people have no control, are used to destroy other conflicting cultures. "Empire" globally swallows the cultures of the world's nations, metabolized, rescripts, metamorphoses and reproduces (favorite words of Marx) them into its own flesh or coin, capturing, possessing, colonizing and replacing the group thought and memory of other less developed worlds with their own group thought and memory.
> (1989: 57)

Making a similar claim that "The Europeanization of human consciousness masquerades as a universal will," Molefi Kete Asante (1987: 126) maintains, rightly in my mind, that Euro-American cultural ideology has had a debilitating effect on the identity formation of the Black population in the United States. What many teachers perceive as school failure among Black and other minority students needs to be seen as a form of cultural adaptation to White racism. Scholars of education, therefore, need to analyze the different cultural patterns of experiences of Whites and Blacks in relation to rhetorical and linguistic practices framed by unequal relationships of power and the institutional and social practices which reproduce them. He argues that:

> If we examine the flow of rhetoric in Western thought, we will see that even when the rhetorician poses as a critic in the interests of the oppressed, that critic seems incapable of the divestment of Eurocentric views. Criticism becomes criticism within a European context, a sort of ruthless intellectual game in which scores are kept but the oppressed are not even represented. Invariably, rhetoric allies itself with the socioeconomic (though not necessarily numerically) dominant culture. Therefore, the dilemma of the scholar who would break out of these restricting chains is fundamentally an ideological one.
>
> (Asante 1987: 167)

Edward Said asserts that "the epic scale of United States global power and the corresponding power of the national domestic consensus created by the electronic media have no precedents" (1993: 323). In fact, he further remarks that "Rarely before in human history has there been so massive an intervention of force and ideas from one culture to another as there is today from America to the rest of the world" (p. 319). But it is important to note with Said that colonialism is no longer a seamless, monolithic structure of social and ideological relations but rather operates within arenas of contestation in the sense that the terms periphery and center no longer apply. History now refuses to follow the unilateral trajectories of the modernist path from East to West, from South to North. Rather, Said tells us that the old cultural map has been replaced by new configurations which should lead us to acknowledge that "the map of the world has no divinely or dogmatically sanctioned spaces, essences, or privileges" (p. 311). Said argues that we cannot make sense out of changing world conditions without taking into account our own relationship to others. He writes:

> [W]e face as a nation the deep, profoundly perturbed and perturbing question of our relationship to others – other cultures, states, histories, experiences, traditions, peoples, and destinies. There is no Archimedean point beyond the question from which to answer it; there is no vantage outside the actuality of relationships among cultures, among unequal imperial and non-imperial powers, among us and others; no one has the epistemological privilege of somehow judging, evaluating, and interpreting the world free from the encumbering interests and engagements of the ongoing relationships themselves. We are, so to speak, *of* the connections, not outside and beyond them. And it behooves us as intellectuals and humanists and secular critics to understand the United

> States in the world of nations and power from *within* the actuality, as participants in it, not detached outside observers.
>
> (1993: 55–6, emphasis in original)

We must begin to face the legacy of postcolonial conflict in terms of its sweeping global context such as mass deportation, forced immigrations, ethnic cleansing, and dispossession on a grand scale. Said writes that:

> it is one of the unhappiest characteristics of the age to have produced more refugees, migrants, displaced persons, and exiles than ever before in history, most of them as an accompaniment to and, ironically enough, as afterthoughts of great post-colonial and imperial conflicts. As the struggle for independence produced new states and new boundaries, it also produced homeless wanderers, nomads, and vagrants, unassimilated to the emerging structures of institutional power, rejected by the established order for their intransigence and obdurate rebelliousness. And insofar as these people exist between the old and the new, between the old empire and the new state, their condition articulates the tensions, irresolutions, and contradictions in the overlapping territories shown on the cultural map of imperialism.
>
> (1993: 332)

When we situate the discourses of postcolonialism geopolitically within the dominant discourse communities in the United States, we witness a privileging of the discourses of the metropolitan center and an undermining of forms of moral or epistemic authority that are attempting to make the often perilous intellectual journey from the hybrid cultural margins inhabited by the Other to the center of Western discursive traditions.

In rather terroristic fashion, the New Right has, for instance, been extremely successful in its ability to conflate patriotism, citizenship, and forms of individualism with the production of consumer desire. Particularly in the context of the United States, the electronic media have facilitated the conflation of older colonialist and anti-communist discourses on character with present-day capitalist entrepreneurial values so that, contrary to Weber, economic production no longer appears inimical to charisma (*wirtschaftsfremd*). This is true to the extent that greater affinities now exist among economies of affect and modes of discursive production under capitalism (through both direct and indirect forms of non-economic legitimating symbols produced within the *cultural sphere of capitalism* such as popular national discourses and their articulation to state apparatuses, the military establishment, and institutions of commerce). Larry Grossberg (1989b: 33) refers to this condition as the "struggle for the 'natural' and 'national' authority of conservative discourses." Grossberg is one of the few social theorists whose writings remain singularly attentive to the dangerous tendencies within strands of contemporary cultural studies to fetishize difference (i.e., through a valorization of the specific, the local, and the particular) and to analyze the current debate over representation *outside of the current conjunctural crisis of cultural authority*. Grossberg's argument is particularly convincing:

> Insofar as the Left continues to locate the audience in a context of difference, and to valorize the local, it cannot even enter into the struggle. For the Right need not offer a singular national identity (although at any moment, and in different discourses, such identities may be offered); rather, it need only negotiate a popular national discourse which can be lived locally, that is, which speaks to and of the lived conditions of people's lives. The right articulates the national to the local by ways of increasingly valorizing the national in defense of the local. In that way, it can also turn its own discourse around and articulate the local out of the national, thus using the local to valorize the national. This discursive strategy, however unconscious and incompletely realized, establishes their claim to political and moral authority as already given in the position from which they speak; for it is a matter of how popular discourses are differentially invested in and taken up.
>
> (1989b: 33)

Grossberg has struck on one of the key issues concerning the condition of knowledge as a form of production, and the discursive and affective alliances that are responsible for knowledge to be actively taken up by various audiences and groups. An extension of his insight has been put forth by Andrew Ross, who suggests that discourses of transformation and liberation must find a way to rearticulate the popular in order to compete with the populist language of the New Right.

> Intellectuals today are unlikely to recognize, for example, what is fully at stake in the new *politics of knowledge* if they fail to understand why so many cultural forms, devoted to horror and porn, and steeped in chauvinism and other bad attitudes, draw their popular appear from expressions of disrespect for the lessons of educated taste. The sexism, racism, and militarism that pervade these genres is never expressed in a pure form (whatever that might be); it is articulated through and alongside social resentments born of subordination and exclusion. A politics that only preaches about the sexism, racism, and militarism while neglecting to rearticulate the popular, resistant appeal of the disrespect will not be a popular politics, and will lose ground in any contest with the authoritarian populist languages that we have experienced under Reaganism and Thatcherism.
>
> (Ross 1989: 231, emphasis in original)

Greil Marcus underscores the almost surreal conditions surrounding the dilemma charted out by both Grossberg and Ross while commenting that

> in the USA today there is only one person – Ronald Reagan, whose genius is his ability to appropriate every appealing cultural manifestation (the Olympics, Dirty Harry, Rambo, random acts of everyday heroism, the saving of random children dying from cancer) – only one American, Ronald, whose genius is his ability to be the supercelebrity whose celebrity is used to legitimize the reality of the cultural manifestations he appropriates, to finally, legitimate or deny the reality of everyone else.
>
> (1990: 477)

I have drawn on the warnings of Grossberg, Ross, and Marcus to emphasize what I consider to be a crucial dilemma for Left educators. However, I do want to point out that such conditions are not cause enough to adopt a politics of retreat or despair. Despite the inability of the Left to undermine the conditions for the current growth of barbarism within the New Right, all is not lost. While the social organization of discursive struggles over the past decade has brought about new forms of domination, it has, to a certain degree, also created space for new freedoms and recreations of relations of power. These have been brought about through various practices of revolt, emancipation, and the postmodern and postcolonial reconstitution of meaning.

Just as every barbarism conceals a hidden referent for hope (Bloch 1986), so too does every social struggle carry the potential for its own inversion. Earlier in this century, for instance, the struggle over the construction of the welfare state by subordinate groups created more humane living conditions for the economically disenfranchised while at the same time it brought about a new and extended pattern of surveillance and control. Abercrombie, Hill, and Turner (1986) have referred to this particular turn of events as "the Foucault Paradox." These authors note that new rights of citizenship were not won without a price, for they brought with them a new panopticism which was linked to a more detailed order of urban administration "made possible by knowledge (criminology, penology, demography) and by institutions (the asylum, factory, penitentiary)" – all of which were enhanced by conditions of mass warfare.

On the other hand, during our present sojourn in predatory culture, dominant discursive structures have created an economic subject which, unlike the economic subject of nineteenth-century industrial capitalism, *is no longer necessarily or mainly tied to the logic of possessive individualism but rather to growing collective discourses* (i.e., collective capitalism and rights of the public citizen). As a result, there exists within the larger public sphere a growing collective tolerance for a plurality of privatized discourses of the individual in which tolerance itself (for instance, tolerance for oppression, humiliation of the weak, and the suffering of the less fortunate) has taken precedence over *what* is tolerated.

I am not suggesting that the potential for a greater variety of economic subjects made possible by the current disorganization of capital is necessarily a good thing since, as Gramsci's theory of hegemony would suggest, a variety of ideological roles for the individual could simply mean more ways to propagate manipulative values and sustain the privileges of the few under the cover of a new pluralism (Offe 1985; Lash and Urry 1987). Rather, I am merely trying to emphasize the urgency brought on by the discursive ruptures in the current historical moment and their implications for a profound revision and transformation of the very idea of the subject given the current transitional period between two stages of capitalism and the appearance of the global proletariat (Jameson 1989b).

I am also keeping in mind the presence not only of the structures of underdevelopment and dependence for which the U.S. is largely responsible in the Third World, but also the presence in the U.S. of what Jameson (1990: 49) refers to as "internal Third World voices, as in black women's literature or Chicano literature" – voices of those whom Spivak (1990b) calls "guest workers." Jameson notes that the particular character of the loss of meaning for the imperial or metropolitan subject – its "dépossession du monde" – brought on by present-day colonialism is due to the fact that

> a significant structural segment of the economic system as a whole is now located elsewhere, beyond the metropolis, outside of the daily life and existential experience of the home country, in colonies over the water whose own life experience and life world – very different from that of the imperial power – remain unknown and unimaginable for the subjects of the imperial power, whatever social class they may belong to.
>
> (Jameson 1990: 50–1)

It is a juncture which is witnessing the dissolution of the transformative possibilities of counterhegemonic struggles as the Left increasingly loses the ideological initiative to the New Right. Given the conditions of the current struggle, I am suggesting that it is important to consider the shifting nature of contemporary discourses on the subject, and their relationship to wider social forces, if we are to contest the rhetorically manipulative and unified view of the world – the late capitalist *Weltanschauung* – in which such a relationship is implicated.

POSTMODERNISM AND POLITICS

Postmodernity can be described as a time of cultural and epistemological *coupure*, a time during which borders are breaking down and disciplinary genres are becoming blurred. Fred Dallmayr describes postmodernism as

> the experience of a certain rupture with, or distantiation from, central features of the "modern area" – an era which was inaugurated culturally by the Renaissance and philosophically by Bacon and Descartes and which reached its political and economic culmination in capitalist market relations and in individualist or bourgeois literalism.
>
> (1986: 145)

Kobena Mercer makes the following distinction between modernity and postmodernity that is appropriate to my discussion:

> If modernity defined a political arena of bourgeois democracy organized around the state and around a particular set of relations of representation – you vote for someone and they're supposed to speak for you and speak for your interests – then one might say that postmodernity involves struggles not only around the state, around legal, socio-economic justice . . . but also around new cultural formations in which new subjects find democratic agency . . . [and] . . . their voices as agents of representation.
>
> (1990: 7)

The Faustian dream of imposing master codes of Enlightenment reasoning (in the guise of a Western hyper-rationalism) on the indeterminacy of social and cultural life has become a nightmare weighing heavily on the brains of those marginalized groups who have suffered the most from the colonizing binary logic who demarcates the relationship between self and the environment. Yet, as symbolic economies continue to proliferate outside of a monolithic causal relationship with capital, creating a greater variety of subject-positions to assume, the possibilities have also increased for what I call global forms of cultural cross-dressing – or what Fredric Jameson (1989b: 41) might call "global decentralization and small group institutionalization." And while the oppressed and oppressors are, to a greater extent, able to visit each other's culture as tourists and travelers, it is nevertheless *at a time in which there exists a widespread sanctioned inarticulateness about the workings of everyday power/knowledge relations.* Here Jameson offers us a description of the current postmodern juncture that is quite apposite to the themes I wish to underscore. In addition to being a "cultural dominant" constructed by the logic of late capitalism, postmodernism is

> a transitional period between two stages of capitalism, in which the earlier forms of the economic are in the process of being restructured

> on a global scale, including the older forms of labor and its traditional organizational institutions and concepts. That a new international proletariat (taking forms we cannot yet imagine) will emerge from this convulsive upheaval it needs no prophet to predict: we ourselves are still in the trough, however, and no one can say how long we will stay there.
>
> (1989b: 44)

Anthony Giddens is more explicit about what globalization entails and he, too, is worth quoting at length:

> Globalisation can . . . be defined as the intensification of worldwide social relations which link distant localities in such a way that local happenings are shaped by events occurring many miles away and vice versa. This is a dialectical process because such local happenings may move in an obverse direction from the very distanciated relationships that shape them. *Local transformation* is as much a part of globalization as the lateral extension of social connections across time and space. Thus whoever studies cities today, in any part of the world, is aware that what happens in a local neighborhood is likely to be influenced by factors – such as world money and commodity markets – operating at an indefinite distance away from that neighborhood itself.
>
> (1990: 64, emphasis in original)

While globalization is very much a part of the postmodern scene, the effect of such global decentralization has been the proliferation of post-colonial social and literary production which has softened the certainty of Western imperial verities woven on the spindle of bourgeois-capitalist high culture. As foundational and universal truths begin to sag under the heavy assault on Western metaphysics by discourses from the margins, we are left with only specific appeals to a particular historical tradition – the language games of our particular cultural heritage (Vattimo 1988) – in order to justify our values and social practices. Steven Best (1989: 361) describes this condition as "the dictatorship of the fragment."

Moral imperatives related to the specificity of our cultural heritage are not enough to justify individual or collective agency; we need a reconstruction of theory itself, through which individuals can make a greater impact on the world as historical agents. The theory which educators must develop and work with must be a bold one, but must also remain studiously attentive to the dangers inherent in re-evoking "the inherently totalizing posture indicative of Western metaphysics" even as it attempts to displace the very metaphysical categories which have given the modernist "sovereign" subject its illusion of autonomy and self-constitution.

QUESTIONS FOR EDUCATORS

In this "postmodern" climate, educators need to ask themselves: What is the task of cultural retrieval in an age of shifting cultural borders, the unmooring of traditional cultural symbols, the blurring of metaphorical and linguistic boundaries, the back and forth crossover of subject positions over dominant discursive regimes, the breaking apart of institutionally bound structures of meaning, and the reterritorialization of desire with respect to the formations of cultural otherness which we have created? In other words, what does it mean to construct pedagogies of resistance on the basis of cultural difference within a cross-national economy that speaks to both the conditions of material necessity and the material density of subjectivity? More specifically, how can critical educators begin to map the question of agency across the various relations of class, gender, race, history, and ideological production in the form of popular memory and narrative forms?

CRITICAL SOCIAL THEORY IN THE AGE OF POSTCOLONIALISM: IMPLICATIONS FOR EDUCATIONAL THEORY

I would like to delineate the concepts of postmodern social theory and situate them in relation to empire and consumption (Angus 1989). That is, I intend to discuss postmodernist social theory as an attempt to understand the failure of the Enlightenment tradition to construct autonomous subjects who are capable of overcoming their alienation by reconciling their "authentic" subjectivity against that of the "other" through the master narratives of identity formation. These narratives, as Lyotard, Foucault, Habermas, and others have pointed out, have been built upon the scientific/technical domination of nature. Postmodernist social theory, as I am describing it, is an effort to reterritorialize the field of social theory through an appropriation of various discursive strategies designed to make sense, and ultimately transform, the social and semiotic contours of what has been described as the "end of modernity" or, as some prefer to call it, "postmodern culture." Ian Angus describes the later condition as a

> self-reproducing end-circuit of modernity. It consists of *staged difference*: The self becomes an other as a token authenticated by experiences postulated by image-sets; the other as a fear for the self, seeking security in toying with global destruction. It demonstrates the failure of the modern search for free and equal autonomous subjects and requires a radical investigation of the formation of identity as relations of dependence between self and others.
>
> (1989: 106, emphasis in original)

Within postmodern culture, domination occurs less through legal–rational legitimation, but rather through what Zygmunt Bauman (1988: 222) identifies as seduction and repression. Seduction occurs when the capitalist marketplace makes consumers dependent on it. Repression means "panoptical" power – surveillance employed at the regimentization of the body which is diffused (made invisible) by the institutionalization of knowledge-based experience. But I would argue that repression occurs in the service of keeping colonialist metanarratives invisible, perpetuating a form of political amnesia. Postmodern social theory has much to offer the critique of colonial discourses within educational research since it assumes the position that the age of modernism was characterized by the geopolitical construction of the center and the margins within the expansive hegemony of the conqueror: it is marked by the construction through European conquest of the foundational "I." Enrique Dussel asserts:

> From the "I conquer" applied to the Aztec and Inca world and all America, from the "I enslave" applied to Africans sold for the gold and silver acquired at the cost of the death of Amerindians working in the depths of the earth, from the "I vanquish" of the wars of India and China to the shameful "opium war" – from this "I" appears the Cartesian *ego cogito.*
>
> (1985: 8)

That is, the *ego cogito* has provided "the empires of the center – England and France as colonial powers, Nazi Germany, and later the United States with its Central Intelligence Agency" – with the ontological expression of the ideology of the bourgeois class. It has provided the discursive support for what in recent times is paradoxically called "free" trade and has helped to justify the repression of the Mayan insurgents in Chiapas.

Bill Ashcroft, Gareth Griffiths, and Helen Tiffin have summarized the major advances in theory and practices in postcolonial literatures, suggesting that such criticism has generally followed two major paths:

> the reading of specific post-colonial texts and the efforts of their production in and on specific social and historical contexts, and on the other, via the "revisioning" of received tropes and modes such as allegory, irony and metaphor and the rereading of "canonical" texts in the light of post-colonial discursive practices.
>
> (1989: 194)

Much of our understanding of postcolonial theory has been helped by the work of the Algerian theorist, Jacques Derrida, who has revealed how the metaphoricity of language does not represent speech; rather, the indeterminacy of language in general, and the fact that meaning cannot precede writing, in particular, subverts the claim of any language or theoretical discourse to possessing a transcendental status. All discourses and discursive formations betray an unpredictable heterogeneity and relations of power/knowledge which inform them are recursively constituted within Eurocentric rules of binary construction. This revelation made by Derrida merely underscores the reality that all discourses – even those of freedom and liberation – carry with them ideological traces and selective interests which must be understood and transformed in the interests of greater justice, democracy, and freedom. It also suggests that one cannot take up any theoretical position with an algorithmic certainty without falsifying or undercutting that position in some way. Such a condition obtains within any theory which mediates the self and the world, however dialectical such a form of mediation might be. Of course, this position can be traced linguistically to the idea, prevalent within postmodernist discourse, that language does not immanently reflect reality but serves as its constituent mechanism, creating, in the words of John Fekete (1984: 234), "a certain anti-empiricist denaturalization of the phenomenal event." One danger, of course, is that postmodernist social theory's preoccupation with the sign has rendered it susceptible to a form of semantic autism. There is the attendant danger also that some variants of postmodernist social theory will ontotheologize its own critical paradigm, creating new, debilitating forms of totalization (cf. Fekete 1984). These dangers serve as a warrant for the critical postmodernist theorist to interrogate discourses of emancipation with the objective of reconstructing their theoretical assumptions in a language that will help to reduce the most debilitating aspects of Eurocentrism and androcentrism.

NEW TRENDS IN CRITICAL SOCIAL THEORY

The 1980s witnessed vivacious new developments in critical social theory that have brought with them important new ways of understanding the relationship between the process of schooling and the reproduction of inequity in the wider society. The present decade will undoubtedly see an extension and, in some cases, a considerable restructuring of such work and a further refinement of theoretical categories.

An increased rejection of the objectivist ideal of presuppositionless self-transparency and a recognition that knowledge is not autonomous but embedded and produced in situations where there exist numerous economic, societal, political, historical, textual, and personal relations that impinge on the production of subjectivity along class, race, gender, and geopolitical lines, is currently helping educators to better understand how patterns of subordination are produced among certain groups. Such a recognition is also revealing how new communities of resistance can be forged within classrooms, schools, and other social and cultural sites, for the purpose of de-othering subjugated groups and enhancing and deepening the project of democracy.

Social theory is currently profiting from various theoretical strands of feminist discourse (e.g. radical and cultural feminism, and post-structuralist feminism) as well as advances in feminist pedagogy and critical pedagogy. Much of this work owes a theoretical debt to the rich legacy of Continental thinkers, such as the projects that occupied the Frankfurt School, S. F. Haug and Frigga Haug's Das Argument group, the New Left in Britain and Ireland (such as the work undertaken by the Birmingham Centre for Contemporary Cultural Studies and *Screen* magazine) and the work of Lévi-Strauss, Barthes, Althusser, Foucault, Lacan, Derrida, Kristeva, and Cixous. Of special significance at present is the development of critical postmodernist and postcolonialist approaches within social and cultural theory. Such approaches, while dispossessing themselves of any grand assurance and loyalty to some epic totality of Hegelian proportions – to the false necessity of an external dialectic – affirm emergent narratives of liberation tied to the particularity and specificity of concrete historical struggles. This raises certain issues which educators will need to engage.

For instance, how can educators begin to discuss the concept of identity and cultural politics with respect to race, class, and gender in non-essentialist ways, that is, without becoming complicitous in the role of the "reluctant imperialist" by denying legitimacy to those heterogeneous subjects which fail to evoke the image of the autonomous meta-subject of the empire? Put another way, how can educators avoid legitimizing the Western masculinist meta-subject as the paradigm of human agency and avoid reading back into human nature what has become "natural" for us as social agents?

This raises a further question to be wrestled over by social theorists in the coming years: How can experience be mediated and understood through a language which refuses to totalize experience and render it homogeneous, unitary, and as one of univocal determination? How can one simultaneously assume a self-reflexive, critical and cautionary attitude with respect to Euro-American systems of dualistic reasoning and androcentric narratives of the self in which the Cartesian *ego cogito* establishes equivalences with the logic of imperialism and fascism?

To adequately respond to such questions, social theorists in education need to expand and refigure the concept of identity/difference such that separate and particular modes of gender, racial, and ethnic oppression are not conflated and the concept of identity/difference does not become totalized into a grand narrative of its own.

Of related and equal importance is the development of a social theoretical perspective in education that recognizes the mutual constitutivity of identity and difference in the formation of human subjectivity. Here educators should increasingly profit from engaging the works of Teresa De Lauretis, Julia Kristeva, bell hooks, Rey Chow, Trinh T. Minh-ha,

Nancy Fraser, Linda Nicholson, Seyla Benhabib, Donna Haraway, Christine DiStephano, Gayatri Spivak, E. Ann Kaplan, E. San Juan, Edward Said, Henry Giroux, Sandra Harding, and others taking up this theoretical challenge.

Cultural studies and research into the constitutive characteristics and effects of colonial discourses and practices should assume a greater importance in university programs in the liberal acts and in colleges of education. Cultural studies is showing signs of increasing importance within the academy. Work currently undertaken by bell hooks, Angela McRobbie, Larry Grossberg, Stuart Hall, Andrew Ross, Constance Penley, Stanley Aronowitz, Michele Wallace, Dick Hebdige, and Paul Gilroy – to name some of the more prominent critical exponents of the cultural studies field – is providing important intellectual and pedagogical resources for critical educators.

Another significant development that is beginning to show signs of burgeoning influence both in Europe and North America involves attempts at formulating a critical pragmatism in which the works of Dewey, Pierce, and the social reconstructionists are able to join forces with critical theorists, Continental social theorists, and Third World social theorists (cf. Miedema and Biesta 1990; and the work of Dieter Misgeld). Not surprisingly, such a development is currently heading in two general directions: aiming at a Habermasian goal of maximally transparent communication among hierarchically divergent subject positions; or, the Foucauldian notion of the "practices of the self" with its Nietzchean lineage (in this case with an emphasis on collective as well as individual self-conducts practiced with a minimum of domination) articulated as a form of mutually enhancing rapprochement between genealogical analysis and feminist discourse. Undoubtedly debate will continue to proliferate concerning the relative worth of Habermas's notion of "differentiation" when compared with postmodern "difference." There should also be related debates concerning questions raised by historicism, the transcendental conditions of objectivity prior to the empirical level, and the notion of a universal pragmatics.

The concept of the global subject (or global proletariat) has been made especially significant as a result of the growth of multinational corporations and neo-corporatist logics, the hypertrophy of science, the system integration and regulatory instruments of late capitalism (and their collective impact on the Third World) not to mention recent developments in Eastern Europe and the implications that these events possess for a restructing of capitalism and a recolonization of the lifeworld of the Other. There can be little question that the shifting balance between the margins and the centers of global power is becoming a much greater concern to critical social theorists. The call has been sounded for more concerted efforts within sociology and anthropology to subvert the colonizer's representations of colonized cultures and the justifications by colonizers of their entitlement to create an expansive hegemonic mission of global dominance (cf. McLaren 1986; Clifford and Marcus 1986).

New forms of narratology emerging from Latin America and minority cultures in North America and elsewhere which challenge current Eurocentrist and metaphysical assumptions in our curricula and pedagogical practices need to be taken more seriously by critical educators. Concurrently, new modes for establishing referentiality need to make further headway into the language of critical educational studies, followed by the development of a new method for establishing evidential claims for new forms of disciplinary knowledge.

As we learned in Chapters 1 and 2, the concept of the body as a site of cultural inscription is growing in prominence as a topic of investigation. The analysis of desire is also generating increased interest among theorists trained in psychoanalytic traditions and those whose work follows poststructuralist and semiotic lines of social and cultural analysis. Efforts are being made to uncouple the idea of the feminine body/subject from the negative and unspoken Other and to recognize the body as a site of enfleshment and intextuation (De Certeau 1984). In other words, bodies are becoming recognized and explored as socially situated and incarnated social practices that are very much semiotically alive. However, I should add here that the importance of studying the body is not to turn it into a textualized, semiotic laboratory but rather to recognize knowledge as a typography of embodiment, that is, to recognize the body as the grounds for our intersubjective relationships and active investment in social life against which all else is a form of discursive elaboration (cf. O'Neil 1989). Important new explorations are being undertaken in terms of how the history of philosophy has been linked to the body and how the body becomes significant in terms of the manner in which individuals invest in their bodies in historical and culturally specific ways.

In a related sense, the notion of gender has become problematized in ways that do not enforce binary divisions and dichotomous and oppositional methods of categorizing which partake of phallocentrism and other forms of patriarchal investment. In this regard, the work of French feminists such as Kristeva, Irigaray, and Cixous have taken on increasing importance, as has the work of Foucault, Deleuze, De Certeau, Spinoza, Nietzsche, and Merleau-Ponty.

Despite current differences, I do not think it unrealistic to foresee a devastatingly powerful politics and praxis of liberation eventually emerging from dialogues between educators who work in the areas of feminist pedagogy and those who work from the perspective of critical pedagogy. A language of possibility (cf. Giroux 1983) and arch of social dreaming constructed within the critical educational tradition are meant to suggest ways of surmounting the divisiveness and disarray currently characterizing the politics of the educational Left, and the disconcerting proliferation of separatist forms of identity politics.

POSTMODERNISM AND RADICAL PEDAGOGY

While the term "postmodernism" is comparatively new to educational research, it has become one of the major preoccupations of social theorists working in critical social theory and literary criticism. This is not to deny that the term denotes a form of theoretical outlawry and a highly unstable concept straddling a number of definitional boundaries – notwithstanding David Bennett's (1990: 30) observation that the prefix "post" entails a temporal distinction suggesting that the adjectives modernist and post-modernist refer to "coexistent moments in any self-reflexive discourse." Although I certainly agree with Dick Hebdige (1988) that postmodernism has become a "buzzword" and "notoriously vertiginous concept," there is no doubt that it has ushered in a whole new range of nascent paradigmatic articulations for rethinking the knowledge industry outside of a framework which reduces it to a homogeneous totality, and for prying open semantic spaces for a subversive and redemptive cultural politics. The term "postmodernism" is a slippery event and its referents are saturated with overlapping significance. It refers simultaneously to the state of contemporary consumer culture, complexes of metropolitan moods, and new trends in contemporary theories of the social subject.

The ambiguities in the meaning of "postmodernism" and the increasing variety of connotations surrounding the concept itself have proliferated enormously in recent years. This confusion, coupled with the looseness of the terminology surrounding postmodernist turns in social theory, has been responsible for much of the opprobrium that the term has accrued over the past few years in becoming one of the au courant topics of academe. While there is often little discernible precision of thought behind its usage, the term both plays on the pretensions of North American haute-bourgeois academicians and serves as a referent for ideological critique and emancipatory politics. The growing interest among educators with respect to the now well publicized debates over whether or not we inhabit a "postmodernist" conjuncture, and the implications these debates have for evaluating the legacy of the modern Enlightenment tradition, are not only unabated, but notably lively. However, it is only in recent years that scholars working in the areas of the philosophy of education and critical education have begun to mine the value of these debates for rethinking the relationships among schooling, culture, language, and power.

There is a danger, of course, in conflating postmodernist social theory with the postmodern condition. As Andrew Goodwin (1990: 272) has recently cautioned: "by conflating postmodernism as *theory* and as *condition*, the former finds itself with a vested interest in promoting the latter, if not morally and/or politically, then as a cultural form of far greater significance than the evidence often suggests." Elsewhere I have addressed the distinction between postmodern theory and postmodern culture and their attendant problematics in detail, and I do not wish to canvass them again here.

Rather than provide the reader with an overview of the recent theoretical debates and positions surrounding what may be loosely called postmodernist social theory, and to attempt to make fine-tooth distinctions between terms such as postmodernist social theory and post-structuralism, I have chosen to focus on the critical appropriation and employment of specific discourses which have emerged from these recent debates. More specifically, I am concerned with drawing attention to aspects of post-structuralist and neo-colonialist discourse which I feel can be critically appropriated into what I am calling a postcolonialist or critical postmodernist pedagogy and what others are calling a postcritical or feminist pedagogy. I am making the claim that the current revolution in social theory demands a new set of critical paradigms within educational theory that can account for the heterogeneity of pedagogical and curricular discourses and complexity of meaning production in postmodern cultures. In this way, postcolonial educational theory can be seen as a form of "travelling theory" which criss-crosses both old and new disciplinary domains, creating new patterns and relations of insight into the connections among power, discourse and pedagogical practice. Postcolonial pedagogy has not only inherited the vocabulary of modernity – i.e., the language of political economy and class struggle – but also extends and transforms its terms.

RELATIVISM, HISTORICISM, AND SOLIDARITY

In this section, I shall be using the theme of historicism, relativism, and solidarity to explore the conditions necessary for a genuine politics of social transformation to occur in a postmodern climate of competing discourses of ethics and epistemology. While a certain species of relativism is inescapable – in that knowledge is always contingent and context specific – the construction of an emancipatory politics of education must eschew any general relativism that refuses to take a stand on issues of human oppression and social injustice.

I would like to begin with a quotation from the discerning Marxist literary critic, Terry Eagleton. Eagleton's comments draw attention to a number of theoretical tensions which both implicitly and explicitly appear in many of the positions taken by exponents of critical social theory.

> Any emancipatory politics must begin with the specific, then, but must in the same gesture leave it behind. For the freedom in question is not the freedom to "be Irish" or "be a woman," whatever that might mean, but simply the freedom now enjoyed by certain other groups to determine their identity as they may wish. Ironically, then, a politics of difference or specificity is in the first place in the cause of sameness and universal identity – the right of a group victimized in its particularity to be on equal terms with others as far as their self-determination is concerned. This is the kernel of truth of bourgeois Enlightenment: the abstract universal right of all to be free, the shared essence or identity of all human subjects to be autonomous. In a further dialectical twist, however, this truth itself must be left behind as soon as seized; for the only point of enjoying such universal abstract equality is to discover and live one's own particular difference. The *telos* of the entire process is not, as the Enlightenment believed, universal truth, right and identity, but concrete particularity. It is just that such particularity has to pass through that abstract equality and come out somewhere on the other side, somewhere quite different from where it happens to be standing now.
>
> (1990: 30)

Eagleton's remarks remind us that we cannot retreat to the politics of the universal where agents are reduced to the role of divine spectators who merely legislate truth without living it; nor can we retreat to the politics of the specific, where our proximity to the event – to the object of knowledge – provides us with the pre-emptive right to measure truth by the norm of experience. Either extreme holds very real dangers for an emancipatory politics of difference. The point is to recognize that both abstract universalism and the politics of particularity and the concrete have contributed to producing the very reality that they enable us to investigate.

Each extreme must serve as a corrective device to disqualify abuses of power committed in the name of truth and freedom. This is not the same thing as arguing that truth is to be found somewhere in the middle. It is to argue that particular universes of meaning and social relations that have directly visible realities generate their own demise unless they are consecrated by a social mission of universalizing what is most noble and virtuous about such meanings and relations.

Eagleton goes on to make the important point that bourgeois ideology has never been able to reconcile difference and identity, the local and the global, the particular and the universal. According to Eagleton, this situation persists because the sensuous particularity of human needs and desires belongs in classical bourgeois thought to the degraded sphere of civil society: the essentially private realms of family and economic production. By contrast, the ethical and political spheres become terrains where men and women encounter one another as abstractly equalized universal subjects. And one of the tasks of bourgeois ideology, notes Eagleton (1990: 30), is "to square the grotesque discrepancy between the two worlds as brazenly as it can." The Right has done a far greater job mediating the tension between universal and specific knowledges – that is, squaring the discrepancies between the two, including local and global discourses – than has the Left.

Eagleton attributes the success of the Right to the Left's surrendering of the aesthetic (i.e., "the intimate, affective depths of the poetic") at the beginning of the nineteenth century. Of course, the pressing issue is how the Left can now mediate this tension within postmodern culture at a time when the boundaries between the universal and specific, the local and the global, are collapsing into new aesthetically pleasing discursive economies of affect.

The Left has endorsed a politics of consensus; but this has only proved more troubling to the construction of a politics of difference. For the politics of consensus the liberal humanists exhort us to adopt is, from the perspective of a critical postmodernist or postcolonial social theory, a politics based on the unstated assumption of conquest. In Sharon Welch's (1990: 133) terms, "the search for consensus is a continuation of the dream of domination." We can see this tendency even in some of the best critical modernist attempts at mediating the universal and the particular. Take, for example, Habermas's well-known project of communicative competency.

I agree enthusiastically with Michael Ryan (1989) when he argues that the priority which Habermas's model for undistorted communication establishes must be reversed. That is, we must create materially equal circumstances necessary for rational discussion. As Ryan cogently points out, social rationalization is not merely an issue of reason, but of need – material need such as housing, food, sexuality, psychological health. Before undistorted communication can occur, an ethical culture must be created in which there exist communities of understanding related to realized material structures of equality. Validity of reason must therefore take into account material norms on the basis of need. Consequently, Habermas's model needs to include a more context-responsible participation in material existence. In Habermas's system, terms like "validity" serve to stabilize social violence and a colonialist politics. Ryan is correct when he argues that validity and reason must not assume a transcendent status over the contingencies of materiality and over the need and desires of the public. The indeterminate contingency of social discussion must not remain subsumed under Habermas's authoritative norms of validity.

Anthony Giddens's critique tellingly illustrates how Habermas fails to extend the bounds of conversation in his model of undistorted communication to include cultural traditions which differ or exist in opposition to Western intellectual cultures – "alternative modes of conversation and interaction in which not only the validity claims but the substantive proposals of each culture could be fairly explained" (Welch 1990: 132). Habermas also fails to take seriously the possibility of mutual critique. Welch argues that material changes are necessary to conversation between groups that conflict in values and political strategies, that are situated within asymmetrical relations of power, and that are privileged with respect to race, gender, and class. Of course, the critique of Habermas's quest for universal pragmatics made by Giddens and Welch has deep philosophical roots.

For instance, historicism has shown the weaknesses of Habermas's search for an answer to relativism and scepticism. Historicism identifies the culturally constructed character of social "facts" – the historical and socially coded frameworks of meaning. It operates under the assumption that all critique and explanation take place within explanatory frames which privilege certain discourses over others, and never serve as transparent media with access to pre-given orders of facticity. Historicism, as I am employing it, can serve as an important framework within critical pedagogy for understanding the local, contingent, and provisional status of all meaning and understanding. Robert D'Amico describes the position as follows:

> Historicism treats knowledge as a culturally significant system. It therefore treats philosophical reflection as an important aspect of that system, but not a privileged vantage point. As a kind of reflection, historicism makes statements about all traditions from the vantage point of some style of inquiry. It admits the role of assumptions and, therefore, does not claim that the world is transparent to its gaze. What is seen, understood, or taken as basic always depends on *when*. . . . [It] does not require that argument, reasoning, and reflection be abandoned. It does require that appeals to such terms as self-evidence, common sense, demonstrative, pure, and a priori be reconstructed. These terms are not floating freely, available eternally for the construction of good reasoning. Reasoning is always local and locatable.
>
> (1989: 147, 146, emphasis in original)

Reflecting the perspective taken by the new historicists, Giddens (1990: 154) tells us that " 'History' is not on our side, has no teleology, and supplies us with no guarantees." Furthermore, there exist "no privileged agents in the process of transformation geared to the realization of values" (pp. 154, 155). The historicist argument that "the world as appearance changes in the manner of a cultural convention or alterable arrangement" (D'Amico 1989: 132), and that there are no intrinsically correct strategies of reasoning, directly challenges Habermas's contention that there exist an invariant point of view, invariant behavioral preconditions for the construction of meaning, and that a certain objectification is necessarily presupposed by all experience, even though concepts themselves are relative. Richard Litchman's brilliant analysis of Habermas makes a similar point:

> I follow Habermas' insistence that categories we impose in nature are not the produce of a Kantian transcendental consciousness, but of human labor. . . . [T]he mode of human labor is not itself a timeless essence, but the concrete result of the particular form of industrialized technology through which it receives its expression and determination. As psychoanalysis remains subservient to the assumptions of capitalist social life, so its practice remains a means for the realization of capitalist power. A truly self-reflective, emancipatory discipline must explore the preconditions of its own categorization, a task that has not been undertaken by psychoanalysis, but which is, on the contrary, the legacy of Marxian critique.
>
> (forthcoming: 12)

D'Amico reveals that Habermas's transcendental strategy does not escape the historicist position about knowledge and representation. D'Amico writes:

> the transcendental strategy does not eliminate an historicist position about knowledge and representation. Historicism does treat the objectivity of knowledge as constituted and internally justified. The diverse historical schemes, however, can only be known partially and provisionally from the vantage point of the present.
>
> (1989: 143)

To be fair to Habermas, he does, as Martin Jay (1988: 168–9) attests, make the distinction between a rational construction of the past and any objective historical account of it, eschewing the goal of unifying all versions of reason and postulating "a reconciled, harmonious reason embodied in a homogeneous, totalized form of life." Nevertheless, it is still difficult to endorse uncritically Habermas's emphasis on idealized consensus under non-coercive and unlimited communication. D'Amico (1989: 148) convincingly makes the claim that as a standard, "it is futile and resolves no essentially contested concept; nor can it guide any historical reconstruction. Further, Habermas's view maintains the hermeneutic project of preventing misunderstanding or misreading; it assumes that historicity can be transcended."

Against new historicism's challenge, does Foucault handle the matter of relativism and the objectivity of knowledge any better than Habermas? While Foucault's defense of the objectivity of knowledge remains problematic (cf. D'Amico 1989), it should be noted that Foucault, to his credit, does reveal an excessive insistence on the discontinuity in history which, for him, includes a critique of continuist histories that have legitimated present social practices and obscured the conflicts and struggles of history; at the same time, Foucault is able to develop a sophisticated criticism of the concept of social totality. Consequently, in our defence of historicism we must be careful not to dismiss Foucault's legacy of articulating the effects of power that theories produce in historically specific ways. And, as critical educators, it makes fundamental sense to work towards what Pheby calls

> a more sophisticated treatment of history, one that recognizes that history is opaque rather than transparent and self-articulating (given that it only comes to us in textualized form), that is, a view of history as an "absent cause," a text-to-be created.
>
> (1988: 106)

Larry Grossberg provides an excellent summary of the historicist understanding of reality which I have been trying to portray.

> Reality here is not defined as a metaphysical or even an historical origin but rather as an interested mapping of the lines of concrete effects. Reality is not "outside" of any apparatus, merely represented within the discourses comprising it. This assumed difference between discourse and reality gives rise to the epistemological problem. But if reality is always articulated through our own fabrication of it, one cannot define the specificity (the difference) of any practice or conjuncture apart from its ongoing articulation within the history of our constructions. Reality is always a construction of and out of the complex intersections and interdeterminations among specific conjunctural effects. Reality in whatever form – as matter, as history or as experience – is not a privileged referent but the ongoing . . . production or articulation of apparatuses. And the only grounds for deciding, in Benjamin's terms, how deeply and precisely one has cut into the body of the real are political and historical.
>
> (1989a: 143)

Of course, historicism necessarily brings with it condemnations that it largely consists of a discourse of ethical relativism. To answer such a charge, some excellent commentary by Paul Hirst and Barbara Hernstein Smith would appear instructive. Hirst (1990: 21) makes the important claim that even though methodological pluralism and a certain species of epistemological and ethical relativism are inescapable facts of life today – that is, that "the form of argument or the type of evidence used will depend on the case at issue, the discipline in question" (p. 20) – we must at all costs avoid a *general relativism* that "dodges the issue of the validity of beliefs in a complete epistemological and social liberalism" (p. 21).

In their attempt to disarm practices of oppression, critical educators need to recognize the ways in which liberalism (with its stress on pluralism and consensus) often remains complicit with that which it attempts to oppose and, in so doing, provides the necessary ideological cover for re-empowering and privileging patriarchy and existing relations of class and race. Hernstein Smith makes a very important point with respect to this concern, which is that consensual and normative reasoning must be pragmatically applied in a specific, case-by-case manner such that transcendentally universalistic consequences of our thought and action must be put aside in favour of decisions which understand knowledge to be rational, that is, historical, cultural, and institutionally individuated. She argues that

> The "autonomous subject freely choosing" is not the only alternative to "transcendental guarantees." To be sure, since not a Marxist, feminist, nor any other analysis can be developed as a transcendental account of the objective wrongness of the current state of affairs, anyone who desires a change must assert her desire and exert her will for it independent of any such presumptively objective justificatory analysis. The crucial point, however, is that, if the theoretical analysis is not transcendental, then it must be historical, and if the justification is not universal and unconditioned, then it must be restricted, partial, and local, which is *not* to say, it must be heavily emphasized, "subjective" in the usual limited objectivist senses of the latter, or "privatized" or "individualistic" in *their* current polemical senses.
>
> (Smith 1988: 175, emphasis in original)

The position that needs to be taken in order to refute objective justificatory analysis involves a conception of the world as "continuously changing, irreducibly various, and multiply configurable" (p. 183). In addition, it must partake of a species of relativism that

> conceives of its own conception of the world as the contingent product of many things: *contingent* in the sense that it is a function not of the "way the world is" but of the states of numerous particular systems interacting at a particular time and place. This conception of the world requires that there be "something" other than itself, other than the process of conceiving-the-world; but it cannot conceive of a single other thing to say, or way to think, about that "something" – not a single feature to predicate of it, or any way to describe, analyze, or manipulate any of its properties – that would be *independent* of that process.
>
> (Smith 1988: 183, emphasis in original)

Smith suggests that, in consequence, relative uniformities and constancies are never strictly absolute but only appear that way within particular communities for which they are *in effect* universal and unconditional. Therefore, it is better to describe such conditions as "contingently absolute" or "contingently objective." This means that social agents who seek change without any transcendental guarantees need to justify their actions. However, such forms of justification are always already a form of manipulation or rhetorical persuasion.

The serious issue ahead for educators struggling to work through a crippling general relativism that undergirds the pluralistic implications of liberal social theory is to elaborate a position for the human subject which acknowledges its embeddedness and contingency in present political and historical conditions without, however, relinquishing the struggle against domination and oppression and the fight for social justice and emancipation. In the context of critical pedagogy, educators must ask "how the discourse of theory [can] intervene in practice without bolstering domination" (Poster 1989: 27).

To further avoid falling into a laissez-faire pluralism, educators must develop a more detailed account of what Nancy Fraser (1989:182) calls an "interpretive justification" of people's needs. This means examining the inclusivity and exclusivity of rival interpretations, and analyzing the hierarchy and egalitarianism of the relations among the rivals who are engaged in debating such needs. Fraser maintains that consequences should also be taken into consideration by comparing alternative distributive outcomes of rival interpretations. This should take the form of procedural considerations concerning the social processes by which various competing interpretations are generated. Fraser elaborates:

> [H]ow exclusive or inclusive are various rival needs discourses? How hierarchical or egalitarian are the relations among the interlocutors? . . . [W]ould widespread acceptance of some given interpretation of a social need disadvantage some groups of people vis-à-vis others? Does the interpretation conform to, rather than challenge, societal patterns of domination and subordination? Are the rival chains of in-order-to relations to which competing need interpretations belong more or less respectful, as opposed to transgressive, of ideological boundaries that delimit "separate spheres" and thereby rationalize inequality?
>
> (1989: 182)

This means, of course, that educators need to recognize that within their own classrooms not all voices are equally valid. To argue the contrary would, in effect, amount to endorsing a facile form of universalism. Experiences give rise to voice at the moment such experiences become informed by language and representation, at which point they are discursively circulated in the larger economies of power/knowledge, and located within the prevailing dependent hierarchies of race, class, and gender. The context in which such articulations recursively take place – that is, the theoretical vernacular that students employ and the conditions that determine which vernaculars are used by which groups of students on the basis of their race, class, and gender – in order for personal and collective meaning to occur, should offer educators a very important focus for the analysis of subjectivity, since it is now apparent that experience is always a problem of historicity and discourse.

It is not surprising to note that recent advances in chaos theory (e.g., non-linear dynamics, fractal geometry, and related mathematical and thermodynamic techniques that observe order and pattern in what was formerly only known as indeterminate, random, and erratic) can be applied to the historicist argument. Lehrer, Serlin, and Amundson (1990: 17) remark that:

> the study of chaos suggests that many events formerly considered as completely unstructured and random have a comparatively simple and elegant mathematic form. For many chaotic processes, although one may be relatively uncertain about the location of the next event in a sequence, the sequence as a whole often has a predictable structure (e.g., strange attractors and the like).

The work of the *Annals* historians bears a resemblance to chaos theory in its treatment of the concept of history. For instance, much of their work breaks with traditional emphasis on linear and causal historical explanation, avoiding the consideration of historical phenomena in familiar neo-Kantian universal terms. The *Annals* historians view such neo-Kantian formulations as long-term historical contingency. In this view, the persistence over time of any phenomenon

> is systematically embedded in the material world, has its stability conditions, and is subject to dissolution, disappearance, or decay. While in place, these contingent historical structures are the source of constraints, enablement, and patternings conceivably operating in all spheres of life from the biological to the intellectual.
>
> (Dyke 1990: 386)

The *Annals* historians challenge the historical particularity of unrepeatable events and cause us to re-examine "the presuppositions under which concatentations of events as strings of independent and dependent variables can provide explanation" (Dyke 1990: 389). In addition, they ask us to "consider the degrees of freedom available in the possibility space of human action, and suggest to us that we are subject to far more constraints than we might like to think" (p. 389). Of course, this position poses a serious problem for those concerned about the efficacy of human agency; it means that

> the *particular* life we lead may be explicable in terms of decisions and

> choices we make, but the *kind* of life we lead is explicable only in the light of structurally embedded phenomena of *longue durée*, and the space offered us by the conjunctural organization of our field of action.
> (Dyke 1990: 389)

However, neither chaos theory nor the new historicism sufficiently answers the charge that the overdetermination of the subject through discourse renders the social agent politically innocuous.

SOLIDARITY OVER CONSENSUS

So, where does this leave us, as educators and cultural workers, in the search for a communicative praxis in which a truly transformative dialogue can take place? Those strands of Nietzschean perspectivism and aestheticism which undergird the works of post-structuralists or critical modernists such as Habermas, or, for that matter, the new historicists such as D'Amico or Hayden White, suggest that a dramatic theoretical shift within educational theory and practice should take place. My first suggestion is to support what Joe Kincheloe (1992) and others have urged: that educational historians improve their ability to uncover the way that power works, subjectivity is produced, disciplinary matrixes are legitimated and objectivity is defined. Kincheloe is suggesting that new developments in social theory be incorporated into present historiographical analysis. In doing so, he is not simply asking that educators understand how certain ideas get legitimated. He recognizes, after Zavarzadeh and Morton, that there is a vast difference between examining how certain ideas get legitimated and asking tough questions about their legitimacy.

My second suggestion is to develop a politics of solidarity among critical educationalists, and here the work of feminist theologian Sharon Welch takes on a singular importance. Welch points out that the material basis of consensus and the materiality of the movement of emancipatory communication need to be examined in order to adequately realize a form of dialogue that truly leads to empowerment. I recommend that critical educators follow Welch in presupposing solidarity *as a step prior to consensus*. Welch (1990: 132) writes that "the intention of solidarity is potentially more inclusive and more transformative than is the goal of consensus." She argues convincingly that in order to develop forms of consensus which take seriously a common recognition of social ills and the necessity of their transformation, solidarity must be established first.

> Solidarity has two aspects in this case: 1) granting each group sufficient respect to listen to their ideas and to be challenged by them and 2) recognizing that the lives of the various groups are so intertwined that each is accountable to the other. These forms of recognition assume working together to bring about changes in social practice.
> (1990: 133)

Welch argues that in order for solidarity to occur, *certain material and structural arrangements in our society must be met, such that minorities and marginalized groups have access to dialogue and can be invited into the conversation.* She further notes that attention must be given to the distribution of power in dialogue, especially when considering the possibilities of silencing others or excluding them on the basis of their "otherness." In Welch's view, an adequate model of transformative interaction through dialogue needs more than Habermas's criterion of "the force of the better argument." Welch writes that when mutual transformation is realized, "there is the power of empathy and compassion, of delight in otherness, and strength in the solidarity of listening to others, bearing together stories of pain and resistance" (1990: 135).

Welch's notion of solidarity differs greatly from that of Richard Rorty. This difference becomes clear in the critiques of Rorty's concept of solidarity by Smith, Fraser, and Cornel West. Smith criticizes Rorty's concept of solidarity as being monolithic, as a single, particular way of giving sense to our lives which denies the "mutually inconsistent and conflictual . . . nature both of our desires, beliefs, and actions and also of the relations among them" (Smith 1988: 167). In Rorty's view, solidarity and community serve as a way of privileging ethnocentrism over relativism. Rorty is thus seen attaching a special privilege to his own community, and pretending an impossible tolerance for non-liberal groups. Rorty's position, therefore, "denies or obscures both *difference* and *dynamics*, including *internal* difference and dynamics, it can only encourage the illusion, undesirable for political theory and dangerous for political practice, that there is some mode of thought or set of principles that would ultimately eliminate all difficult and disagreeable encounters with other people" (p. 168). It is in this context that Smith understands Rorty's valorization of community as a replacement for objective reality.

Similarly, Fraser asserts that Rorty's move from objectivity to solidarity "homogenizes social space, assuming tendentiously that there are no deep social cleavages capable of generating conflicting solidarities and opposing 'we's' " (1989: 104). Furthermore, she accuses Rorty of aestheticizing, individualizing, oedipalizing, and masculinizing radical discourses, and condemning any discourse which departs from a bourgeois liberalism. She asks: "[W]hy assume a quasi-Durkheimian view according to which society is integrated by way of a single monolithic and all-encompassing solidarity? Why not rather assume a quasi-Marxian view according to which modern capitalist societies contain a plurality of overlapping and competing solidarities?" (p. 98).

Rorty, it has been shown, manages to turn his own brand of ethnocentrism into a philosophical defense of Western civilization. Cornel West (1985: 267) has astutely observed that Rorty's "ethnocentric posthumanism" can only "kick the philosophical props from under bourgeois capitalist societies and require no change in our cultural and political practices." West (1989a: 208) additionally criticizes Rorty for defending a bourgeois way of life and for detranscendentalizing the transcendental subject and historicizing and demythologizing philosophy "without acknowledging and accenting the oppressive deeds done under the ideological aegis of these notions" and remaining "silent about forms of political, economic, racial, and sexual privilege."

What are the implications of this discussion for pedagogy? It would seem that the critiques of Rorty's position on solidarity offered by Smith, Fraser, and West, and the radicalizing of solidarity by Sharon Welch, make a considerable case for a pedagogy that is prepared and able to avoid the liberal trap of positing all groups and individuals as a "generalized other" (see Benhabib in Welch 1990: 127). This entails taking up the task of accounting for the concrete identity and individuality of the Other and recognizing the determinative differences in the Other's access to political power. This becomes particularly important in relation to the construction of norms and categories of the subject that educators employ in teaching and working with students.

Part of the problem with current attempts by Left social theorists to address political agency in the age of postmodernism is that too often critical social theory is seen as just one more "language game" in the postmodern celebration and fetishization of difference and its eschatological declarations of the end of the human subject. The question of whether postcolonial pedagogy is modern or postmodern is therefore a secondary one. Rita Felski's commentary on feminism's relation to postmodernism is apposite to my discussion of postcolonial pedagogy. Felski writes that:

> Such investigation is not significantly furthered by assimilating feminism to the notion of a "postmodern condition" defined as a radical rupture with the modern, a definition which is often grounded in reified oppositions of hierarchy vs. anarchy, reason vs. desire, depth vs. surface, identity vs. difference, etc. Such a conception of a postmodern era subsumes and simplifies diverse political and cultural standpoints within a single periodizing structure and in turn betrays an exaggerated belief in the radical novelty of contemporary positions. . . . The postmodern ideology of the rupture, the apocalyptic appeal to deaths and endings, merely reinforces the very tradition which it is trying to subvert, re-enacting one of the most enduring topoi of modernity, the radical negation of the past.
>
> (1989: 52–3)

If postcolonial pedagogy is going to escape the impasse faced by postmodern theories of subjectivity, it will need what Sandra Harding calls a preferential option for a view of the oppressed from a "standpoint epistemology." This speaks directly to the call for praxis and "entails greater attention to the knowledge of those who are oppressed at many levels – by reason of gender, sexual orientation (gays and lesbians), race, class, nationality, and degree of physical limitations" (Welch forthcoming). This becomes especially important at a time when postmodernism has become a predatory cultural movement that includes an "enormous pluralization of tastes, practices, enjoyments, and needs . . . patterns of consumption . . . [that] have become embedded in a variety of lifestyles" (Heller 1990: 10) and where grounding these values and lifestyles takes the form of an entrenched cultural pluralism. In an era in which "cultures are becoming pluralized to the degree of total particularization" and in which "meaningful, rational decision-making" is becoming less possible (Heller 1990: 11), educators need a sophisticated concept of pedagogy that can lay the ground for non-coercive dialogue with consumer tastes, the politics of conquest, and a Eurocentric and androcentric view of the meta-subject. This means that teachers must begin to challenge Western male views of subjectivity and agency.

Are we forever suspended in Barthes's "dark night of history" where the postmodern apotheosis of human identity has become the eroded, the splintered, the parodic and disseminatory self – the shattered *image* of self-identity seeking out residual, atopic spaces of perversion? Can the "split-I" (*Ich-Spaltung*) forged amidst the semiotic debris in the postmodern wasteland be healed and transformed by pedagogies not yet written, not yet conceived? Can we even begin to conceptualize what such a challenge would look like? Readers should not be surprised at discovering in Terry Eagleton's remarks a particular theoretical resonance. Nor should they be surprised when educators begin to ask questions of pedagogy and politics again in light of the social's postmodern turn.

> Where human subjects politically begin, in all their sensuous specificity, is with certain needs and desires. Yet need and desire are also what renders us nonidentical with ourselves, opening us up to some broader social dimension; and what is posed within this dimension is the question of what *general* conditions would be necessary for our particular needs and desires to be fulfilled. Mediated through the general in this way, particular demands cease to be self-identical and return to themselves transformed by a discourse of the other. The feminist, nationalist, or trade unionist might now come to recognize that in the long run none of their desires is realizable without the fulfillment of the others'.
>
> (Eagleton 1990: 37–8)

Chapter 7

Multiculturalism and the postmodern critique

Towards a pedagogy of resistance and transformation

SOCIAL JUSTICE UNDER SIEGE: SLOUCHING TOWARDS ATZLÁN

We inhabit skeptical times, historical moments spawned in a temper of distrust, disillusionment, and despair. Social relations of discomfort and diffidence have always existed, but our own time is particularly invidious in this regard, marked as it is by a rapture of greed, untempered and hyper-eroticized consumer will, racing currents of narcissism, severe economic and racial injustices, and heightened social paranoia. The objective conditions of Western capitalism now appear so completely incompatible with the realization of freedom and liberation that it is easy to see the two as mutually antagonistic enterprises. Situated beyond the reach of ethically convincing forms of accountability, capitalism has dissolved the meaning of democracy and freedom into glossy aphorisms one finds in election campaign sound bites or at bargain basement sales in suburban shopping malls. The American public has been proffered a vision of democracy that is a mixture of Sunday barbecue banality, American Gladiator jocksniffery, AMWAY enterprise consciousness, and the ominous rhetoric of "New World Order" jingoism.

The heroic cult of modernism which has naturalized the power and privilege of "dead white men" and accorded the pathology of domination the status of cultural reason has all but enshrined a history of decay, defeat, and moral panic. As illustrated so vividly in Oliver Stone's television mini-series *Wild Palms*, greed, avarice, and cynicism have insinuated themselves into virtually every aspect of cultural life, and have become rationalized and aestheticized as necessary resources that must be fed into a vast technological machine known as Western civilization. It is history that has installed Willie Horton into our structural unconscious and helped make possible and desirable the legal torture and dehumanization of Rodney King and people of color in general. That the fortified, postmodern noir metropolises of this fin-de-siècle era have grown more Latinophobic, homophobic, xenophobic, sexist, racist, and bureaucratically cruel is not reflective of the self-understanding of the public at large but of the way that the public has been constructed within predatory culture through a politics of representation linked to the repressive moralism of successive conservative political regimes and counterattacks from the Right against cultural democracy. We should not forget, either, the spectatorial detachment of those postmodern free-floating intellectuals who, despite their claim to be part of a collective deconstructive project, often fail to mobilize intellectual work in the interest of a liberatory praxis.

The present moral apocalypse, perhaps most vividly represented by the maelstrom of anger and violence under the smoke-filled skies of Los Angeles – what Mike Davis calls the "L.A. Intifada" (Katz and Smith 1992) – has not been brought on simply by the existence of midnight hustlers, the drug trade, skewed ambition, or gang members taking advantage of public outrage over the justice system, but by shifting economic, political, and cultural relations that have worsened over the last two decades. We have been standing at the crossroads of a disintegrating culture, and have witnessed a steady increase in the disproportionate level of material wealth, economic dislocation, and intergenerational poverty suffered by African-Americans, Latinos, and other minorities. Such conditions have been brought about by the frenetic and, at times, savage immorality of the Reagan and Bush administrations, as evidenced in their direct attacks on the underclass, the disintegration of social programs, and the general retreat from civil rights that occurred during their tenure in office.

Other characteristics of this current juncture include: changes in the structure of the U.S. economy; the declining inner-city job market; growing national unemployment rates; a drastic decline in the number of unskilled positions in traditional blue-collar industries in urban areas; the increasing numbers of youth competing for fewer and fewer entry-level unskilled jobs; the automation of clerical labor; the movement of the African-American middle class out of the once multiclass ghetto; the shifting of service-sector employment to the suburbs (Kasinitz 1988); the destructive competition among nations that results from a free-trade policy fueled by the retrograde notion that other nations can achieve economic growth by unbalanced sales to the U.S. market; increased global competition provoking capitalist manufacturing firms to reduct cost by exploiting immigrant workers in U.S. cities or "out-sourcing" to Third World countries; and a post-Fordist de-monopolization of economic structures and the deregulation and globalization of markets, trade, and labor as well as deregulated local markets "that [make] local capital vulnerable to the strategies of corporate raiders" (Featherstone 1990: 7).

In addition, we are faced with an increasing assault on human intelligence by the architects of mass culture, an increasing dependency on social cues manufactured by the mass media to construct meaning and build consensus on moral issues, and the strengthening of what Piccone (1988: 9) has called the "unholy symbiosis of abstract individualism and managerial bureaucracies." The white-controlled media have ignored the economic and social conditions responsible for bringing about in African-American communities what Cornel West has called a "walking nihilism of pervasive drug addiction, pervasive alcoholism, pervasive homicide, and an exponential rise in suicide" (cited in Stephanson 1988: 276).

THE DILEMMA OF POSTMODERN CRITIQUE AND THE DEBATE OVER MULTICULTURALISM

I have begun with social and cultural oppression as a background for my discussion, since I share Michele Wallace's conviction that the debates over multiculturalism cannot afford to have their connection to wider material relations occulted by a focus on theoretical issues divorced from the lived experiences of oppressed groups:

> Many individual events on the current cultural landscape conspire to make me obsessed with contemporary debates over "multiculturalism" in both the art world and the culture at large, but my concern is grounded first and foremost in my observation of the impact of present material conditions on an increasing sector of the population. These material conditions, which include widespread homelessness, joblessness, illiteracy, crime, disease (including AIDS), hunger, poverty, drug addiction, alcoholism as well as the various habits of ill health, and the destruction of the environment are (let's face it) the myriad social effects of late multinational capitalism.
>
> (1991: 6)

A focus on the material and global relations of oppression can help us to avoid reducing the "problem" of multiculturalism to simply one of attitudes and temperament or, in the case of the academy, to a case of textual disagreement and discourse wars. It also helps to emphasize the fact that in the United States the concoction called "multiculturalism," which has resulted from a forensic search for equality and the political ladling of the long-brewing "melting pot," has produced an aversion to rather than a respect for difference. Regrettably, multiculturalism has been too often transformed into a code word in contemporary political jargon that has been fulsomely invoked in order to divert attention from the imperial legacy of racism and social injustice in this country and the ways in which new racist formations are being produced in spaces culturally de-differentiated and demonized by neo-conservative platforms that anathematize difference through attacks on the concept of heterogeneous public cultures (see Ravitch 1990, 1991; Kimball 1991; Browder 1992).

In the sections that follow, I want to discuss recent articulations of the postmodern critique in order to examine the limitations of current conservative and liberal formulations of multiculturalism. In doing so, I should like to pose an alternative analysis. I shall argue that, despite its limitations for constructing an emancipatory politics, postmodern criticism can offer educators and cultural workers a means of problematizing the issue of difference and diversity in ways that can deepen and extend existing debates over multiculturalism, pedagogy, and social transformation. Certain new strands of postmodern critique that fall under the rubric of "political" and "critical" postmodernism deserve serious attention in this regard. I will be expanding some ideas discussed in Chapter 4.

More specifically, I shall redraw the discussion of multiculturalism from the perspective of new strands of postmodern critique that emphasize the construction of "a politics of difference." I shall conclude by urging critical educators to reclaim the importance of relational or global critique – in particular the concept of "totality" – in their efforts to bring history and materiality back into theoretical and pedagogical discourses.

SUBALTERN AND FEMINIST CHALLENGES TO THE POSTMODERN CRITIQUE

Enlightenment reason mocks us as we allow it to linger in our educational thinking and policies; some of the most painful lessons provided by postmodern criticism have been that a teleological and totalizing view of scientific progress is antipathetic to liberation; that capitalism has posited an irrecuperable disjunction between ethics and economics; and that, paradoxically, modernity has produced an intractable thralldom to the very logic of domination which it has set out to contest and in doing so has reproduced new forms of the repression to which it has so disdainfully pointed.

The riot of contradictory perspectives surrounding the lush profusion of rival claims about what exactly constitutes the postmodern condition is perhaps one of the ironic outcomes of the condition itself. Broadly speaking, the postmodern critique concerns itself with a rejection or debunking of modernism's epistemic foundations or metanarratives; a dethronement of the authority of positivistic science that essentializes differences between what appear to be self-possessing identities; an attack on the notion of a unified goal of history; and a deconstruction of the magnificent Enlightenment swindle of the autonomous, stable, and self-contained ego that is supposed to be able to act independently of its own history, its own indigenist strands of meaning-making and cultural and linguistic situatedness, and its inscriptions in the discourses of, among others, gender, race, and class.

Postmodern social theory has rightly claimed that we lack a vocabulary or epistemology that is able to render the world empirically discoverable or accurately mappable, and that experience and reason cannot be explained outside of the social production of intelligibility. It emphasizes the indissociability of language, power, and subjectivity. Meaning does not inhere stratigraphically within a text or in the abstract equivalence of the signified. The labyrinthine path of Enlightenment rationality has been shown to function not as an access to but rather as a detour from the iterability of meaning – from its connection to human suffering and oppression. Further, the postmodern critique has been exemplary in revealing the hopelessness of attempts by empiricists to transcend the political, ideological, and economic conditions that transform the world into cultural and social formations. While postmodern social theory has advanced our understanding of the politics of representation and identity formation, the fashionable apostasy of certain postmodern articulations and inflections of critical social theory have noticeably abandoned the language of social change, emancipatory practice, and transformative politics. In fact, many of them carry in their intoxication with the idea of "cultural surplus" a mordantly pessimistic and distinctively reactionary potential.

Postmodern criticism's attempt to transform the concept of the political through its emphasis on signification and representation, its preoccupation with the dispersion of history into the after-image of the text, and its challenge to logocentric conceptions of truth and experience have not gone uncontested. For instance, Paul Gilroy has made clear some of the problems with theorizing under the banner of postmodernism – if under such a banner one assumes one has constructed a politics of refusal, redemption, and emancipation. Gilroy writes:

> It is interesting to note that at the very moment when celebrated Euro-American cultural theorists have pronounced the collapse of "grand narratives" the expressive culture of Britain's black poor is dominated by the need to construct them as narratives of redemption and emancipation. This expressive culture, like others elsewhere in the African diaspora, produces a potent historical memory and an authoritative analytic and historical account of racial capitalism and its overcoming. (1990: 278)

What some prominent cultural critics view as the constituent features of postmodernism – depthlessness, the retreat from the question of history, and the disappearance of affect – do not, in Gilroy's view, take seriously enough what is going on in black expressive culture. Blatantly contradicting this supposed "cultural dominant" of postmodernism is "the repertoire of 'hermeneutic gestures'." Gilroy points out that widely publicized views of the postmodern condition held by such prominent critics as Fredric Jameson may simply constitute another form of Eurocentric master narrative, since black expressive cultures use all the new technological means at their disposal "not to flee from depth but to revel in it, not to abjure public history but to proclaim it" (1990: 278). Similarly, Cornel West (1989b: 96) qualifies black cultural practices in the arts and intellectual life as examples of a "potentially enabling yet resisting postmodernism" that has grown out of

> an acknowledgment of a reality that [black people] cannot not know – the ragged edges of the real, of necessity; a reality historically constructed by white supremacist practices in North America during the age of Europe. These ragged edges – of not being able to eat, not to have shelter, not to have health care – all this is infused into the strategies and styles of black cultural practices.
>
> (1989b: 93)

Important concerns about the postmodern critique have also been posed by feminist theorists. They have questioned why men, in particular, find the new gospel of postmodernism to be so significantly compelling. Their objections are related not least to the fact that a theoretical conversion to the postmodern critique in many instances allows men to retain their privileged status as bearers of the Word precisely because it distracts serious attention from the recent concentration on feminist discourse (Kaplan 1987: 150–2). Dominant strands of the postmodern critique also tend to delegitimize the recent literature of peoples of color, black women, Latin Americans, and Africans (Christian 1987: 55). In addition, we are reminded that just at a time in history when a great many groups are engaged in "nationalisms" which involve redefining their status as marginalized Others, the academy has begun to legitimize a critical theory of the "subject" which holds the concept of agency in doubt, and which casts a general skepticism on the possibilities of a general theory which can describe the world and institute a quest for historical progress (Harstock 1987, 1989; DiStephano 1990).

It is difficult to argue against calls to decapitalize the registers of Patriarchy, Manhood, and Truth as they manifest themselves within dominant variants of the postmodern critique. With such a consideration in mind, I would ask if it is at all possible to recuperate and extend the project of postmodernist critique within the context of a critical pedagogy of multiculturalism in a way that remains attentive to the criticisms posed above. To attempt to answer such a question demands that I establish at the outset both by my own convergences with and departures from the discourse genre of postmodernism.

LUDIC AND RESISTANCE POSTMODERNISM

I will now expand on the idea of critical postmodernism that I introduced in Chapter 4. Postmodernist criticism is not monolithic and for the purposes of this essay I would distinguish between two theoretical strands. The first has been astutely described by Teresa Ebert (1991b: 115) as "ludic postmodernism" – an approach to social theory that is decidedly limited in its ability to transform oppressive social and political regimes of power. Ludic postmodernism generally focuses on the fabulous combinatory potential of signs in the production of meaning, and occupies itself with a reality that is constituted by the continual playfulness of the signifier and the heterogeneity of differences. As such, ludic postmodernism (e.g., Lyotard, Derrida, Baudrillard) constitutes a moment of self-reflexivity in deconstructing Western metanarratives, asserting that "meaning itself is self-divided and undecidable" (Ebert, forthcoming b).

Politics, in this view, is not an unmediated referent to action that exists outside of representation. Rather, politics becomes a textual practice (e.g., parody, pastiche, fragmentation) that unsettles, decenters, and disrupts rather than transforms the totalizing circulation of meaning within grand narratives and dominant discursive apparatuses (Ebert, forthcoming b; Zavarzadeh and Morton 1991). While ludic postmodernism may be applauded for attempting to deconstruct the way that power is deployed within cultural settings, it ultimately represents a form of detotalizing micro-politics in which the contextual specificity of difference is set up against the totalizing machineries of domination. The contingent, in this case, determines necessity as ludic postmodernism sets up a "superstructuralism" that privileges the cultural, discursive, and ideological over the materiality of modes and relations of production (Zavarzadeh and Morton 1991).

Educators should assume a cautionary stance toward ludic postmodernism because, as Ebert notes, it often simply reinscribes the status quo and reduces history to the supplementarity of signification or the free-floating trace of textuality (1991b: 115). As a mode of critique, it rests its case on interrogating specific and local enunciations of oppression but often fails to analyze such enunciations in relation to larger, dominating structures of oppression (Aronowitz and Giroux 1991).

Ludic postmodernism is akin to what Scott Lash (1990) calls "spectral postmodernism" – a form of critique that deals with the de-differentiation and blurring of disciplinary knowledge and genres (e.g., literature and criticism) and involves the implosion of the real into representation, the social into the mediascape, and exchange-value into sign-value. For the spectral postmodernist, the social is sucked up and dissolved into the world of signs and electronic communication while depth of meaning is imploded into superficiality. Pauline Marie Rosenau (1992) refers to this as "sceptical postmodernism" – a strand of postmodernism that reflects not only an ontological agnosticism that urges a relinquishing of the primacy of social transformation but also an epistemological relativism that calls for a tolerance of a range of meanings without advocating any one of them. Ludic postmodernism often takes the form of a triumphalistic and hoary dismissal of Marxism and grand theory as being hopelessly embroiled in a futile project of world-historical magnitude that is out of place in these new times. Such an endeavor often brings new forms of "totalization" into the debate through the back door of antifoundationalist theorizing (Lyotard's universalization of local stories, for example).

The kind of postmodern social theory I want to pose as a counterweight to skeptical and spectral postmodernism has been referred to as "oppositional postmodernism" (Foster 1983), "radical critique-al theory" (Zavarzadeh and Morton 1991), "postmodern education" (Aronowitz and Giroux 1991), "resistance postmodernism" (Ebert 1991b, forthcoming b) and "critical postmodernism" (Giroux 1992; McLaren and Hammer 1989). These forms of critique are not alternatives to ludic postmodernism but appropriations and extensions of this critique. Resistance postmodernism brings to ludic critique a form of materialist intervention since it is not solely based on a textual theory of difference but rather on one that is social and historical. In this way, postmodern critique can serve as an interventionist and transformative critique of U.S. culture. Following Ebert, resistance postmodernism attempts to show that "textualities (significations) are material practices, forms of conflicting social relations" (1991b: 115). The sign is always an arena of material conflict and competing social relations as well as ideas, and we can "rewrite the sign as an ideological process formed out of a signifier standing in relation to a matrix of historically possible or suspended signifieds" (Ebert, forthcoming b). In other words, difference is politicized by being situated *in* real social and historical conflicts rather than simply being textual or semiotic contradictions.

Resistance postmodernism does not abandon the undecidability or contingency of the social altogether; rather, the undecidability of history is understood as related to class struggle, the institutionalization of asymmetrical relations of power and privilege, and the way historical accounts are contested by different groups (Zavarzadeh and Morton 1991; Giroux 1992; McLaren and Hammer 1989). On this matter Ebert remarks: "We need to articulate a theory of difference in which the differing, deferring slippage of signifiers is not taken as the result of the immanent logic of language but as the effect of the social conflicts traversing signification" (1991b: 118). In other words, to view difference as simply textuality, as a formal, rhetorical space in which representation narrates its own trajectory of signification, is to ignore the social and historical dimensions of difference. Ebert elaborates this point as follows:

> A postmodern analytic of difference would enable us to move beyond the theory of difference as reified experience, and to critique the historical, economic, and ideological production of difference itself as a slipping, sliding series of relations that are struggled over and which produce the significations and subjectivities by which we live and maintain existing social relations.
>
> (1991b: 118)

She further describes resistance postmodernism as a politics of difference, as a theory of practice and a practice of theory:

> A resistance postmodern cultural critique – interrogating the political semiosis of culture – would be an oppositional political practice produced through the activity of reading, of making sense of cultural texts. However, opposition does not lie within – in other words it is not inherent in – a text or individual but is produced out of the practice of critique itself. Moreover, the critic herself is always already interpellated in the hegemonic subject positions of the culture, and contestation derives not from some will to resist but again is produced through the practice of critique.
>
> (1991b: 129)

Resistance postmodernism takes into account both the macro-political level of structural organization and the micro-political level of different and contradictory manifestations of oppression as a means of analyzing global relations of oppression. As such, it bears a considerable degree of affinity to what Scott Lash (1990) has termed "organic postmodernism," which tries to move beyond epistemic skepticism and explanatory nihilism to concern itself with issues related not just to the commodification of language but to the commodification of labor and the social relations of production. According to Lash, it attempts to reintegrate the cultural into the natural, material environment. From this perspective, rationality is not panhistorical or universal but is always situated in particular communities of discourse. In addition, organic postmodernism argues that high modernism articulates reality in a way that often serves as a cover for validating a Cartesian universe of discrete parts disconnected from wider economics of power and privilege. In other words, high modernism is accused of collapsing difference into the uneasy harmony we know as white patriarchal privilege – a privilege inextricably bound up with nationalism, imperialism, and the state.

MULTICULTURALISM AND THE POSTMODERN CRITIQUE

In this section I want to bring a critical or resistance postmodernist perspective to bear on the issue of multiculturalism. For me, the key issue for critical educators is to develop a multicultural curriculum and pedagogy that attends to the specificity (in terms of race, class, gender, sexual orientation, etc.) of difference (which is in keeping with ludic postmodernism) yet at the same time addresses the community of diverse Others under the law with respect to guiding referents of freedom and liberation (which is in keeping with resistance postmodernism).

According to Rosemary Hennessy (1993), difference needs to be discussed from a materialist feminist perspective as a form of ideological signification. Her work, heavily inflected by French feminism, neo-Marxism, and Gramsci's theory of hegemony, attempts to rethink the meaning of difference outside of its empiricist forms of capture and a postmodern neo-formalist hermeneutics, in order to articulate difference as an act of symptomatic reading, a critical counterhegemonic practice. By rewriting the materiality of discourse from a feminist critical standpoint as a form of ideology, and by reimagining the feminist standpoint as the collective subject of ideology critique, Hennessy is able to reconsider the boundaries of social totality in a convincing and important manner by conceiving them as uneven and contested ensembles of discourses grounded in the materiality of class struggle against the exploitative and oppressive social relations under patriarchal capitalism. For Hennessy, as for Ebert and other feminist theorists, differences are not "essential connections" but the product of "mediated and uneven historical positions" (1993: 99).

Too often liberal and conservative positions on diversity constitute an attempt to view culture as soothing balm – the *aftermath* of historical disagreement – some mythical present in bourgeois dreamtime where the irrationalites of historical conflict have been smoothed out. This view of culture is profoundly dishonest. The liberal and conservative positions on culture also assume that justice already exists and needs only to be evenly apportioned. However, both teachers and students need to realize that justice does not already exist simply because laws exist. Justice needs to be continually created, constantly struggled for. The question that I want to pose to teachers is this: Do teachers and cultural workers have access to a language that allows them to sufficiently critique and transform existing social and cultural practices that are defined by liberals and conservatives as democratic? Atzlán may await us but as the events in Chiapas portend, our arrival will not be without revolutionary struggle.

THE SUBJECT WITHOUT PROPERTIES

The critical postmodernist critique provides us with a way of understanding the limitations of a multiculturalism trapped within a logic of democracy that is under the sway of late capitalism. One of the surreptitious perversions of democracy has been the manner in which citizens have been invited to empty themselves of all racial or ethnic identity so that, presumably, they will all stand naked before the law as *unvermögender*. Others, in effect, citizens are invited to become little more than disembodied consumers. As Joan Copjec points out:

> Democracy is the universal quantifier by which America – the "melting pot," the "nation of immigrants" – constitutes itself as a nation. If *all* our citizens can be said to be Americans, this is not because we share any positive characteristics, but rather because we have all been given the right to *shed* these characteristics, to present ourselves as disembodied before the law. I divest myself of positive identity, therefore I am a citizen. This is the peculiar logic of democracy.
>
> (1991: 30)

Renato Rosaldo (1989) refers to this process as "cultural stripping," wherein individuals are stripped of their cultures in order to become "transparent" American citizens. While the embodied and perspectival location of any citizen's identity has an undeniable effect on what can be said, democracy has nevertheless created formal identities which give the illusion of identity while simultaneously erasing difference. David Lloyd (1991: 70) refers to this cultural practice as the formation of the "Subject without properties." As the dominated are invited to shed their positive identities, the dominators unwittingly serve as the regulating principle of identity itself by virtue of their very indifference.

The universality of the position of dominator is attained through its literal indifference and it "becomes representative in consequence of being able to take anyone's place, of occupying any place, of a pure exchangeability" (Lloyd 1991: 70). Such a subject without properties governs the distribution of humanity into the local (native) and the universal by assuming the "global ubiquity of the white European" which, in turn, becomes the very "regulative idea of Culture against which the multiplicity of local cultures is defined" (p. 70). Lloyd notes that the domination by the white universalized subject "is virtually self-legitimating since the capacity to be everywhere present becomes an historical manifestation of the white man's gradual approximation to the universality he everywhere represents" (p. 70).

Against this peculiar logic of democracy, resistance postmodernism argues that individuals need always to *rethink the relationship between identity and difference*. They need to understand their ethnicity in terms of a politics of location, positionality, or enunciation. Stuart Hall argues that "there's no enunciation without positionality. You have to position yourself *somewhere* in order to say anything at all" (1991: 18). One's identity, whether as black, white, or Latino, has to do with the discovery of one's ethnicity. Hall calls this process of discovery the construction of "new ethnicities" or "emergent ethnicities." Entailed in such a discovery is the

> need to honor the hidden histories from which . . . [people] . . . come. They need to understand the languages which they've been not taught to speak. They need to understand and revalue the traditions and inheritances of cultural expression and creativity. And in that sense, the past is not only a position from which to speak, but it is also an absolutely necessary resource in what one has to say. . . . So the relationship of the kind of ethnicity I'm talking about to the past is not a simple, essential one – it is a constructed one. It is constructed in history, it is constructed politically in part. It is part of narrative. We tell ourselves the stories of the parts of our roots in order to come into contact, creatively, with it. So this new kind of ethnicity – the emergent ethnicities – has a relationship to the past, but it is a relationship that is partly through memory, partly through narrative, one that has to be recovered. It is an act of cultural recovery.
>
> (Hall 1991: 18–19)

While the discourse of multiculturalism has tended to oppose hierarchical exclusiveness with arguments in favor of unrestricted inclusiveness (Wallace 1991: 6), a resistance postmodernist critique further problematizes the issue of exclusion and inclusion by articulating a new relationship between identity and difference. Not only can a resistance postmodernist articulation of difference theorize a place where marginalized groups can speak *from* but it can also provide groups a place from which to move *beyond* an essentialized and narrow ethnic identity since they also have a stake in global conditions of equality and social justice (Hall 1991).

Homi Bhabha (1990b, 1990c) has articulated an important distinction between "difference" and "diversity." Working from a post-structuralist perspective, Bhabha breaks from the social-democratic version of multiculturalism where race, class, and gender are modeled on a consensual conception of difference and locates his work within a radical democratic version of cultural pluralism which recognizes the essentially contested character of the signs and signifying apparatuses that people use in the construction of their identities (Mercer 1990: 8).

Bhabha is critical of the notion of diversity used in liberal discourse to refer to the importance of plural, democratic societies. He argues that with diversity comes a "transparent norm" constructed and administered by the "host" society that creates a false consensus. This is because the normative grid that locates cultural diversity at the same time serves to *contain* cultural difference: the "universalism that paradoxically permits diversity masks ethnocentric norms" (Bhabha 1991b: 208). Differences, on the other hand, do not always speak to consensus but are often incommensurable. Culture, as a system of difference, as symbol-forming activity, must in Bhabha's view be seen as "a process of translations" (1990a: 210). From this follows the observation that while cultures cannot be simply reduced to unregulatable textual play, neither do they exist as undisplaceable forms in the sense that they possess "a totalised prior moment of being or meaning – an essence" (1990a: 210).

Otherness in this sense is often internal to the symbol-forming activity of that culture and it is perhaps best to speak of culture as a form of "hybridity." As was pointed out in Chapter 3, within this hybridity, there exists a "third space" that enables other discursive positions to emerge – to resist attempts to normalize what Bhabha refers to as "the time-lagged colonial moment" (1991a: 211). This "third space" opens up possibilities for new structures of authority, and new political vistas and visions. Identity from this perspective is always an arbitrary, contingent, and temporary suturing of identification and meaning. Bhabha's distinction makes it clear why people such as Ravitch, Bloom, Hirsch, and Bennett are so dangerous when they talk about the importance of building a common culture. Who has the power to exercise meaning, to create the grid from which Otherness is defined, to create the identifications that invite closures on meanings, on interpretations and traditions?

I have suggested here that conservative and liberal multiculturalisms are really about the politics of assimilation; both assume that we really do live in a common egalitarian culture. Such an understanding of difference implies, as Iris Marion Young (1990: 164) notes, "coming into the game after the rules and standards have already been set, and having to prove oneself according to those rules and standards" – which are not set as culturally and experientially specific among the citizenry at large because within a pluralist democracy privileged groups have occluded their own advantage by invoking the ideal of an unsituated, neutral, universal common humanity of self-formation in which all can happily participate without regard to differences in race, class, age, or sexual orientation. Resistance postmodernism, in particular, unsettles such a notion of universal common humanity by exploring identity within the context of power, discourse, culture, experience, and historical specificity.

DIFFERENCE AND THE POLITICS OF SIGNIFICATION

Resistance postmodernism has been especially significant in reformulating the meaning of difference as a form of signification. Differences in this view do not constitute clearly marked zones of auto-intelligible experience or a unity of identity as they do within most conservative and liberal forms of cultural pluralism. Rather, differences are understood through a politics of signification, that is, through signifying practices that are both reflective and constitutive of prevailing economic and political relations (Ebert 1991b). Against the conservative multiculturalist understanding of difference as "self-evident cultural obviousness," as a "mark of plurality," or "the carefully marked off zones of experience – the privileged presence – of one group, one social category against another that we faithfully cultivate and reproduce in our analyses", Teresa Ebert defines difference as

> culturally constituted, made intelligible, through signifying practices. [For postmodern theories] "difference" is not a clearly marked zone of experience, a unity of identity of one social group against another, taken as cultural pluralism. Rather, postmodern differences are relations of opposing signifiers.
>
> (1991b: 117)

Liberal and conservative attacks on multiculturalism constitute a flawed politics of seeing; they work to seal over the fault-lines of difference, by failing to historicize the epistemological and ethical contradictions in which differences are inscribed. Liberalism, for instance, simply re-scripts existing practices of domination by trying to manage the contradictions within a politics of difference by, first of all, denying that such fundamental contradictions exist. Differences are not linked to asymmetric structures of power and privilege in the larger social formation. Liberal approaches to difference constitute, furthermore, a form of crisis management pluralism in which the boundaries of plurality are celebrated as indices of cultural interest. Yet these approaches ultimately fail to explore how capitalist social arrangements and patriarchal economics are imbricated in the politics of race, class gender and sexuality in ways that are further shaped by political and social patterns of production and consumption – patterns which, in turn, betray their own levels of specificity and periodization. Differences are produced according to the ideological production and reception of cultural signs. As Zavarzadeh and Morton point out, "Signs are neither eternally predetermined nor panhistorically undecidable: they are rather 'decided' or rendered as 'undecidable' in the moment of social conflicts" (1990: 156). Difference is not "cultural obviousness" such as black versus white or Latino versus European or Anglo-American; rather, differences are historical and cultural constructions (Ebert 1991b).

A resistance postmodernist critique can help teachers explore the ways in which students are differentially subjected to ideological inscriptions and multiply organized discourses of desire through a politics of signification. Student identities are produced by a type of discursive ventriloquism in that they are creatures of the languages and knowledges that students have inherited and which unconsciously exert control over their thinking and behavior. As James Donald (in press) points out, social norms often surface as personal and guilt-provoking desires since they have gone through a process that Foucault referred to as "folding." Donald points out that the

> norms and prohibitions instituted within social and cultural technologies are folded into the unconscious so that they "surface" not just as "personal desires" but in a complex and unpredictable dynamic of desire, guilt, anxiety, and displacement. Subjects have desires that they do not want to have; they reject them at the cost of guilt and anxiety.

While subjects are invariably prisoners of a male monopoly of language and knowledge production (Grosz 1990: 332), they are also active agents who are capable of exercising deliberate historical actions in and on the world (Giroux 1992). The point, of course, is that conscious knowledge is not exhaustive of either identity or agency. We need to acknowledge what is not so obvious about how difference is constitutive of both identity and agency.

Attempting to abandon all vestiges of the dominant culture in the struggle for identity can lead to a futile search for premodern roots that in turn leads to a narrow nationalism, as in the case of what Hall calls the "old ethnicity." Refusing to attempt to decolonize one's identity in the midst of the prevailing ideological and cultural hegemony can serve as a capitulation to assimilation and the loss of forms of critical historical agency. We should seek a view of multiculturalism and difference that moves beyond the "either/or" logic of assimilation and resistance. To make a claim for multiculturalism is not, in the words of Trinh T. Minh-ha

> to suggest the juxtaposition of several cultures whose frontiers remain intact, nor is it to subscribe to a bland "melting pot" type of attitude that would level all differences. [The struggle for a multicultural society] lies instead, in the intercultural acceptance of risks, unexpected detours, and complexities of relation between break and closure.
>
> (1991: 232)

ALWAYS TOTALIZE!

In this section I want to focus my analysis of multiculturalism on the concept of totality introduced in Chapter 1. I would like to emphasize that while educators must affirm students' "local" knowledges of sociopolitical and ethnic locations, the concept of totality must not be abandoned altogether. Not all forms of totalization are democratically deficient. Not all forms truncate, oppress, and destroy pluralism. As Fredric Jameson remarks

> Local struggles . . . are effective only so long as they also remain figures or allegories for some larger systemic transformation. Politics has to operate on the micro- and the macro-levels simultaneously; a modest restriction to local reforms within the system seems reasonable, but often proves politically demoralizing.
>
> (1989a: 386)

George Lipsitz underscores this idea, arguing that while totality can do violence to the specificity of events, a rejection of all totality would likely "obscure real connections, causes, and relationships – atomizing common experiences into accidents and endlessly repeated play . . . [and that] only by recognizing the collective legacy of accumulated human actions and ideas can we judge the claims to truth and justice of any one story" (1990: 214).

Without a shared vision (however contingent or provisional) of democratic community, we risk endorsing struggles in which the politics of difference collapses into new forms of separatism. As Steven Best points out, post-structuralists rightly deconstruct essentialist and repressive wholes, yet they often fail to see how crippling the valorizing of difference, fragmentation, and agonistics can be. This is especially true of ludic postmodernism. Best writes:

> The flip side of the tyranny of the whole is the dictatorship of the fragments. . . . [W]ithout some positive and normative concept of totality to counter-balance the poststructuralist/postmodern emphasis on difference and discontinuity, we are abandoned to the seriality of pluralist individualism and the supremacy of competitive values over communal life.
>
> (1989: 361)

As I noted in Chapter 1, what needs to be abandoned is the reductive use of totality, not the concept of totality itself.

Teresa Ebert (forthcoming b) argues brilliantly that we need to reassert the concept of totality not in the Hegelian sense of an organic, unified, oppressive unity, but rather "as both a system of relations and overdetermined structure of difference." Difference needs to be understood as social contradictions, as difference in relation, rather than dislocated, free-floating difference. Systems of differences, notes Ebert, always involve patterns of domination and relations of oppression and exploitation. We need to concern ourselves, therefore, with economies of relations of difference within historically specific totalities that are always open to contestation and transformation. As structures of difference that are always multiple and unstable, the oppressive relations of totalities (social, economic, political, legal, cultural, ideological) can always be challenged within a pedagogy of liberation. Ebert argues that totalities shouldn't be confused with Lyotard's notion of universal metanarratives.

Only when they are used unjustly and oppressively as all-encompassing and all-embracing global warrants for thought and action in order to secure an oppressive regime of truth, should totality and universality be rejected. We need to retain some kind of moral, ethical, and political ground – albeit a provisional one – from which to negotiate among multiple interests. Crucial to this argument is the important distinction between universal metanarratives (master narratives) and metacritical narratives. The resistance postmodernist critique repudiates the necessity or choice of any one master narrative because master narratives suggest that there is only one public sphere, one value, one conception of justice that triumphs over all others. Resistance postmodernism suggests that, on the contrary, "different spheres and rival conceptions of justice must be accompanied to each other" (Murphy 1991: 124). In other words, the "communitarian, the liberal or social democrat, the developmental liberal or humanist, the radical, and the romantic must find ways of living together in the same social space" (p. 124). This does not mean trying to press them all into a homogeneous cultural pulp but to suggest that there must be a multiplication of justices and a pluralistic conception of justice, politics, ethics, and aesthetics.

Again, the crucial question here is one that deals with the notion of *totality*. While I would argue against one grand narrative, I believe that there exists a primary metadiscourse that could, in fact, offer a *provisional* engagement with discourses of the Other in a way that can be unifying without dominating and that can provide for supplementary discourses. This is the metacritical narrative of rights or freedom. Peter Murphy distinguishes between a master discourse and a metadiscourse, arguing that "a master discourse wants to impose itself on all the other discourses – it is progressive, they are reactionary; it is right, they are wrong. A metadiscourse, on the other hand, seeks to understand society as a *totality*" (1991: 126). Murphy, like Ebert, argues against a Lyotardian rejection of the grand narrative of emancipation. Instead, he embraces the idea of totality as set forth by Charles Jencks. This distinction is worth emphasizing.

> Postmodernism, Jencks, following Venturi, argues is concerned with complexity and contradiction, and precisely because it is concerned with complexity and contradiction, it in fact has a special obligation to the whole. This is not the "harmonious whole" of canonic classicism, but rather the "difficult whole" of a pluralized and multi-dimensional world. Postmodernism, Jencks argues, is committed to synthesizing a "difficult whole" out of different fragments, references, and approaches.

> Its truth lies not in any part, but, as Venturi puts it, *in its totality or implications of totality.*
>
> (Murphy 1991: 126; italics in original)

Here I am not reclaiming or rewriting totality as a synonym for political economy or suggesting that a critical postmodernism resist narrating the location of the theorist or abandon local struggles. I am not setting up a Manichean contest between the *méta récits* of liberation and social justice and the polyvocality and positionality of an antifoundational approach to difference. I also want to make clear that I am not using the concept of "totality" to mean an act of generalizing from the law of intelligibility of one phenomena to the level of all social or cultural phenomena (Zavarzadeh and Morton 1991). Nor am I using it to mean some forgotten plenitude, formalized auratic experience, or bygone world that needs to be recovered for the sake of some noble nostalgia. Rather, I am using "totality" in the manner that Zavarzadeh and Morton (1991) have described as "global." Global understanding is a "form of explanation that is *relational* and *transdisciplinary* and that produces an account of the 'knowledge-effects' of culture by *relating* various cultural series" (p. 155). It is a mode of inquiry that attempts to address how the ludic postmodernist critique serves as a strategy of political containment, by privileging forms of "local" analysis which center the subject in experience as the Archimedean site of truth and posit ideology as the sole "reader" of experience.

Global or relational knowledge points to the existence of an underlying logic of domination within the signifying practices that constitute the cultural products of late capitalism and for this reason it sets itself against ludic postmodernism's dismissal of knowledge as integrative and political because of the supposed incommensurability of cultural, political, and economic phenomena. It moves beyond the cognitivism and empiricism of the dominant knowledge industry by dispossessing individuals of their imaginary sense of the autointelligibility of experience. Further, it reveals that *différance* is not an inherent condition of textuality but a socially overdetermined historical effect that acquires its tropicity only within given historical and cultural modes of intelligibility. Zavarzadeh and Morton argue that:

> in the ludic space of playfulness, the social relations of production are posited not as historically necessary but as subject to the laws of the alea: chance and contingency. In ludic deconstruction chance and contingency perform the same ideological role that "native" (i.e., non-logical, random, inscrutable) difference plays in traditional humanistic discourses. Both posit a social field beyond the reach of the logic of necessity and history.
>
> (1991: 194)

Resistance postmodernism offers teachers working in multicultural education a means of interrogating the locality, positionality, and specificity of knowledge (in terms of the race, class, and gender location of students) and of generating a plurality of truths (rather than one apodictic truth built around the invisible norm of Eurocentrism and white ethnicity), while at the same time situating the construction of meaning in terms of the material interests at work in the production of "truth effects" – that is, in the production of forms of intelligibility and social practices. Consequently, teachers working within a resistance postmodernism are able to call into question the political assumptions and relations of determination upon which social truths are founded in both the communities in which they work and the larger society of which they are a part. Ludic postmodernism, in contrast, effectively masks the relationship between dominant discourses and the social relations that they justify through an immanent reading of cultural texts (reading texts on their own terms) in which their internal and formal coherence takes priority over the social relations of their production. In fact, Zavarzadeh and Morton go so far as to suggest that ludic postmodernism gained ascendancy in the academy just at the time when capitalism became deterritorialized and multinational. In effect, they are arguing that the ludic postmodern critique has suppressed forms of knowing that "could explain multi-national capitalism's trans-territoriality and its affiliated phenomena" (Zavarzadeh and Morton 1991: 163).

Viewed from the perspective of the construction of a global or relational understanding, the idea of organizing postmodern critique around the referents of freedom and emancipation is an attempt to avoid a unifying logic that monolithically suppresses or forecloses meaning. Conversely, it is a determined effort to retain and understand the "difficult whole" of a pluralistic and global society. It is to take up a position against reactionary pluralists such as William Bennett, Diane Ravitch, and Allan Bloom, who embrace and advocate the idea of a harmonious common culture.

I have tried to argue that in order to have a liberating narrative informing our pedagogies, educators need to address the concept of totality. The idea of a master narrative's "phallic projectory" into the telos of historical destiny needs to be discredited, yet the idea of totality as a heterogeneous and not homogeneous temporality must be recuperated. The concepts of totality and infinity need to be dialectically positioned within any pedagogy of liberation. Emmanuel Levinas (1969: 25) notes that "the idea of infinity delivers subjectivity from the judgment of history to declare it ready for judgment at every moment" (cited in Chambers 1990: 109). Isn't this precisely what Frantz Fanon was trying to describe when he urged us to *totalize infinitely* as a communicative act (Taylor 1989: 26)? For me, spaces for rewriting dominant narratives come into being by the very fact of the patience of infinity, the diachrony of time which, as Levinas observes, is produced by our situatedness as ethical subjects and our responsibility to the Other. The problem, of course, is that the remarking of the social and the reinvention of the self must be understood as dialectically synchronous – that is, they cannot be conceived as unrelated or only marginally connected. They are mutually informing and constitutive processes.

According to Patrick Taylor (1989: 25), the essential ingredient of a narrative of liberation is the recognition of freedom in necessity. In this sense, the necessity of freedom becomes a *responsible totalization* – not a master narrative, but a metadiscourse or discourse of possibility (Giroux 1992). If we talk about totalization in the sense of a master narrative, we are referring to a type of discursive homogenization, a premature closure on meaning, a false universalism (what Taylor calls an "ordered totality") that leads to a categorical utopia – that is, to one or another inflection of fascism. Infinite totalization, which is an asymptotical approach, refers to a hypothetical or provisional utopia. As P. B. Dauenhauer (1989) notes, the hypothetical embrace of utopian representation must be distinguished from the categorical embrace. To embrace ideology or utopia categorically is a form of "bad infinity" by denying alternatives to the present reality. Of course, in saying this, attention must be given to the specific structural differences that exist in various national contexts today.

Teachers need to stress in their teaching (following Ernst Bloch 1986) the hypothetical or provisional and not the categorical embrace of utopia. Paradoxically, hypothetical utopias based on infinite totalization are the most concrete of all because they offer through their negative content (i.e., the concrete negation of domination) *the end of ordered totalities.* Patrick Taylor, citing Jameson, notes that "the ultimate interpretive task is the understanding of symbolic works in relation to a demystifying, open-ended narrative of liberation that is grounded in the imperative of human freedom" (1989: 19). Ann Game makes a similar point when she locates inquiry as a "disturbing pleasure" in which "the risks of infinity, with hints of madness . . . are far preferable to the safety (and, possibly, bad faith) of closure" (1991: 191).

Narratives of freedom are ways of transcending those social myths (with their pre-given narrative orders) that reconcile us, through the resolution of binary oppositions, to lives of subordination. Narratives of liberation are those that totalize infinitely, but not by integrating difference into a monolithic executive identity produced by modernity's colonial or neo-colonial situation – by forcing difference into silence precisely when it is asked to speak (Sáenz 1991: 158). They do not simply negate the difference produced by identity secreted in a situation of domination, because this simply saps the sustenance of the identity of the dominator

(Sáenz 1991). Narratives of liberation do not merely construct an identity that

> runs counter to Eurocentric identity; for such would be a mere resurrection of the racist European myth of the "noble savage" – a millenarianism in reverse, the expression of Eurocentric self-dissatisfaction and self-flagellation over its own disenchantment with the "modernity" produced by its project of "possessive individualism."
>
> (1991: 159)

Rather, narratives of liberation point to the possibility of new, alternative identities contemporaneous with modernity but not simply through inverting its normative truths.

The educator as historical agent is positioned within the tension produced by modernist and postmodernist attempts to resolve the living contradiction of being both the subject and the object of meaning. But our mode of critical analysis needs to move beyond the tropological displacement of discursive familiarity or a hijacking of meaning in the back alleys of theory (as is the case with ludic postmodernism). Educators require narratives of liberation that can serve a *metacritical* function – that can metaconceptualize relations of everyday life – and that do not succumb to the transcendental unity of subject and object or their transfiguring coalescence (Saldivar 1990: 173). In other words, such narratives promote a form of analectic understanding in addition to a dialectical understanding. As Enrique Dussel (1980/1985) has argued, analectics reaches exteriority not *through* totality (as does dialectics) but rather beyond it. Sáenz (1991: 162) remarks that the "beyond" that Dussel speaks about must not be interpreted as an absolute beyond all criticism (i.e., God) but rather as a "beyond" that has its roots "in the midst of domination," that is, in suffering of the oppressed "understood within its colonial textuality." Analectics could be thus described as a form of "pluritopic" dialectical critique aimed at revealing the monotopic understanding of Eurocentrism as merely contingent to its own cultural traditions (Sáenz 1991).

Through a praxis of infinite totalization educators can provide analectically a new vision of the future that is contained in the present, immanent in this very moment of reading, in the womb of the actual. Such a praxis can help us understand that subjective intentions do not constitute the apodictical site of truth. Subjectivities and identities of students and teachers are always the artifacts of discursive formations; that is, they are always the products of historical contexts and language games (Kincheloe 1991; Carspecken 1991). Students and teachers are all actors in narrative configurations and emplotments that they did not develop but that are the products of historical and discursive struggles that have been folded back into the unconscious. Teachers need to learn to recognize those internalized discourses, not only those that inform the ritualization of their teaching practices, but that organize their vision of the future. They must recall, too, that human agency is not a substrate that props them up like the crutches in a Dali painting, but has *imperative force*. The theater of agency is *possibility*.

Agency is informed by the stereotypical ways in which subjectivities have been allegorized by historical discourses which have been gridded in the subject-positions teachers and students take. These discourses differentially enable and enact specific forms of practice. Yet while there is a logos immanent to the discourses that constitute teachers as functionaries within modern technologies of power, this does not mean that educators and cultural workers cannot foster and realize potentialities within the discursive and material conditions of their own communities. Educators have a heritage of possibilities from which to work. While these possibilities affect the ground of teachers' subjectivism they do not saturate their will, nor do they prevent them from struggling against the constraints that bind freedom and justice. Identities may thus be considered both mobile structures and structured mobilities and as such are dialectically re-initiating. David Trend speaks to this issue when he emphasizes the importance of understanding the productive character of knowledge. While one's influence on the process of knowledge production is always partial, cultural workers do exert considerable influence:

> Acknowledging the role of the "learning subject" in the construction of culture, we affirm processes of agency, difference, and, ultimately, democracy. We suggest to students and audiences that they have a role in the making of their world and that they need not accept positions as passive spectators or consumers. This is a position that recognizes and encourages the atmosphere of diverse and contradictory opinions so dreaded by the conservative proponents of a "common culture." It functions on the belief that a healthy democracy is one that is always being scrutinized and tested.
>
> (Trend 1992: 150)

To exert an influence over cultural production we must find ways of speaking and acting outside the totalizing system of logocentric thought by creating metacritical and relational perspectives linked to the imperative of a unifying project (in Sartre's sense). Educators need to get outside the admixtures and remnants of languages – the multiplicity of stereotypical voices that already populate their vocabulary and fill up all the available linguistic spaces – in order to find different ways of approaching or mediating the real. Educators and cultural workers need to cross borders into zones of cultural difference rather than construct subjectivities that simply reassert themselves as monadic forms of totality facilitated by consumerist ethics and marketplace logic (Giroux 1992).

This means developing a more effective theory for understanding pedagogy in relation to the workings of power in the larger context of race, class, and gender articulations. It means advancing a theory that does not elevate the teacher–other as individual knower and devalue the student as an objectified, unknowing entity. Students must not be constructed as the zombified ideal "always already" open to manipulation for passive acquiescence to the status quo. We should not forfeit the opportunity of theorizing both teachers and students as historical agents of resistance.

CRITICAL PEDAGOGY: TEACHING FOR A HYBRID CITIZENRY AND MULTICULTURAL SOLIDARITY

Resistance postmodernism has figured prominently in the development of new forms of pedagogical praxis concerned with rethinking educational politics in a multicultural society (Giroux 1992; McLaren and Leonard 1993; Aronowitz and Giroux 1991). Of particular significance is Giroux's concept of a "border pedagogy" which enables educators to affirm and legitimate local meanings and constellations of meaning that grow out of particular discursive communities but at the same time interrogate the interests, ideologies, and social practices that such knowledges serve when viewed from the perspective of more global economies of power and privilege.

A pedagogy informed significantly by resistance postmodernism suggests that teachers and cultural workers need to take up the issue of "difference" in ways that don't replay the monocultural essentialism of the "centrisms" – Anglocentrism, Eurocentrism, phallocentrism, androcentrism, and the like. They need to create a politics of alliance-building, of dreaming together, of solidarity that moves beyond the condescension of, say, "race awareness week," that actually serves to keep forms of institutionalized racism intact. A solidarity has to be struggled for that is not centered around market imperatives but develops out of the imperatives of liberation, democracy, and critical citizenship.

The notion of the citizen has been pluralized and hybridized, as Kobena Mercer notes, by the presence of diversity of social subjects. Mercer points out that "solidarity does not mean that everyone thinks the same way, it begins when people have the confidence to disagree over issues of fundamental importance precisely because they 'care' about constructing a common ground" (1990: 68). Solidarity is not impermeably solid but depends to a certain degree on antagonism and uncertainty. Timothy Maliqualim Simone calls this type of multiracial solidarity "geared to maximizing points of interaction rather than harmonizing, balancing, or equilibrating the distribution of bodies, resources, and territories" (1989: 191).

While guarding against the privileging of a false universalism, a false unity that denies the internal rifts of bodily desire, both teachers and students need to open themselves to the possibility of Otherness so that the particularity of individual being can become visible in relations of power and privilege. Students especially need to be provided with opportunities to devise different assemblages to the self by dismantling and interrogating the different kinds of discursive segmentarity that inform their subjectivities, subverting those stratified and hierarchized forms of subjectivity that code the will, and developing nomadic forms of individual and collective agency that open up new assemblages of desire and modes of being-in-the-world (Grossberg 1988a).

A critical pedagogy that embraces resistance postmodernism needs to construct a politics of refusal that can provide both the conditions for interrogating the institutionalization of formal equality based on the prized imperatives of a white, Anglo male world and for creating spaces to facilitate an investigation of the way in which dominant institutions must be transformed so that they no longer serve simply as conduits for a motivated indifference to victimization, for a Euroimperial aesthetics, for depredations of economic and cultural dependency, and for the production of asymmetrical relations of power and privilege.

Here it is important to contest the charge made by some liberal humanist educators that teachers should only speak for themselves and not for others. Those who claim that teachers can and should only speak for themselves – a claim that is at the very least implied by many critics of critical pedagogy – forget that "when I 'speak for myself' I am participating in the creation and reproduction of discourses through which my own and other selves are constituted" (Alcoff 1991/92: 21). Linda Alcoff notes that we need to promote a *dialogue with* rather than a *speaking for* others (although this does not preclude us from speaking for others under certain restricted circumstances). Drawing upon the work of Gayatri Chakravorty Spivak, Alcoff maintains that we can adopt a "speaking to" the other that does not essentialize the oppressed as non-ideologically constructed subjects. Summarizing Spivak, Alcoff stresses how important it is that the intellectual "neither abnegates his or her discursive role nor presumes an authenticity of the oppressed but still allows for the possibility that the oppressed will produce a 'countersentence' that can then suggest a new historical narrative" (Alcoff 1991/92: 23). As educators we need to be exceedingly cautious about our attempts to speak for others, questioning how our discourses as events position us as authoritative and empowered speakers in ways that unwittingly constitute a reinscription of the discourse of colonization, of patriarchy, of racism, of conquest – "a reinscription of sexual, national, and other kinds of hierarchies" (Alcoff 1991/92: 29). Educators also need to avoid a "tolerance" that appropriates the difference of the Other in the name of the colonizer's own self-knowledge and increased domination. This is a lesson Paulo Freire has taught us so well.

Critical pedagogy does not work toward some grandiose endpoint of an ideologically perceived world history but rather attempts to make understandable the indefinite and to explore other models of sociality and self-figuration that go beyond dominant language formations and social organizations. In doing so, it has often been accused of being inaccessible to rank-and-file teachers. Trinh T. Minh-ha (1991) issues a very telling warning against such calls for accessibility of language. She writes that resistance to the language of complex theory can reinstitute "common sense" as an alternative to theory – that is, it can usher in a new dictatorship of pre-theoretical nativism in which experience supposedly speaks for itself. To be "accessible," writes Trinh, often suggests that

> one can employ neither symbolic and elliptical language, as in Asian, African, or Native American cultures (because Western ears often equate it with obscurantism); nor poetic languages (because "objective" literal thinking is likely to identify it with "subjective" aestheticism). The use of dialogical analytical language is also discouraged (because the dominant worldview can hardly accept that in the politics of representing marginality and resistance one might have to speak at least two different things at once).
>
> (1991: 228)

Trinh further notes, after Isaac Julien, that resistance to theory is embodied in white people's resistance to the complexity of black experience. Not only does such resistance point to the illusion that there exists a natural, self-evident language, but it can also lead to forms of racism and intolerance and the politics of exclusion. The "diversely hybrid experiences of heterogeneous contemporary societies are denied" by such a form of binary thinking, which would reduce the languages of analysis to white, hegemonic forms of clarity (Trinh 1991: 229).

INTENSIFYING THE OBVIOUS AND ACCELERATING THE MUNDANE

A pedagogy that takes resistance postmodernism seriously does not make the nativist assumption that knowledge is pre-ontologically available and that various disciplinary schools of thought may be employed in order to tease out different readings of the same "common-sense" reality in a context of impartiality. Rather, the discourses that inform the educator's problematics are understood as constitutive of the very reality that he or she is attempting to understand. Consequently, the classroom is the site of the teacher's own embodiment in theory/discourse, ethical disposition as moral and political agent, and situatedness as a cultural worker within a larger narrative identity. In recording the important role played by "place" in any critical pedagogy, it should be clear that we are talking not about physical milieu where knowledge is made visible within pre-ordained and circumscribed limits but rather the textual space that one occupies and the affective space one creates as a teacher. In other words, the discursive practice of "doing pedagogy" does not simply treat knowledge outside of the way that it is taken up by both teachers and students as *a form of dialogue.* I am referring here to the multi-voicedness of democratic discourse not in the sense of unrestrained intersubjective exchange but rather as challenging "the logic of dialogue as equal linguistic exchange." Such a challenge involves interrogating the ideological interests of the speaker, the social overdeterminations of utterances, and the social context in which utterances are both historically produced and culturally understood (Hitchcock 1993: 7). Knowledge can never be treated as a cultural artifact or possession that serves as a pristine, prefigurative source of cultural authenticity inviting unbiased analysis.

The project of critical pedagogy means bringing the laws of cultural representation face to face with their founding assumptions, contradictions, and paradoxes. It also means encouraging teachers to participate in affective as well as intellectual cultures of the oppressed, and to challenge in the spirit of Ernst Bloch's "militant optimism" ethical and political quietism in the face of operating homilies such as the "inevitability of progress" or what might seem like historical inevitability – a perspective that leads to the cult of the mausoleum. Educators can no longer project onto the student-as-Other that part of themselves which out of fear and loathing they rejected or subtracted from their identity in their attempt to become unified subjects – that "split-off" part of themselves which prevents them from becoming whole, that disfiguring surplus that they cast out in order to become white or live in the thrall of racelessness, that metaphysical double that guarantees their own self-regarding autonomy. From this point of view, liberation is never an encapsulated fulfillment of some prefigured end constructed in the temple of memory, but the lived tension between the duration of history and the discourse of possibility. It resides in an approach to the *Aufhebung* – our passing into the "not-yet," and seeking the immanent utopia in the crisis of meaning and the social relations that inform it. It is found, too, in the proleptic consciousness of liminality – the liberating intention of the reflective will caught in the "subjunctive" moment of the "ought" and disabused of metaphysical illusion. It is formed out of an ethical intent commensurable with the love that Paulo Freire and Che Guevara both argue constitutes the wellspring of all revolutionary action.

Educators need to do more than to help students redescribe or represent themselves in new ways. As Sander L. Gilman has pointed out in his study of stereotypes of sexuality, race, and madness, "we view our own images, our own mirages, our own stereotypes as embodying qualities that exist in the world. And we act upon them" (1985: 242). More specifically, a pedagogy must be available to teachers that will enable them along with their students to outface the barrenness of postmodern culture by employing a discourse and set of social practices that will not be content with infusing their pedagogies with the postmodern élan of the ludic metropolitan intellectual, with resurrecting a nostalgic past that can never be reclaimed, or with redescribing the present by simply textualizing it, leaving in place its malignant hierarchies of power and privilege, its defining pathologies. For these latter acts only stipulate the lineage of and give sustenance to those social relations responsible for the very injustice against which critical educators are trying to struggle. Educators need to stare boldly and unflinchingly into the historical present and assume a narrative space where conditions may be created for students to tell their own stories, to listen closely to the stories of others and dream the dream of liberation. Identity formation must be understood in terms of how subjectivity is contextually enacted within the tendential forces of history (Grossberg 1992). The exploration of identity should consist of mapping one's subject position in the field of multiple relations and should be preceded by a critique of hegemony (San Juan, Jr. 1992: 128). This suggests that educators and students need to uncouple themselves from the "disciplined mobilizations" that regulate their social lives and rearticulate the sites of their affective investments in order to create new strategies and alliances of struggle.

A critical pedagogy also demands political and cultural tactics that can fight multiple forms of oppression yet achieve a cohesiveness with divergent social groups working toward liberation goals. To this end, Chela Sandoval (1991) suggests that cultural workers develop "tactical subjectivities" which she describes as form of oppositional and differential consciousness and counterhegemonic praxis (which she discusses in the context of feminism). Tactical subjectivity enables teachers as social agents to recenter their multiple subjectivities with respect to the kind of oppression that is being confronted and "permits the practitioner to choose tactical positions, that is, to self-consciously break and reform ties to ideology, activities which are imperative for the psychological and political practices that permit the achievement of coalition across differences" (Sandoval 1991: 15).

RESISTANCE AS "*LA CONCIENCIA DE LA MESTIZA*"

The invitation posed by critical pedagogy is to bend reality to the requirements of a just world – requirements that shift the contexts of justice while interrogating the meaning behind such requirements and to decenter, deform, disorient, and ultimately transform modes of authority that domesticate the Other, that lay siege to the power of margins. Educators would do well to consider Gloria Anzaldúa's (1987) project of creating *mestizaje* theories that create new categories of identity for those left out or pushed out of existing ones. The sites of our identity within postmodernity are various. As seekers of liberation, we recognize the heterogeneous character of our inscription into colonial texts of history and cultural discourses of empire. Those of us who are *blan*[1] need to caution against the redissemination of oppression in our attempts to give others a "voice." New sites of agency are erupting at the borderlines of cultural instability, in the transgressive act of remembering, and through the disavowal and refashioning of predatory consciousness in the in-between spaces of cultural negotiations and translation. Marcos Sanchez-Tranquilino and John Tagg (1991) refer to this as the borderland, the "in-between" space that Gloria Anzaldúa calls *la frontera*. It is the space of borders that was discussed in Chapter 3, a space we need to revisit not only in the border theories of academics but also in the lived contingencies of revolutionary struggle. Border identities are all about doing, about engaging ideas and relationships through bodily, enacted knowing, a knowing emulated in the lives of Paulo Freire, Rosa Luxembourg, Rosa Parks, Che Guevara, Malcolm X, subcommandante Marcos and others, including Jesus.

The rhythm of the struggle for educational and social transformation can no longer be contained in the undaunted, steady steps of the workers' army marching towards the iron gates of freedom but is being heard in the hybrid tempos of border town bands; in the spiraling currents of an Aster Aweke Kabu vocal; in the sounds of the *ason* and the *priyè Deyò* in the percussive polyrhythms of prophetic black rap; in the invocations to Ogum, Iansã and Obaluaiê, in meaning that appears in the deafening silences of cultural life where identities are mapped not merely by diversity but through difference.

Chapter 8

Critical pedagogy and the pragmatics of justice[1]

> ... there are times when philosophy cannot afford to be a "gay science," for reality itself becomes deadly serious.
>
> (Selya Benhabib)

CRITICAL PEDAGOGY AND THE POLITICS OF MEANING

The economic collapse of the Soviet Union and its eventual disintegration has become the prized testimony of Cold War hawks in their impassioned verdict that capitalism has defeated socialism due in part to the immanent democratic nature of the free market. The orgy of smug self-congratulation that has surrounded the rhetoric of conservatives and liberals in the United States has led many to proclaim that history is on the side of international capitalism and political leadership of the United States. Western capitalism has become the most successful claimant of the right to determine the new world order. The cultural apparatuses of the West have represented the dismantling of the Soviet bloc as the triumph of individualism over the hegemony of the totalitarian state. The image of the communist has been hypertrophied into that of a global *ideologue troleur* living off the detrius of capitalism in the back alleys of the crumbling Eastern marketplace. In fact, what has been described as the autonomous logic of the free market has been accorded a sacerdotal status despite the misprision surrounding such claims and the proliferation of corruption scandals involving business and government leaders. While capitalism produces its own limits and creates conditions that work immanently against its success, its socially reproductive effects on schooling show little sign of abatement at this present historical conjuncture. Successful as a *trompe-l'oeil* for the great social equalizer, schools still serve as vigorous mechanisms for the reproduction of dominant race, class, and gender relations and the imperial values of the dominant sociopolitical order.

While it is important to recognize the conceptual limits of Marxian analysis for reading certain aspects of the postmodern condition (such as the non-synchronous production of race, class, and gender inequalities) I believe that the main pillars of Marxian analysis remain intact: the primacy of economics and the identification of contradictions and antagonisms that follow the changing forces of capitalism (Nagara 1993), including new regimes of capital accumulation that reflect an expansion of the informal economy and service sectors. I also believe, along with Lyotard, that information will become a major component in global struggles for power and competitive advantage. It is important that critical educators do not lose sight of these foci in their move to incorporate into their curricula and policy deliberations insights from Continental social theorists who write under the sign of postmodernism.

This chapter focuses the work of Jean François Lyotard and its potential for rethinking critical pedagogy – which has its roots in Marxian analyses of class but which has recently made efforts to appropriate deconstructive readings of discursive formations as well as certain strands of post-structuralism. Let's rehearse critical pedagogy's central ideas.

While there are now many different articulations of critical pedagogy (i.e., Freirean pedagogy, feminist pedagogies, ludic and resistance postmodernist pedagogies), most of them endorse to a greater or lesser extent the following axioms: that pedagogies should constitute a form of social and cultural criticism; that all knowledge is fundamentally mediated by linguistic relations that inescapably are socially and historically constituted; that individuals are synechochically related to the wider society through traditions of mediation (family, friends, religion, formal schooling, popular culture, etc.); that social facts can never be isolated from the domain of values or removed from forms of ideological production as inscription; that the relationship between concept and object and signifier and signified is neither inherently stable nor transcendentially fixed and is often mediated by circuits of capitalist production, consumption, and social relations; that language is central to the formation of subjectivity (unconscious and conscious awareness); that certain groups in any society are unnecessarily and often unjustly privileged over others and while the reason for this privileging may vary widely, the oppression which characterizes contemporary societies is most forcefully secured when subordinates accept their social status as natural, necessary, inevitable or bequeathed to them as an exercise of historical chance; that oppression has many faces and focusing on only one at the expense of others (e.g., class oppression vs. racism) often elides or occults the interconnection among them; that an unforeseen world of social relations awaits us in which power and oppression cannot be understood simply in terms of an irrefutable calculus of meaning linked to cause and effect conditions; that domination and oppression are implicated in the radical contingency of social development and our responses to it; and that mainstream research practices are generally and unwittingly implicated in the reproduction of systems of class, race, and gender oppression (Kincheloe and McLaren, in press).

For the criticalist in the classroom, meaning is not self-generated. It is not, in other words, wholly available to the active consciousness of autonomous agents. Nor does it reside in some pre-ontological netherworld of Orphic harmony and bliss where power circulates in a self-contained, self-referencing universe. Power is viewed by the criticalist as partaking of relations among persons who are differentially enabled to act by virtue of the opportunities afforded them on the basis of their race, ethnicity, class, gender, and sexual orientation. Mainstream pedagogy simply produces those forms of subjectivity preferred by the dominant culture, domesticating, pacifying, and deracinating agency, harmonizing a world of disjuncture and incongruity, and smoothing the unruly features of daily existence. At the same time, student subjectivities are rationalized and accommodated to existing regimes of truth. To see the classroom as a contestatory, agonistic site of competing discourses that structure what is questioned and what is taken for granted is not easily recoverable within a pedagogy that views knowledge as something external to human discourse. Critical pedagogy, on the other hand, brings into the arena of schooling practices insurgent, resistant, and insurrectional modes of interpretation which set out to imperil the familiar, to contest the legitimating norms of mainstream social life and to render problematic the common discursive frames and regimes within which "proper" behavior, comportment, and social interactions are premised.

Critical pedagogy attempts to analyze and unsettle extant power configurations, to defamiliarize and make remarkable what is often passed off as the ordinary, the mundane, the routine, the banal. In other words, critical pedagogy ambiguates the complacency of teaching under the sign of modernity, that is, under a sign in which knowledge is approached as ahistorical and neutral and separated from value and power.

For the criticalist educator, agency is structurally located and socially inscribed, and while every formation of agency is an arbitrary imposition of meaning and value and not a transparent reflection of universal selfhood, it cannot be denied that subjectivities are shaped overwhelmingly by articulatory practices that include the social relations of production and consumption, as well as the social construction of race, gender, and sexuality. The overall project of critical pedagogy is directed towards inviting students and teachers to analyze the relation among their own quotidian experiences, classroom pedagogical practices, the knowledges they produce, and the social, cultural and economic arrangements of the larger social order (Giroux 1983, 1992; McLaren 1993a, 1993b, 1994; Giroux and McLaren 1994; Lankshear and McLaren 1993). Critical pedagogy is engaged in assisting students to interrogate the formation of their subjectivities in the context of advanced capitalist formations with the intention of generating pedagogical practices that are non-racist, non-sexist, non-homophobic and which are directed towards the transformation of the larger social order in the interests of greater racial, gender, and economic justice.

Critical pedagogy reveals how omnipotent mainstream approaches to meaning in school settings instantiate the formalistic and formulaic repetition of sameness and essay a world that ontologizes its own representation, valorizing its iteration as natural and commonsensical. It prevents liberating instruction with the injunction to accept what is inevitable, to pass off intellectual scarcity as plenitude. Possibility is denied in the act of turning the inert present into a social fate. The result is the demarginalization of the political in pedagogy.

Not only is it impossible to disinvest pedagogy of its relationship to politics, it is theoretically dishonest. The belief that knowledge is removed from history, above politics, and immune from ethical questioning has had the political effect of disqualifying and de-authorizing the voices of criticalists who work in schools of education. Classrooms are complex cultural sites neither ripe for revolution nor for mindless complicity with oppression, but rather possess the potential for transgressive practice where identities are constantly negotiated: they are places of counter-pressure and counternarrative. Critical educators occupy the borderlands – liminal zones, between places of hybrid possibilities, sites of cultural struggle and of crossing that mix meaning and knowledge, aesthetics and politics, fact and value. Outside of the borderlands these characteristics or qualities remain highly demarcated, separated out and kept apart by the unified, predictive logic of identity of scientific empiricism and the will to totality in modern science – all of which rationalize difference through forms of domination.

From the borderlands, it becomes clearer that all knowledge, all awareness is contaminated by prior knowledge which has "officially" disappeared but whose traces remain in the tangled arcs of prior meaning. All knowledge contains the afterglow of lost worlds. All sign systems are populated by silent interlocutors. Criticalists work against the traditional role of teachers as museum curators of the mind. They criticize the museumization of classrooms as places where knowledge is salvaged from its "primitive" beginnings, admired in its "advanced" stages, and mounted as display: on chalkboards, in reading centers, language laboratories, as visual catechism. Only what can be seen can be evaluated. Even the most liberal variants of mainstream pedagogy only reproduce aporetically through their practices their own relations of subordination with respect to dominant social and cultural relations. Only the finished form counts. Critical pedagogy, on the other hand, tries to make thematic its own situatedness, its own contingency, its own enmeshedness in moral and political positions and practices.

O TEMPORA! O MORES! PERVERSITY AND SCHOOLING

Capitalist schooling is generally perverse. It is perverse precisely in that it

> solicits desire not with the purpose of obtaining its consent but instead with the intention of hiding from us the yawning gap through the play of an object/answer/disavowal that, from this point of view at least, bears all the characteristics of the perverse object.
>
> (Haineault and Roy 1993: 184)

What schooling hides in its solicitation of desire is the field of difference and alterity. Perverts cannot tolerate difference so they "invent, in its place and instead of this difference, a quasi-delirious image of a nonlack" (p. 184). Under the sign of capitalism, an image of common culture is cultivated in order to "avoid what is intolerable about desire" (p. 186). In other words, the commodified forms of culture become "half-truths that seem intolerable not to perceive as absolute" (p. 187). That is, culture is turned into an idealized relationship to an imaginary other. In this light we become aware of the similarity between teaching as a form of advertising and the role of propaganda:

> The object advertising offers to us is *not the object of desire, but an alibi for no longer desiring the object*. . . . The place where it consolidates collective thought is the conviction it propagates that this world of free circulation of goods contains all of the objects necessary to satisfy us. Thanks to advertising, therefore, it is no longer necessary to desire.
>
> (Haineault and Roy 1993: 193)

In the sense that it is premised on a perverse advertisement for a common culture populated by an enforced tolerance for difference, schooling too often becomes an alibi for not exploring otherness, for not engaging in a politics of difference. It becomes an alibi for not desiring. Contemporary schooling dares students to become productive, loyal citizens. Whilst students are exhorted to "be all they can be" such a transgressive challenge – of saying "no" to drugs and "yes" to books, for instance – is always already situated within a total obedience to normative codes of conduct and standardized regimes of valuing. This is not empowering education, but a perverse form of prohibition in which desire as human agency is not permitted to explore its own constitutive possibilities. Students are treated as objects of consumption just as they are simultaneously taught the value of becoming consuming subjects. In this way, schooling transforms itself into a perverse ritual in which students disavow the enablement of their own destiny in order to remain subjectively compatible with the commodity form.

DISSOLUTION IN THE WORKPLACE

According to Lyotard, the very act of work takes place within a libidinal economy in which slavery is invested with a strange form of pleasure experienced in the destruction of the inorganic bodies imposed by capital on workers. According to Lyotard:

> And if one does *this* [work], if one becomes a slave of the machine, the machine of the machine, the screwer screwed by it, eight hours a day, twelve in the last century, is it because one is forced to do it, constrained because one clings to life? Death is not an alternative to *that*, it is part of it, it attests that there is a *jouissance* in it. The workless English did not become workers in order to survive, they were – buckle up tightly and spit on me later – delighted [*joui*] by the hysterical exhaustion, masochism, who knows, of *staying* in the mines, in the foundries and workshops, in hell. They were delighted in and by the insane destruction of their inorganic body which was of course imposed on them, delighted by the decomposition of their personal identity which the peasant tradition had constructed for them, delighted by the dissolution of families and villages and delighted by the new and monstrous anonymity of the suburbs and the pubs in the morning and evening.
>
> (cited in Pefanis 1991: 98)

Pefanis describes the "prostitutive relationship imposed by capital" which – although perverse – changes nothing "because, according to Lyotard, it was always so" (p. 98). For Lyotard, to start a revolution that was simply a reversal of the sphere of economic and political power only gives ultimate validity to capital and serves to maintain that very sphere which is responsible for domination and oppression. He notes that capitalism, in its attempt to universalize exchangeability "creates a différend for the specific, the unexchangeable, and so on" (During 1990: 123). Simon During captures Lyotard's perspective as follows:

> [C]apitalism itself works to undo the force of the order of discourse. In capitalism, money, rather than language, installs exchangeability as the dominant relation between objects in the world. But money is also stored time and security – one might add, stored pleasure. Thus capitalism disburdens itself from notions such as humanity and progress which underpin high-cultural imperialism. But it also discounts the formations which resist these ideas: in particular, nationalism and philosophic deliberation. Ultimately, for Lyotard, capitalism even implies the end of effective political institutions. The play of exchange, the production of money as security, will delegitimate the discursive presuppositions of institutions too.
>
> (During 1990: 124)

Lyotard sees the laws of exchange – the exchangeability of all values – as capitalism's only universal law. It is the law of "indifferent exchange" according to which profits exchange lost "labor" time for "real" time and value becomes equivalent to the rate of transaction rather than the objects of transaction. For Lyotard, capitalism levels singularity through the logic of exchangeability and equivalence. Peter Dews captures his criticism of capitalism as follows:

> The world of capitalism . . . is not an alienated world. Rather, the cynicism and polymorphous perversity of an economy which can absorb any object, any capacity, any experience into the circuit of commodity exchange parallels the aimless voyage of intensities on the libidinal band, indeed – because forms of order are now themselves seen as merely stases of energy – is indistinguishable from the great ephemeral pellicule itself. Admittedly, in this respect capitalism, like every system of signification and exchange, dissimulates. The capitalist is concerned not with the product as such, but only with the constant augmentation of production, so that capital as a whole functions as a "great totalizing Zero" which neutralizes the singularity of the object into the indifferently exchangeable sign of a value.
>
> (1987: 137)

Critical pedagogy must enable a sustained criticism of the effects of global capitalism. Further, it must renounce and contest the production of race, class, and gender injustices through capitalism's terroristic logic of production and consumption linked to the commodity form as described by Lyotard. The conceptual advances of continental thinkers like Lyotard have added significantly to the seriousness and urgency of this and other challenges posed by critical pedagogy. One pressing question which we believe Lyotard's work raises for critical educators is: How do we move away from current strategies of liberation in order to give pedagogy a tactical centrality? This chapter attempts to evaluate Lyotard's potential contribution to a pedagogy of liberation in light of this question.

THE QUESTION OF AGENCY

The central challenge posed by critical education has been an analysis of the conceptual ground upon which subjectivity rests in what is becoming known as the era of global capitalism. While the terrain of postmodern social theory is admittedly abyssal and heteronomous, and reads like an itinerary of unpredictable epistemological excursions, ruptured genres of criticism, and of dramatic discursive inflections, it has shed exciting new light on the constitution of subjectivity. Few criticalists in education still subscribe to the notion of the freestanding autonomous subject self-fashioned through free will and good intentions. Subjectivity is now recognized as bearing a constitutive relationship to social power and the relationships to which it gives rise. One issue concerns the extent to which subjectivity as it is manufactured socially must be articulated in a totalizing opposition to otherness (i.e., male versus female; African-American versus white; First World versus Third World) or whether it can be self-reflexive with respect to its own constitutive elements. Another important issue that stems from this debate involves identifying and examining the social relations, cultural contradictions, and antagonisms that organize and shape the constitution of difference with respect to personal, local, and situated knowledges and experiences. These issues center themselves around the question of agency – a question that is one of Lyotard's central concerns in that "he sees it as underlying the historical epoch we call modernity" (Godzich 1992: 112).

I am sympathetic to the conjunctural view of agency set forth by Judith Butler, that agency is immanent to power and not opposed to it:

> agency belongs to a way of thinking about persons as instrumental actors who confront an external political field. But if we agree that politics and power exist already at the level at which the subject and its agency are articulated and made possible, then agency can be *presumed* only at the cost of refusing to inquire into its construction. Consider that "agency" has no formal existence or, if it does, it has no bearing on the question at hand. In a sense, the epistemological model that offers us a pregiven subject or agent is one that refuses to acknowledge that *agency is always and only a political prerogative.* As such, it seems crucial to question the conditions of its possibility, not to take it for granted as an a priori guarantee.
>
> (1992: 13)

Butler poses a number of questions which speak to the possibility of agency as both collective and historical, and potentially transformative of existing relations of power and privilege. She asks:

> [W]hat possibilities of mobilization are produced on the basis of existing configurations of discourse and power? Where are the possibilities of reworking that very matrix of power by which we are constituted, of reconstituting the legacy of that constitution, and of working against each other those processes of regulation that can destabilize existing power regimes?
>
> (1992: 13)

It should be emphasized that agency is never complete, as subjects are continually being produced within and by relations of power and systematic structures of exclusion, disempowerment, abjection, deauthorization and erasure. According to Butler, subjects are produced to a considerable extent *in advance* of the political field in which they are engaged. She writes, in fact, that "agency can never be understood as a controlling or original authorship over that signifying chain, and it cannot be the power, once installed and constituted in and by that chain, to set a sure course for its future" (1993: 219). In other words, a political signifier is always re-signified in that it derives from the sedimentation of prior signifiers, of a repetitive citation of prior instances of itself. Agency, then, is located for Butler in the performativity of signifiers which are repeated or cited. To be constituted by a discourse is not the same thing as being determined by it.

Paradoxically, according to Butler, identity seeks to foreclose the very contingency upon which it depends. She notes that "agency is the hiatus in iterability, the compulsion to install an identity through repetition, which requires the very contingency, the undetermined interval, that identity insistently seeks to foreclose" (1993: 220). To claim that the subject is constituted as such is not to claim that agency is determined or that the subject is dead; rather, it is to understand that the belief in an autonomous subject is induced; the notion of subjectivity must be approached as a problematic, and its constitution within discursive formations seen as the very precondition of its agency. Lyotard's concept of the self as a constellation of language games in constant collision subverts settled assumptions with respect to agency and generally affirms the politics of contingency articulated by Butler and other post-structuralists. The self is viewed as fragmented, living at the unstable intersection of a series of language games which become absorbed into the ever-expanding commodity form. Lyotard applies the presumption of incommensurability of language games relentlessly to the concept of subjectivity and in doing so debunks imperial signifiers and pushes the practice of judgment against the frayed limits of reason. However, Lyotard's privileging of quasi-theory over theory, his location of *jouissance* as an unmediated site of sensational self-reading or auto-intelligibility and of a "post-political bodily ecstasy" or "corporeal subjectivity" tends to deflect an interrogation of those capitalist relations of production and consumption that are complicitous in the formation of experience (Zavarzadeh and Morton 1991: 157).

PERSONS, INDIVIDUALS, AND SUBJECTS

It is important that I situate the problematic of agency and my own discussion of Lyotard's challenges to critical pedagogy within a larger discussion of historical agency. Recently, Wlad Godzich (1993) has provided a tentative frame for considering these issues in his discussion of premodern, modern and postmodern structures of identity. In doing so, he traces different forms of sociopolitical regulation. According to Godzich, premodern or oral cultures produced *persons* rather than *individuals* who, generally speaking, were discursively constituted in pre-established roles. Persons may be described as those occupying the subject positions of a particular hegemonic discourse or a discursive regime. Here emphasis is placed on the primacy of the group and its collective well-being. Whereas premodern persons tended not to view themselves as autonomous entities who possessed the power or the right to associate freely, modern individuals consider themselves to be the coherent bearers of a unified, universal consciousness.

There exists within modernity a rationalization of the social sphere anchored in a politics of individualism in which individuals are seen as reflections and constitutive elements of civil and political society. Within Godzich's conceptualization, the individual is defined not so much culturally as politically – as, for instance, a normative, abstract, and universal subject. This form of individualism is referred to by Godzich as principled individualism and requires the submission of individuals to specifiable social regulations and forms of socialization, marked by a steady encroachment of the state into the civil sphere. Modern individuals are also submitted to preferred forms of socialization.

Postmodern identity formations are different still. They are formed through new modalities of social regulation which do not construct individuals but rather *subjects.* Abstract individualism is replaced by concrete, empirical subjects that have differentiated needs and desires produced through "new machines of production and consumption" (1993: xvii). The genesis of this form of agency can be traced to the eighteenth century and to development of the idea that the economy is autonomous, separate from the public sphere. The public sphere (the sphere of intellectual deliberation) came into being as a symptom of and as a corrective to the alienation and "rejectionary forces" brought on by the autonomization of the economy. We inhabit a new world of postmodern modalities of social regulation that work not from a premodern collectivist cultural paradigm of human agency or a modernist individualist political paradigm but from a paradigm centered on new forms of global capitalism grounded in new global technocratic machineries of production and consumption. Here, individual subjectivity is exploited not for collective ends but for private rituals of self-fashioning.

Godzich's typology raises numerous implications for educational criticalists which may be summarized in the following questions: What does it mean to educate students who are no longer individuals in the modernist sense of being co-extensive with the sphere of civil politics but rather subjects produced by an autonomous economy? To what extent can the school, as a public sphere, serve as a "site in which what is felt to be in common is defined and where a nonalienated form of society comes into being and delineates its own course of action?" (p. xviii). If, in a global economy, there can be only subjects and no society – subjects permanently confined to their subjection – are schools then simply destined to continue serving as compensatory and ultimately reproductive mechanisms for new forms of subjectivity based on a merging of identity and the fetishized consumer object?

LYOTARD'S SUBALTERN

Lyotard's work on subjectivity and discourse gives supportive emphasis to the typology outlined by Godzich. With Lyotard, Kant's transcendental subject has been hijacked and brought from the firmament to the terra firma where it is constructed within a politics of incongruences, incommensurables, and impossible possibilities. Lyotard's pagan subject is not grounded in a metaphysics of presence; rather, it deictically anchors itself in a political pragmatics of reading. Godzich summarizes Lyotard's position on agency as follows:

> Lyotard challenges the idea of the autonomy of the subject as enunciator of the law by showing that such an act of enunciation always presupposes a chain of prior enunciations and enunciators, none of which can claim originary status except as a character in a mythic discourse that needs to be enunciated in any case.
>
> (1992: 126)

Lyotard's perspectives on agency generally affirm the post-structuralist critique of autonomous subjectivity offered by Butler (1992; 1993) and others and share a certain limited affinity with a number of the more "postcolonialist" approaches within critical pedagogy, Postcolonial educationalists remain sympathetic to the position on the subaltern "other" taken by Rey Chow, Gayatri Spivak, and other postcolonial critics in the sense that they agree that the "speaking self [of the subaltern] belongs to an already well-defined structure of history and domination" (Chow 1993: 36). Drawing upon Lyotard's notion of the *différend*, Chow maintains that "a radical alternative can be conceived only when we recognize the essential untranslatability from the subaltern discourse to imperialist discourse" (p. 35). She further recognizes that "the 'identity' of the native is inimitable, beyond the resemblance of the image" (p. 36). Efforts to situate the subaltern in new and specific contexts in an attempt to resurrect the native's victimized voice/self too often makes those who would render the native visible complicitous in simultaneously neutralizing "the untranslatability of the native's experience and the history of that untranslatability" (p. 38). The problem of modernity, notes Chow, is

> the confrontation between what are now called the "first" and "third" worlds in the form of the *différend*, that is, the untranslatability of "third world" experiences into the "first world." This is because, in order for her experience to become translatable, the "native" cannot simply "speak" but must also provide the justice/justification for her

> speech, a justice/justification that has been destroyed in the encounter with the imperialist. The native's victimization consists in the fact that the active evidence – the original witness – of her victimization may no longer exist in any intelligible, coherent shape. Rather than saying that the native has already spoken because the dominant hegemonic discourse is split/hybrid/different from itself, and rather than restoring her to her "authentic" context, we should argue that it is the native's silence which is the most important clue to her displacement. That silence is at once the *evidence* of imperialist oppression (the naked body, the defiled image) and what, in the absence of the original witness to that oppression, must act in its place by *performing* or *feigning* as the pre-imperialist gaze.
>
> (1993: 38)

I take a position similar to Chow with respect to the concept of cultural hybridity – a concept gaining a great deal of currency in cultural studies. Chow warns that the idea of cultural hybridity is limited to the idea that cultural texts are invariably split or resistant; that the native's voice is *always already* present in the ambivalence of the discourse of the dominator. Too often this position unwittingly

> revives, in the masquerade of deconstruction, anti-imperialism, and "difficult" theory . . . an old functionalist notion of what a dominant culture permits in the interest of maintaining its own equilibrium. Such functionalism informs the investigatory methods of classical anthropology and sociology as much as it does the colonial policies of the British Empire. The kind of subject-constitution it allows, a subject-constitution firmly inscribed in Anglo-American liberal humanism, is the other side of the process of image-identification, in which we try to make the native more like us by giving her a "voice".
>
> (1993: 35)

Faye Harrison (1993) underscores Chow's observation in her discussion of postmodern experiments in ethnographic writing. She argues that

> Although postmodernist experiments in ethnographic writing highlight difference, Otherness, power and authority – issues originally foregrounded by Third World and feminist thinkers – many of these experiments inadvertently reinscribe neocolonial domination, wherein the Other is objectified and appropriated. Textual and representational strategies and literary techniques tend to privilege the force of rhetoric over substantive concern with concrete/institutional relations of power. . . . For example, the concern with dispersing authority and engaging in dialogue is often reduced to a polyphonic style whereby a form of narrative ventriloquism is performed, creating the magical illusion of the Other's coming to voice.
>
> (1993: 407)

MULTICULTURALISM MATTERS

Lyotard's notion of justice built on the regulatory principle of the differend, his effort to become more appreciative of and alert to the modernist illusion of perfecting subjectivity, and his attempt to lay bare the swindle of the modernist dream of self-mastery and his probing of the dissonance of the self have given us conceptual tools to reexamine established frames for making judgments. Bill Readings has attempted to capture Lyotard's pragmatics of justice in the context of examining the untranslatability of subaltern discourses into majority discourses. He has done this through a discussion of Werner Herzog's film, *Where the Green Ants Dream*. The film focuses on a small mining station in Australia in which a young white mining engineer is conducting blasting tests for mineral deposits. Local Aborigines believe these blasts will disturb the "dreaming" of the green ants and will hasten the end of the "universe world." The Supreme Court rules on the dispute in favor of the mining company.

Readings follows Lyotard's paralogical approach to postmodern aesthetic experience to analyze the film. According to Readings the film accommodates a Lyotardean approach to the *incommensurability of language games* in the way it chooses not to represent the Aborigines but rather to foreground the *differend* in the act of representation itself. Readings is able to make some important observations about Lyotard's approach to the subaltern through his analysis of this film. For instance, he claims that the film illustrates Lyotard's insistence on promoting justice rather than representing the truth by bearing witness to an otherness without attempting to represent the truth of such otherness; further, that it is the film-maker's intent to displace the governing frames of reference with which such otherness is normally understood. A comparison can be made between the film-maker's techniques and Lyotard's paganism consisting of quasi-aesthetic experiments. Readings notes (in general sympathy with the film-maker) that an incommensurability exists between the landscape of green ants and the rational discourse that seeks to represent it, the latter referring to a republican discourse founded on the Idea of Man. The film captures "the heterogeneity of Aboriginal to western argument" (Readings 1992: 179), and "refuses to identify the Aborigines as simply the inchoate or primitive opposite of the rationality of technological man" (p. 179). The Aborigines are unrepresentable. Readings makes an effective case against the idea of common humanity and Western liberal democratic tolerance. Differences arising from cultural diversity must, in this view, be overcome. Common law will arbitrate in the name of liberation what counts as human freedom. Readings notes that each claimant in the dispute is "right in their own terms" (p. 183). According to Readings,

> Injustice in the proceedings of translation comes not from the fact of

> simply speaking a different language but from the fact that the language of the Aborigines is untranslatable into the language of the court, heterogeneous to the language of common law, of common humanity. An encounter takes place, it happens, but no language is available to phrase it, for the Aboriginal language is insistently local, rooted in the land from which it comes; it cannot become multinational. It cannot, that is, become modern: no one can immigrate into Aboriginal culture.
>
> (1992: 183)

Lyotard's stress on the incommensurability of phrase regimes or language games can certainly be applied to the struggle over multiculturalism, especially as I have defined this struggle in earlier chapters. Lyotard's work can be appropriated as a means of guarding against the translation of otherness into the discourse of Western imperialism. Similarly, Lyotard's call for diversity can effectively serve to challenge the restoration and recuperation of sameness in the attempt by conservative multiculturalists to foster a common humanity or culture. Conservative multiculturalism assumes that difference is commensurable with democratic citizenship in the sense that citizenship is capable of welding diverse voices into a unity within differences. It ignores that agency is constructed within differentially constituted relations of power. In liberal pluralistic approaches to multicuturalism differences become important in that they can all be equally shed in order to reveal a common humanity – a relation of pure exchangeability which, of course, universalizes white culture as having privileged status. In Lyotard's politics of incommensurables, there is an implicit appeal for dissensus rather than harmony.

His position on cultural difference would appear to support Trinh T. Minh-ha's statement that

> Cultural difference is not a totemic object. It does not always announce itself to the onlooker; sometimes it stands out conspicuously, most of the time it tends to escape the commodifying eye. Its visibility depends on how much one is willing to inquire into the anomalous character of the familiar . . .
>
> (1991: 159)

However, Lyotard's celebration of multiplicity and plurality and his call for a radical tolerance of incommensurability can fall prey to the very liberal pluralist stance he is criticizing. For instance, an uncritical celebration of multiplicity and heterogeneity can be used in the politics of multiculturalism as an alibi to exoticize "otherness" in a nativistic retreat that locates difference in a primeval past of cultural authenticity. We see a tendency in Lyotard to romanticize the pagan theater of the subversive and the unknown in which the elimination of grand narratives would lead to the dissolution of power and confrontation. It is a dream of the pre-political arena, the artistic and the literary over the theoretical, experimentation over determinate concepts, the decadent over the transcendent, local validity over official standards of judgment, the mythic over the narratological, the aesthetics of the sublime over practical reason, figural narrativity over discursive efficiency, and radical singularity over heterogeneity. Lyotard seems to presume that conflicts over differences will somehow eventually cancel themselves out if the horizon of possibility for new forms of subjectivities and social practices is kept open. On this note, Peter Dews remarks that Lyotard is dangerously wrong in his assumption that once the aspiration to cognitive or moral universality is abandoned, "a harmonious plurality of unmediated perspectives" will result. The danger carried by this assumption lies in the inability of Lyotard's position to "prevent the perspective of one minority from including its right to dominate others: the Empire which Lyotard so vehemently denounces is simply the minority which has fought its way to the top" (1987: 218).

What is ultimately troubling in Lyotard's view of the subaltern subject is that it refuses all attempts to name such a subject, even provisionally, on the grounds that any form of naming is an act of appropriation and ultimately an act of violence. Anti-dialecticians such as Lyotard effectively expel the other, often in a well-intentioned attempt to protect the singularity of the other. This position can ultimately lead to both political and pedagogical paralysis as the subaltern is continually exiled into the realm of the uncodifiable, the non-human, the undecidable.

Lyotard is correct in arguing that the eventhood that is being repressed in every act of representation betrays the utter impossibility of representation. Such a position warns against constructing an underlying unity among incommensurable regimes of representation which can be politically abused. For instance, the notion that "we are all alike under the skin" offers white culture the alibi it needs to define oppressed groups against the invisible legitimating norms of whiteness. Yet there is a sense in which Lyotard's activation of the differences recuperates a neo-liberal move towards unity and consensus under the cover of agonistics and dissensus. Lyotard's refusal to name otherness suggests a tolerance of difference rather than an engagement with it, and intractable difference becomes something to be endured rather than activated as a common ground of struggle against structures of domination.

While it is true that African-Americans, Latinos/Latinas, and Anglos may speak incommensurable ideolects, Lyotard's idea of incommensurability does not take into account the cultural production of intersubjectivity – the fact that Third World cities such as Los Angeles are inhabited by groups who, unlike Herzog's Aborigines, have influenced each other historically for generations (which is not to deny the overdetermination of structures of difference within capitalist imperialism, the reality of domination and the violence of hegemonic social relations). Best and Kellner speak to this deficit in Lyotard's work in the following passage:

> Postmodern theories of language often omit or downplay concrete communication practices and while Lyotard – unlike some other postmodern theorists – does stress the importance of a pragmatic dimension of language analysis, his stress on agonistics covers over the problem of how understanding is produced in language, how language helps produce intersubjectivity and mutual understanding.
>
> (1991: 178)

I regard Lyotard's refusal of representation as exceedingly noble in that he is sensitively trying to avoid the imposition of colonial or neo-colonial idioms on the voice of the other, and the terrorism that is implied in all forms of identification with the other. Yet Lyotard's position betrays a discomfiting silence with respect to understanding how agency can be linked to a pedagogical project of social justice that must include some prescriptive components, even if on a provisional and contingent basis. I agree with Lyotard that there is no true or just way of representing the other and that to argue otherwise could lead to a prescription for fascism. Yet I feel that there must be some sense in which the self must acknowledge the movement of non-identity in its own identity. In other words, critical self-reflexivity is a necessary but certainly not sufficient component of critical pedagogy – a position that cuts across Lyotard's intellectual trajectory that rejects reason as a form of imperialism.

A critical pedagogy dedicated to a critical multiculturalism needs to be formulated within a goal-oriented social praxis. Lyotard's u-topos, wherein "differences may converge without fusing" (Kearney 1991: 219) needs to be grounded in a riposte to the totalizing narratives of modernity which refuse to admit a politics of doubt. This demands a project of political praxis in which every group is encouraged to distrust its own certainties and yet strive to solve the conflict of needs among competing groups situated asymmetrically in relations of power. This demands a theory of agency that not only forswears and terminates representations, or forfeits all purchase on their historical meaning, but vigorously transforms existing representations in the interests of the dispossessed. I believe critical pedagogy must have a preferential option for the poor, the marginalized and disenfranchised. Lyotard's project helps us to guard against dogmatism but lacks the substantive elements necessary for guiding our choices towards these ends.

There are also problems associated with Lyotard's implosion of the self into the social. Lyotard's imploded subject is one constructed out of the ruins of modernity, out of an entrapment in the machine logic of speed technology. The dissolution of individuals in so-called consumer society should, in Lyotard's view, be affirmed (Dews 1987). This parallels Adorno's view of post-liberal capitalism as the progressive liquidation of the distinction between the unconscious and the ego, resulting in the narcissistic personality type (Dews 1987). Agency at times appears to be reduced in Lyotard's work to unbridled subjectivity, to the sundered realms of the self crashing through the gates of identity and official knowledge, to difference left unfettered in an aesthetic field. We are asked to invigilate this terrain to make sure nobody claims a greater purchase on the truth than anybody else. As we shall explore later, this becomes a daunting if not impossible task.

WHAT A DIFFERENCE JUSTICE MAKES

It is a mark of neither exaggeration nor romanticization to consider Lyotard's work as a type of taboo, a transgression of sorts. According to Julian Pefanis who is commenting on Bataille:

> Transgression, and the thought for which it was a rhetorical figure, would ultimately come to replace the dialectical thought of contradiction. Transgression is the game of limits: a play at the conventional frames of language, at the border of disciplines, and across the line of taboo. . . . Transgression maintains the taboo, since without it it would lose its fundamental violence. A society without taboos would be outside human society. And the taboo also maintains transgression, since the concept of a limit, such as a taboo, is only possible on the condition of its infringement: an unpassable limit would require no social constraint to prevent its crossing.
>
> (1991: 85–6)

Pefanis's phrase, "lurching at the abyss of *unreason*" is, in my estimation, an appropriate description of the way in which Lyotard is able to position his work outside of any existing genres of criticism and in a position of radical incredulity towards reason and the critique.

Lyotard moves us beyond a flirtation with abstract negation to face militantly the question of ethics in a world that betrays an attitude of skepticism toward all grand narratives. Through his incredulity toward emancipatory metanarratives and his dismissal of rational metadiscourses of legitimation, Lyotard challenges the very politics of the political in that he refuses to be concerned with who or what is represented. According to Readings (1991), he concerns himself with the violence inherent in the very act of representation (i.e., the function of representation in the West since Plato). To critically interrogate the act of representation is, for Lyotard, yet another form of representation (and in this sense his work cannot avoid recuperating that which it attempts to critique). Consequently, Lyotard calls for a politics of the irrepresentable. Bill Readings (1991) argues that, for Lyotard,

> the political is not the final meaning of representations, but one kind of apparatus, along with others (such as visual perspective, realist narrative, theoretical discourse) for the reduction of heterogeneous singularities to a unifying rule of representability within which all is recognizable. Politics, then, is not simply a question of who is represented, since the exercise of domination is the effect of the representational *apparati* that have governed the understanding of cultural experience. For example, under capitalism the function of commodification is to submit all events to the rule of capital by reducing them to representations of value within a system of exchange. Existence is thus determined as an effect of representation. The politics that seeks to "represent legitimate aspirations" is itself the subjection of desire to the rule of capitalist commodification and exchange. Theoretical "critique" is itself merely the nihilistic inversion of this movement, either the simple attempt to make commodities circulate in the opposite direction within a system itself functioning in terms of binary oppositions, or the ultimate capitalization whereby the system may know itself as commodity. According to Lyotard any politics that remains within the realm of representation is necessarily complicit with the exclusionary politics that have oppressed women, workers, ethnic and sexual minorities, and others as yet unrecognizable.
>
> (1991: xxvii–xxviii)

According to Lyotard, all representation (including images representing metalinguistic prescriptive commands) inhabits discourse as a radical alterity to any meaning assigned to it. Lyotard calls for a transgression of the very order of the concept and the cognitive idiom itself. Lyotard effectively and at times capriciously pulls the ethico-cognitive safety net from under the ontological readings of the metanarratives (emancipation of humanity, liberation through science, self-autonomy, etc.) within a modernism dominated by the logic of identity manifested in the exchange principle. His work serves to dispossess us of the representational ground upon which we negotiate the real. Lyotard calls for the "suspension of symbolicity" (Cohen 1993: 142) through a type of exteriorization in which privileged representations are frustrated. This amounts on Lyotard's part to provoking "symbolic 'indifference' toward every type of official culture" (Cohen 1993: 145). Lyotard stops at nothing short of trying to radically unsettle the social bond of official culture – "the social bond that is reasserted in the face of the difficulty of communication" (Cohen 1993: 145). Following the writings of his libidinal economy phase, Lyotard no longer sought the ground of unintelligibility in transgressive desire; he could discover it instead in the incommensurability of language games

(Jay 1993: 580). Lyotard would argue that "the ethical language game, that of prescriptives based on the command from the other, could never be reconciled with the language game of description based on the visible presence of ontological reality" (Jay 1993: 580).

Resistance to capitalism involves not political organization but the temporality of ethics – he wants to disrupt the synthesis of sense impressions into knowledge by means of concepts. Lyotard seeks, in other words, a temporal alterity (Readings 1991). This is the basis of materiality for Lyotard – the insertion of resistant time into the system. Time must be inserted that capitalism can't account for or make accountable. Reading must be given the status of an event – an experiment. Reading is ethical in that it always encounters laws which are indeterminate, which are yet to be determined and which can never be determined in advance. According to Bill Readings, "Lyotard is not advocating simply an oppositional wasting of time; rather, he proposes an opening of historical or sociological (modernist) time to a temporal otherness that displaces its accounting, that is untamable, irreconcilable" (1991: 133).

Abandoning a concern with agency as materially constitutive of social relations of production and the new social physics of consumption brought on by a post-Fordist variety of flexible specializations, Lyotard discovers agency in the fissures and fault-lines of language games or phrase regimes. Society as a totality slips from the focus of investigation to be replaced by an emphasis on language and discourse. Lyotard is correct in arguing that it is both impossible and undesirable to give specific or universal content to the category of the subject, since agency demands a continual openness and resignifiability. All normative foundations for building a politics of social justice and transformative agency must necessarily be contingent and provisional. Here Lyotard evokes a palpably diminished faith in critical self-reflexivity and transformative praxis.

Lyotard's rhetorical moves are made within a philosophy of language and not a philosophy of consciousness. However, within his pragmatics of discourse, rules are viewed as unable to provide any advance criteria for judgment of any language game. Rules only apply to games which have already been played. Only the rules germane to a particular language game have any legitimacy (not within themselves but as part of an implicit contract among players) yet ironically all judgments precede their own rules. Lyotard's sentiment here is captured by Godzich:

> It is the games that turn us into their players and not we who constitute the games. Players are immanent to the games they play; as a result they cannot extricate themselves from these games and cannot produce a metadiscourse that could dominate this plurality. The only option that remains is that of an indefinite experimenting with language games,

> somewhat on the order of the scientific inventivenesss that operates by rupture rather than continuous derivation.
>
> (1992: 127)

Lyotard's preference for small narratives as distinct from master narratives privileges a society of micro-events over one resulting from a master plan. In a very profound sense Lyotard's position is radically important precisely because the modern claim of autonomy has wreaked so much havoc in the name of universal social justice. This idea is worth exploring further.

According to Lyotard, it is reading which is our mode of constitution of the subject and this yields the structure of the postmodern (Godzich 1992). However, during the act of reading the notion of the freestanding subject is induced. Lyotard advocates a notion of agency in which the subject relearns the practice of reading so as to understand the constitutive moment of subjecthood in the act of reading itself. According to Godzich,

> reading is not actualizing something that lies there; it is deictically to anchor ourselves in relation to that which is around us, and such a deictic anchoring requires that to the phrase we voice we counterpose another phrase, that is, we become the link in the concatenation of these phrases, with all this implies in terms of selection, organization, and ruse. It is not the transcendental positions of meaning that matter; it is how we deictically anchor such meaning as obtains around us.
>
> (1992: 133)

The type of justice which is advocated by Lyotard is the justice of heteronomy, of irreducible difference. This is a justice which is not lawless but which does not legislate. It results in an "unresolvable dissensus" in which no individual is subjected to a law that is alien to him or her. This is the justice of *Le Différend*, in which the Kantian Ideal of Reason is invoked only to serve as a regulatory mechanism that maintains the preservation of the idea of incommensurability of language games or phrase regimes. It means recognizing a world of pluralized logics and heterogeneous value systems and engaging in a politics with no criteria or normativity, a politics of indeterminate or experimental judgment in which agonistics becomes the founding principle. This may seem odd for a man whose early writings had stressed political action and a revolutionary praxis: "Man is the work of his works" (Pefanis 1991: 87) and equally strange for someone who "had long been torn between the life of writing and the life of militant political action" (Godzich 1992: 110), who had been one of the founding members of the neo-Trotskyist left-wing group, *Socialisme ou barbarie* (a tradition of non-P.C.F. French Marxism and socialism that included such members as Claude Lefort and Cornelius Castoriadis), who worked on behalf of Algerian freedom fighters in the 1950s, who was active in

Mouvement du 22 Mars, and who took part in storming the administration building that ensconced Dean Paul Ricoeur at Nanterre in May, 1968.

LYOTARD'S WAR ON TOTALITY

Lyotard's "war on totality," his activation of the differences, has led to a serious problem that we are now facing in many current articulations of postmodern discourses – articulations that have taken us from the realm of abstract negation to a more determinate form of negation in order to attempt to destabilize and unsettle the *archai* of modernism. This problem may be described as the privileging of an entirely new set of fixed binary oppositions – an anti-metaphysical move in name only. Have we not witnessed in Lyotard's work the metaphysical endorsement of a new set of reified binarisms, a valorization of otherness over sameness, of contingency over necessity, of singularity and particularity over universality, of fragmentation over wholeness (Bernstein 1992: 310)?

Lyotard's search for a theory of political judgment is premised on a semiurgical grammar. His call for a multiplication of justices is, on the one hand, an admirable one given his attempt to recover minority discourses by rescuing the social pluralities that have been "suppressed in the West by the commodity terrorism of capitalist hegemony and in the East by the 'rational terrorism' of bureaucratic Communism" (Kroker 1992). Underlying such a project is Lyotard's important recognition that justice is plural. Justices must be understood as contextually specific and in relation to the many different spheres of society they need to be seen in their incommensurability. However, there is a problem in Lyotard's refusal not to privilege any of these justices, subjects or positions. Best and Kellner write:

> In a sense, Lyotard's celebration of plurality replays the moves of liberal pluralism and empiricism. His "justice of multiplicities" is similar to traditional liberal pluralism which posits a plurality of political subjects with multiple interests and organizations. He replays tropes of liberal tolerance by valorizing diverse modes of multiplicity, refusing to privilege any subjects or positions, or to offer a standpoint from which one can choose between opposing political positions. Thus he comes close to falling into a political relativism, which robs him of the possibility of making political discriminations and choosing between substantively different political positions.
>
> (1991: 174–5)

What regulates the idea of politics in the arena of the Lyotardian postmodern is not the "piety" of a transformative praxis but rather the idea of multiplicity and the plurality of language games. Minority discourses would prevail; that is, no one language game would prevail. The problem with this perspective, notes Peter Murphy, is Lyotard's repudiation of the idea of totality. Lyotard believes that there should be no Mother Of All Games, only the maintenance of all known games regulated by the idea of minority. Every discourse would remain a minority discourse such that none of the *petits récits* would be situated in a conceptual hierarchy or prevail as the majority. The metaphysical claim of identity subjugating difference is therefore ruptured and in its place would be a "multifold history of narrative clusters" (Kearney 1991: 200) – a narrative imagination purged of injustices. Lyotard writes:

> Destroy all monopolies of narrative, destroy the exclusivist themes of parties and markets. Remove from the Narrator the privilege he gives himself and show there is just as much power in narrative listening and narrative action (in the socially narrated world).... Struggle for the inclusion of all Master Narratives, of theories and doctrines, particularly political ones, within the (little) narratives. So that the intelligentsia may see its task not to proclaim the truth or save the world, but to seek the power of playing out, listening to, and telling stories. A power that is so common that peoples will never be deprived of it without riposte. And if you want an authority – that power is authority. Justice is wanting it.
>
> (cited in Kearney 1991: 201)

Peter Murphy asks if there is "a discourse that draws together all the other discourses or systems of knowledge without destroying them, without imposing a reign of tyranny over them" (1991: 126). In answering his own question he affirms that "the discourse of rights or freedom" is such a discourse because it is always in need of being supplemented with other stories, other narratives. As I mentioned in earlier chapters, such a discourse recognizes the importance of understanding how domination can be eliminated "in the relations between the pluralistic cultures of modernity" (p. 126). Murphy criticizes Lyotard's antagonism towards totality as follows:

> Lyotardian postmodernism... is scandalized by the idea of totality. Yet, in a totality, we see the fragments of modernity *in relation to each other*: confronting, avoiding, colliding, remonstrating, debating, accommodating, outwitting, and judging each other. It is this – the drama of modernity and its mediations – that a Lyotardian postmodernism cannot convey....
>
> The Lyotardian postmodernist may honor divergence. But there is divergence and divergence. Whatever their differences, the pluralistic cultures of modernity *need* to "hang together." They need each other. And, in fact and in deed, these fragments *can* "hang together," *only* insofar as they participate in the idea of freedom. A metadiscourse is

> a reflection on the relations between the fragments of modernity, *a reflection which, moreover*, judges these relations – relations which are sometimes domineering, sometimes tragic, sometimes mutually enriching. But to judge we must have a *criterion of judgment* – a criterion that will justify us not only in refusing colonizing relations between the plural cultures of modernity, but will also allow those cultures to speak to, to argue with, and to understand each other, however gropingly. This criterion is the idea of freedom. Freedom is the common measure of all the discourses of modernity.
>
> (Murphy 1991: 126–7)

According to Norman K. Denzin (1991), Lyotard "promotes a kind of neo-liberal pluralism" (p. 39) which "ignores the very structures of oppression other metanarratives, including feminism, make problematic" (p. 40). He concludes that "Lyotard's is an *existential pragmatism* which by making no appeal to grand narrative, only personal conscience and local narratives, always leaves open the potential of the very reign of terror he (and Sartre, Merleau-Ponty, and Rorty) so vehemently opposes" (p. 41). Murphy's answer to Lyotard's existential pragmatism is the construction of a metadiscourse of freedom. This means, in Murphy's view, that we need to distinguish between a master discourse and a metadiscourse. He claims that

> A master discourse wants to impose itself on all the other discourses – it is progressive, they are reactionary; it is right, they are wrong. A metadiscourse, on the other hand, seeks to understand society as a *totality*. By this I mean, it sets out to portray the contradictory nature of society and the complex interactions between the different spheres of society – their dramatic collisions and their dialogues, their tensions and reconciliations, their conflicts and accommodations.
>
> (1991: 126)

The problem in Lyotard's work of reconciling "a multiplicity of justice with a justice of multiplicity" (Kearney 1991: 196) is a formidable one. To judge without criteria, as Lyotard urges, affirms the imagination as the ground for making ethical decisions. Yet ethical decisions presuppose, in our view, the construction of an ethical imagination. Whilst the "scruple of undecidability" set forth by Lyotard and other post-structuralist thinkers offers us an important means of resisting metaphysical absolutes stored in the narrative archives of the nation-state and helps us to unsettle the dominant tropes and schematizing power of the sovereign imagination responsible for the standards that have historically terrorized our judgments (witness Auschwitz), it does little to help us construct the criteria for what constitutes an ethical imagination. Surely, critical education must move beyond simply affirming a proliferation of language games, or effecting new moves, new efficacies, and new intensities. Critical pedagogy calls for an ethical imagination that, following Kearney, "suffers the other to be other while suffering with (*com-patire*) the other as other" (1991: 225). Kearney writes:

> One must ask, at some point, what guides our evaluation of conflicting interpretations? What standards form or inform our judgments? And a post-modern ethic of dissemination which dismisses such questions as "futile and wrong-headed" is itself futile and wrong-headed. If it is true that we cannot possess knowledge of what is good in any absolute sense, it is equally true that we have an ethical duty to decide between what is better and what is worse.
>
> (Kearney 1991: 221)

The problem with Lyotardian analysis of difference is that it tends unwittingly to support a notion of difference reduced to its particularity such that concepts such as class, capital, and patriarchy are seen as totalizing master concepts and unhelpful in its understanding. Overall social organization, notes Himani Bannerji, becomes unnamable from such a perspective. She writes that attempts at viewing society as an overall social organization

> are dismissed as totalizing and detrimental to individuality, uniqueness of experience and expression. Concepts such as capital, class, imperialism, etc., are thus considered as totalizing, abstract "master narratives," and untenable bases for political subjectivity since they are arrived at rationally and analytically, moving beyond the concreteness of immediate experience. And the master narrative of "patriarchy" . . . fractured through experience and locked into identity circles, also cannot offer a general basis for common action for social change, without sinking into a fear of "essentialism" or "totalization."
>
> (1991: 84)

Critical pedagogy needs what Benhabib calls "a regulative principle of hope" without which a radical transformation of morality and social life is unthinkable. Benhabib writes:

> What scares the opponents of utopia, like Lyotard for example, is that in the name of such future utopia the present in its multiple ambiguity, plurality, and contradiction will be reduced to a flat grand narrative. I share some of Lyotard's concerns insofar as utopian thinking becomes an excuse either for the crassest instrumentalism in the present – the end justifies the means – or to the extent that the coming utopia exempts the undemocratic and authoritarian practices of the present from critique. Yet we cannot deal with these political concerns by rejecting the ethical impulse of utopia but only by articulating the

> normative principles of democratic action and organization in the present. Will the postmodernists join us in this task or will they be content with singing the swan-song of normative thinking in general?
>
> (1992: 229)

CONCLUSION: TOWARDS A RADICAL IMAGINARY AND EXPERIMENTAL PRAXIS

Bannerji echoes the concern of critical educationalists in her call for the creation of "an actively revolutionary knowledge" which will lead to the transformation of the conditions and social relations which give rise to our experience. She writes that "[t]his new theorization must challenge binary or oppositional relations of concepts such as general and particular, subject and object, and display a mediational, integrative, formative or constitutive relation between them which negates such polarization" (1991: 93). Drawing on Marx, Bannerji notes that the purpose of the concept of mediation is

> to capture the dynamic, showing how social relations and forms come into being in and through each other, to show how a mode of production is an historically and socially concrete formation. This approach ensures that the integrative actuality of social existence is neither conceptually ruptured and present fragmentarily nor abstracted into an empty universalism. Neither is there an extrapolation of a single aspect – a part standing in for the whole – nor the whole erasing the parts. Within this framework the knowledge of the social arises in the deconstruction of the concrete into its multiple mediations of social relations and forms which displays "the convergence of many determinations."
>
> (1991: 93)

The important objective here is to show "how the social and the historical always exist *as* and *in* "concrete" forms of social being and knowing" (p. 94). Bannerji is able to express a notion of self and agency in which everything that is local and immediate and concrete is "specific" rather than "particular." Agency that is "specific" is spacio-temporally present yet also the product of history and the politics of social relations. It is both singular and general. In this sense, experience becomes the starting point for politics since experience must then be read critically through a recounting of experience "within a broader socio-political and cultural framework that signals the larger social organization and forms which contain and shape our lives" (1991: 94).

Bannerji advocates cutting through the "false polarity posited between the personal/the private/the individual and the mental, and the social/collective/the public and the political, and find a formative mediation between the two" (p. 96). Here one can see the emergence of an "inter-constitutive relation between the mental and the social" (p. 96). Experience, then, becomes a point of departure for critical knowledge. It becomes a form of interpretation, "a relational sense-making" that has the potential to both create and transform. Bannerji notes that "[e]xperience, therefore, is that crucible in which the self and the world enter into a creative union called 'social subjectivity' " (p. 97).

Bannerji's position is not unfamiliar to many criticalists engaged in the project of transformative pedagogy, especially those who work from a Freirean perspective that invites the critical interrogation of experience as the starting point for developing a transformative praxis. Read against this critical interrogation and transformation of experience, there is something troubling in the way Lyotard's subject luxuriates in its inevitable and intractable cultural contradictions and the singularity of its own production. Further, there is something unsettling in Lyotard's attempt to marshal a respect for difference as an antidote to the normalizing conventions of formulaic commodity narratives and fetishized self-identity. Difference tends to self-destruct if it is not linked to some constitutive outside. For Lyotard, experience constitutes an irreducible complexity which can never be grasped since the sublime always occupies the gap between the experimental and the conceptual. This makes it exceedingly difficult to mount a pedagogy of critical self-reflexivity.

The underlying political project that informs the production of meaning constitutes the fundamental characteristics of knowledge production. If the construction of meaning is always already undergirded by ethico-political imperatives (which could also be read as motivated "absences") it is possible that teaching can be informed by a project of social transformation such that the forms of knowledge produced will be radically more liberating than those resulting from a pedagogy designed simply to promote membership in certain sanctioned communities of discourse, predicated on the joint task achievement of assuming monolithic executive identities, entrepreneurial agents of capital and modernity's colonial and neo-colonial situation. It is possible a priori to stipulate ethically yet still advance relationally and contingently a pedagogical project that cautions against rationalizing the social sphere based on the idea of individualism or taking as its normative subject the obedient, hard-working and creative citizen whose goal is to preserve existing relations of social privilege that have been produced out of the blood and mortar of official history. In making such a claim, we fully acknowledge with Lyotard that individuals engaged in such a project unconsciously accept roles they did not write and submit unwittingly to certain forms of social regulation which they consciously decry. Our motivations and actions are never fully transparent to our reason.

I am with Lyotard when we maintain that transformative pedagogy begins with the local, concrete and situated knowledges of the students themselves – an approach that validates the construction of their historical agency. But I diverge when, as criticalists, we seek to move beyond the specificity of experience – beyond local narratives – as the central referent for political action. Critical pedagogy seeks to uncover the social relations that organize experience and as such must seek to interrogate the social as a totality while simultaneously avoiding the terrorism that totalization often entails. Ernesto Laclau has suggested a way to understand the relationship between particularism and universalism that I find instructive. Arguing that "there is no real alternative between Spinoza and Hegel," Laclau remarks that "if a particularity asserts itself as a mere particularity, in a purely differential relation with other particularities, it is sanctioning the status quo in power relations between the groups" (1992: 88). For instance, the identity of an ethnic minority group can only be fully achieved within a context such as a nation or state. If that minority succeeds in establishing a complete identity within such a context then it becomes integrated into that context. If identity does not become fully achieved then this is due to unsatisfied demands within such a context (equal access to education, employment, etc.). Laclau notes that such demands cannot be made in terms of difference but "on the basis of some universal principles that the ethnic minority shares with the rest of the community" (p. 89). Consequently, the universal is part of the identity of this ethnic minority group insofar as their differential identity has failed in the process of constituting itself – that is, insofar as such an identity is "penetrated by a constitutive lack" (p. 89). This means that the universal "emerges out of the particular not as some principle underlying and explaining it, but as an incomplete horizon suturing a dislocated particular identity." Here, the universal is not an imposed metanarrative but rather "the symbol of a missing fullness." Consequently, "the particular exists only in the contradictory movement of asserting a differential identity and simultaneously canceling it through its subsumption into a nondifferential medium" (p. 89). This perspective offers us a way of contesting Western Eurocentrism insofar as Eurocentrism is the result of universalistic values being imposed on concrete social actors whose incommensurability with such values is not taken into consideration. In other words,

> If the social struggles of new social actors show that the concrete practices of our society restrict the universalism of our political ideals to limited sectors of the population, it becomes possible to retain the universal by widening the spheres of its application – which, in turn, will redefine the concrete contents of such a universality.
>
> (p. 90)

Laclau points to an apparent paradox in his formulation of the relationship between particularism and universalism: "that universalism is incommensurable with any particularity yet cannot exist apart from the particular." Such a condition does not represent a terminal paradox but rather, as Laclau puts it, "the very precondition of democracy" (p. 90). "If democracy *is* possible," writes Laclau, "it is because the universal does not have any necessary body, any necessary content. Instead, different groups compete to give their particular aims a temporary function of universal representation" (p. 90). This view reflects that of Eagleton in Chapter 6.

I have tried to make the case that, for the purposes of constructing a critical pedagogy, Lyotard does not stipulate adequately the need to make critical discriminations among incommensurable discourses. So long as claims of substantiation remain unredeemable and criteria of obligation for making judgments remain absent, it is difficult to develop a transformative praxis (Van Reijen 1990). I believe, following Selya Benhabib, that there are more conceptual and normative options to the death of Man, History, and Metaphysics than allowed by Lyotard and as such a fallibilistic and procedural concept of rationality needs to be developed in order that a certain "reasonable and ethical conversation" be made available, that is, in order for the admission of certain normative options that are necessary for an emancipatory educative praxis. In other words, "the agonistics of language" and a "polytheism of values" are not the only options following the end of metanarratives and the demise of the episteme of representation.

There may be no foundational criteria of truth transcending local discourses – no commensurability of language games or discursive means that can derive an "ought" from an "is" – but this need not rule out, *mutatis mutandis*, provisionally normative human coexistence and the construction of warranted assertions about what constitutes oppression and liberation. Ethics and epistemology speak of standards of justification and such standards are always imbricated in politics. Ethics and epistemology have political effects as discursive interventions and we need to be able to stipulate which effects are oppressive and which are productive of social transformation.

Here I wish to repeat again what Benhabib calls the standpoint of "interactive universalism" which allows us to recognize "the dignity of the generalized other through an acknowledgment of the moral identity of the concrete other" (1992: 164). This is not a prescriptive moral theory that sets out to unqualifiedly defend the standpoint of the concrete other. Rather, its purpose is to recognize the reversibility of perspectives between the concrete and generalized other. It is important to distinguish this position from "substitutionalist universalism" which "dismisses the concrete other behind the facade of a definitional identity of all as rational beings" (pp. 164–5).

I believe that defending the value of emancipation means more than simply speaking differently, but rather involves understanding difference *relationally*. While Lyotard's articulation of the *différend* as a principle of justice in which minority and subaltern voices are allowed to speak is an important corrective to totalitarian narratives that silence the other, we must make certain that not all voices are celebrated for the simple sake that they remain *unfettered by a priori rules of judgment*.

What is necessary, according to Benhabib, is to examine the radical situatedness and contextualization of the subject. This is a project that I believe Bannerji has engaged with considerable success. Such a project entails the proposition that the subject is more than the sum total of its signifying practices, more than an unstable ensemble of shifting subject positions. What is important here is that subjects are invited to explore the constitutive possibilities of their own desiring such that they are able to disavow the foreclosure of their own destinies. This is not a call for transforming students into versions of postmodern refuseniks who simply "zone out" when confronted with normative political, ethical, and social demands, but for a conjunctural politics in which agents, while refusing assigned roles produced by fixed determinations, are able to act in oppositional ways. Lyotard's call to think liberation otherwise, to tell another story, demands a self-reflexive agent who is able to make sure that the *other stories* we tell ourselves about ourselves have less painful historical consequences for those generally left out of such stories or who are generally unwittingly narrativized as the victims. It also suggests the importance of constructing pedagogical tactics as opposed to strategies.

Strategies, notes Rey Chow (after De Certeau), deal with subjects who wish to solidify a place or barricade a field of interest. Tactics, on the other hand, deal with calculated actions outside of specific sites. Strategic solidarities only repeat "what they seek to overthrow" (Chow 1993: 17). Michael Shapiro (following De Certeau) describes strategies as belonging "to those (e.g., the police) who occupy legitimate or what is recognized as proper space within the social order" (1992: 103). Further, he describes them as "part of a centralized surveillance network for controlling the population." Tactics, on the other hand, are described as belonging "to those who do not occupy a legitimate space and depend instead on time, on whatever opportunities present themselves." Describing tactics as "weapons of the weak," De Certeau is worth quoting at length:

> [A] *tactic* is a calculated action determined by the absence of a proper locus. . . . The space of a tactic is the space of the other. Thus it must play on and with a terrain imposed on it and organized by the law of a foreign power. It does not have the means to *keep to itself*, at a distance, in a position of withdrawal, foresight, and self-collection: it is a maneuver "within the enemy's field of vision," . . . and within enemy

> territory. It does not, therefore, have the option of planning, general strategy. . . . It operates in isolated actions, blow by blow. It takes advantage of opportunities and depends on them, being without any base where it could stockpile its winnings, build up its own position, and plan raids. . . . This nowhere gives a tactic mobility, to be sure, but a mobility that must accept the chance offerings of the moment, and seize on the wing the possibilities that offer themselves at any given moment. It must vigilantly make use of the cracks that particular conjunctions open in the surveillance of proprietary powers. It poaches them. It creates surprises in them. . . . It is a guileful ruse.
>
> (cited in Conquergood 1992: 82)

Lyotard's pragmatics of justice uncannily embodies many of the characteristics of De Certeau's tactics. Lyotard's anti-monism and celebration of plural rationalities makes use of the zones of uncertainty, creating the possibility for tactical maneuvers that work like the shock effect of Dada. Here, the constitutive space of resistance is realized in the rootlessness of the temporal and the contingent, the realm of atopia, of some other realm that cannot be defined or represented but can be glimpsed. As the self implodes under the impact of multiple stories en route to the circuit of commodification, new spaces of possibilities are seized, powers are poached. The methodological provocation advanced by Lyotard helps to remind us that all representations as forms of violence must be ceaselessly interrogated and continually reinvented outside the totalizing logic of grand narratives. Our postmodern imaginary must be placed in the service of dreaming beyond the acceptance of such violence and seek new forms of social, political, and ethical relations: in short, new forms of human community hitherto unimaginable. Yet because Lyotard has renounced a general theory of politics, we need to turn elsewhere to fulfill the challenge he has put before us.

We need to infuse critical pedagogy with a subversive power that is able to effect new cultural transgressions and that cannot be brought within the fateful orbit of commodity exchange. There is no natural destiny to critical pedagogy or to the communities to which it dedicates itself. As Sadie Plant (1992) notes, "the scenario in which theorists trip over people asleep on the streets on their way to declare the impossibility of changing anything is merely the tip of an absurd and tragic iceberg with which we cannot continue to live" (p. 185). Like Benjamin's flâneur, we need to abandon the metropolitan salons of bourgeois intellectuals which barricade us from the pulsations of other stories and begin again to walk the tremulous streets of desire; aware of the culpability of our theoretical practices, we nevertheless need to become *troleurs* of hope.

Perhaps Lyotard and Baudrillard would tell us not to worry, that the new revolutionaries are here in the form of cyberpunk "hackers" who create the new information public forums through interactive "town hall" bulletin boards. Or they are xerox pirates or the inhabitants of dropout culture who create fanzines, "detourned" advertisements, irreverent political/aesthetic manifestos, and oppositional social networks. Do we then rely for liberation on the "negative ecstasy" of new technologies and high tech cybernetic systems, the telechtronic talents of cyborg protagonists shaking their super-highway protheses in the face of the life-subverting megacorporate barons? Do we wait for a new, hyperreal, video-thrill, tongue-flicking, hipster Ché, techno homeboy of hope, swaddled in electronic circuitry and sporting a neon codpiece and nipple ring to challenge the megastate? Do we listen to cultural snipers in *Vanity Fair* or gunfire from the towns of Chiapas? Is the only choice left between Lyotard and el subcomandante Marcos en San Cristobal de las Casas? How do we ratify this new covenant of nihilism? Through the ecstasy of self-mutilation and the thrill-seeking of predatory culture? Is there room in accelerated culture for Obatalá, Changó, Yemayá, Oshún, Babalú-Ayé, Oggún? If we follow Lyotard in moving away from our ancestral gods and in opposing current corporate, legal and institutionalized constructions of who we are through claims of decentered subjectivity, then we need to guard against the process of incorporation in which resistant subjectivities are denuded through appropriation into the commodity form of capital and transformed into the high-return alienation of promotional culture. If we define ourselves as postmodern mobile subjects, multiply constituted and negotiated on a daily basis, for whom do we make our demands for social justice?

In a world where the prospect of living has become more fearful than the mystery of death, such questions can only engender the dystopic ridicule and mockery that comes with the times.

Notes

INTRODUCTION: EDUCATION AS A POLITICAL ISSUE

1 The term "predatory culture" was inspired by reading Mick Farren's "Theater of the disturbed" (Farren 1993).

1 RADICAL PEDAGOGY AS CULTURAL POLITICS

1 See Aronowitz and Giroux (1985: 69–114) for a review and critical analysis of this literature. See also Giroux (1988a).
2 For a critical treatment of the social reconstructionists, see Giroux (1988b). A version of this discussion of the critical pedagogical tradition appears in McLaren (1989b).
3 The relationship between curriculum and the logic and process of commodification and capital accumulation has been emphasized in the writings of Michael W. Apple (1979, 1982, 1987).
4 We have discussed this issue extensively in Giroux and McLaren (1986a).
5 Versions of this section appear in Giroux and McLaren (1987a, 1987b, forthcoming).
6 A critique of this position can be found in McLaren (1986).
7 Versions of this section appear in McLaren (1988, 1989a).
8 Not all resistance is linked to a politics of emancipation. See Giroux (1983) and McLaren (1986).
9 On the question of affective investment, see Grossberg (1987: 28–45).
10 See Liston (1988).
11 Wayne Hudson (p.50) has summarized the standard critique of utopian thinking as follows:

> The standard critique of utopia rests on the ontological claim that the nature of things is given, on the regional claim that utopia is not grounded in the world at hand, and on the psychological claim that men depart from reality when they dream of perfection beyond the limitations which the reality at hand imposes. It maintains that utopia is not only unrealistic and impractical, but potentially dangerous; since it encourages men to give vent to totalistic, adolescent psychological states, and provides an illusory basis for human action. According to this critique, utopia is a form of unbridled subjectivism which ignores the fact that man cannot reshape the objective world in his own image, make it conform to abstract plans and schemata, or base his practical activities on maximally preferred values. It is *irrational* in its

refusal to acknowledge the authority of objective reality, *immature* in its inability to realize the limited nature of the possible, and *irresponsible* in its failure to understand the role of fallibilism in the realization of the good. The standard critique, summed up in the smart phrase "That's rather utopian," recognizes that there are different kinds of utopians and that utopianism can adopt a scientific as well as Messianic guise; but it maintains that all utopians err in preferring the fulfillment of ideal representations to the more mundane improvements which are possible in their time.

(Hudson 1982: 50–1)

12 Wells (1984: 82). See also the response to Wells by Gregory Baum in the same issue.
13 Bernstein (1988: 271). See also Kolakowski (1982), McLaren (1988a: 64–5), and McLaren and Da Silva (1993).
14 Bloch, cited in Rabinbach (1977: 11).
15 Our notion of utopia is derived from Ernst Bloch, *The Principle of Hope* (1986).
16 Ernst Bloch, *Das Princip Hoffnung*, as quoted in Hudson (1982: 51–2).
17 For a discussion of the concept of "dangerous memory," see Welch (1985: 82–3).
18 See Henry A. Giroux (1991); see also McLaren (1991a, 1992b); for a discussion of enfleshment, see McLaren (1991b).

2 SCHOOLING THE POSTMODERN BODY

This idea of the schooled body first came to mind in a 1980 seminar taught by Michel Foucault. Since then I have profited from the ideas of many colleagues, especially Henry Giroux.

1 For a summary of some of the major themes of postmodernism, see Dick Hebdige (1986). I believe that postmodernism is a conflicting and contradictory sphere of ideological and cultural manifestations within and pronouncements about the constitution of late capitalism both with respect to the possibilities of cultural criticism and the development of an oppositional political project. It is clearly the case that there are both socially reactionary and socially emancipatory strains of postmodern social theory as Henry Giroux, Hal Foster (1983), Linda Hutcheon (1988), and others have argued. There exist, I would argue, both utopian and dystopian potentialities within the current heterotopian character of postmodern society. While classical modernist dichotomies of Left vs. Right fail to adequately characterize these strains, there is, unarguably, a subversive element in the free-play of the signifier as well as a disabling potential. The freeing of the signifier from its link to a mythic signified can certainly be used both to attack dominant signifying practices such as the notion of the transcendental self as existing outside articulation, and collapse the boundaries between high and low culture. Yet there is also a danger that postmodernism can be co-opted for commercial and ideological ends (Kaplan 1987). And while I essentially agree with Scott Lash and John Urry that "Postmodernism on one side, with its glorification of commercial vulgarity, its promotion of 'authoritarian populism,' reinforces relations of domination [and] on the other side, with its opposition to hierarchy, it is a cultural resource for resistance to such domination" (1987: 14), this chapter will essentially forgo an extended discussion of the enabling possibilities of the latter and will,

instead, concentrate on a critique of the authoritarian servility, pronounced anti-utopianism, and incipient nihilism of the former.

2 In order to avoid a "blaming the victim" explanation of the noncontestedness within the ideological formation of today's youth, we need to acknowledge that while ideological hegemony in the United States is irredeemably condemnable and undeniably powerful, it is not without its contradictory moments. A critical reading of social reality often becomes, for many students, a self-contesting exercise not because they enjoy living a yuppie narcosis but because, as Grossberg points out, "youth inserts cultural texts into its public and private lives in complex ways" (1988b: 139). Grossberg rightly recognizes that in our postmodern culture, youth exists within the space between subjectification (boredom) and commodification.

3 In this context, the T.V. screen symbolizes a new era of recycled reality – what Baudrillard refers to as a "narcissistic and protean era of connections, contact, contiguity, feedback and generalized interface" (1983: 127) – where we witness the spectacle of meanings imploding into the flat, seamless surface of hyperreality while at the same time watch helplessly as subjectivity becomes terrorized into political inaction by the baleful dictates of commodity logic and "the constant promise of a plentitude forever deferred" (Kaplan 1987: 50).

4 Our consumption of signs is but itself a sign of cultural illness and is symptomatic of postmodern pathologies: narcissistic character disorders, schizophrenias, and depressions (Levin 1987). Richard Litchman (1982) has revealed to us how the very structure of capitalism condemns us from living its own moral truth by pathologizing our everyday subjectivity and provoking a deluded complicity with an often oppressive consensus reality. The "structural unconscious," which helps shape our everyday identity and disposition, is informed largely by the structural contradictions of capitalism which help to construct needs, mobilize desires, and then deny all of these (p. 229).

5 For a similar analysis of the New Right, see McLaren and Smith (1989). Left social theorists are currently attacking a host of sacrosanct modernist themes which range from the grand myth of science as a self-correcting, self-perfecting, and apodictic universal methodology, to the transparency of the sign, to the transcendental constitutivity of the subject and its fictive stability and unitary identity across time, to the teleological myth of progress (McLaren 1986). Left educational theorists have been slow to respond to such an attack, but in some cases they have occupied the front ranks of the foray, since many of these myths have been responsible for fuelling the logic which has made objectivism and certainty into the new demiurge of late capitalist schooling. Yet an unintended consequence of current deconstructive assaults and attempts to construct a form of ethics outside traditional moral and political codes has been the fostering of a public climate regulated by tribunals of normalcy reflecting a brutish and often belligerent self-righteousness.

Forces on the Right, which have taken a swift and punishing advantage of the growing moral ambivalence on the Left, are not pausing to take account of which strand of postmodernism – emancipatory or reactionary – has the temporary leverage in the academy. They are smoothly injecting their ideology directly into the cultural veins of the nation through the electronic media. It's now in fashion to be "Right Wing," as George Bush made clear in his 1986 election campaign during which time he easily derailed the Democratic platform with spectral images of Willy Horton and video clips of Mike Dukakis riding shotgun in an army tank. With the exception of Jesse Jackson and a handful of others, Liberal Democrats under Dukakis were unable to speak from a moral position that was able to evoke either the sympathy or the support of the American public. In this sense postmodern culture has been especially kind to the New Right, whose political effectiveness can be largely credited to its ability to use the media to mobilize consent around a normative moral vision of the future and to recontextualize difference into a consensus ideology. The often frenzied political and ideological allegiance among such a wide spectrum of individuals – which includes, among others, West Coast evangelists in natty business suits, East Coast private-sector executives, Midwestern service technicians, and primary labor market workers from the South – is as much a function of the way desires and needs are constituted through the body and sedimented discourses invest themselves in the flesh through what Raymond Williams called "structures of feeling" (1977) as it is a matter of making deliberate choices between conflicting discourses.

The inability of leftist social theorists to establish a politics of praxis strong enough to contest the broad and sweeping constituency of the New Right has imperiled their goal of social transformation and justice that should, ideally, provide the springboard for all social theorizing and practice. What gets unintentionally softened as a result of the relentless attack on the sovereignty of identity and the transparency of society is the very grounds of political opposition and social transformation. Without a new language of ethics and authority it is hard to construct the grounds for what Henry Giroux (1983; 1988b) has called a counterpublic sphere and pedagogy for the opposition.

6 It should be pointed out that, with minor exceptions, the Left has failed to develop a critical language that is able to speak directly to the contradictions and particularities of everyday life. In other words, to maintain the requisite complexity of its concepts and formulations its language has paid a price in suggestive power. Undoubtedly, this has also been aggravated by "academic assimilation that neutralizes oppositional writing in a society that provides room for intellectual battles but little for the uses of theory as an ally of actual political resistance" (Merod 1987: 186).

Politics has now taken on a strange, hybrid meaning among social and political theorists of the Left within the academy, who vary enormously in their opinion and appropriation of postmodern strategies of critique. On the one hand, there are critics such as Fredric Jameson who warn against a simplistic, reductionistic view of the political (1982: 75); on the other hand, there are critics such as Jim Merod, who feel that much academic work that falls into the category of "postmodern," decidedly fails to move the reader "from the academic world of texts and interpretations to the vaster world of surveillance, technology, and material forces" (1987: 146). Harsher antagonists, such as Robert Scholes, claim that the deconstructive enterprise often operates as a form of left mandarin terrorism, both displacing "political activism into a textual world where anarchy can *become* the establishment without threatening the actual seats of political and economic power" (1988b: 284) and sublimating political radicalism "into a textual radicalism that can happily theorize its own disconnection from unpleasant realities" (p. 284). Cornel West argues that some current Left allegiances satisfy "a pervasive need for Left-academic intellectuals . . . for the professional respectability and rigor that displace political engagement and this-worldly involvement . . . [while at the same time providing] an innocuous badge of radicalism" (Stephanson 1988: 274).

If we take these critics of present-day Left theorizing seriously, and I believe that we should, then we should also consider the possibility that by evacuating the fallen gods of modernity and by adopting what is essentially an anti-utopian discourse, Left educational theorists may have unwittingly reinstated the worst ideological dimensions of the very discourses they are attempting to renounce. In their fully-fledged frontal attack on metaphysics, a new subterranean metaphysics may have seeped into existence.

7 See Kroker and Cook (eds) (1986).

8 For an excellent analysis of this dilemma in feminist discourse, see Alcoff (1988).

9 In confronting the vast power of the myth of identity, and in questioning the unity of the liberal, humanist subject, Left social theorists have failed to secure a stable platform from which to speak to the role of the individual as an active political agent. Their failure to situate individuals as political and ethical agents has contributed to the broader failure of constructing a public language and critical vernacular capable of speaking effectively to the daily, lived concerns of the body politic (Giroux 1988). As a result of these failures, Left social theorists have paved the way for a system grounded in absolute ethical certainty and moral closure which has turned schools into laboratories for character engineering based on a reactionary political vision. Here, subjectivities are policed, ethics is dispensed, and nationalism celebrated. Here, the discursive underpinnings are provided for a national character formation which can best expedite the production and flow of capital in tough, competitive, economic times and resist the threat of the omnipresent Marxist or Third World Other. The school takes on the hybrid ethos of the local legion hall and fundamentalist revival meeting: America will prevail on the basis of sound, unflinching, moral fibre and die-hard courage in the face of physical threat.

Translated into a curriculum directive on a national scale, the victory of the New Right has been devastating. A sweeping rearguard action to promote and bolster the simplification and infantilization of the good vs. evil morality of the mass spectacle has been accomplished with little effective resistance. School success in the postmodern era is located within the iron determinism of the capitalist will and achieved by effecting a closure of the sign to a univocal and monodimensional reading. The election of Clinton has changed little.

10 It is useful here to draw attention to the distinction Bryan Turner has made between Freud's pessimistic view of desire as its own object, and the Marxian notion of need which implies an object that can satisfy it (1984: 11). While desires are always already in the order of the signifier as protolinguistic demands (in the sense that they cannot be conceived independently of their representations) (Turner and Carter 1986), objects of desire are never fully assimilable into desire, as desire is never wholly contained in social forms. Desire is always displaced (as in Lacan's notion that in language desire is metonymically and metaphorically displaced).

11 As cited in Turner and Carter (1986).

12 Postmodernism is very much about the noise of the body which is evident in performance art, minimalism and neo-tonality. Fred Pfeil has remarked on the "scandalously ambivalent" aspect of postmodern forms of pleasure (which he has experienced in the performances of Laurie Anderson and the production of the Wilson/Glass opera, *Einstein on the Beach*) which is "characterized both by the release of new sociopolitical forces through de-Oedipalization of middle-class American life *and* by the hegemony of this same de-Oedipalization social–sexual structure that tends to block the further development of those social forces" (1988: 399). What Pfeil is referring to is the "Omnipotent" return to pre-Oedipal wholeness and pleasure produced in avant-garde ima-

gery and productions. But if we take the Oedipus complex to be more of a linguistic rather than a primarily intrafamilial phenomenon, as does Eugene Holland (following Lacan's lead), then we can make a link between such a phenomenon and certain types of social formation. Utilizing the typology of social forms developed by Gilles Deleuze and Felix Guattari (1988) Holland notices that the "name-of-the-Father" does not govern the Symbolic order in capitalist societies as it does under 'primitive' communistic and despotic societies. Under capitalism, the Symbolic order has no fixed center, no established authority figure, and no transcendental signified since "exchange value and the market ruthlessly undermine and eliminate all traditional meanings and pre-existing social codes" (1988: 407). In other words, the "abstract calculus of capital itself" knits together the social order not by providing universal codes but by "decoding" pre-existing meanings and codes (which "frees desire from capture and distortion by social coding") and "recoding... libidinal energy back onto factitious codes so as to extract and realize privately appropriable surplus value" (p. 408). In other words, continuous revolution under capitalism of the means of production generates a massive decoding which liberates creative consumption and production – even revolutionizing and socializing productive forces – yet the libidinal energy which escapes the constraints of social coding nevertheless becomes recolonized through bureaucratization, the nuclear family, and consumerism.

3 BORDER DISPUTES

1 *Rasquachismo* means the aesthetics of the dispossessed or downtrodden. It is a chicano/a term.

4 WHITE TERROR AND OPPOSITIONAL AGENCY

Slightly altered versions of this chapter will appear in Christine Sleeter and Peter McLaren (eds), *Critical Pedagogy and Multiculturalism*, Albany, NY, State University of New York Press; and Peter McLaren, Rhonda Hammer, Susan Reilly and David Sholle, *A Critical Pedagogy of Representation*, New York, Peter Lang Publishers. Some sections of this paper have appeared in Peter McLaren, "Multiculturalism and the postmodern critique: towards a pedagogy of resistance and transformation," *Cultural Studies* 7(1), 1993, 118–46 and Peter McLaren, "Critical pedagogy, multiculturalism, and the politics of risk and resistance: a response to Kelly and Portelli," *Journal of Education* 173(3), 1991, 29–59.

1 Africa is still demonized as a land uncivilized, corrupt, and savage, divided into countries that are viewed as not evolved enough to govern themselves without Western guidance and stewardship. We shamefully ignore Africa's victims of war and famine in comparison, for instance, to the "white" victims of Bosnia. When the U.S. media does decide to report on Africa, much of the image it reinforces is a land of jungle, wildlife, famine, poachers, and fierce fighting among rival tribes/factions (Naureckas 1993). The white supremacist and colonialist discourses surrounding the recent intervention in Somalia by heroic U.S. troops and relief workers (referred to by Colin Powell as sending in the "cavalry") is captured in comments made by Alan Pizzy of CBS when he described the intervention in "humanitarian" terms as "just a few good men trying to help another nation in need, another treacherous country where all the members of all the murderous factions look alike" (cited in Naureckas

1993: 12). Described as a land populated by helpless and history-less victims and drug-crazed thugs high on khat (a mild stimulant) who ride around in vehicles out of a *Mad Max* movie, an implicit parallel is made between Somalia youth and the cocaine-dealing gangs of toughs who participated in the L.A. uprising (ibid.). This "othering" of Africa encouraged a preferred reading of Somalia's problems as indigenous and camouflaged the broader context surrounding the famine in Somalia and its subsequent "rescue" by U.S. marines. Occluded was the fact that the U.S. had previously obstructed U.N. peacekeeping efforts in Somalia, Angola, Namibia, and Mozambique because it was too costly (the U.S. still owes $415 million to the U.N., including $120 million for peacekeeping efforts) – a factor absent in nearly all the media coverage (ibid.). From a U.S. foreign policy perspective, Somalia still plays an important role geopolitically, not simply because of its potential interest to Israel and Arab nations, but because of its rich mineral deposits and potential oil reserves. As Naureckas notes, Amoco, Chevron and Sunoco are engaged in oil exploration there (ibid.).

The media have rarely reported on other factors surrounding the famine in Somalia. For instance, they have virtually ignored the U.S. support (to the sum of $200 million in military aid and half a billion in economic aid) to the Siad Barre regime (1969–91). The U.S. ignored its corruption and human rights abuses because the dictatorship kept Soviet-allied Ethiopia embroiled in a war. Naureckas also points out that until the 1970s, Somalia was self-sufficient in grain and its agricultural land productive enough to withstand famine. However, U.S. and international agencies like the I.M.F. pressured Somalia to shift agriculture from local subsistence to export crops (ibid.).

5 PEDAGOGIES OF DISSENT AND TRANSFORMATION

1 McLaren (1992a).
2 Kroker (1992).
3 Davis (1990). McLaren's discussion of L.A. draws from Davis (1993).
4 West (1993).
5 Gates (1989).
6 Massumi (1993).
7 Coupland (1991).
8 Chow (1993).
9 I will use "we" to talk about this research because research assistants have always been an important part of the ongoing study. Assistants such as Joanne Larson, Marc Pruyn, Williams Saunders, Terese Karnafel, Cindy Tuttle, Tracy Rone, and Claudia Ramirez should be acknowledged for their contributions.
10 Goodwin (1993).
11 Goldberg (1993).
12 Telles and Murguia (1990).
13 See Gutierrez and Larson (1994) for more discussion.
14 Ruiz (1992).
15 Williams (1993).
16 Deloria (1987).
17 See Gutierrez (1994) for a comparison of the effects of various contexts for learning on bicultural children.
18 See Moll (1990) for more discussion of the notion of "funds of knowledge" in Chicano communities.

19 See Marc Pruyn (1994) for a discussion of the social construction of critical pedagogy in elementary school classrooms.
20 Scott (1992).
21 Delpit (1988).

7 MULTICULTURALISM AND THE POSTMODERN CRITIQUE

1 A Haitian Creole term meaning "whitey" or "white person."

8 CRITICAL PEDAGOGY AND THE PRAGMATICS OF JUSTICE

1 This chapter is dedicated to El Ejército Zapatista de Liberación Nacional. It is also dedicated to my comrades in Latin America who are continually teaching me important lessons dealing with hope and the need for struggle at the level of everyday, institutional and political life. The examples of their everyday lives has helped to give me the strength and conviction to continue writing and working. These wonderful friends have helped me to see the role of the professor in a much broader light – not as a practice that is consumed by self-interest and the politics of self-aggrandizement but rather as a political project guided by humility, self-sacrifice and a love of others.

References

Abercrombie, N., Hill, S., and Turner, B. (1986) *Sovereign Individuals of Capitalism*, London: Allen & Unwin.

Adorno, T. (1974) "Culture industry reconsidered," *New German Critique* 6: 13–19.

Alcoff, L. (1988) "Cultural feminism versus poststructuralism: the identity crisis in feminist theory," *Signs* 13(3): 405–36.

Alcoff, L. (1991/92) "The problem of speaking for others," *Cultural Critique* 20: 5–32.

Alvez, R. A. (1975) *A Theology of Human Hope*, St Meinrad, IN: Abbey Press.

Angus, I. (1989) "Media beyond representation," in I. Angus and S. Jhally (eds) *Cultural Politics in Contemporary America*, London and New York: Routledge.

Anzaldúa, G. (1987) *Borderlands/La Frontera: The New Mestiza*, San Francisco: Spinsters/Aunt Lute.

Anzaldúa, G. (1990) "Haciendos caras, una entrada: an introduction," in G. Anzaldúa (ed.) *Making Face, Making Soul: Creative and Critical Perspectives by Women of Color*, San Francisco: Aunt Lute.

Appiah, A. (1991) "Tolerable falsehoods: agency and the interests of theory," in J. Arac and B. Johnson (eds) *Consequences of Theory*, Baltimore, MD: Johns Hopkins University Press.

Apple, M. W. (1979) *Ideology and Curriculum*, London and Boston, MA: Routledge & Kegan Paul.

Apple, M. W. (1982) *Education and Power*, London and Boston, MA: Routledge & Kegan Paul.

Apple, M. W. (1987) *Teachers and Texts: A Political Economy of Class and Gender Relations in Education*, London and New York: Routledge & Kegan Paul.

Arac, T. (ed.) (1986) *Postmodernism and Politics*, Minneapolis, MN: University of Minnesota Press.

Aronowitz, S. (1981) *The Crisis in Historical Materialism: Class, Politics and Culture in Marxist Theory*, New York: J. F. Bergin.

Aronowitz, S. (1983) "Mass culture and the eclipse of reason: the implications for pedagogy," in D. Lazere (ed.) *American Media and Mass Culture*, Berkeley and Los Angeles, CA: University of California Press.

Aronowitz, S. (1993) "Paulo Freire's radical democratic humanism," in P. McLaren and P. Leonard (eds) *Paulo Freire: A Critical Encounter*, London: Routledge.

Aronowitz, S. and Giroux, H. (1985) *Education Under Siege: The Conservative, Liberal, and Radical Debate Over Schooling*, South Hadley, MS: Bergin & Garvey.

Aronowitz, S. and Giroux, H. (1991) *Postmodern Education*, Minneapolis, MN: University of Minnesota Press.

Asante, M. (1987) *The Afrocentric Idea*, Philadelphia, PA: Temple University Press.

Ashcroft, B., Griffiths, G., and Tiffin, H. (1989) *The Empire Writes Back*, London and New York: Routledge.

Attali, J. (1987) *Noise: The Political Economy of Music*, Minneapolis, MN: University of Minnesota Press.

Auni, O. (1991) "Narrative subject, historic subject: Shoah and La Place de l'Etoile," *Poetics Today* 3(12): 495–516.

Auster, L. (1990) *The Path to National Suicide: An Essay on Immigration and Multiculturalism*, American Immigration Control Foundation.

Baker, H. A. (1985) "Caliban's triple play," in H. L. Gates, Jr. (ed.) *"Race," Writing, and Difference*, Chicago: The University of Chicago Press.

Bakhtin, M. M. (1986) *Speech Genres and Other Late Essays* (M. Holquist (ed.) and C. Emerson and M. Holquist (trans.)), Austin: University of Texas Press.

Bannerji, H. (1991) "But who speaks for us? Experience and agency in conventional feminist paradigms," in H. Bannerji, L. Carty, K. Delhi, S. Heald, and K. McKenna (eds) *Unsettling Relations*, Toronto: Women's Press.

Barker, F. (1984) *The Tremulous Private Body*, London: Methuen.

Baudrillard, J. (1975) *The Mirror of Production*, St Louis: Telos Press.

Baudrillard, J. (1983) *Simulations*, trans. P. Foss, P. Patton, and J. Johnston, New York: Semiotext(e).

Baudrillard, J. (1988) *America*, London: Verso.

Baudrillard, J. (1990) *Seduction*, New York: St Martin's Press.

Baum, G. (1987) *Compassion and Solidarity: The Church for Others*, Montreal and New York: C.B.C. Enterprises.

Bauman, Z. (1988) "Is there a postmodern sociology?," *Theory, Culture & Society* 5(2–3): 217–37.

Bauman, Z. (1988/89) "Strangers: the social construction of universality and particularity," *Telos* 78: 7–42.

Benhabib, S. (1992) *Situating the Self: Gender, Community and Postmodernism in Contemporary Ethics*, London and New York: Routledge.

Benjamin, A. (1992) *Judging Lyotard*, London and New York: Routledge.

Benjamin, W. (1968) "The work of art in the age of mechanical reproduction," in H. Arendt (ed.) *Illuminations*, New York: Schocken Books.

Benjamin, W. (1973) "Program for a proletarian children's theater," *Performance* 1(5): 28–32, trans. S. Buck-Morss.

Bennett, D. (1990) "Wrapping up postmodernism: the subject of consumption versus the subject of cognition," in A. Milner, P. Tompson, and C. Worth (eds) *Postmodern Conditions*, Providence, RI: Berg Publishers Ltd.

Bennett, T. (1986) "Texts in history: the determinations of readings and their text," in D. Attridge, G. Bennington, and R. Young (eds) *Post-Structuralism and the Question of History*, Cambridge: Cambridge University Press.

Bennett, T. and Wollacott, J. (1987) *Bond and Beyond: The Political Career of a Popular Hero*, New York: Methuen.

Berman, R. A. (1989) *Modern Culture and Critical Theory*, Madison, WI: University of Wisconsin Press.

Bernstein, R. J. (1988) "Metaphysics, critique, and utopia," *Review of Metaphysics* 42(2): 255–73.

Bernstein, R. J. (1992) *The New Constellation*, Cambridge, MA: MIT Press.

Best, S. (1989) "Jameson, totality, and the post-structuralist critique," in D. Keller (ed.) *Postmodernism/Jameson/Critique*, Washington, DC: Maisonneuve Press.

Best, S. and Kellner, D. (1991) *Postmodern Theory: Critical Interrogations*, New York: Guilford Press.

Bhabha, H. K. (1984) "Of mimicry and man: The ambivalence of colonial discourse," *October* 28: 125–33.

Bhabha, H. K. (1987) "Interrogating identity," in *The Real Me: Post-Modernism and the Question of Identity*, London: ICA Documents 6: 5–12.

Bhabha, H. K. (1988) "The commitment to theory," *New Formations* 5: 5–23.

Bhabha, H. K. (1990a) "The Third Space: Interview with Homi Bhabha," in Jonathan Rutherford (ed.) *Identity: Community, Culture, Difference*, London: Lawrence & Wishart.

Bhabha, H. K. (1990b) "Dissemination: time, narrative, and the margins of the modern nation," in H. K. Bhabha (ed.) *Nation and narration*, London and New York: Routledge.

Bhabha, H. K. (1990c) "Introduction: narrating the nation," in H. K. Bhabha (ed.) *Nation and Narration*, London and New York: Routledge.

Bhabha, H. K. (1991) " 'Race', time, and the revision of modernity," *Oxford Literary Review* 13(1–2): 193–219.

Bhabha, H. K. (1992) "A good judge of character: men, metaphors, and the common culture," in T. Morrison (ed.) *Race-ing Justice, En-gendering Power*, New York: Pantheon Books.

Bloch, E. (1986) *The Principle of Hope* (3 vols), trans. N. Plaice, S. Plaice, and P. Knight, Cambridge, MA: MIT Press.

Bradford, P. V. and Blume, H. (1992) *Ota Benga: The Pygmy in the Zoo*, New York: St Martin's Press.

Brenkman, J. (1979) "Mass media: from collective experience to the culture of privatization," *Social Text* 1: 94–109.

Brenkman, J. (1985) *Culture and Domination*, Ithaca, NY: Cornell University Press.

Brodkey, L. (1987) *Academic Writing as Social Practice*, Philadelphia, PA: Temple University Press.

Brookhiser, R. (1991) *The Way of the WASP: How it Made America, and How it Can Save it, So to Speak*, New York: Free Press.

Browder, L. H. (1992) "Which America 2000 will be taught in your class, Teacher?," *International Journal of Educational Reform* 1(2): 111–33.

Brown, R. H. (1987) *Society as Text: Essays on Rhetoric, Reason, and Reality*, Chicago: The University of Chicago Press.

Bruner, J. (1991) "The narrative construction of reality," *Critical Inquiry* 18(1): 1–78.

Burger, P. (1984) *Theory of the Avant-gard*, Minneapolis, MN: University of Minnesota Press.

Burger, P. (1989) "The disappearance of meaning: a postmodern reading of Michel Tournier, Botho Strauss, and Peter Handke," *Polygraph* 2(3): 124–39.

Butler, J. (1991) "Contingent foundations: feminism and the question of 'postmodernism,' " *Praxis International* 11(2): 150–65.

Butler, J. (1992) "Contingent foundations: feminism and the question of postmodernism," in J. Butler and J. W. Scott (eds) *Feminists Theorize the Political*, New York and London: Routledge.

Butler, J. (1993) *Bodies That Matter*, New York and London: Routledge.

Carspecken, P. F. (1991) *Community Schooling and the Nature of Power: The Battle for Croxteth Comprehensive*, London and New York: Routledge.

Cascardi, A. (1990) "Narration and totality," *The Philosophical Forum* 21(33): 277–94.

Castoriadis, C. (1992) "The retreat from autonomy: postmodernism as generalized conformism," *Thesis Eleven* 31: 14–23.

Chambers, I. (1990) *Border Dialogues: Journeys in Postmodernity*, London and New York: Routledge.

Cherryholmes, C. (1988) *Power and Criticism*, New York: Teachers' College Press.

Chopp, R. (1985) *The Praxis of Suffering*, Maryknoll, NY: Orbis.

Chow, R. (1993) *Writing Diaspora*, Bloomington and Indianapolis, IN: Indiana University Press.

Christian, B. (1987) "The race for theory," *Cultural Critique* 6: 51–63.

Clegg, S. R. (1989) *Frameworks of Power*, Beverly Hills, CA: Sage Publications.

Clifford, J. and Marcus, G. (eds) (1986) *Writing Culture: The Poetics and Politics of Ethnography*, Berkeley, CA: University of California Press.

Cohen, J. and Rogers, J. (1983) *On Democracy: Toward a Transformation of American Society*, New York: Penguin Books.

Cohen, S. (1993) *Academia and the Luster of Capital*, Minneapolis, MN: University of Minnesota Press.

Connerty, J. P. (1990) "History's many cunning passages: Paul Ricoeur's *Time and Narrative*," *Poetics Today* 2(2): 383–403.

Conquergood, D. (1992) "Ethnography, rhetoric, and performance," *Quarterly Journal of Speech* 78: 80–123.

Conquergood, D. (1993) "Storied worlds and the work of teaching," *Communication Education* 42: 337–48.

Conquergood, D. (in press) "Homeboys and hoods: gang communication and cultural space," in L. Frey (ed.) *Group Communication in Context*, Hillsdale, N.J.: Erlbaum.

Cooper, B. M. (1989) "Cruel and the gang: exposing the Schomburg Posse," *The Village Voice* 34(19): 27–36.

Copjec, J. (1991) "The Unvermogender Other: hysteria and democracy in America," *New Formations* 14: 27–41.

Cortázar, J. (1963) *Hopscotch*, trans. G. Rabassa, New York: Random House.

Coste, D. (1989) *Narrative as Communication*, Minneapolis, MN: University of Minnesota Press.

Coupland, D. (1991) *Generation X: Tales for an Accelerated Culture*, New York: St Martin's Press.

Dallmayr, F. (1986) "Democracy and postmodernism," *Human Studies* 10: 143–70.

D'Amico, R. (1989) *Historicism and Knowledge;* London: Routledge.

Darder, A. (1992) *Culture and Power in the Classroom*, South Hadley, MS: Bergin & Garvey.

Darnovsky, M. (1991) "The new traditionalism: repacking Ms. Consumer," *Social Text* 9(4): 72–91.

Dauenhauer, P. B. (1989) "Ideology, utopia, and responsible politics," *Man and World* 22: 25–41.

Davis, M. (1990) *City of Quartz*, New York: Verso.

Davis, M. (1993) "Who killed L.A.? A political autopsy," *New Left Review* 197: 3–28.

De Certeau, M. (1984) *The Practice of Everyday Life*, Berkeley, CA: University of California Press.

De Lauretis, T. (1987) *Technologies of Gender*, Bloomington, IN: Indiana University Press.

De Lauretis, T. (1990) "Eccentric subjects: feminist theory and historical consciousness," *Feminist Studies* 16(1): 115–50.
Deleuze, G. and Guattari, F. (1983) *Anti-Oedipus: Capitalism and Schizophrenia*, Minneapolis, MN: University of Minnesota Press.
Deloria, V., Jr. (1987) "Identity and culture," in R. Takaki (ed.) *From Different Shores: Perspectives on Race and Ethnicity in America*, New York: Oxford University Press.
Delpit, L. (1988) "The silenced dialogue: power and pedagogy in educating other people's children," *Harvard Educational Review* 58(3): 280–98.
Denzin, N. K. (1991) *Images of Postmodern Society: Social Theory and Contemporary Cinema*, Newbury Park, CA: Sage Publications in association with *Theory, Culture & Society*.
Dews, P. (1987) *Logics of Disintegration*, London and New York: Verso.
DiStephano, C. (1990) "Dilemmas of difference: feminism, modernity, and postmodernism," in L. J. Nicholson (ed.) *Feminism/Postmodernism*, New York and London: Routledge.
Donald, J. (in press) "The natural man and the virtuous woman: reproducing citizens," in C. Jencks (ed.) *Cultural Reproduction*, London and New York: Routledge.
During, S. (1990) "Postmodernism or post-colonialism today," in A. Milner, P. Thomson, and C. Worth (eds) *Postmodern Conditions*, Oxford: Berg.
Dussel, E. (1985) *Philosophy of Liberation*, trans. A. Martinez and C. Morkovsky, Maryknoll, NY: Orbis Books, 1985.
Dyer, R. (1988) "White," *Screen* 29(4): 44–64.
Dyke, C. (1990) "Strange attraction, curious liaison: Clio meets Chaos," *Philosophical Forum* XXI (4): 369–92.
Dyson, M. E. (1993) *Reflecting Black: African-American Cultural Criticism*, Minneapolis and London: University of Minnesota Press.
Eagleton, T. (1981) *Walter Benjamin*, London: Verso.
Eagleton, T. (1985/86) "The subject of literature," *Cultural Critique*, Winter, 2: 95–104.
Eagleton, T. (1986) *William Shakespeare*, Oxford: Basil Blackwell.
Eagleton, T. (1990) "Nationalism: irony and commitment," in *Nationalism, Colonialism, and Literature*, Minneapolis, MN: University of Minnesota Press.
Eagleton, T. (1991) *Ideology: An Introduction*, New York: Verso.
Ebert, T. (1991a) "Writing in the political: resistance (post)modernism," *Legal Studies Forum* XV(4):291–303.
Ebert, T. (1991b) "Political semiosis in/of American cultural studies," *The American Journal of Semiotics* 8(1/2): 113–35.
Ebert, T. (in press a) "Ludic feminism, the body, performance and labor: bringing materialism back into feminist cultural studies," *Cultural Critique*.
Ebert, T. (in press b) "Writing in the political resistance (post)modernism".
Ellsworth, E. (1988) Why doesn't this feel empowering? Working through the repressive myths of critical pedagogy. Paper presented at the Tenth Conference on Curriculum Theory and Classroom Practice, Dayton, Ohio, October 26–9.
Estrada, K. and McLaren, P. (in press) "A dialogue on multiculturalism and democracy," *Educational Researcher*.
Everhart, R. (1983) "Reading, writing and resistance: adolescence and labor in a junior high school," London and Boston, MA: Routledge & Kegan Paul.
Farren, M. (1993) "Theater of the disturbed," *Los Angeles Reader* 16(8): 8–11, December 3.
Fay, B. (1987) *Critical Social Science*, Ithaca, NY: Cornell University Press.

Featherstone, M. (1990) "Global culture: an introduction," *Theory, Culture & Society* 2/3: 1–14.

Feher, M. (1987) "Of bodies and technologies," in H. Foster (ed.) *Discussions in Contemporary Culture* no. 1, Seattle: Bay Press.

Fekete, J. (1984) "Modernity in the literary institution: strategic anti-foundational moves," in J. Fekete (ed.) *The Structural Allegory*, Minneapolis, MN: University of Minnesota Press.

Feldman, A. (1991) *Formations of Violence: The Narrative of the Body and Political Terror in Northern Ireland*, Chicago: The University of Chicago Press.

Felski, R. (1989) "Feminism, postmodernism, and the critique of modernity," *Cultural Critique* 13: 33–56.

Fine, M. (1988) "Sexuality, schooling, and adolescent females: the missing discourse of desire," *Harvard Educational Review* 51(i): 29–83.

Fine, M. (1989) "Silencing and nurturing voice in an improbable context: urban adolescents in public schools," in H. A. Giroux and P. McLaren (eds) *Critical Pedagogy, the State and Cultural Struggle*, Albany, NY: SUNY Press.

Fish, S. (1992) "Bad company," *Transition* 56: 60–7.

Fiske, T. (1986) "MTV: post-structural, post-modern," *Journal of Communication Inquiry* 10: 74–9.

Fiske, T. (1989) *Understanding Popular Culture*, Sydney: Unwin Hyman, Inc.

Foster, H. (1983) "Postmodernism: a preface," in H. Foster (ed.) *The Anti-aesthetic: Essays in Postmodern Culture*, Port Townsend, WA: Bay Press.

Foucault, M. (1980) *Power/Knowledge: Selected Interviews and Other Writings, 1972–77*, New York: Pantheon.

Foucault, M. (1991) *Remarks on Marx: Conversations with Duccío Trombadori*, New York: Semiotext.

Frank, A. W. (1990) "Bringing bodies back in: a decade review," *Theory, Culture & Society* 7(1): 131–62.

Fraser, N. (1989) *Unruly Practices*, Minneapolis, MN: University of Minnesota Press.

Freire, P. (1985) *The Politics of Education*, South Hadley: Bergin and Garvey.

Fuss, D. (1989) *Essentially Speaking: Feminism, Nature, and Difference*, London and New York: Routledge.

Game, A. (1991) *Undoing the Social: Towards a Deconstructive Sociology*, Toronto and Buffalo, NY: University of Toronto Press.

Gardiner, M. (1992) *The Dialogues of Critique: M. M. Bakhtin and the Theory of Ideology*, London and New York: Routledge.

Gardner, H. (1985) *Frames of Mind*, New York: Basic Books.

Garneski, J. (1993) "In town with Jose Ebert," *The Westwood News*, p. 13 (December).

Gates, H. L., Jr. (1989) Transforming of the American mind. Paper presented at the Annual Meeting of the Modern Language Association, San Francisco.

Geoghegan, V. (1987) *Utopianism and Marxism*, London: Methuen.

Gerbner, G. (1989/90) "TV vs. reality," *Adbusters* 1: 12.

Gergen, K. J. (1991) *The Saturated Self: Dilemmas of Identity in Contemporary Life*, New York: Basic Books.

Giddens, A. (1990) *The Consequences of Modernity*, Stanford, CA: Stanford University Press.

Gilman, S. L. (1985) *Difference and Pathology*, Ithaca, NY: Cornell University Press.

Gilroy, P. (1990) "One nation under a groove: the cultural politics of 'race' and racism in Britain," in D. T. Goldberg (ed.) *Anatomy of Racism*, Minneapolis, MN: University of Minnesota Press.

Giroux, H. A. (1983) *Theory and Resistance in Education*, South Hadley, MA: Bergin & Garvey.

Giroux, H. A. (1988a) *Teachers as Intellectuals: Towards a Critical Pedagogy of Learning*, South Hadley, MA: Bergin & Garvey.

Giroux, H. A. (1988b) *Schooling and the Struggle for Public Life*, Minneapolis, MN: University of Minnesota Press.

Giroux, H. A. (ed.) (1991) *Postmodernism, Feminism, and Cultural Politics*, Albany, NY: SUNY Press.

Giroux, H. A. (1992) *Border Crossings*, New York and London: Routledge.

Giroux, H. A. (1994) "Living dangerously: identity politics and the new cultural racism," in H. A. Giroux and P. McLaren (eds) *Between Borders*, London and New York: Routledge.

Giroux, H. A. (forthcoming) "Border pedagogy and the politics of postmodernism," in P. McLaren (ed.) *Postmodernism, Postcolonialism and Pedagogy*, Albert Park, Australia: James Nicholas Publishers.

Giroux, H. A. and McLaren, P. (1986a) "Teacher education and the politics of engagement: the case for democratic schooling," *Harvard Educational Review* 56(3): 213–38.

Giroux, H. A. and McLaren, P. (1986b) "Critical pedagogy and rethinking teacher education," *Ontario Public School Teachers Federation News*, February 1.

Giroux, H. A. and McLaren, P. (1987a) "Teacher education as a counterpublic sphere: notes towards a redefinition," in T. S. Popkewitz (ed.) *Critical Studies in Teacher Education: Its Folklore and Practice*, New York and London: Falmer Press.

Giroux, H. A. and McLaren, P. (1987b) "Teacher education as a counter sphere: radical pedagogy as a form of cultural politics," *Philosophy and Social Criticism* 12(1): 51–69.

Giroux, H. A. and McLaren, P. (1989) "Schooling, cultural politics, and the struggle for democracy: introduction," in H. A. Giroux and P. McLaren (eds) *Critical Pedagogy, the State, and Cultural Struggle*, New York: SUNY Press.

Giroux, H. A. and McLaren, P. (1991a) "Leon Golub's radical pessimism: toward a pedagogy of representation," *Exposure* 28(12): 18–33.

Giroux, H. A. and McLaren, P. (1991b) "Media hegemony," introduction to J. Schwoch, M. White, and S. Reilly, *Media Knowledge*, Albany, NY: SUNY Press.

Giroux, H. A. and McLaren, P. (1991c) "Radical pedagogy as cultural politics: beyond the discourses of critique and anti-utopianism," in D. Morton and M. Zavarzadeh (eds) *Theory/Pedagogy/Politics*, Champaigne, IL: University of Illinois Press, pp. 152–86.

Giroux, H. A. and McLaren, P. (1994) "Teacher education and the politics of democratic life: beyond the Reagan agenda in the era of 'good times'," in C. C. Yeakey and G. Styles Johnston (eds) *Schools as Conduits: Educational Policymaking During the Reagan Years*, New York: Praeger Press.

Giroux, H. A. and McLaren, P. (forthcoming) "Paulo Friere, postmodernism, and the utopian imagination: a Blochian reading," in J. Owen Daniel and T. Moylan (eds) *Bloch in Our Time*, London and New York: Verso.

Giroux, H. A. and Simon, R. (1984) "Curriculum study and cultural politics," *Boston University Journal of Education* 166(3): 226–38.

Giroux, H. A. and Simon, R. (1988) "Critical pedagogy and the politics of popular culture," *Cultural Studies* 2(3): 294–320.

Godzich, Wlad (1990) "Foreword: the time machine," in D. Coste (ed.) *Narrative as Communication*, Minneapolis, MN: University of Minnesota Press.

Godzich, Wlad (1992) "Afterward," in J.-F. Lyotard, *The Postmodern Explained*, Minneapolis, MN: University of Minnesota Press.

Godzich, Wlad (1993) "Introduction," in D.-L. Haineault and J.-Y. Roy, *Unconscious For Sale*, Minneapolis, MN and London: University of Minnesota Press.

Goldberg, D. T. (ed.) (1990) *Anatomy of Racism*, Minneapolis, MN: University of Minnesota Press.

Goldberg, D. T. (1993) *Racist Culture: Philosophy and the Politics of Meaning*, Oxford: Blackwell.

Goldfield, M. (1992) "The color of politics in the United States: white supremacy as the main explanation for the peculiarities of American politics from colonial times to the present," in D. LaCapra (ed.) *The Bounds of Race*, Ithaca, NY and London: Cornell University Press.

Goodwin, Andrew (1990) "Sample and hold: pop music in the digital age of reproduction," in S. Frith and A. Goodwin (eds) *On Record*, New York: Pantheon Books.

Goodwin, Charles (1993) The Discursive Constitution of Rodney King. Paper presented at the annual meeting of the American Anthropological Association, Washington, DC.

Goodwin, Marjorie H. (1990) *He-Said-She-Said: Talk as Social Organization among Black Children*, Bloomington, IN: Indiana University Press.

Grossberg, L. (1986a) "History, politics and postmodernism: Stuart Hall and cultural studies," *Journal of Communication Inquiry* 10(2), Summer.

Grossberg, L. (1986b) "Teaching the popular," in C. Nelson (ed.) *Theory in the Classroom*, Urbana, IL: University of Illinois Press.

Grossberg, L. (1987) "The in-difference of television," *Screen* 28(2): 28–45.

Grossberg, L. (1988a) *It's A Sin*, Sydney: Power Publications.

Grossberg, L. (1988b) "Rockin' with Reagan, or the mainstreaming of postmodernity," *Cultural Critique* 10: 123–49.

Grossberg, L. (1988c) "Patrolling frontiers: the articulation of the popular," in L. Grossberg, *It's A Sin*, Sydney: Power publications.

Grossberg, L. (1989a) "The formations of cultural studies: an American in Birmingham," *Strategies* 2: 115–49.

Grossberg, L. (1989b) "The context of audiences and the politics of difference," *Australian Journal of Communication* 16: 13–35.

Grossberg, L. (1992) *We Gotta Get Out Of This Place: Popular Conservatism and Postmodern Culture*, New York and London: Routledge.

Grosz, E. (1990) "Conclusion: notes on essentialism and difference," in S. Gunew (ed.) *Feminist Knowledge: Critique and Construct*, London: Routledge.

Guattari, F. and Negri, T. (1990) *Communists Like Us: New Spaces of Liberty, New Lines of Alliance*, Columbia University: Semiotext(e).

Gutierrez, Gustavo (1983) "Liberation praxis and Christian faith," in R. Gibellini (ed.) *Frontiers of Theology in Latin America*, Maryknoll, NY: Orbis.

Gutierrez, Kris (1994) "How talk, context and script shape contexts for learning: a cross-case comparison of journal sharing," *Linguistics and Education* 5: 335–65.

Gutierrez, Kris and Larson, J. (1994) "Language borders: recitation as hegemonic discourse," *International Journal of Educational Reform* 3(1): 22–36.

Haineault, D.-L. and Roy, J.-Y. (1993) *Unconscious For Sale*, Minneapolis, MN and London: University of Minnesota Press.

Hall, S. (1987) "Minimal selves," in *The Real Me: Modernism and the Question of Identity*, London: ICA Documents 6: 44–6.

Hall, S. (1988) "New ethnicities," in *Black Film/British Cinema*, London: ICA Documents 7: 27–31.

Hall, S. (1990) "The meaning of our times," in S. Hall and M. Jacques (eds) *New Times: The Changing Face of Politics in the 1990s*, New York: Verso.

Hall, S. (1991) "Ethnicity: identity and difference," *Radical America* 23(4): 9–20.

Hammer, R. and McLaren, P. (1991) "Rethinking the dialectic," *Educational Theory* 41(1): 23–46.

Hammer, R. and McLaren, P. (1992) "The specularization of subjectivity: media knowledges, global citizenry and the new world order," *Polygraph* 5: 46–66.

Hanna, J. L. (1983) *The Performer/Audience Connection*, Austin: University of Texas Press.

Haraway, D. (1988) "Situated knowledges: the science question in feminism as a site of discourse on the privilege of partial perspective," *Feminist Studies* 14: 575–99.

Haraway, D. (1991) *Simians, Cyborgs, and Women: The Reinvention of Nature*, New York: Routledge.

Harding, S. (1986) *The Science Question in Feminism*, Ithaca, NY: Cornell University Press.

Harris, A. (1990) "Race and essentialism in feminist theory," *Stanford Law Review* 42: 581–616.

Harrison, E. (1994) "Principal's race comments spur small-town uproar," *Los Angeles Times*, March 16.

Harrison, F. (1993) "Writing against the grain," *Critique of Anthropology* 13(4), December.

Harrison, P. R. (1989) "Narrativity and interpretation: on hermeneutical and structuralist approaches to culture," *Thesis Eleven* 22: 61–78.

Harstock, N. (1987) "Rethinking modernism: Minority vs. majority theories," *Cultural Critique* 7: 187–206.

Harstock, N. (1989) "Foucault on power: a theory for women?" in L. J. Nicholson (ed.) *Feminism/Postmodernism*, New York and London: Routledge.

Hassan, I. (1987) *The Postmodern Turn*, Columbus: Ohio State University Press.

Haymes, S. (forthcoming a) "Community-based education and the politics of urban development," *Educational Foundations*.

Haymes, S. (forthcoming b) *Race, Culture and the City: A Pedagogy for Black Urban Struggle*, Albany, NY: State University of New York Press.

Heath, S. (1990) "The ethics of sexual difference," *Discourse* 12(2): 128–53.

Hebdige, D. (1986) "Postmodernism and 'the other side'," *Journal of Communication Inquiry* 10(2): 78–98.

Hebdige, D. (1988) *Hiding in the Light*, London and New York: Commedia/Routledge.

Heller, A. (1988) *General Ethics*, Oxford: Basil Blackwell.

Heller, A. (1990) "Existentialism, alienation, postmodernism: cultural movements as vehicles of change in the patterns of everyday life," in A. Milner, P. Thomson, and C. Worth (eds) *Postmodern Conditions*, Providence, RI: Berg Publishers Ltd.

Hennessy, R. (1993) *Materialist Feminism and the Politics of Discourse*, London and New York: Routledge.

Hicks, E. D. (1988) "Deterritorialization and border writing", in R. Merrill (ed.) *Esthetics/Aesthetics: Post-Modern Positions*, Washington: Maisonneuve Press.

Hicks, E. D. (1991) *Border Writing*, Minneapolis, MN: University of Minnesota Press.

Hillesheim, J. (1990) "Nietzschean images of overcoming," *Educational Theory* 140(2): 211–15.

Hirst, P. (1990) "An answer to relativism," *New Formations* 10: 12–23.

Hitchcock, P. (1993) *Dialogics of the Oppressed*, Minneapolis, MN and London: University of Minnesota Press.

Hochschild, A. R. (1983) *The Managed Heart*, Berkeley, CA: University of California Press.

Holland, E. (1988) "Schizoanalysis: the postmodern contextualization of psychoanalysis," in C. Nelson and L. Grossberg (eds) *Marxism and the Interpretation of Culture*, Chicago: University of Illinois Press.

Holt, D. (1989) "Complex, ontology and our stake in the theatre," in J. Shotter and K. Gergen (eds) *Texts of Identity*, London: Sage.

Honneth, A. (1992) "Pluralization and recognition: on the self-misunderstanding of postmodern social theorists," *Thesis Eleven* 31: 224–33.

hooks, bell (1989) *Talking Back: Thinking Feminist/Thinking Black*, Boston, MA: South End Press.

hooks, bell (1990) *Yearning: Race, Gender, and Cultural Politics*, Toronto: Between The Lines.

hooks, bell (1992) *Black Looks*, Boston, MA: South End Press.

Hudson, W. (1982) *The Marxist Philosophy of Ernst Bloch*, New York: St Martin's Press.

Hunter, I. (1992) *Culture and Government: The Emergence of Literary Education*, Basingstoke: The Macmillan Press.

Hunter, I. (1993) "Mind games and body techniques," *Southern Review* 26(2): 172–85.

Hutcheon, L. (1980) *Narcissistic Narrative: The Metafictional Paradox*, London: Methuen.

Hutcheon, L. (1988) "The politics of postmodernism: parody and history," *Cultural Critique* 5: 179–208.

Jameson, F. (1982) Interview, *Diacritics* 12(3): 72–91.

Jameson, F. (1983) "Postmodernism and consumer society," in H. Foster (ed.) *The Anti-aesthetic: Essays in Postmodern Culture*, Port Townsend: Bay Press.

Jameson, F. (1987) Foreword, in J. Attali, *Noise*, Minneapolis, MN: University of Minnesota Press.

Jameson, F. (1989a) "Afterword – Marxism and postmodernism," in D. Kellner (ed.) *Postmodernism/Jameson/Critique*, Washington, DC: Maisonneuve.

Jameson, F. (1989b) "Marxism and postmodernism," *New Left Review* 176: 31–46.

Jameson, F. (1990) "Modernism and imperialism," in *Nationalism, Colonialism and Literature*, Minneapolis: University of Minnesota Press.

Jay, M. (1982) "Anamnestic totalization," *Theory and Society* 11: 1–15.

Jay, M. (1988) *Fin de siècle Socialism*, London and New York: Routledge.

Jay, M. (1993) *Downcast Eyes: The Denigration of Vision in Twentieth-century French Thought*, Berkeley, CA and Los Angeles: University of California Press.

Johnson, R. (1983) "What is cultural studies anyway?" *Anglistica* 26(1–2): 7–81.

Kalogeras, Y. D. (1991) "Historical representation and the cultural legitimation of the subject in ethnic personal narratives," *College Literature* 18(3): 30–43.

Kaplan, E. A. (1987) *Rocking Around the Clock: Music, Television, Postmodernism, and Consumer Culture*, New York: Methuen.

Kasinitz, P. (1988) "Facing up to the underclass," *Telos* 76: 170–80.

Katz, C. and Smith, N. (1992) "L.A. Intifada: interview with Mike Davis," *Social Text* 33: 19–33.

Kearney, R. (1987) "Ethics and the postmodern imagination," *Thought* 62(244): 39–58.

Kearney, R. (1991) *Poetics of Imagining*, London: HarperCollins Academic.

Kellner, D. (1990) *Television and the Crisis of Democracy*, Boulder, CO: Westview Press.

Kemp, P. T. (1989) "Toward a narrative ethics: a bridge between ethics and the narrative reflection of Ricoeur," in P. T. Kemp and D. Rasmussen (eds) *The Narrative Path: The Later Works of Paul Ricoeur*, Cambridge, MA: MIT Press.

Kimball, R. (1991) "Tenured radicals: a postscript," *The New Criterion* 9(5): 4–13.

Kincheloe, J. (1991) *Teachers as Researchers: Qualitative Inquiry as a Path to Empowerment*, London: Falmer.

Kincheloe, J. (1992) "Educational historiographical meta-analysis: rethinking methodology in the 1990s," *International Journal of Qualitative Studies in Education* 5(1):

Kincheloe, J. and McLaren, P. (1994) "Rethinking critical theory and qualitative research," in Y. Lincoln and N. Denzin (eds) *Handbook of Qualitative Research*, Beverly Hills, CA: Sage, pp. 138–57.

Kolakowski, L. (1982) "The death of utopia reconsidered," The Tanner Lectures on Human Values, Salt Lake City: University of Utah Press.

Kovel, J. (1991) *History and Spirit: An Inquiry into the Philosophy of Liberation*, Boston, MA: Beacon Press.

Kroker, A. (1992) *The Possessed Individual: Technology and the French Postmodern*, Montreal: New World Perspectives.

Kroker, A. and Cook, D. (eds) (1986) *The Postmodern Scene: Excremental Culture and Hyper-aesthetics*, New York: St Martin's Press.

Krupat, A. (1991) *Ethnocentrism: Ethnography, History, Literature*, Berkeley, CA: University of California Press.

Laclau, E. (1988) "Building a New Left: an interview with Ernesto Laclau," *Strategies* 1: 10–28.

Laclau, E. (1992) "Universalism, particularism, and the question of identity," *October* 61 (Summer): 83–90.

Laclau, E. and Mouffe, C. (1985) *Hegemony and Socialist Strategy*, London: Verso.

Lamb, N. (1982) *Solidarity with Victims*, New York: Crossroad.

Lankshear, C. and McLaren, P. (1993) *Critical Literacy: Politics, Praxis, and the Postmodern*, Albany, NY: SUNY Press.

Larmore, C. (1981) "The concept of a constitutive subject," in C. McCabe (ed.) *The Talking Cure: Essays in Psychoanalysis and Language*, New York: St Martin's Press.

Larsen, N. (1990) *Modernism and Hegemony: A Materialist Critique of Aesthetic Agencies*, Minneapolis, MN: University of Minnesota Press.

Larsen, N. (1991) Foreword to E. Hicks, *Border Writing*, Minneapolis, MN: University of Minnesota Press.

Lash, S. (1990) "Learning from Leipzig . . . or politics in the semiotic society," *Theory, Culture & Society* 7(4): 145–58.

Lash, S. and Urry, J. (1987) *The End of Organized Capitalism*, Madison, WI: The University of Wisconsin Press.

Lave, J. and Wenger, E. (1991) *Situated Learning: Legitimate Peripheral Participation*, Cambridge: Cambridge University Press.

Lefèbvre, H. (1990) *Everyday Life in the Modern World*, New Brunswick and London: Transaction Publishers.

Lehrer, R., Serlin, R. and Amundson, R. (1990) "Knowledge or certainty? A reply to Cziko," *Educational Researcher* 19(5): 16–19.

Levin, C. (1987) "Carnal knowledge of aesthetic states," in A. Kroker and M. Kroker (eds) *Body Invaders*, New York: St Martin's Press.
Levinas, E. (1969) *Totality and Infinity*, Pittsburgh: Duquesne University Press.
Lichtman, R. (forthcoming) "Psychoanalysis: critique of Habermas' prototype of critical social sciences," *New Ideas in Psychology* 2(6).
Lippard, L. R. (1987) "Feminist space: reclaiming territory," in L. Falk and B. Fischer (eds) *The Event Horizon*, Toronto: The Coach House Press and Walter Phillips Gallery.
Lippard, L. R. (1990) *Mixed Blessings: New Art in a Multicultural America*, New York: Pantheon Books.
Lipsitz, G. (1990) *Time Passages*, Minneapolis, MN: University of Minnesota Press.
Liston, D. P. (1988) *Capitalist Schools: Explanation and Ethics in Radical Studies of Schooling*, New York: Routledge, Chapman & Hall.
Litchman, R. (1982) *The Production of Desire*, New York: Free Press.
Lloyd, D. (1991) "Race under representation," *Oxford Literary Review* 13(1–2): 62–94.
Lusted, D. (1986) "Why pedagogy?", *Screen* 27(5): 4–5.
Lyotard, J. F. (1973) *Des dispositifs pulsionnels*, Paris: Union Générale d'Editions.
McCabe, C. (1981) "On discourse," in C. McCabe (ed.) *The Talking Cure: Essays in Psychoanalysis and Language*, New York: St Martin's Press.
MacCannell, D. (1989) *The Tourist*, New York: Basic Books.
MacCannell, D. (1992) *Empty Meeting Grounds: The Tourist Papers*, London and New York: Routledge.
McCarthy, C. (1988) "Rethinking liberal and radical perspectives on racial inequality in schooling: making the case for nonsynchrony," *Harvard Educational Review* 58(3): 265–79.
Macedo, D. (forthcoming) "Literacy for stupidification: the pedagogy of big lies," *Harvard Educational Review*.
McGovern, A. F. (1981) *Marxism: An American Christian Perspective*, Maryknoll, NY: Orbis Books.
MacIntyre, A. (1981) *After Virtue*, London: Duckworth.
McLaren, P. (1985) "Contemporary ritual studies: a post-Turnerism perspective," *Semiotic Inquiry* 5(1): 78–85.
McLaren, P. (1986) *Schooling as a Ritual Performance: Towards a Political Economy of Educational Symbols and Gestures*, London and New York: Routledge (reprinted 1994).
McLaren, P. (1987) "Postmodernism and Politics: a Brazilian reprieve," *Educational Theory* 36(4): 389–401.
McLaren, P. (1988a) "Review of Clodovis Boff's theology and praxis: epistemological foundations," *Small Press* 5(4): 64–5.
McLaren, P. (1988b) "On ideology and education: critical pedagogy and the politics of education," *Social Text* 19/20: 153–85.
McLaren, P. (1989a) "On ideology and education: critical pedagogy and the politics of resistance," in H. Giroux and P. McLaren (eds) *Critical Pedagogy, the State, and Cultural Struggle*, Albany, NY: SUNY Press.
McLaren, P. (1989b) *Life in Schools. An Introduction to Critical Pedagogy in the Social Foudations of Education*. White Plains, NY: Longman.
McLaren, P. (1991a) "Decentering culture: postmodernism, resistance, and critical pedagogy," in N. Wyner (ed.) *Current Perspectives on School Cultures*, Boston, MA: Brookline Books.
McLaren, P. (1991b) "Schooling the postmodern body," in H. A. Giroux (ed.) *Postmodernism, Feminism, and Cultural Politics*, Albany, NY: SUNY Press.

McLaren, P. (1992a) "What is the political role of education?" in J. Kinchenloe and S. Steinberg (eds) *Thirteen Questions: Reframing Education's Conversation*, New York and Berlin: Peter Lang.

McLaren, P. (1992b) "Critical literacy and the postmodern turn," in R. Beach, J. Green, M. Kamil, and T. Shanahan (eds) *Multidisciplinary Perspectives on Critical Literarcy*, Urbana, IL: National Council of Teachers of English.

McLaren, P. (1993a) "Border disputes: multicultural narrative, identity formation, and critical pedagogy in postmodern America," in D. McLaughlin and W. Tierney (eds) *Naming Silenced Lives*, London and New York: Routledge.

McLaren, P. (1993b) "White terror and oppositional agency: towards a critical multiculturalism," *Strategies* 7.

McLaren, P. (1994) "Multiculturalism and the postmodern critique: towards a pedagogy of resistance and transformation," in H. Giroux and P. McLaren (eds) *Between Borders*, London and New York: Routledge.

McLaren, P. (ed.) (forthcoming) *Postmodernism, Postcolonialism, and Pedagogy*, Albert Park, Australia: James Nicholas Publishers.

McLaren, P. and Dantley, M. (1990) "Leadership and a critical pedagogy of race: Cornel West, Stuart Hall, and the prophetic tradition," *Journal of Negro Education* 59(1): 29–44.

McLaren, P. and Da Silva, T. (1993) "Decentering pedagogy: critical literacy, resistance, and the politics of memory," in P. McLaren and P. Leonard (eds) *Paulo Friere: A Critical Encounter*, New York and London: Routledge.

McLaren, P. and Hammer, R. (1989) "Critical pedagogy and the postmodern challenge," *Educational Foundations* 3(3): 29–69.

McLaren, P. and Lankshear, C. (eds) (1994) *Politics of Liberation: Paths from Freire*, London and New York: Routledge.

McLaren, P. and Leonard, P. (1993) "Absent discourses: Paulo Freire and the dangerous memories of liberation," in P. McLaren and P. Leonard (eds) *Paulo Freire: A Critical Encounter*, New York and London: Routledge.

McLaren, P. and Smith, R. (1989) "Televangelism as pedagogy and cultural politics," in H. A. Giroux and R. Simon (eds) *Popular Culture, Schooling, and Everyday Life*, South Hadley, MA: Bergin & Garvey.

McLuhan, M. (1973) *Understanding Media*, London: Abacus.

Mandel, E. (1975) *Late Capitalism*, London: New Left Books.

Marcus, G. (1989) *Lipstick Traces*, Cambridge, MA: Harvard University Press.

Marcus, G. (1990) "Corrupting the absolute," in Frith, S. and Goodwin, A. (eds) *On Record*, New York: Pantheon Books.

Massumi, B. (1993) "Everywhere you want to be: Introduction to fear," in B. Massumi (ed.) *The Politics of Everyday Fear*, Minneapolis: University of Minnesota Press, pp. 3–37.

Mauss, M. (1979) *Sociology and Psychology: Essays*, London.

Mayer, M. (1991) "Politics in the post-Fordist city," *Socialist Review* 21(1): 105–24.

Megill, A. (1985) *Prophets of Extremity*, Berkeley, CA: University of California Press.

Mercer, K. (1990) "Welome to the jungle: identity and diversity in postmodern politics," in J. Rutherford (ed.) *Identity: Community, Culture, Difference*, London: Lawrence & Wishart.

Mercer, K. (1992) "1968: periodizing politics and identity," in L. Grossberg, C. Nelson, and P. Treichler (eds) *Cultural Studies*, London and New York: Routledge.

Merod, J. (1987) *The Political Responsibility of the Critic*, Ithaca, NY and London: Cornell University Press.

Miedema, S. and Biesta, G. (1990) The Opportunities for a Critical-Pragmatic Pedagogy. Paper presented at the annual meeting of the John Dewey Society, Boston, April 17.

Minh-ha, T. T. (1987) "Difference: a special Third World issue," *Feminist Review* 25: 5–22.

Minh-ha, T. T. (1988) "Not you/like you: post-colonial women and the interlocking questions of identity and difference," *Inscriptions* 3/4: 71–7.

Minh-ha, T. T. (1989) *Women, Native, Other: Writing Post-colonially and Feminism*, Bloomington and Indianapolis, IN: Indiana University Press.

Minh-ha, T. T. (1991) *When the Moon Waxes Red: Representation, Gender, and Cultural Politics*, New York and London: Routledge.

Mohanty, C. T. (1989/90) "On race and voice: challenges for liberal eduation in the 1990s," *Cultural Critique* 19, Winter: 179–208.

Mohanty, C. T. (1991) "Introduction: cartographies of struggle: Third World women and the politics of feminism," in C. T. Mohanty, A. Russo, and L. Torres (eds) *Third World Women and the Politics of Feminism*, Bloomington, IN: Indiana University Press.

Moll, L. (1990) "Introduction," in L. Moll (ed.) *Vygotsky and Education: Instructional Implications and Applications of Sociohistorical Psychology*, New York: Cambridge University Press.

Morrison, T. (1993) *Playing in the Dark: Whiteness and the Literary Imagination*, Cambridge, MA and London: Harvard University Press.

Muñoz, C., Jr. (1989) *Youth, Identity, Power*, London and New York: Verso.

Murphy, P. (1991) "Postmodern perspectives and justice," *Thesis Eleven* 30: 117–32.

Nagara, B. (1993) "Economics, politics, and socioeconomics: drifting to a new paradigm?", paper delivered at the International Conference, "Communication and development in a postmodern era: re-evaluating the Freirean legacy," Universiti Sains Malaysia, 6–9 December.

Naureckas, J. (1993) "The Somalia intervention: tragedy made simple," *Extra* 6(2): 10–13.

Nieto, S. (1992) *Affirming Diversity: The Sociopolitical Context of Multicultural Education*, White Plains, NY: Longman.

Norris, C. (1990) *What's Wrong With Postmodernism*? Baltimore, MD: Johns Hopkins University Press.

Ochs, E. (1988) *Culture and Language Development*, Cambridge: Cambridge University Press.

Offe, C. (1985) *Disorganized Capitalism*, Massachusetts: The MIT Press.

Ogbu, J. (1990) "Minority education in comparative perspective," *Journal of Negro Education* 59(1): 45–57.

O'Neil, J. (1989) *The Communicative Body*, Evanston: Northwestern University Press.

Parry, B. (1987) "Problems in current theories of colonial discourse," *The Oxford Literary Review* 9: 27–58.

Patton, P. (1986) "Ethics and postmodernity," in E. A. Grosz, T. Threadgold, D. Kelly, A. Cholodenko, and E. Colless (eds) *Future Fall: Excursions into Postmodernity*, Sydney: Power Institute of Fine Arts, University of Sydney.

Pêcheux, M. (1975/82) *Language, Semantics and Ideology: Stating the Obvious*, trans. H. Nagpal, New York: St Martin's Press.

Pecora, V. P. (1991) Nietzsche, genealogy, critical theory, *New German Critique* 53: 104–30.

Pefanis, J. (1991) *Heterology and the Postmodern*, Durham, NC: Duke University Press.

Perez, R. (1990) *On An(archy) and Schizoanalysis*, Brooklyn, NY: Autonomedia.

Pfeil, F. (1988) "Postmodernism as a 'structure of feeling'," in C. Nelson and L. Grossberg (eds) *Marxism and the Interpretation of Culture*, Chicago: University of Illinois Press.

Pheby, K. (1988) *Interventions: Displacing the Metaphysical Subject*, Washington, DC: Maisonneuve.

Piccone, P. (1987/88) "The crisis of American conservatism," *Telos* 74: 3–29.

Piccone, P. (1988) "Roundtable on communitarianism," *Telos* 76: 2–32.

Pieterse, J. N. (1992) *White On Black: Images of Africa and Blacks in Western Popular Culture*, New Haven, CT and London: Yale University Press.

Plant, S. (1992) *The Most Radical Gesture: The Situationist International in a Postmodern Age*, London and New York: Routledge.

Polan, D. (1986) "Brief encounters: mass culture and the evacuation of sense," in T. Modleski (ed.) *Studies in Entertainment*, Bloomington and Indianapolis, IN: Indiana University Press.

Porter, C. (1988) "Are we being historical yet?" *South Atlantic Quarterly* 87: 744–86.

Poster, M. (1989) *Critical Theory and Poststructuralism*, Ithaca NY and London: Cornell University Press.

Pruyn, M. (1994) "Becoming subjects through critical practice," *International Journal of Educational Reform* 3(1): 37–50.

Przybylowicz, D. (1987) "Contemporary issues in feminist theory," in J. A. Buttigieg (ed.) *Criticism Without Boundaries*, Notre Dame, IN: University of Notre Dame Press.

Rabinbach, A. (1977) "Unclaimed heritage: Ernst Bloch's heritage of our times and the theory of fascism," *New German Critique* 11 (Spring).

Ravitch, D. (1990) "Multiculturalism," *The American Scholar* 59: 337–54.

Ravitch, D. (1991) "A culture in common," *Educational Leadership* (December): 8–16.

Readings, B. (1991) *Introducing Lyotard: Art and Politics*, London: Routledge.

Readings, B. (1992) "Pagan, perverts or primitives? Experimental justice in the empire of capital," in A. Benjamin (ed.) *Judging Lyotard*, London and New York: Routledge.

Ricoeur, P. (1984) *Time and Narrative*, Chicago: The University of Chicago Press.

Rigney, A. (1991) "Narrative and historical representation," *Poetics Today* 12(3): 591–605.

Rogin, M. (1990) " 'Make my day!': spectacle as amnesia in imperial politics," *Representations* 29: 99–123.

Rogoff, B. (1990) *Apprenticeship in Thinking: Cognitive Development in Social Context*, New York: Oxford University Press.

Rorty, R. (1991) "Feminism and pragmatism," *Radical Philosophy* 59: 3–14.

Rosaldo, R. (1989) *Culture and Truth: The Remaking of Social Analysis*, Boston, MA: Beacon Press.

Rosen, H. (1986) "The importance of story," *Language Arts* 63(3): 226–37.

Rosenau, P. M. (1992) *Post-modernism and the Social Sciences: Insights, Inroads, and Intrusions*, Princeton, NJ: Princeton University Press.

Ross, A. (1988) "Introduction," in A. Ross (ed.) *Universal Abandon*?, Minneapolis, MN: University of Minnesota Press.

Ross, A. (1989) *No Respect: Intellectuals and Popular Culture*, London and New York: Routledge.

Ruiz, R. (1992) "Language and public policy in the United States," in W. A. Van Horne (ed.) *Ethnicity and Public Policy Revisited: Selected Essays*, Milwaukee: Institute on Race and Ethnicity.

Rutherford, J. (1990) "A place called home: identity and the cultural politics of difference," in J. Rutherford (ed.) *Identity: Community, Culture, Difference*, London: Lawrence & Wishart.

Ryan, M. (1989) *Politics and Culture*, Baltimore, MD: Johns Hopkins University Press.

Saénz, Mario (1991) "Memory, enchantment, and salvation: Latin American philosophies of liberation and the religions of the oppressed," *Philosophy and Social Criticism* 17(2): 149–73.

Said, E. (1993) *Culture and Imperialism*, New York: Alfred A. Knopf.

Saldivar, R. (1990) *Chicano Narrative: The Dialectics of Difference*, Madison, WI: University of Wisconsin Press.

Sanchez-Tranquilino, M. and Tagg, J. (1991) "The pachuco's flayed hide: the museum, identity and Buenas Garras," in R. Griswold del Castillo, T. McKenna, and Y. Yarbro-Bejarano (eds) *Chicano Art: Resistance and Affirmation, 1965–1985*, Los Angeles: Wight Art Gallery, University of California.

Sandoval, C. (1991) "U.S. Third World feminism: the theory and method of oppositional consciousness in the postmodern world," *Genders* 10: 1–24.

San Juan, Jr., E. (1992) *Racial Formations/Critical Formations*, New Jersey and London: Humanities Press.

Sarup, M. (1989) *An Introductory Guide to Post-structuralism and Postmodernism*, Athens, GA: University of Georgia Press.

Sawicki, J. (1991) *Disciplining Foucault: Feminism, Power, and The Body*, New York: Routledge.

Scherpe, K. R. (1986/7) "Dramatization and de-dramatization of the end: the apocalyptic consciousness of modernity and postmodernity," *Cultural Critique* 5 (Winter): 124.

Schlesinger, A. M., Jr. (1991) *The Disuniting of America: Reflections on a Multicultural Society*, Knoxville: Whittle Direct Books.

Scholes, R. (1988) "Deconstruction and comminication," *Critical Inquiry* 14 (Winter): 278–95.

Schulte-Sasse, J. (1986/87) "Imagination and modernity: or the taming of the human mind," *Cultural Critique* 5: 23–48.

Schulte-Sasse, J. (1987/88) "Electronic media and cultural politics in the Reagan era: the attack on Libya and Hands Across America as postmodern events," *Cultural Critique* 8: 123–52.

Scott, J. W. (1992) "Experience," in J. Butler and J. W. Scott (eds) *Feminists Theorize the Political*, New York and London: Routledge.

Sears, J. T. (1987) "Peering into the Well of Loneliness: the responsibility of educators to gay and lesbian youth," in A. Molnar (ed.) *Social Issues and Education*, Alexandria, VA: Association for Supervision and Curriculum Development.

Segundo, J. L. (1980) *Our Idea of God*, Dublin: Gill & Macmillan.

Seljak, D. (1991) "Alan Davies on racism," *The Ecumenist* 29: 13–14.

Shaviro, M. J. (1992) *Reading the Postmodern Polity*, Minneapolis, MN and Oxford: University of Minnesota Press.

Sholle, D. J. (1988) "Critical studies: from the theory of ideology to power/knowledge," *Critical Studies in Mass Communication* 5: 16–35.

Shumway, D. (1989) "Reading rock 'n roll in the classroom: a critical pedagogy," in H. A. Giroux and P. McLaren (eds) *Critical Pedagogy, the State, and Cultural Struggle*, Albany, NY: SUNY Press.

Silverman, K. (1988) *The Acoustic Mirror: The Female Voice in Psychoanalysis and Cinema*, Bloomington, IN: Indiana University Press.

Simon, R. (1986) "Work experience and the production of subjectivity," in D. Livingstone (ed.) *Critical Pedagogy and Cultural Power*, South Hadley, MS: Bergin & Garvey.

Simon, R. (1987) "Empowerment as a pedagogy of possibility," *Language Arts* 64(4): 370.

Simone, T. M. (1989) *About Face: Race in Postmodern America*, Brooklyn, NY: Autonomedia.

Sleeter, C. E. (1991) *Empowerment Through Multicultural Education*, Albany, NY: SUNY Press.

Smith, B. H. (1988) *Contingencies of Value*, Cambridge, MA: Harvard University Press.

Smith, S. (1987) *A Poetics of Women's Autobiography: Marginality and the Fictions of Self-representations*, Bloomington, IN: Indiana University Press.

Spivak, G. C. (1990a) *The Post-colonial Critic*, London and New York: Routledge.

Spivak, G. C. (1990b) "The making of Americans, the teaching of English, and the future of cultural studies," *New Literary History* 21(4): 781–98.

Stephanson, A. (1988a) "Regarding postmodernism – a conversation with Fredric Jameson," in A. Ross (Ed.) *Universal Abandon? The Politics of Postmodernism*, Minneapolis, MN: University of Minnesota Press.

Stephanson, A. (1988b) "Interview with Cornel West," in A. Ross (ed.) *Universal Abandon? The Politics of Postmoderism*, Minneapolis, MN: University of Minnesota Press, pp. 269–86.

Taylor, P. (1989) *The Narrative of Liberation: Perspectives on Afro-Caribbean Literature, Popular Culture, and Politics*, Ithaca, NY: Cornell University Press.

Telles, E. and Murguia, E. (1990) "Phenotypic discrimination and income differences among Mexican-Americans," *Social Science Quarterly* 71(4): 682–96.

Torres, C. A. (1990) *The Politics of Non-formal Education in Latin America*, New York: Praeger.

Toufexis, A. (1994) *Time*, April: 64–6.

Trend, D. (1992) *Cultural Pedagogy: Art/Education/Politics*, New York: Bergin & Garvey.

Turner, B. (1984) *The Body and Society*, Oxford: Basil Blackwell.

Turner. C. and Carter, E. (1986) "Political somatics: notes on Klaus Theweleit's male fantasies," in V. Burgin, J. Donald, and C. Kaplan (eds) *Formations of Fantasy*, London and New York: Metheun.

Turner, D. (1983) *Marxism and Christianity*, Oxford: Basil Blackwell.

Unger, R. (1987) *Social Theory: Its Situation and Its Task*, New York: Cambridge University Press.

Van Reijen, W. (1990) "Philosophical-political polytheism: Habermas versus Lyotard," *Theory, Culture & Society* 7(4).

Vattimo, G. (1988) *The End of Modernity*, trans. J. R. Synder, Baltimore, MD: Johns Hopkins University Press.

Villa-Vincencio, C. (1989) "South Africa: a Church within the Church," *Christianity and Crisis*, Jan. 9, p. 463.

Wallace, M. (1991) "Multiculturalism and oppositionality," *Afterimage* (October): 6–9.

Walzer, M. (1987) *Interpretation and Criticism*, Cambridge, MA: Harvard University Press.

Welch, S. (1985) *Communities of Resistance and Solidarity: A Feminist Theology of Liberation*, Maryknoll, NY: Orbis.

Welch, S. (forthcoming) *A Feminist Ethic of Risk*, Minneapolis, MN: Fortress Press.

Wells, H. (1984) "Political theology in conflict," *The Ecumenist* 22(6): 82.

West, C. (1985) "Afterword: the politics of American neo-pragmatism," in J. Rachman and C. West (eds) *Post-analytic Philosophy*, New York: Columbia University Press.

West, C. (1989a) *The American Evasion of Philosophy*, Madison, WI: University of Wisconsin Press.

West, C. (1989b) "Black culture and postmodernism," in B. Kruger and P. Mariani (eds) *Remaking History*, Seattle: Bay Press.

West, C. (1990) "The new cultural politics of difference," in R. Ferguson, M. Gever, T. Min-ha, and C. West (eds) *Out There: Marginalization and Contemporary Cultures*, Cambridge, MA: The MIT Press and the New Museum of Contemporary Art, New York.

West, C. (1993) *Race Matters*, Boston, MA: Beacon Press.

White, H. (1987) *The Content of the Form: Narrative Discourse and Historical Representation*, Baltimore, MD: Johns Hopkins University Press.

Williams, B. (1993) "The impact of the precepts of nationalism on the concept of culture: making grasshoppers of naked apes," *Cultural Critique* 24:143–91.

Williams, R. (1977) *Marxism and Literature*, Oxford: Oxford University Press.

Willis, P. (1990) *Common Culture*, Boulder, CO: Westview Press.

Witkowski, L. (1990) Education and the Universal Challenge of Border. Paper presented at the Second International Symposium for Universalism, Max-Planck-Institut für Bildungsforschung.

Young, I. M. (1986) "The ideal of community and the politics of difference," *Social Theory and Practice* 12(1): 1–26.

Young, I. M. (1990) *Justice and the Power of Difference*, Princeton, NJ: Princeton University Press.

Yudice, G. (1988) "Marginality and the ethics of survival," in A. Ross (ed.) *Universal Abandon?*, Minneapolis, MN: University of Minnesota Press.

Yudice, G. (1992) "We are not the world," *Social Text* 31/32: 202–16.

Yurick, S. (1989) "How the Athenians planned to colonize the mind of the West and immortalize themselves," *Social Text* 23: 29–85.

Zavarzadeh, M. and Morton, D. (1990) "Signs of knowledge in the contemporary academy," *American Journal of Semiotics* 7(4): 149–60.

Zavarzadeh, M. and Morton, D. (1991) *Theory, (Post) modernity, Opposition*, Washington, DC: Maisonneuve.

Zavarzadeh, M. and Morton, D. (forthcoming) *Theory (Un)limited: Writings in (Post)modern Theory and Radical Pedagogy*, Bloomington, IN: Indiana University Press.

Žižek, S. (1989) *The Sublime Object of Ideology*, London and New York: Verso.

Index